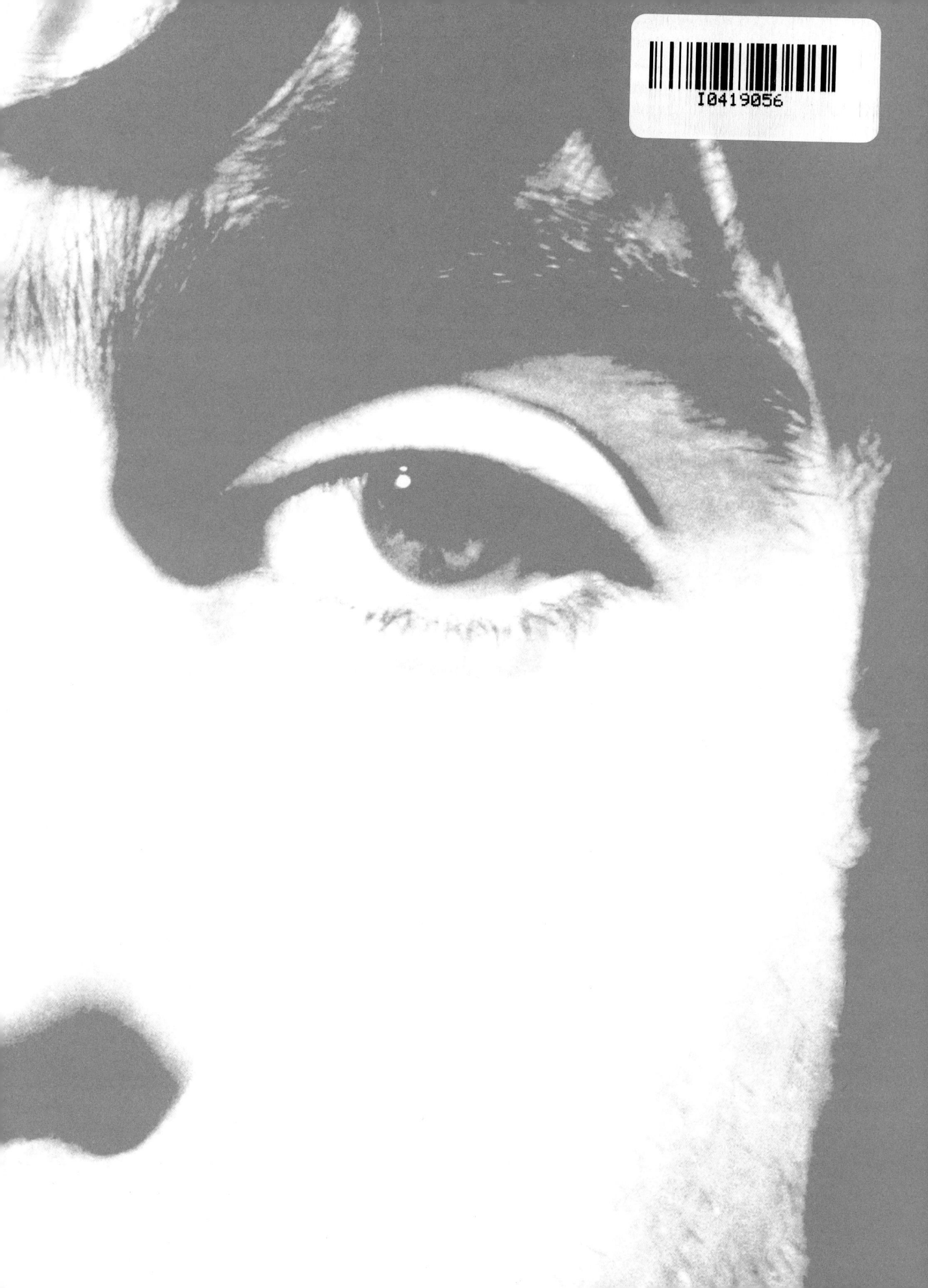

OASIS

THE MASTERPLAN

OASIS

THE MASTERPLAN

PHOTOGRAPHS BY

KEVIN CUMMINS

weldon**owen**

weldon**owen**

an imprint of Insight Editions

P.O. Box 3088

San Rafael, CA 94912

www.weldonowen.com

CEO Raoul Goff

SVP Group Publisher Jeff McLaughlin

VP Publisher Roger Shaw

Executive Editor Edward Ash-Milby

VP Creative Chrissy Kwasnik

Art Director Megan Sinead Bingham

VP Manufacturing Alix Nicholaeff

Senior Production Manager Joshua Smith

Strategic Production Planner Lina s Palma-Temena

First published in Great Britain in 2025 by Cassell,

an imprint of Octopus Publishing Group Ltd

Carmelite House

50 Victoria Embankment

London EC4Y 0DZ

www.octopusbooks.co.uk

An Hachette UK Company

www.hachette.co.uk

ISBN: 979-8-88674-299-2

Printed and bound in China

10 9 8 7 6 5 4 3 2 1

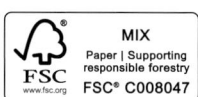

 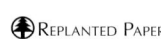

Insight Editions, in association with Roots of Peace, will plant two trees for each tree used in the manufacturing of this book. Roots of Peace is an internationally renowned humanitarian organization dedicated to eradicating land mines worldwide and converting war-torn lands into productive farms and wildlife habitats. Roots of Peace will plant two million fruit and nut trees in Afghanistan and provide farmers there with the skills and support necessary for sustainable land use.

CONTENTS

7 **INTRODUCTION** *Kevin Cummins*

10 **OASIS: THE MASTERPLAN** *Gail Crowther with commentary by Noel Gallagher*

253 **OASIS & MUSIC TODAY** *Noel Gallagher in conversation with Kevin Cummins*

256 **ACKNOWLEDGEMENTS**

INTRODUCTION
KEVIN CUMMINS

In early 1994, before Oasis broke through to become the biggest band in the UK, I was commissioned by their label, Creation Records, to take their photo in different locations and use different lighting techniques in the studio, to see what kind of look would suit them best.

That February, I flew to Amsterdam for an initial shoot. They were supposed to be there opening for The Verve, but on my arrival only Noel was there to meet me. I assumed the others were still out from the previous night, but Noel told me they had all been arrested on the ferry over for fighting with some Chelsea fans (not West Ham fans as has been erroneously reported) and sent back to England. He claimed to have missed it all as he'd gone to bed early. I took a photo of Noel by the poster for the gig, to prove that I had turned up, and to use as a news feature picture for *NME*.

Finally, a few weeks later, we took some shots in a photo studio in East London, and then some more around Soho and the West End.

The Gallaghers are big Manchester City fans, as am I, and I was keen to shoot them in City shirts for *NME*. So, a month later, we took photos in and outside the studio for a session, which I still really love, that was to be the cover and lead feature. My editor at the time – a Southampton fan – decided against using the session on the front cover, saying he didn't want the paper to be associated with "losers".

That aged well, didn't it?

A first *NME* cover was important to any band. It had to be perfect. Eventually we settled on a photo I'd taken of Liam under the Oasis Bar sign in a hotel in Newport, Gwent. The coverline was: "TOTALLY COOL. OASIS: What the world is waiting for".

In spite of this, the Man City shoot became one of my best-known sessions. It is still used on magazine covers worldwide (*NME* finally used it on their cover on 2 January 2010, when they ran a retrospective of the band) and Manchester City and Oasis have become inextricably linked. In September 1994, on their first tour of Japan and the USA, many Oasis fans at the gigs were wearing Man City shirts bearing the brother logo (some of them had no idea it was a brand name for an electronics company, and a few even asked me if it signified that they were a brotherhood). While the session on pages 52–61 was shot on Flitcroft Street, off Charing Cross, as a nod to Garry Flitcroft who was playing in midfield for Man City at the time.

I've worked with Oasis, as well as with Noel and Liam in their solo careers, on and off for 30 years, shooting them editorially for music titles and *Esquire* magazine, for a Man City kit launch, and several times for adidas SPZL, as well as shooting Noel Gallagher's High Flying Birds' *Council Skies* album sleeve. It's a professional relationship I enjoy immensely and I'm really proud of this body of work.

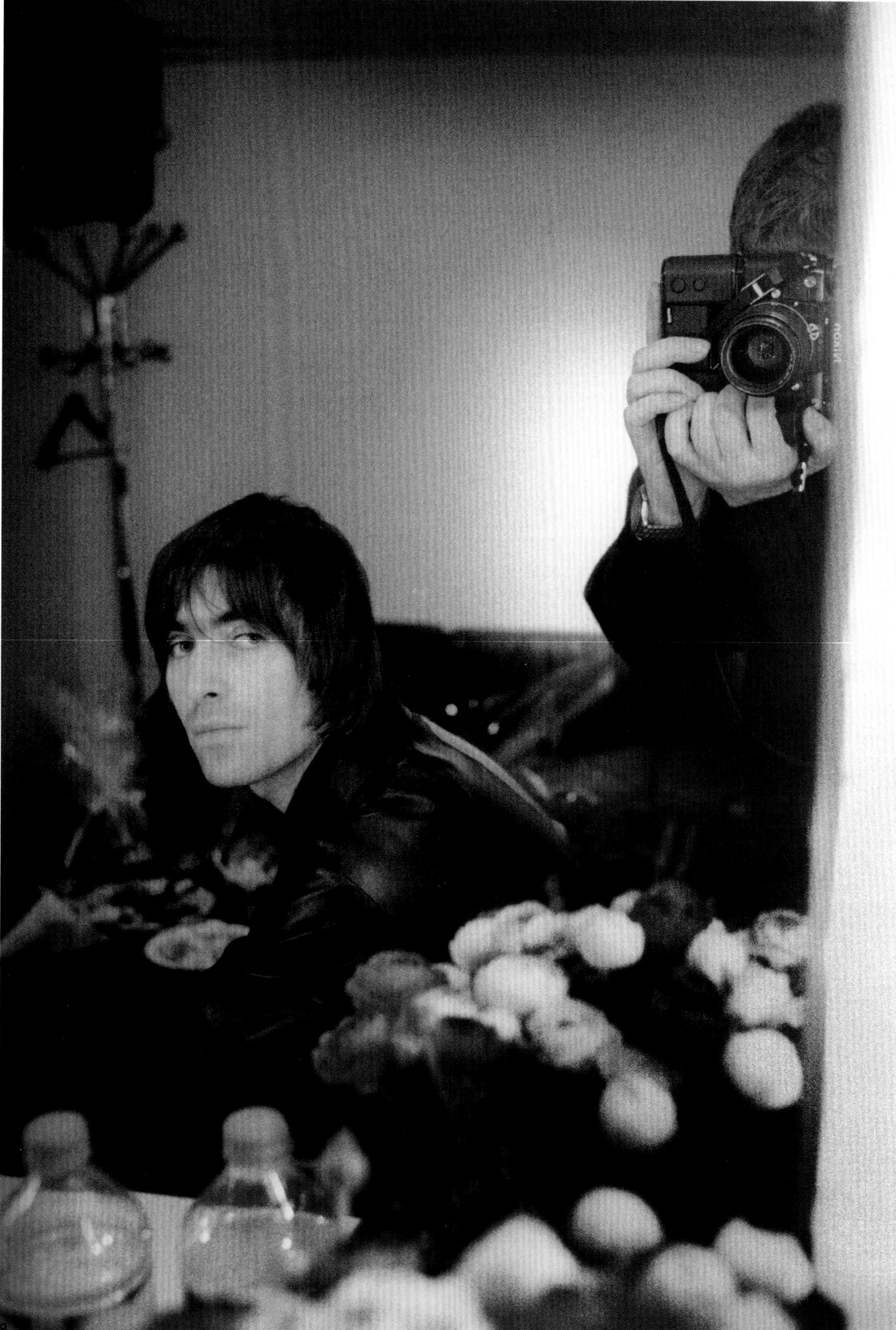

This opening photograph (see opposite) of me shooting Liam was taken in Paris back in 2000. I wanted to use something different for an author picture, and this seemed to be the most appropriate. The final two shots in the book are from an *NME* awards night in 1995 and signify the upward trajectory the band were embarking on after that formative year.

Everything in this book was shot on film, and the occasional inconsistency in colour is due to different processing techniques and questionable storage temperatures. The band shot on pages 22–3 is damaged, as it was a clip test (a short piece of film processed to check exposure). It's the only colour shot remaining from that session, so I wanted to use it, and photoshopping the damage would have made it less authentic, in my opinion. Therefore I left it as it is, damage intact.

Many people have told me they got into Oasis because of that Man City photoshoot, and because the band's members dressed like their mates dressed. The clothes gave them an immediate connection; they made them seem approachable. Throughout the book, all the clothes worn by the band are their own. The only exceptions are the two Man City shirts, which were mine, and the Armani blue denim shirt Liam is wearing on pages 225–9, which is also mine. I had been wearing it, but I wanted some shots with Liam wearing a similar colour to Noel. So, I lent him my shirt and it brings a bit more coherence and harmony to the image and backdrop.

Oasis were also the first band my daughter Ella, who was eight in 1994, identified with. She told me recently why they are still her favourite band:

I grew up with bands, with listening to music and, I suppose, knowing bands an eight-year-old wouldn't usually know. It somehow wasn't cool to like different bands, those who weren't boy bands.

In addition, being a City fan at primary school in Manchester was hard. In 1994 we weren't very good, in 1996 we were worse. I got mercilessly teased about it. I always say it was character-building – you had to be resilient and develop a sense of humour.

And then suddenly there was this band who didn't care, who were from five minutes down the road, and, most importantly, they supported City and were proud of it. And they were going to be "the biggest band on the planet".

Then I met them and started to spend time with them with my dad. They made me feel cool, that it was OK to be different and not give a shit. Oasis at Maine Road was a dream come true, and everyone wanted to be there. And somehow suddenly everything changed.

It changed for fans like Ella, and for the band too.

These photographs are a document to those twelve months of seismic change.

OASIS: THE MASTERPLAN

GAIL CROWTHER
WITH COMMENTARY BY NOEL GALLAGHER

Masterplan

*Noun: a comprehensive, long-term strategy; to construct
a masterplan for*
Verb (used with object): to master-plan one's career

Photographs, like careers, don't simply happen. They
take planning, skill, art, and sometimes they take risks.
But when photographs are taken well, as are the ones
by Kevin Cummins in this book, they can not only
take us back in time but also help us travel through
time. In this case, we are about to journey through the
days of a particular year: 1994.

It's odd to think of a global phenomenon like Oasis
being created, they seem almost timeless. Yet there
was a cultural moment when those songs didn't
exist. There was a time when their record company,
Creation, was getting ready to launch the band into,
and onto, the world. Cummins's book tells the visual
story of the transformation that took place.

If you want to see the immediate results, you
can turn to the first full-band photograph in this
book, a two-page spread. We see a light-blue studio
background, oversized jackets of the Nineties, Liam
leaning forward, in red, expression deadpan. Noel to
the right, frowning and sucking his finger. The rest
of the band looking like they've possibly never had
their photograph taken before. There is a real beauty
in the ordinariness of their style. On reflection, Noel
recognizes that in many ways, unintentionally, this
was part of the appeal of Oasis: "We looked like any

average working-class lads of our age, from our area.
Nothing special." But leap ahead now to the two
photos of the band taken right at the end of the year at
Maine Road. That uncertainty is gone. They all look
sharper, there's better hair, and Noel in a smart, fitted
coat staring directly into the camera lens holding
a football. If ever you were to read meaning into an
image, you would say he has the look of a man who
knows the world is about to become his.

This, of course, can be the unreliability of
interpreting photos, because Noel doesn't like having
his photograph taken and he isn't interested in fashion
beyond an admiration for the style of Al Pacino in
Scarface. When asked what his favourite image is from
the selection in this book he replies, "Hmm...you're
asking the wrong person really. Photographs and
photographers and photoshoots don't bring out the
best in me. I'm not a poser, see?" Neither is he much
bothered about fashion: "I never thought Oasis had
a look. Other people did and that's cool, but I'll put
tunes over trainers EVERY DAY. Trainers last for six
months. The melodies live forever."

Yet Oasis did have a look, and part of that is because
of the way Kevin Cummins photographed them. This
goes a bit deeper than fashion. Certainly, the just-
bought-at-Afflecks-Palace attainability of their look
was hugely important. As was the football (sometimes
called "terrace-chic") sportswear, the highlight of this
surely being the renowned photographs of Noel and
Liam in the brother-sponsored Man City shirts. But

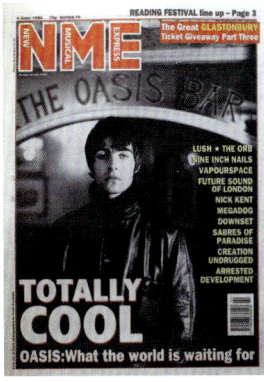
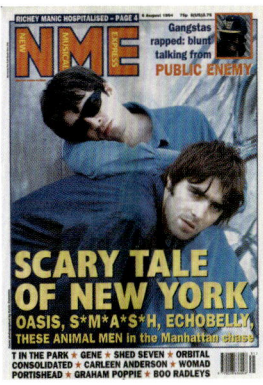
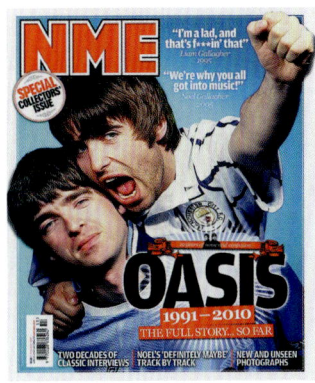

it is not just the fashion that is enduring, it is these photographs of it too. Cummins helped to shape our expectations of Oasis, not only how they looked, but also our anticipation of how they might sound. It may seem a little odd to merge the visual and the aural in this way. It may seem even odder to ask the question: can you "hear" a photograph? But look at any image in this book and you get more than a hint of what Oasis will sound like. We see the different experiments with style, from V-neck jumpers to City tops to button-down shirts; clothing that was as much to do with financial restrictions as preference. "We were as broke as fuck so we wore what we could afford. Nothing more, nothing less," comments Noel. We know they will be singing about something relatable.

In this book we also see the story of a backdrop changing from the brick terraces of Manchester, the stands of Maine Road and the escalators in the Arndale Centre, through to the narrow streets of Soho and the red buses of London. Could Oasis have existed if they had been brought up anywhere other than Manchester? "Absolutely not," replies Noel. They are formed by their geography but neither trapped nor restricted by it. They are equally at home in Back George Street in Manchester's Chinatown, surrounded by overflowing cardboard boxes of rubbish, as they are a month later wearing shades and performing at the Virgin Megastore on Oxford Street, London. So many possibilities, so many paths, *"There's four and twenty million doors/On life's endless corridors."*

These endless possibilities are what this book documents as Cummins shows how the origins of a band – how a masterplan grows and develops, building on the foundations of where it all began. Or, as Noel puts it, "We're Mancunians. We have a thing. The rest of the world LOVES that thing. Why? Fuck knows." Cummins produces some of the most memorable images of the band as they travel from obscurity to global fame; images that bring to mind the famous observation by the artist Joan Miró, who claimed that you can look at a picture for a week and never think of it again, or you can look at a picture for a second and think of it all your life. These are images that people will think of all their lives: Liam beneath the sign for The Oasis Bar; the brothers stood outside of the Peveril of the Peak pub; the soon-to-be-rock stars eating candyfloss and ice cream; Liam and Noel in their City shirts, arms around each other, everything in their lives about to change.

There is poignancy and celebration. And there is art. Life's possibilities captured for a full year. This is the power of photography. Diane Arbus saw what she called the "act of photography" as an adventure, and here Cummins takes us on his adventure for this seminal moment in time. In this case, we know the end of the story. We know exactly what happened by the end of 1994. But the adventure and the journey offer us a reminder that whoever you are, wherever you are from: *"We're all part of a masterplan."*

"If I was to art direct an Oasis shoot, I'd have the band shot while they weren't aware they were being shot. Posing is fake. Fly on the wall is real. That's when you see some kind of truth."

—*Noel Gallagher*

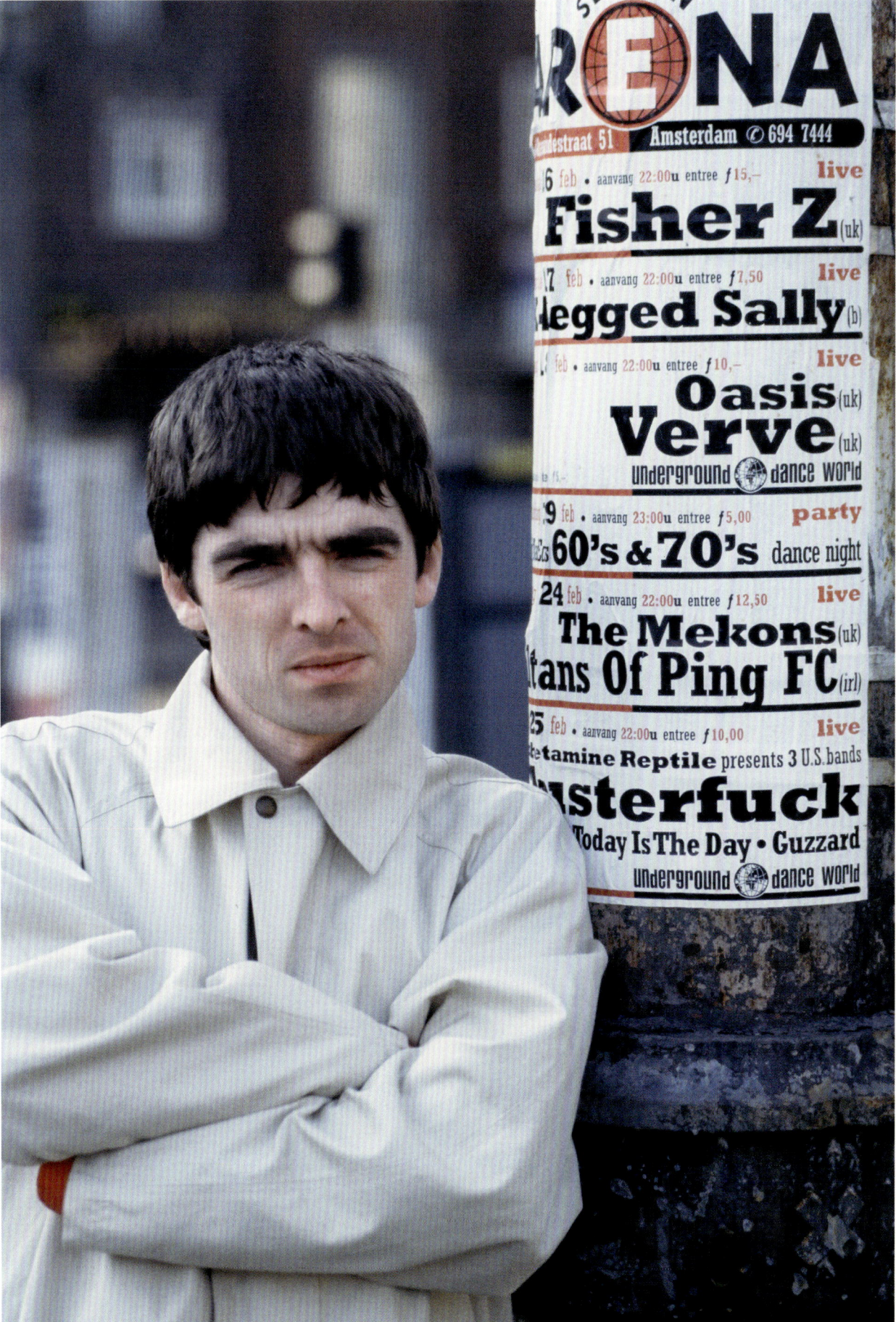

21 FEBRUARY
SLY STREET STUDIO, LONDON

This is a shot from Oasis's first session in a photo studio. It was commissioned by their record label to get them used to the environment and to try out different lighting techniques to see which style suited them.

   They arrived in the clothes they were wearing with nothing else. Liam wore a light-coloured raincoat, a school-style jumper, and adidas tracksuit bottoms. I shot him with lots of 1930s-style shadowy lighting, but it was clear to me that if you wanted to sell the band, a close-up would work best.

   He had an angelic face back then. It was a perfect look for the British music magazine market – and so it was proven to be.

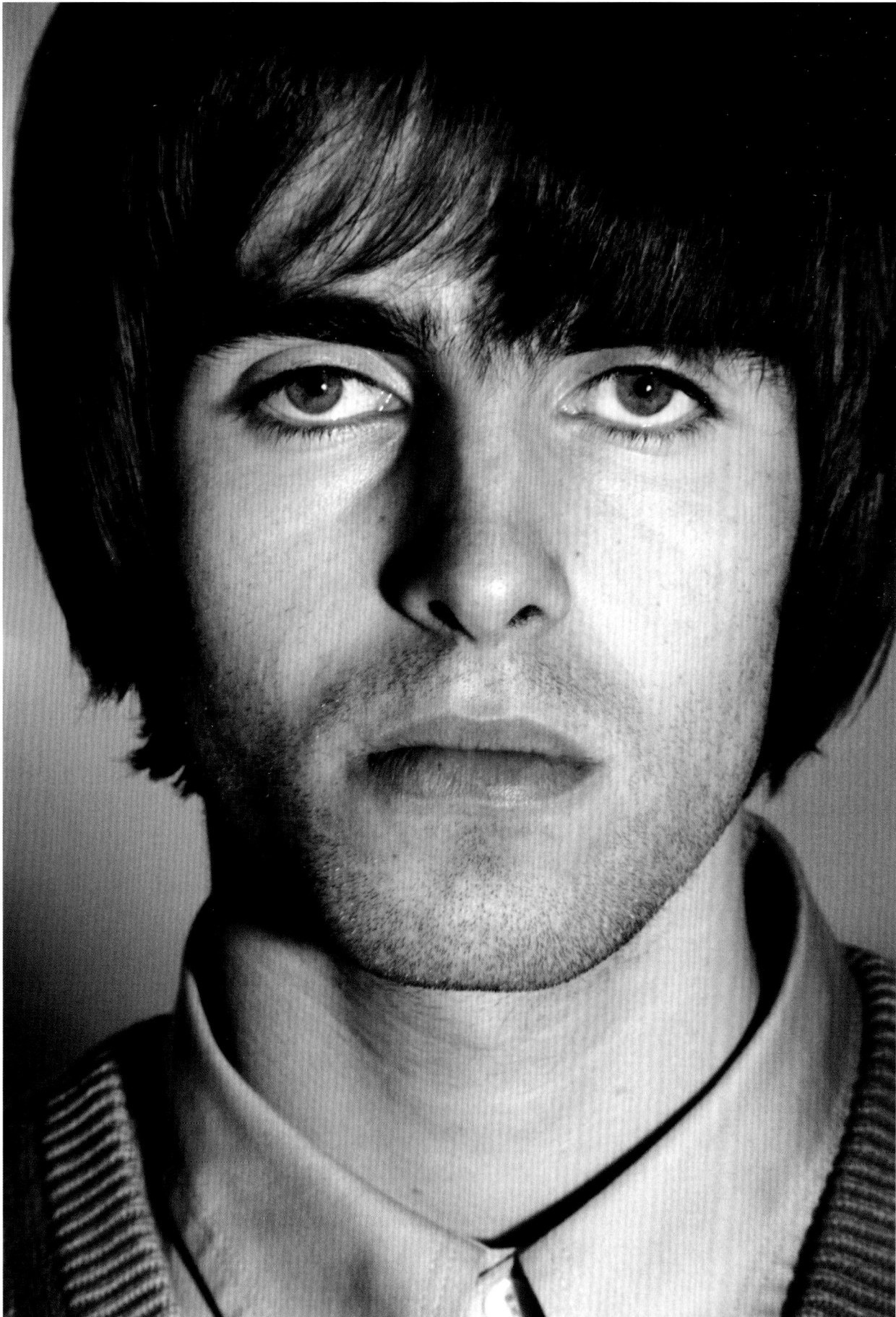

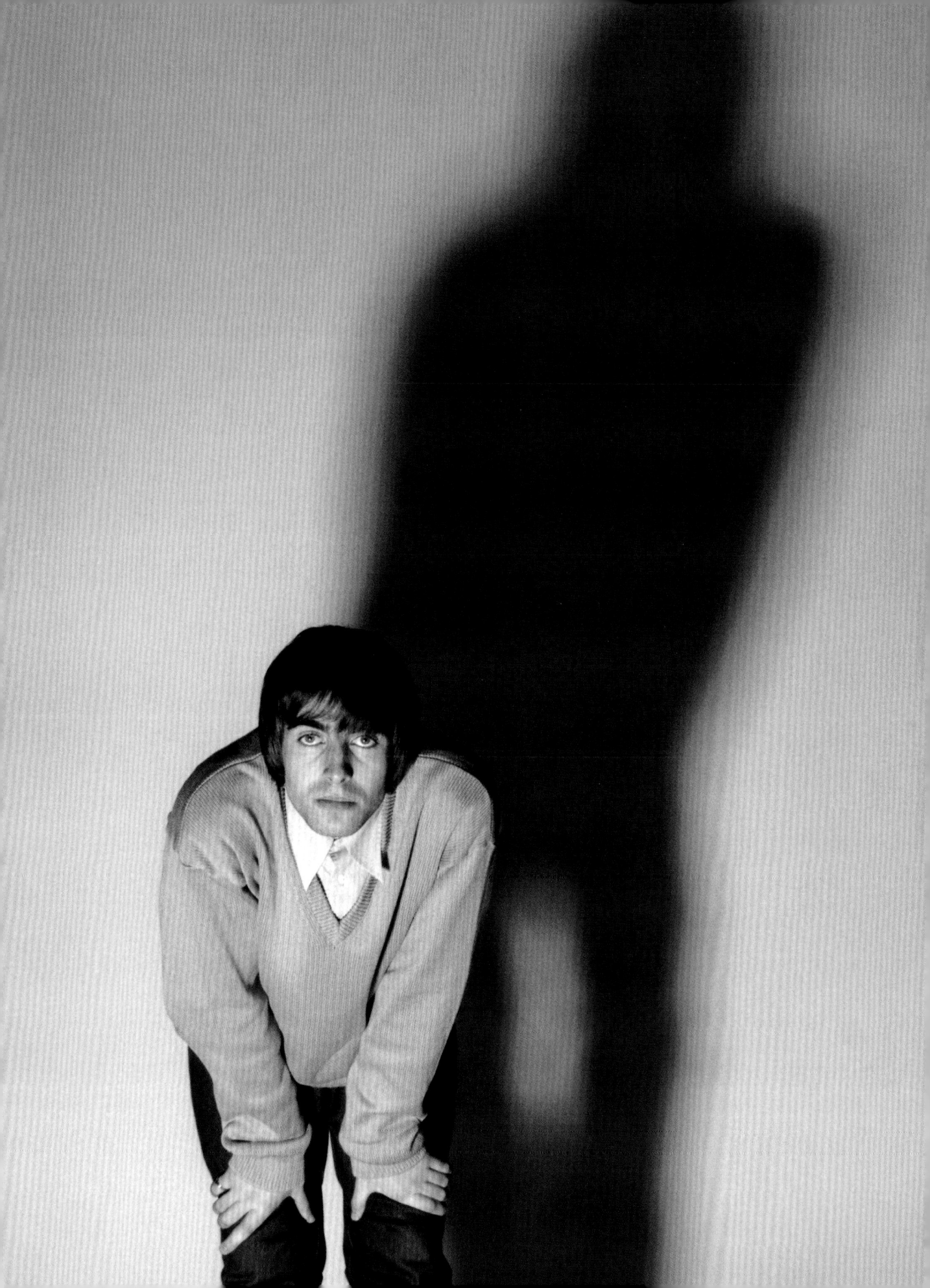

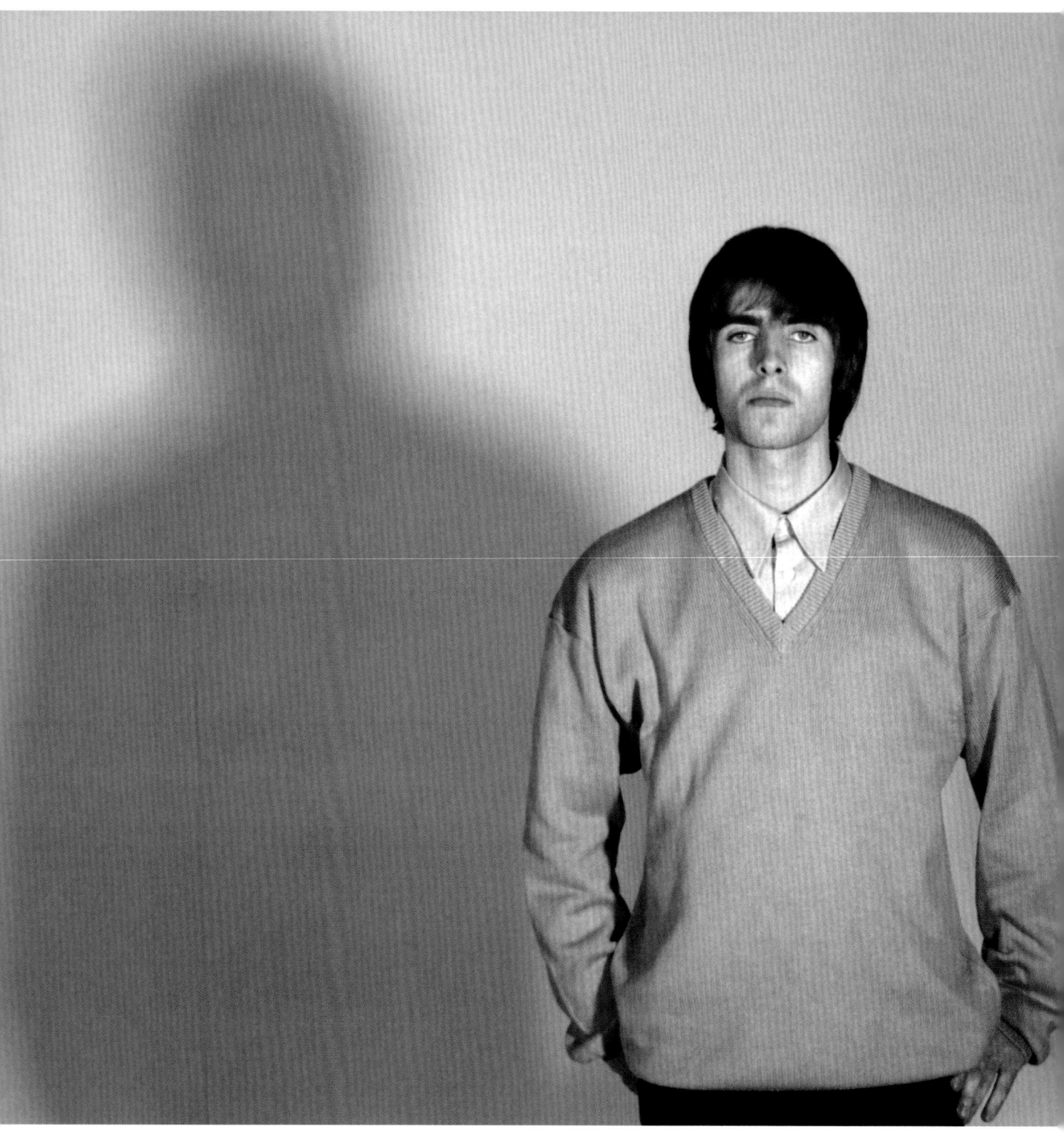

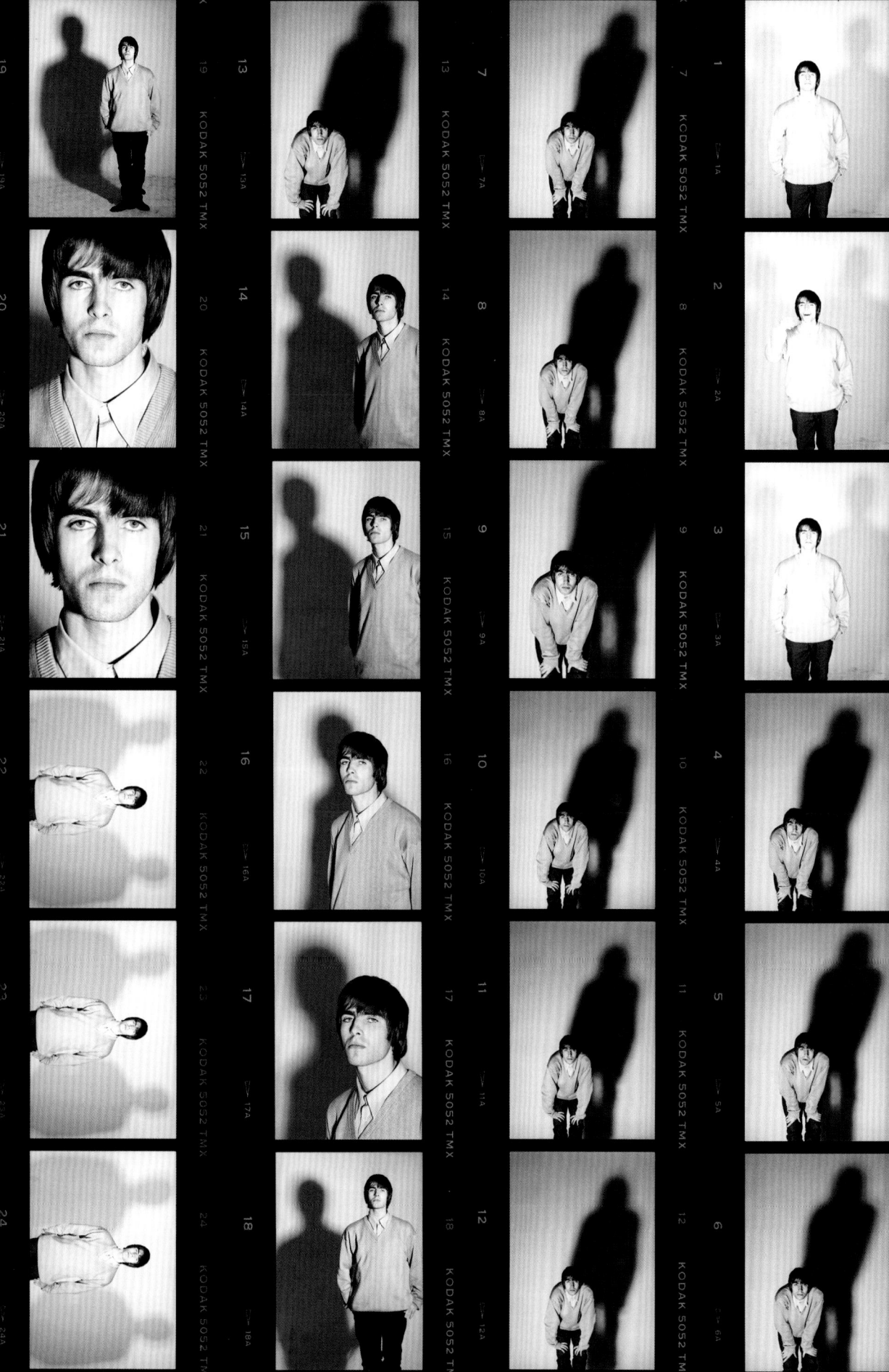

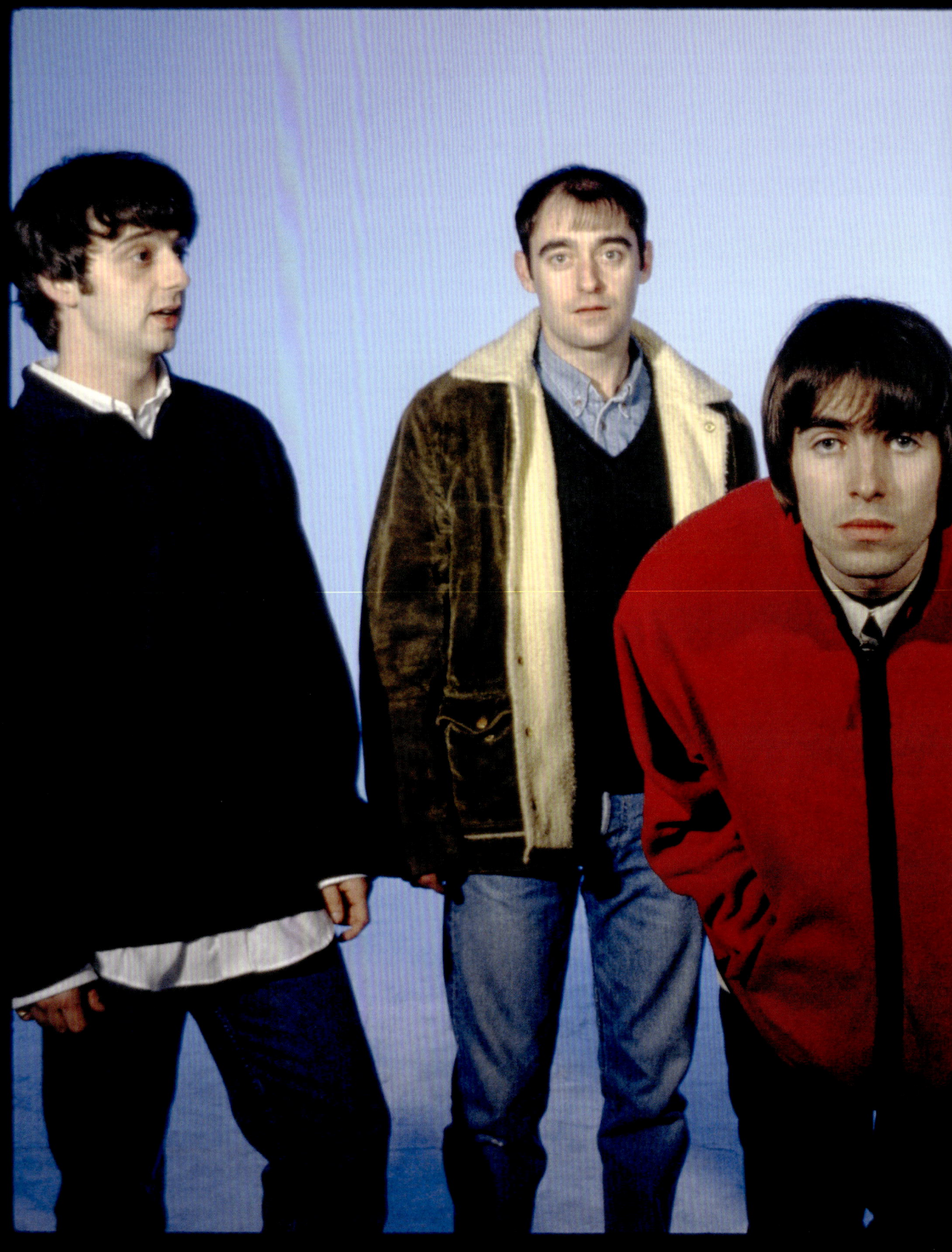

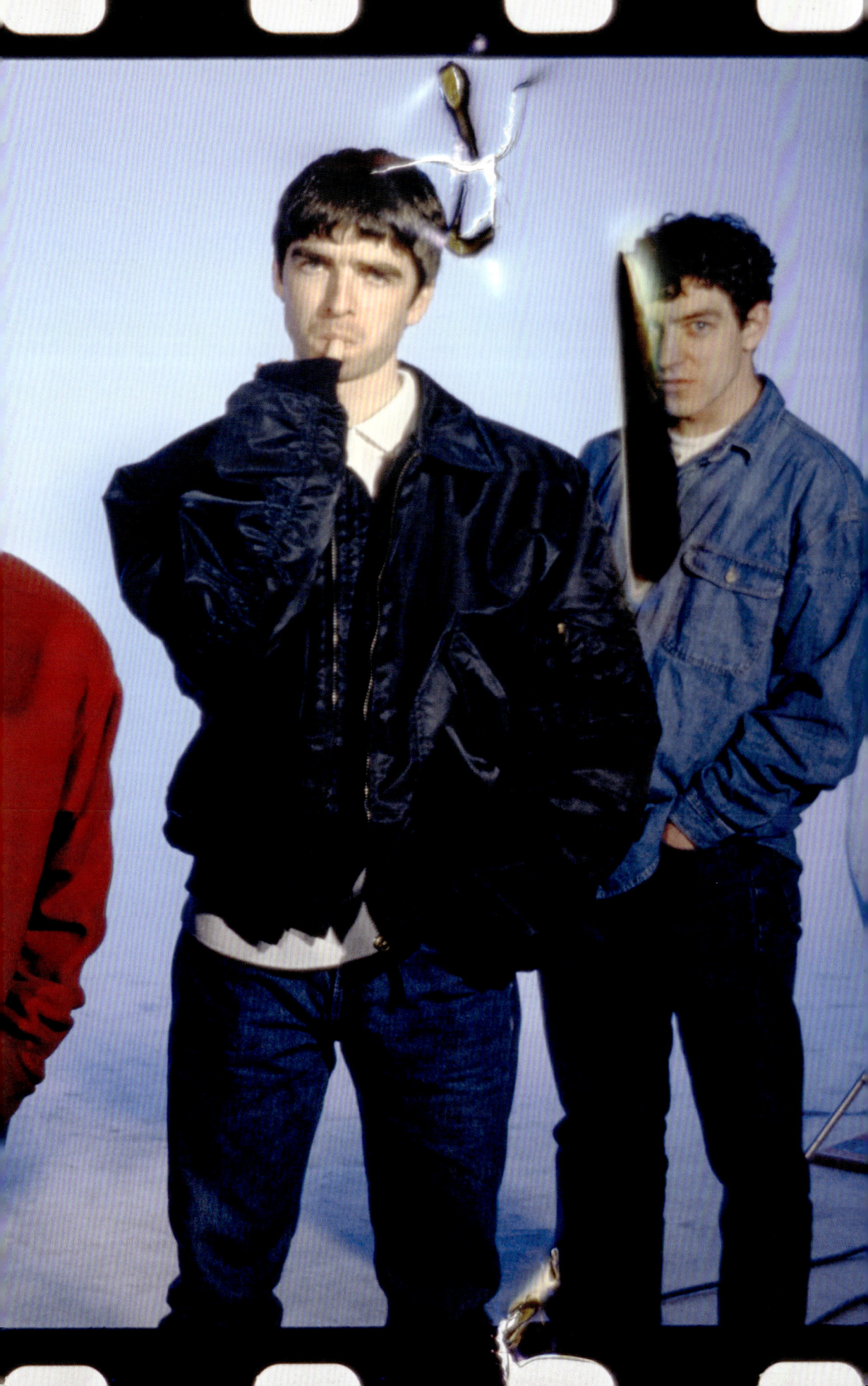

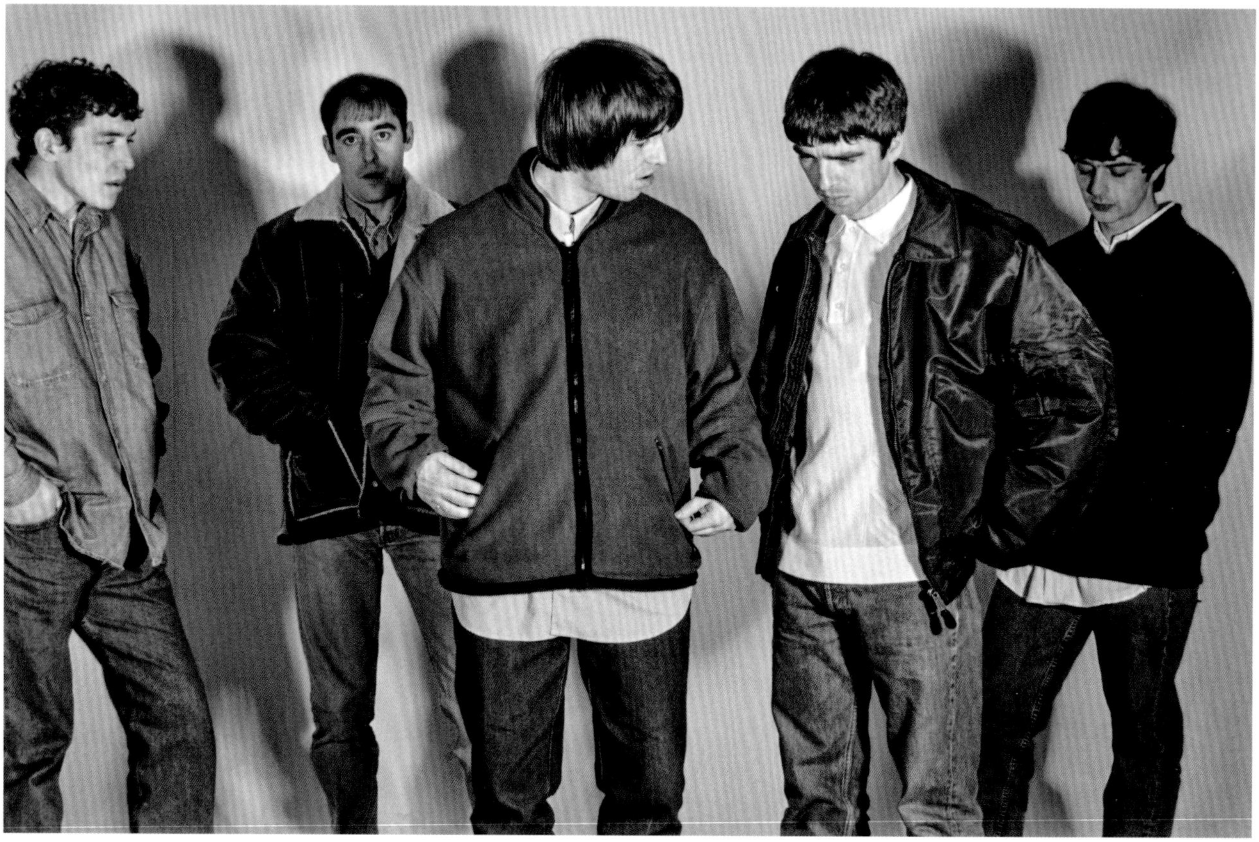
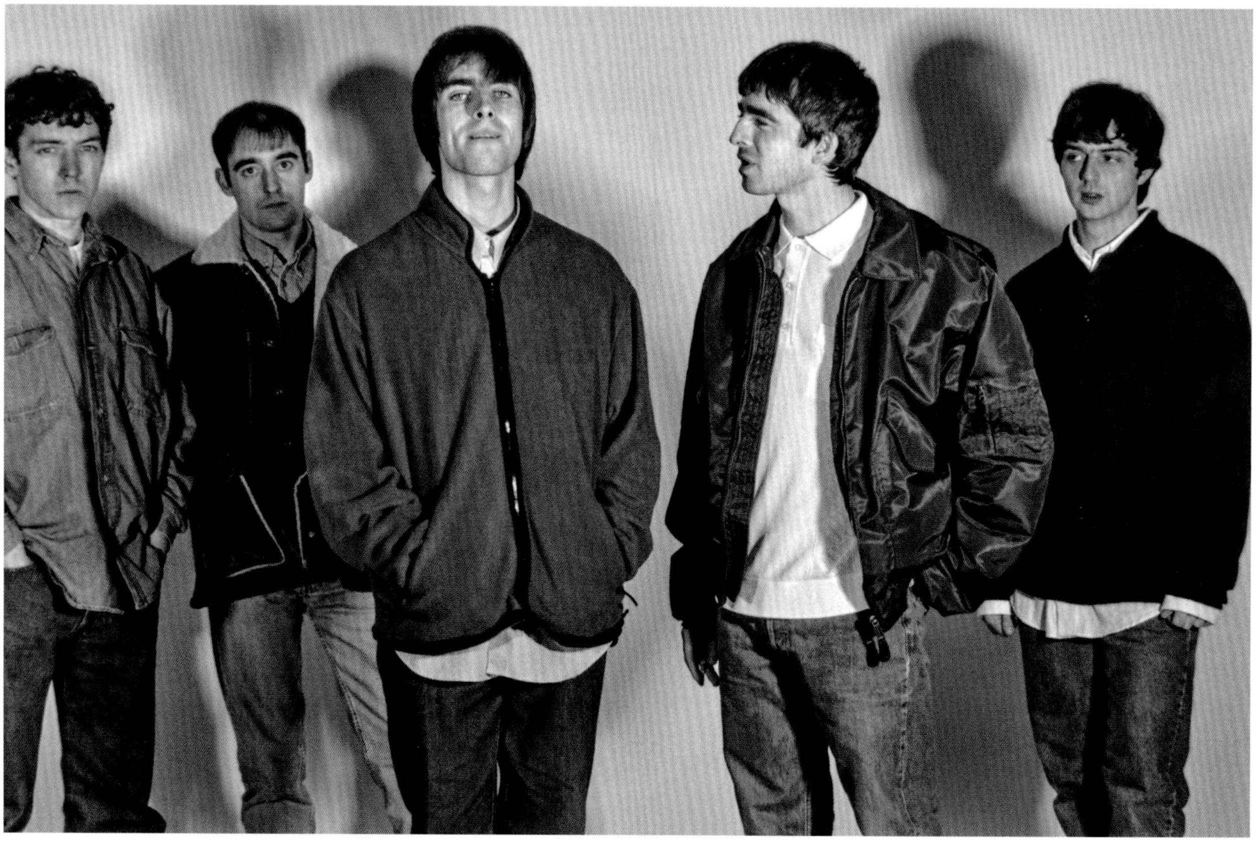

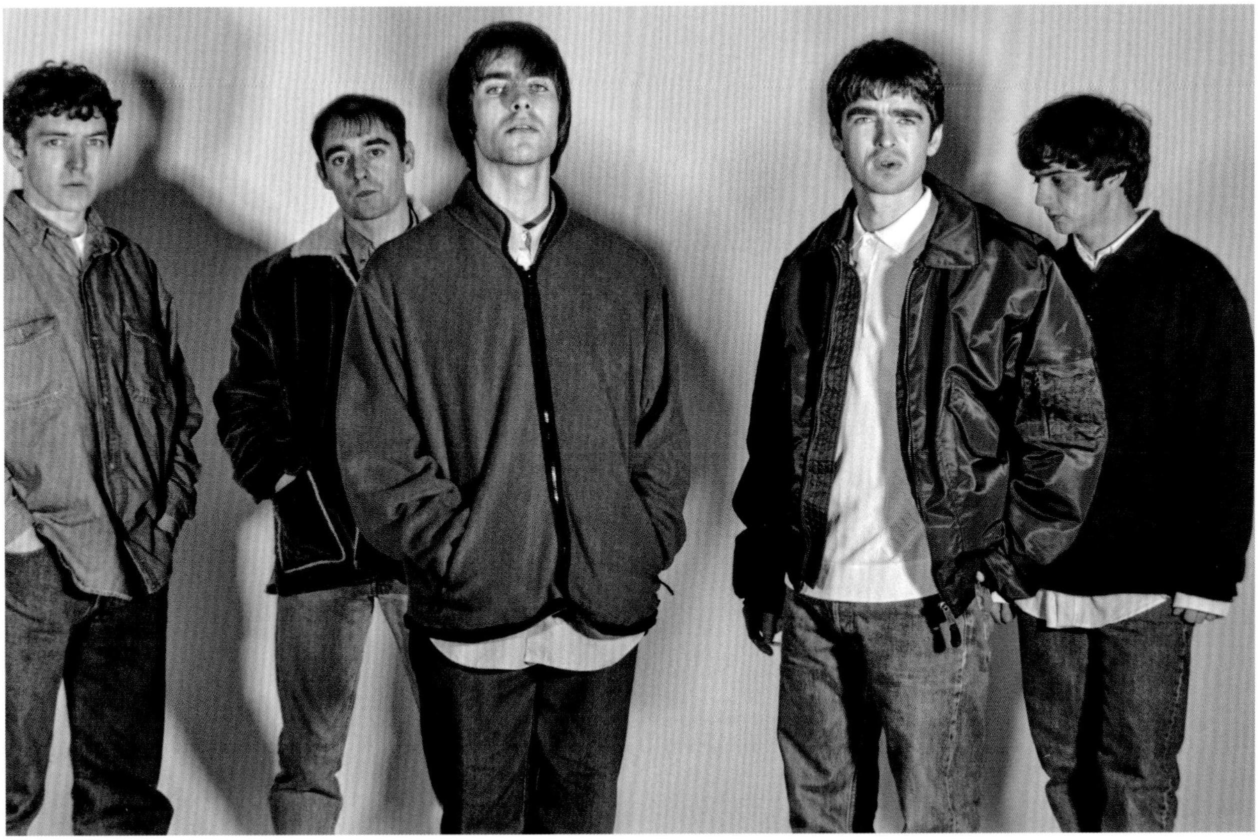

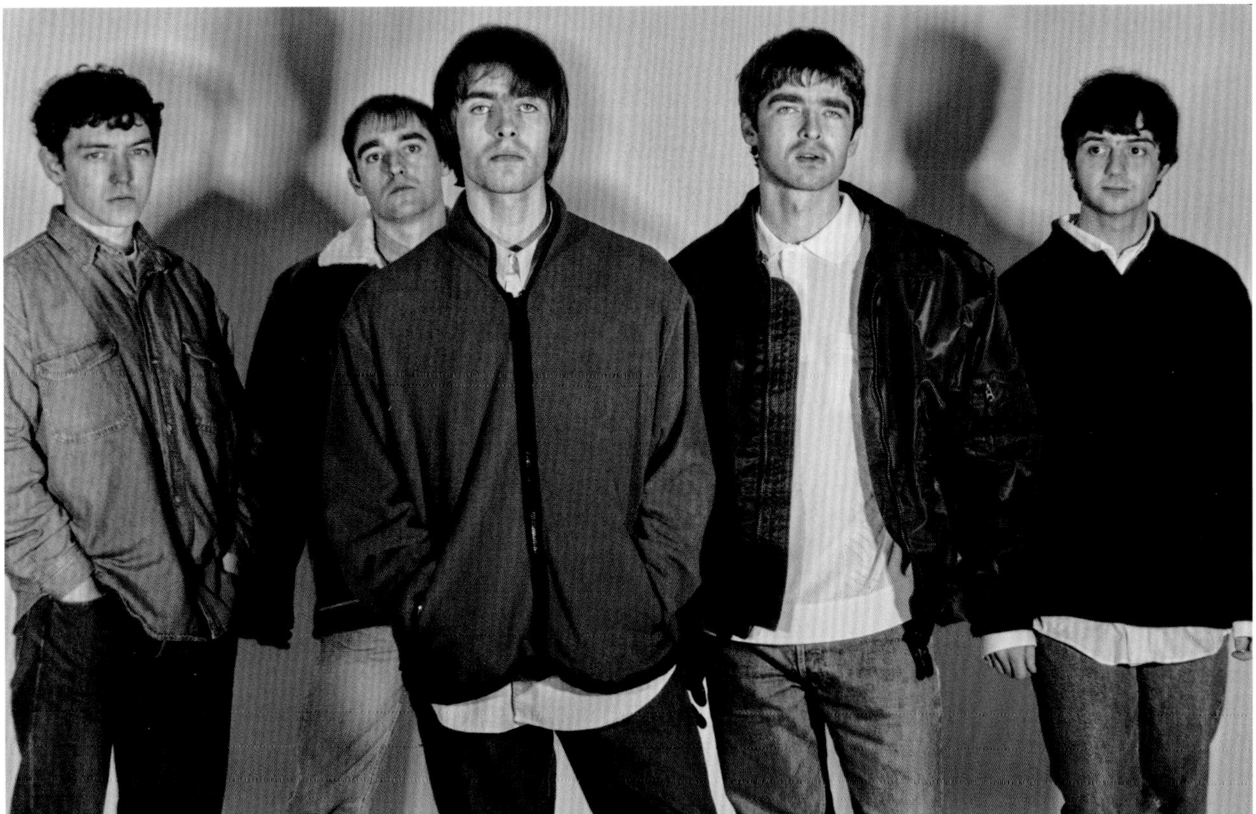

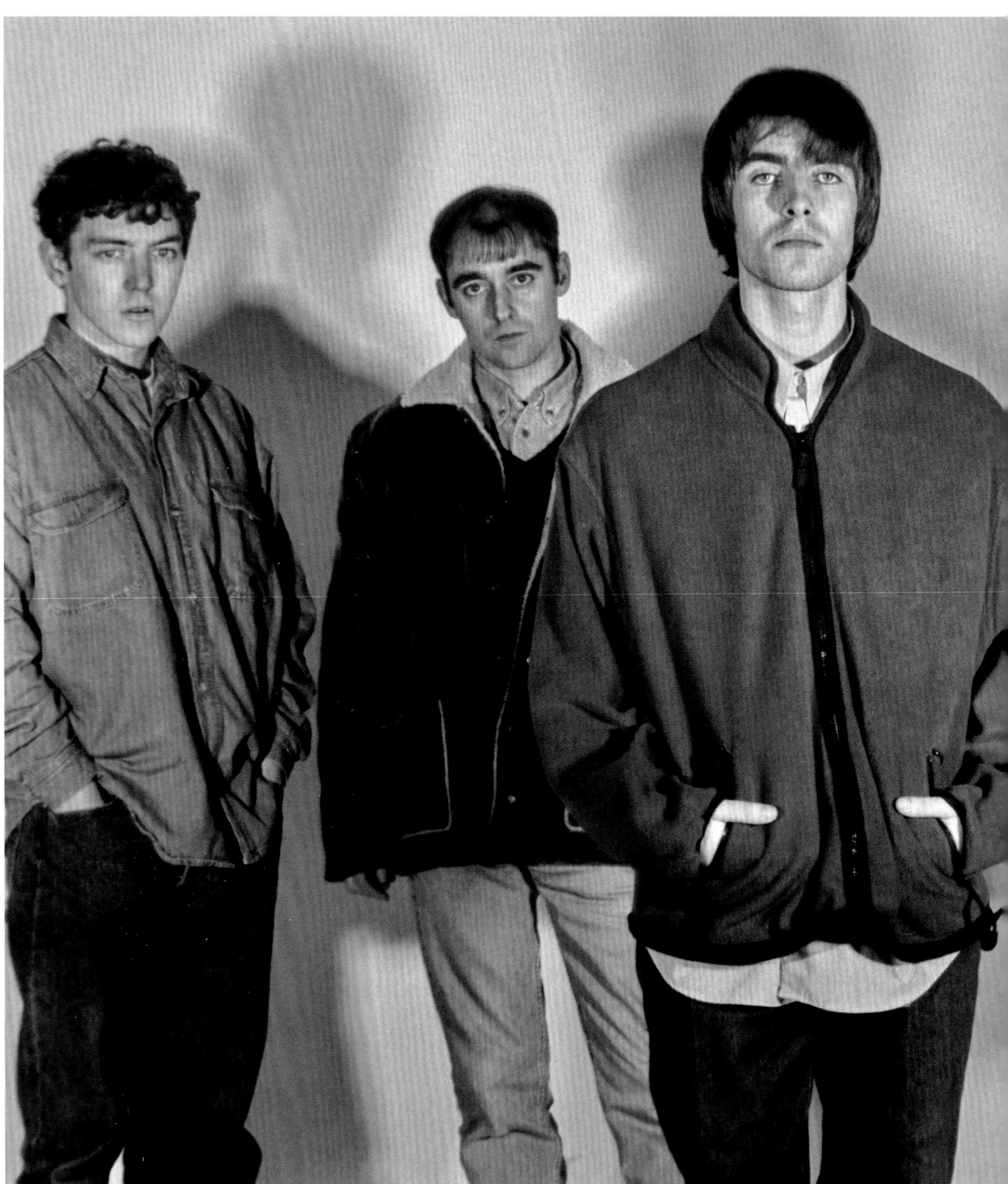

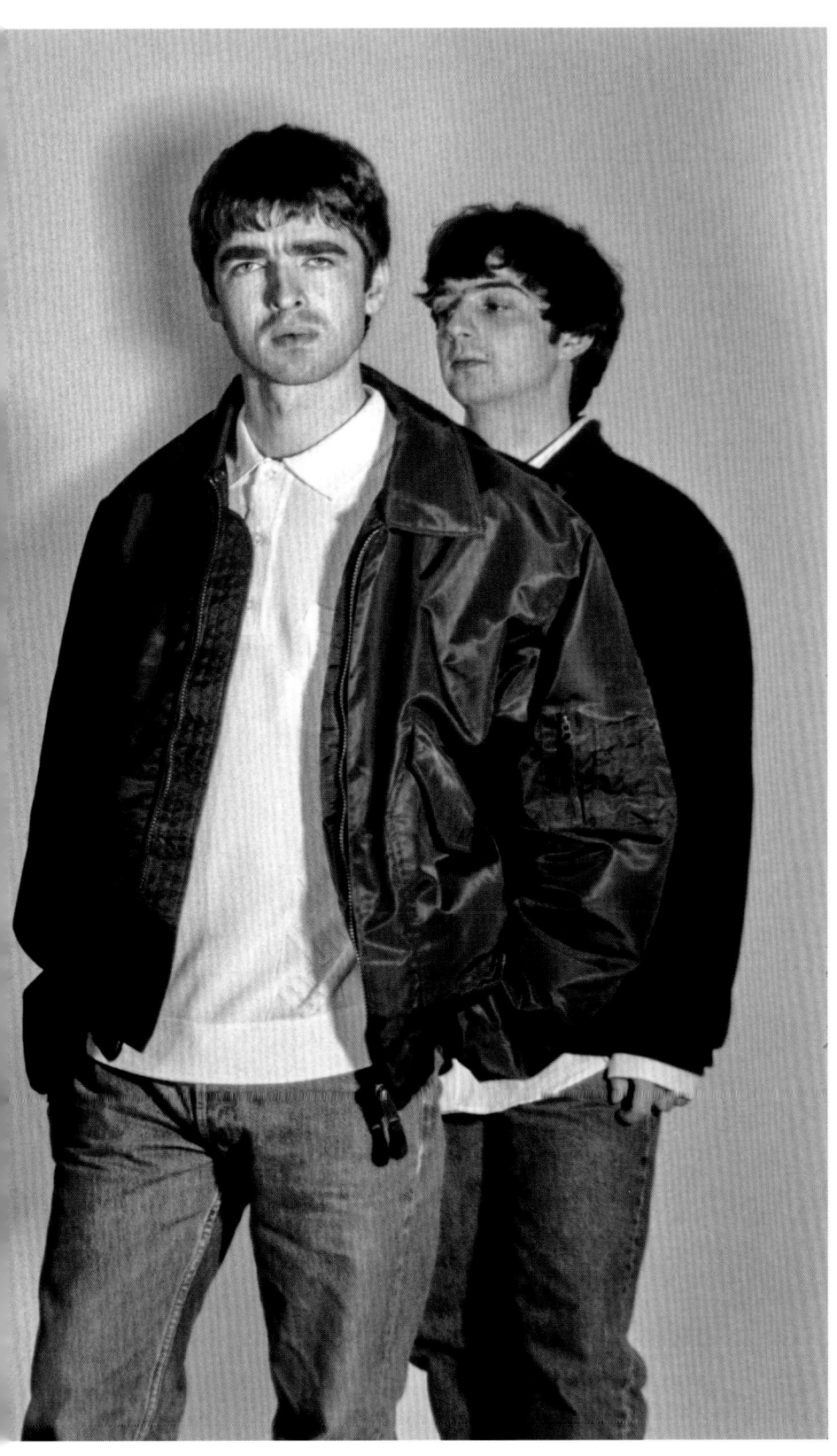

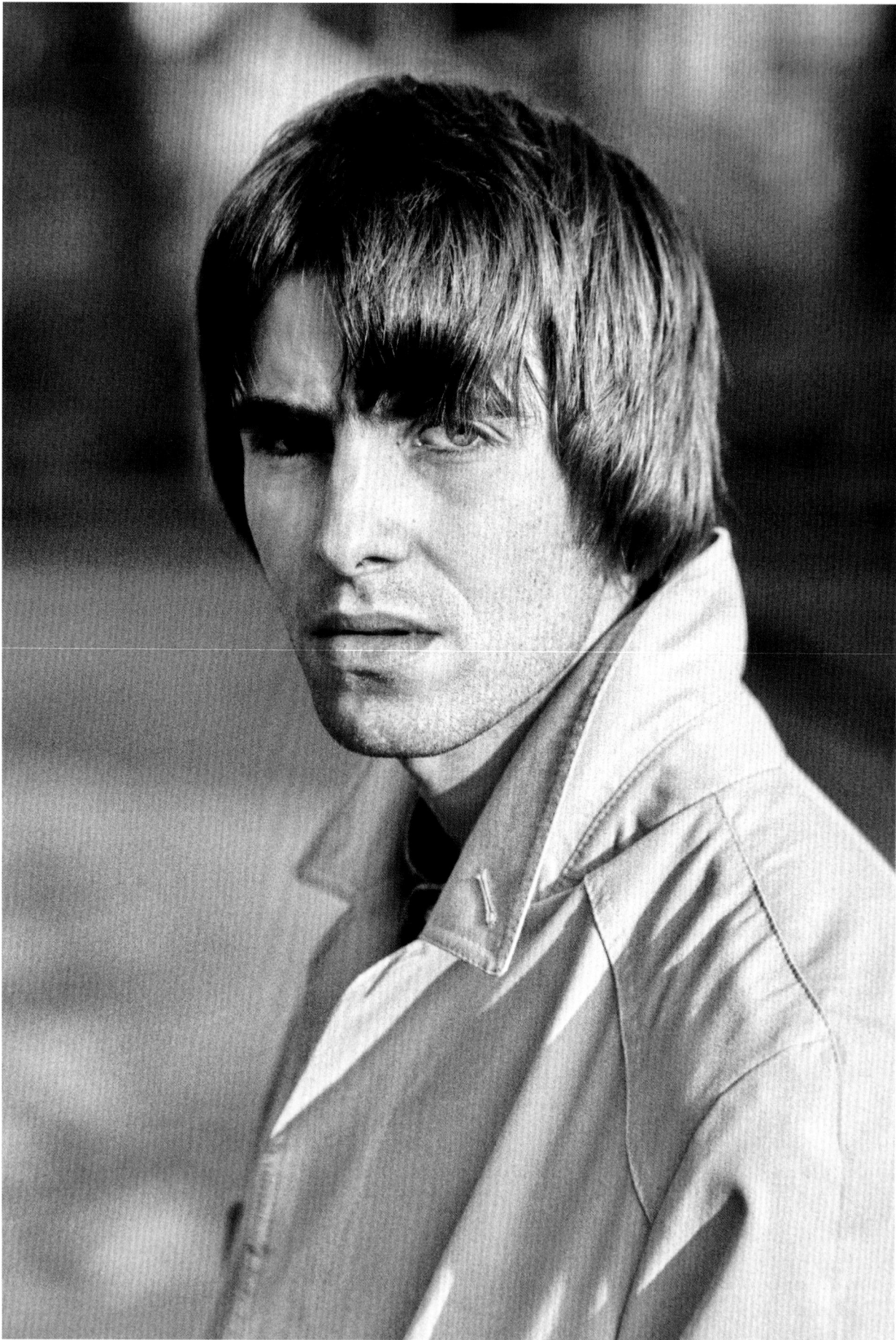

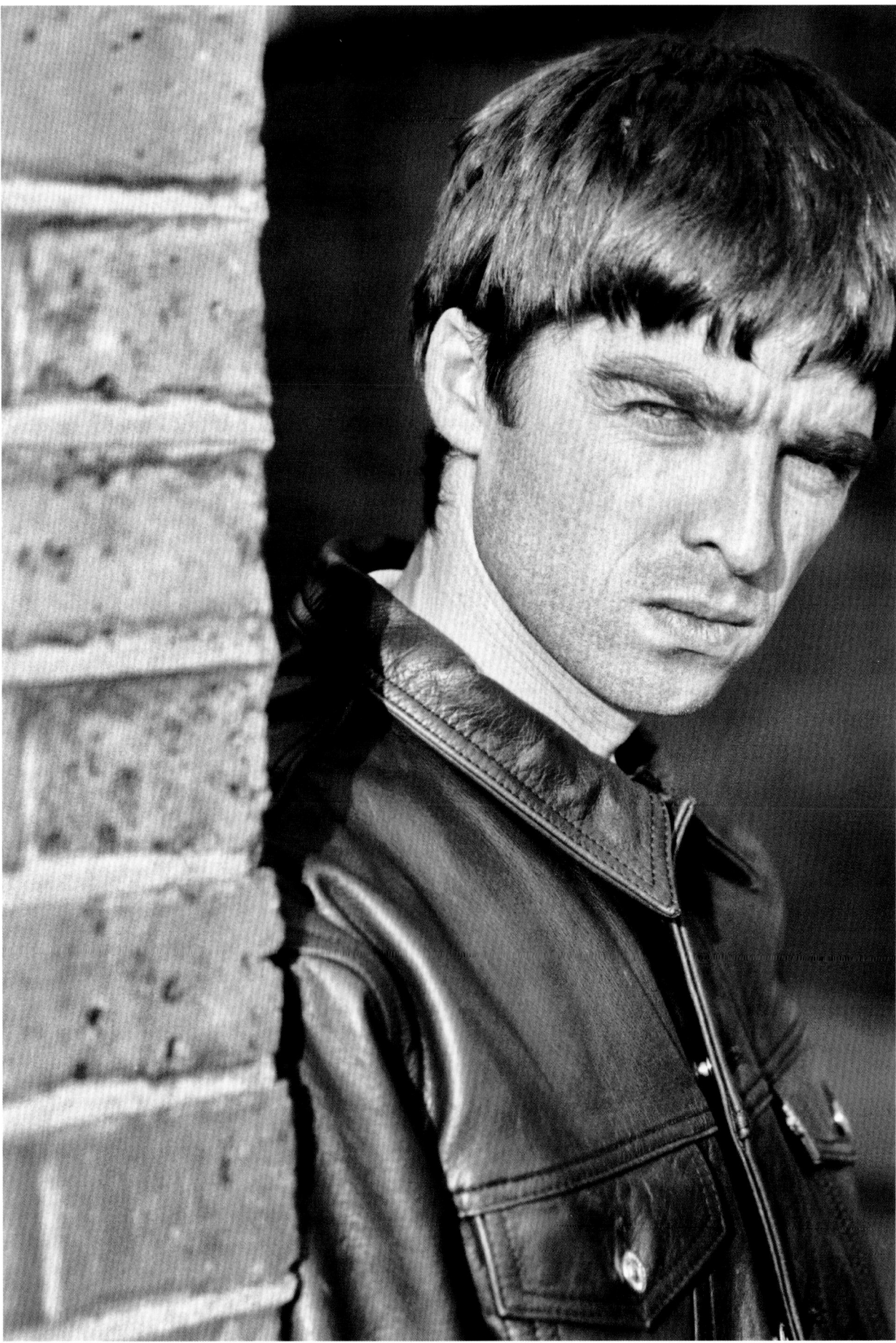

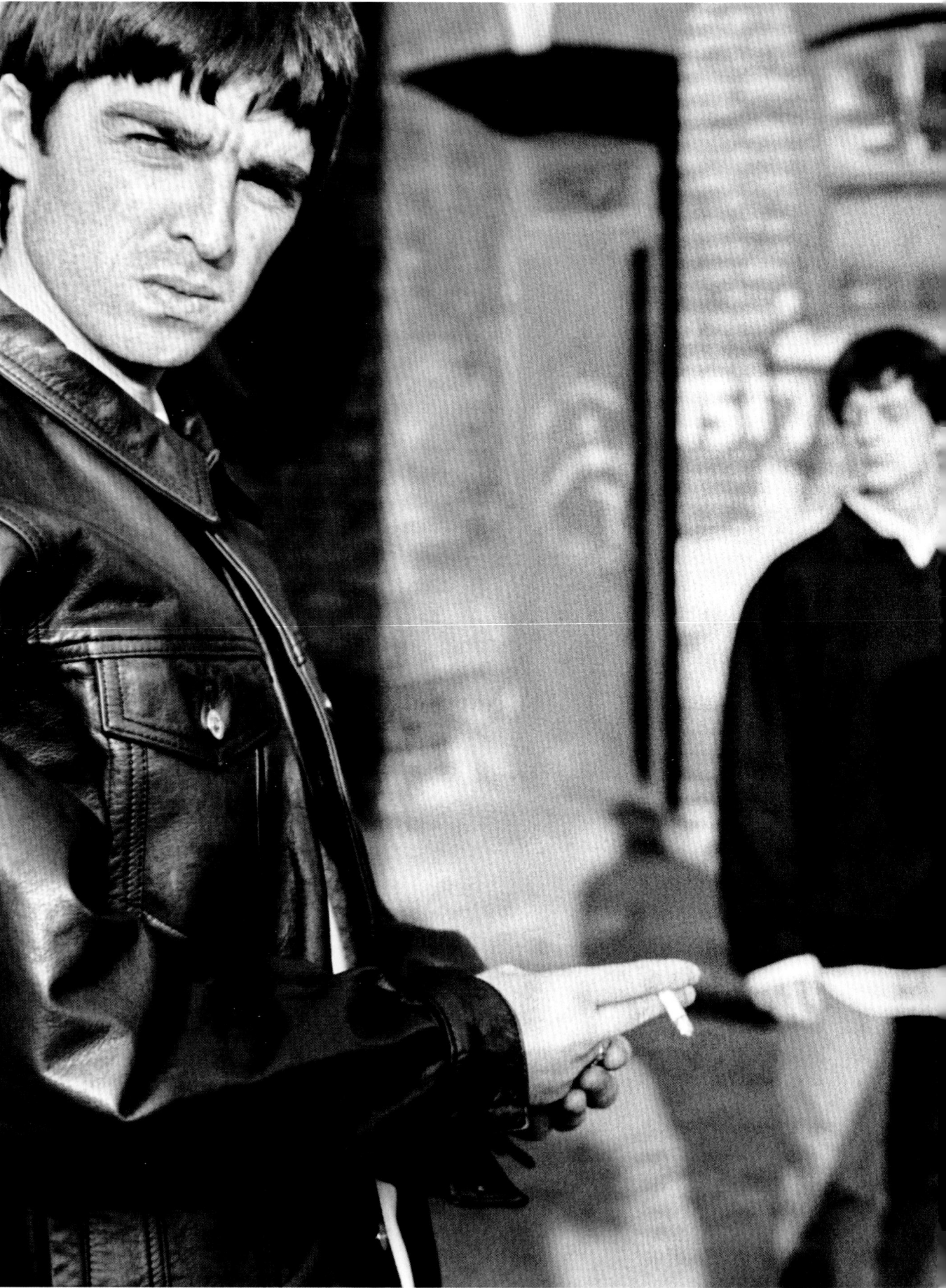

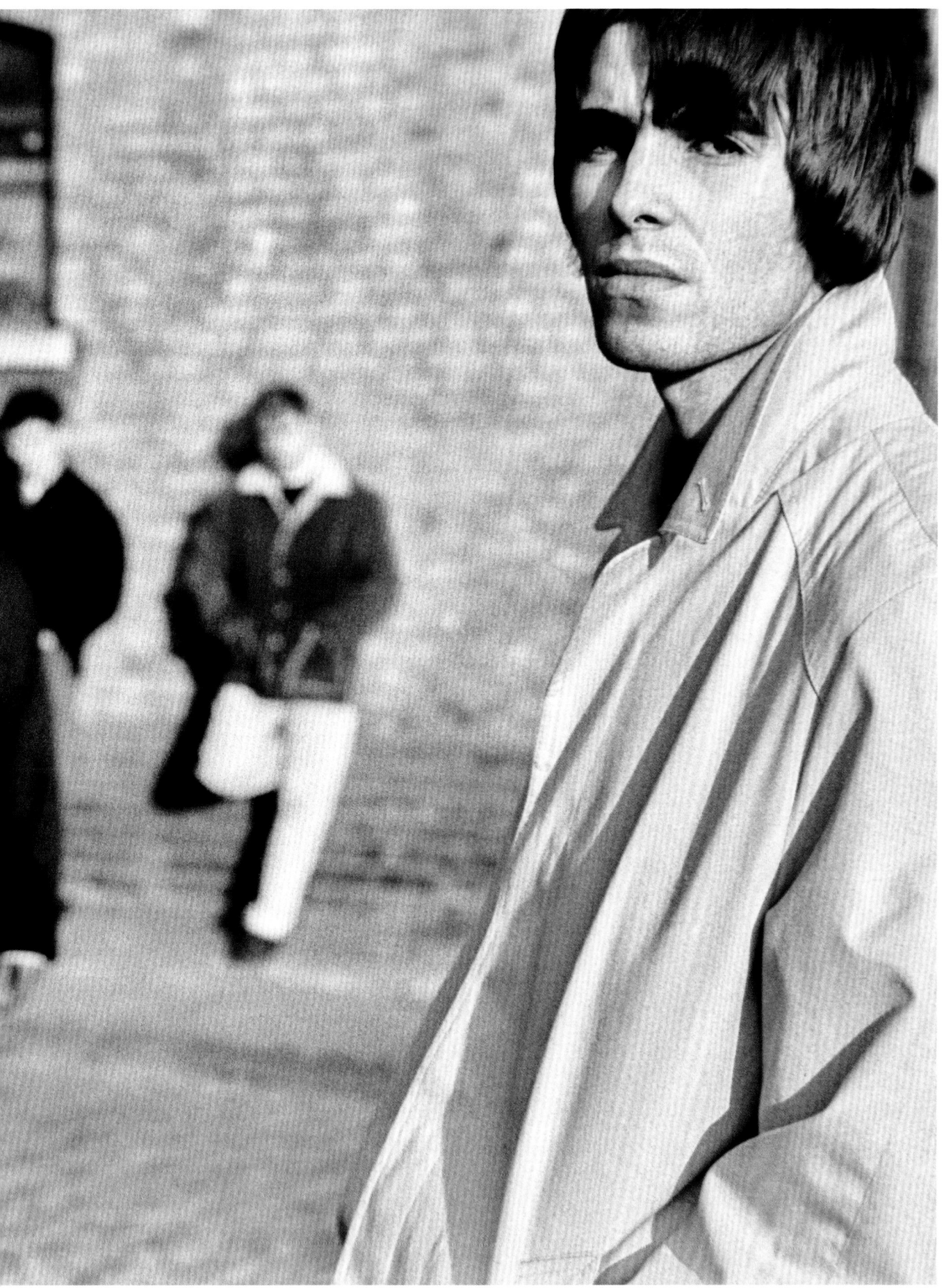

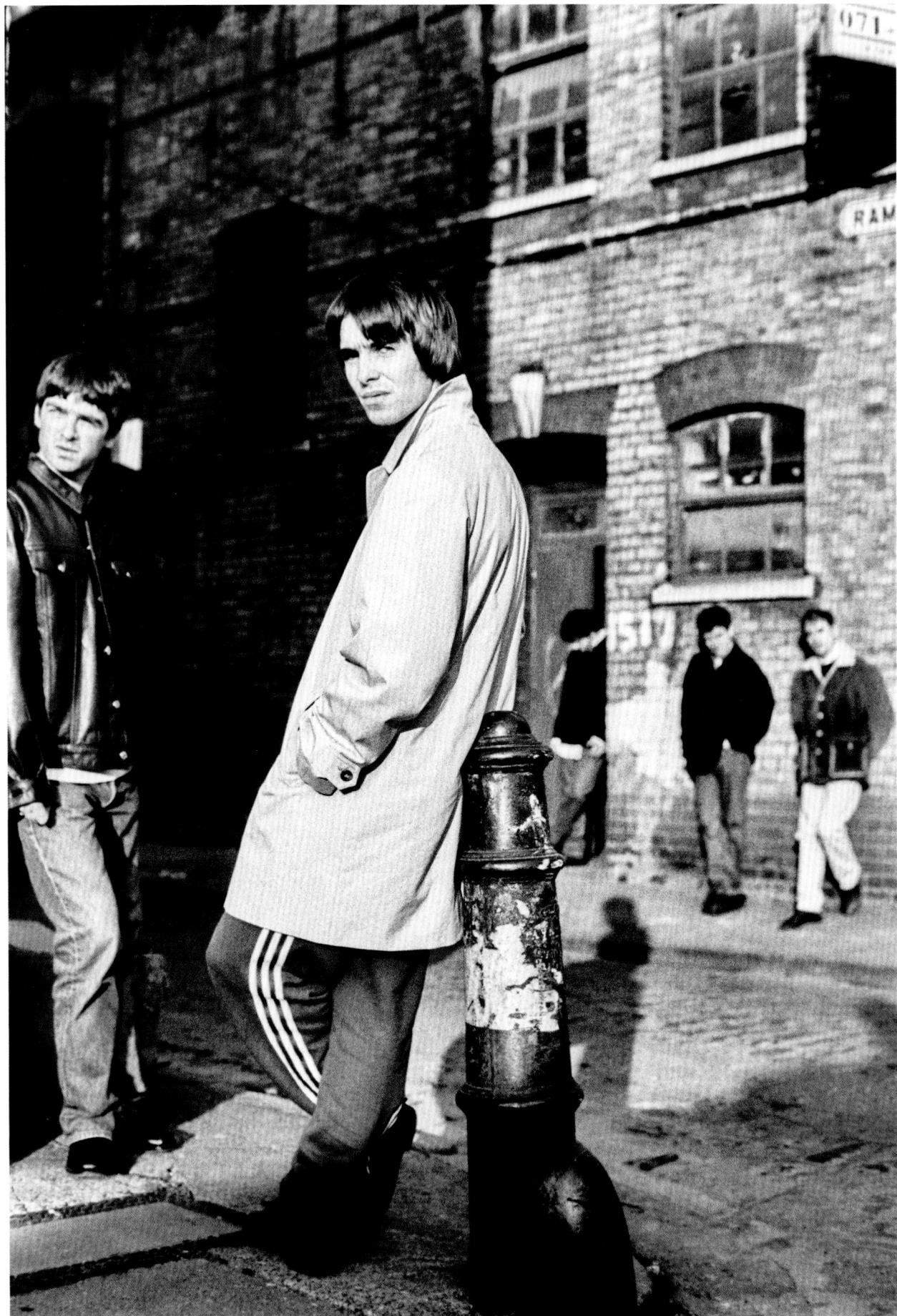

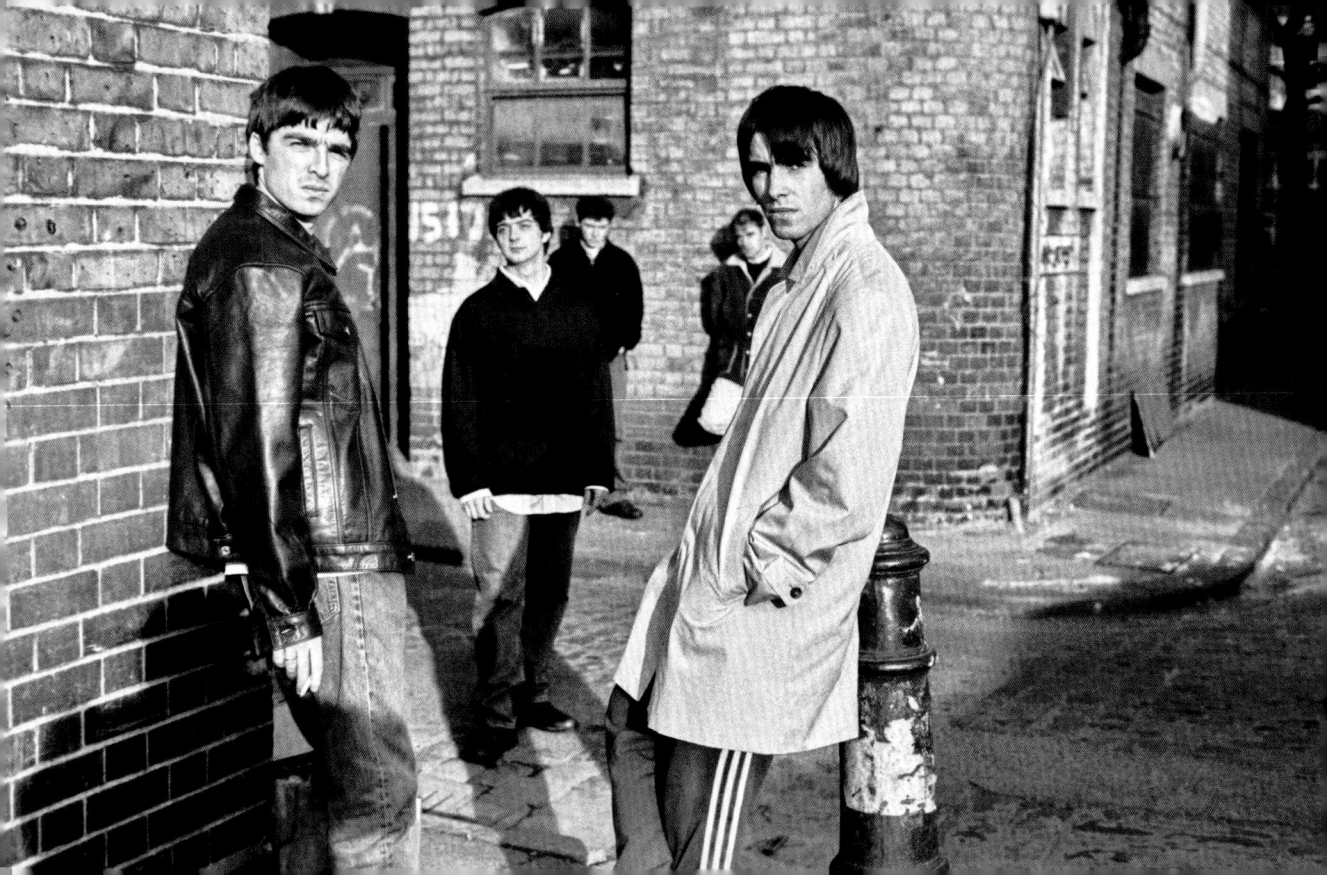

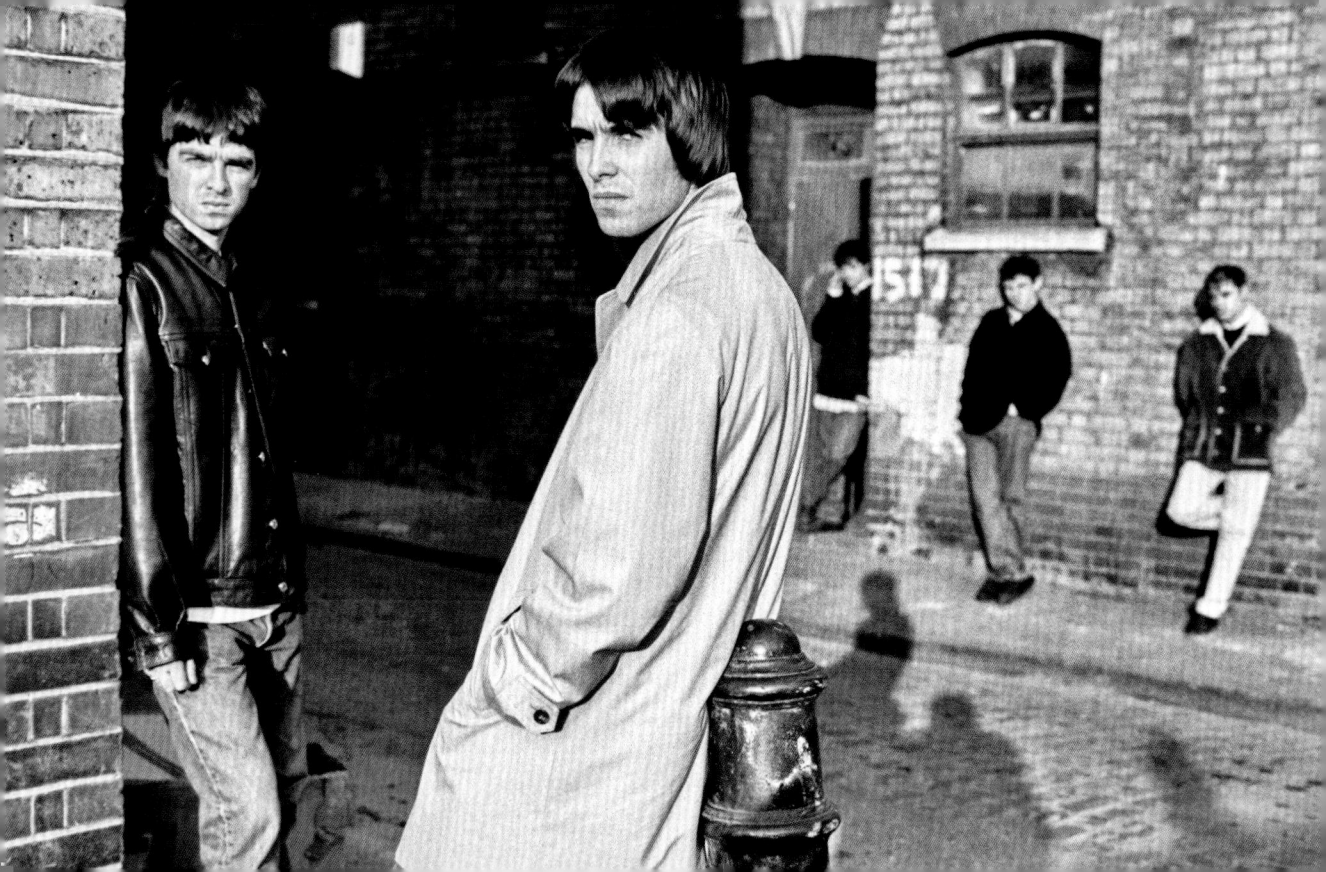

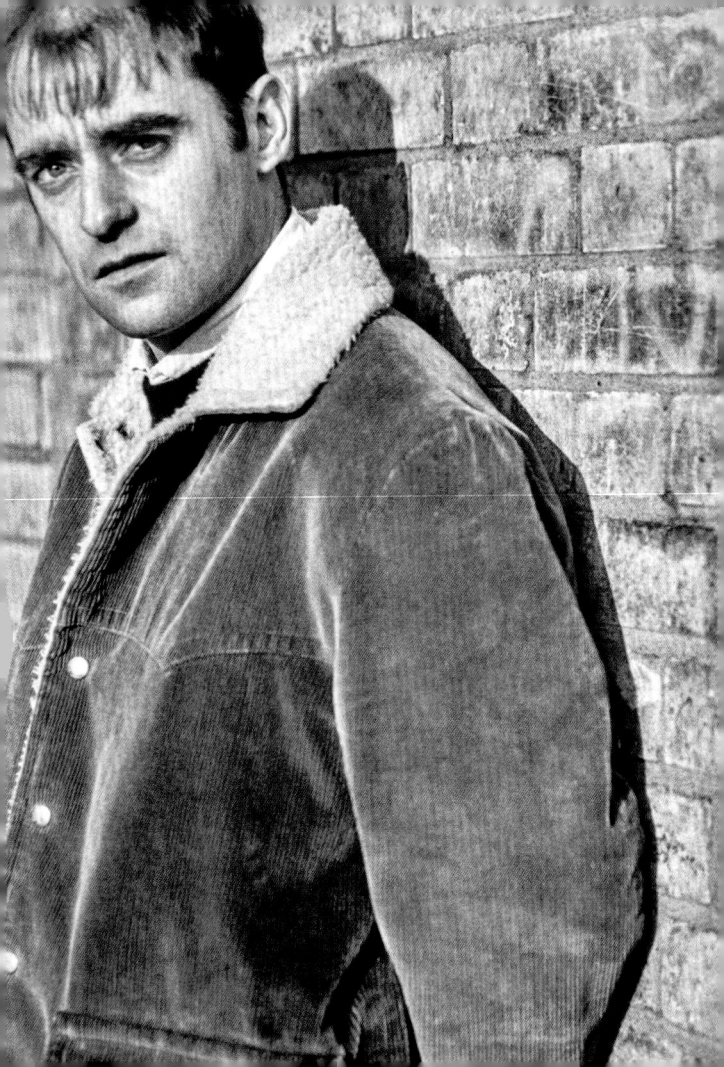

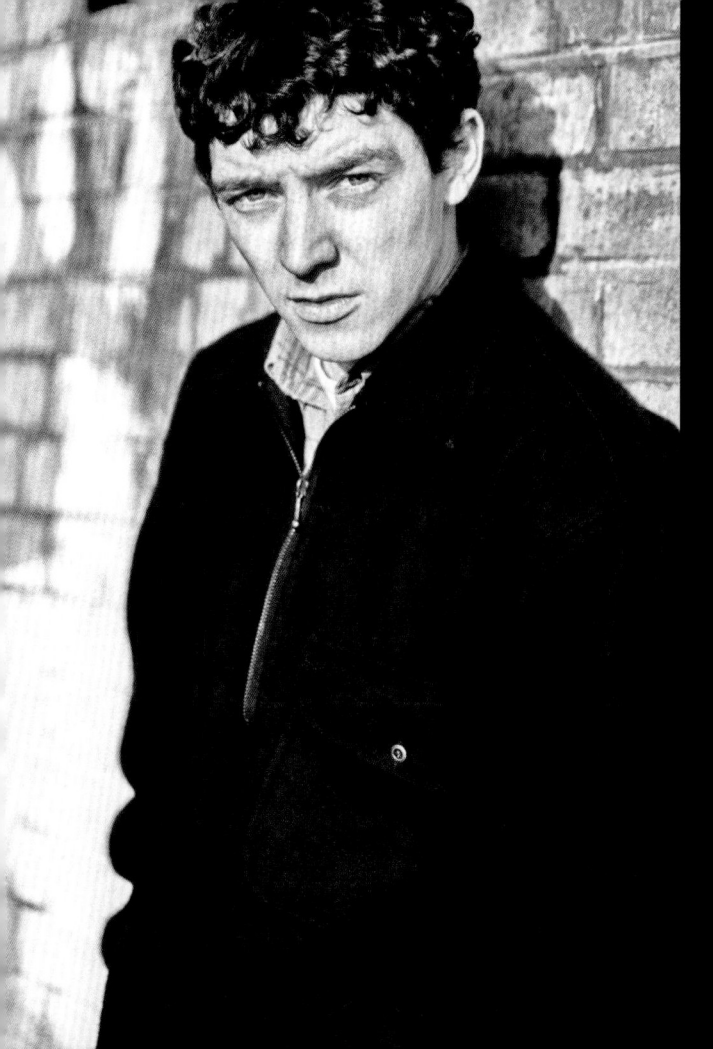

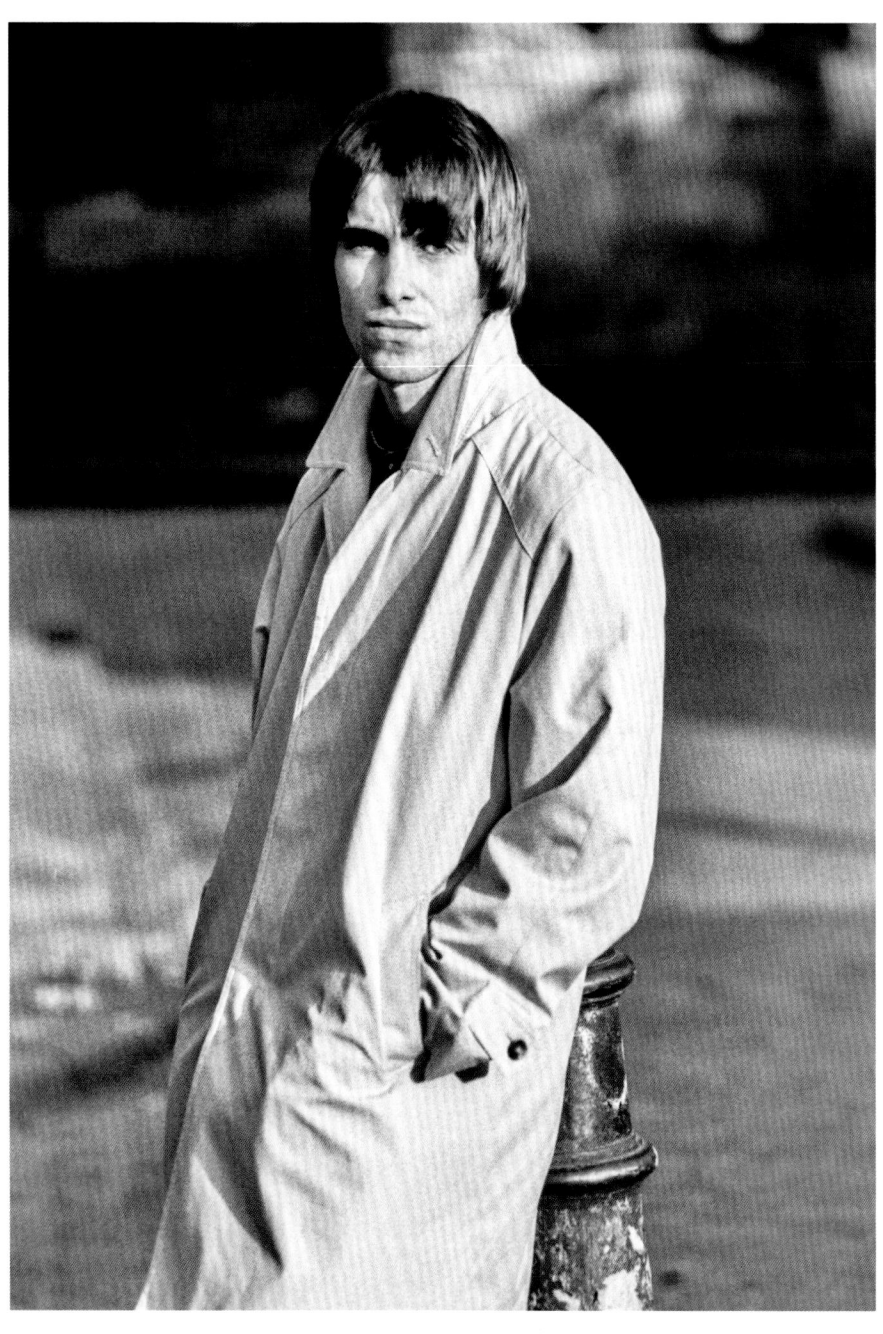

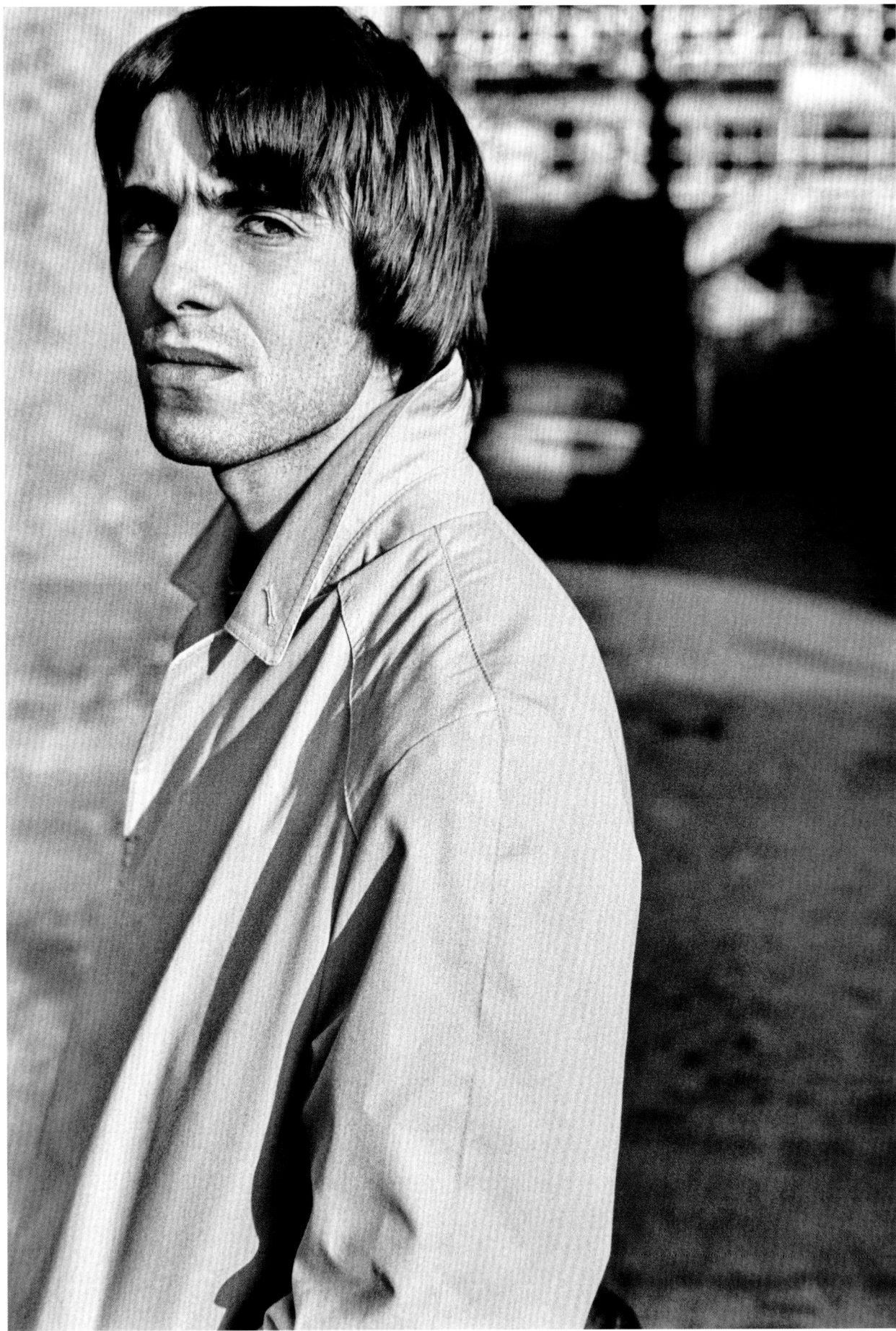

15 MARCH
CAFÉ ROUGE, FRITH STREET,
SOHO, LONDON

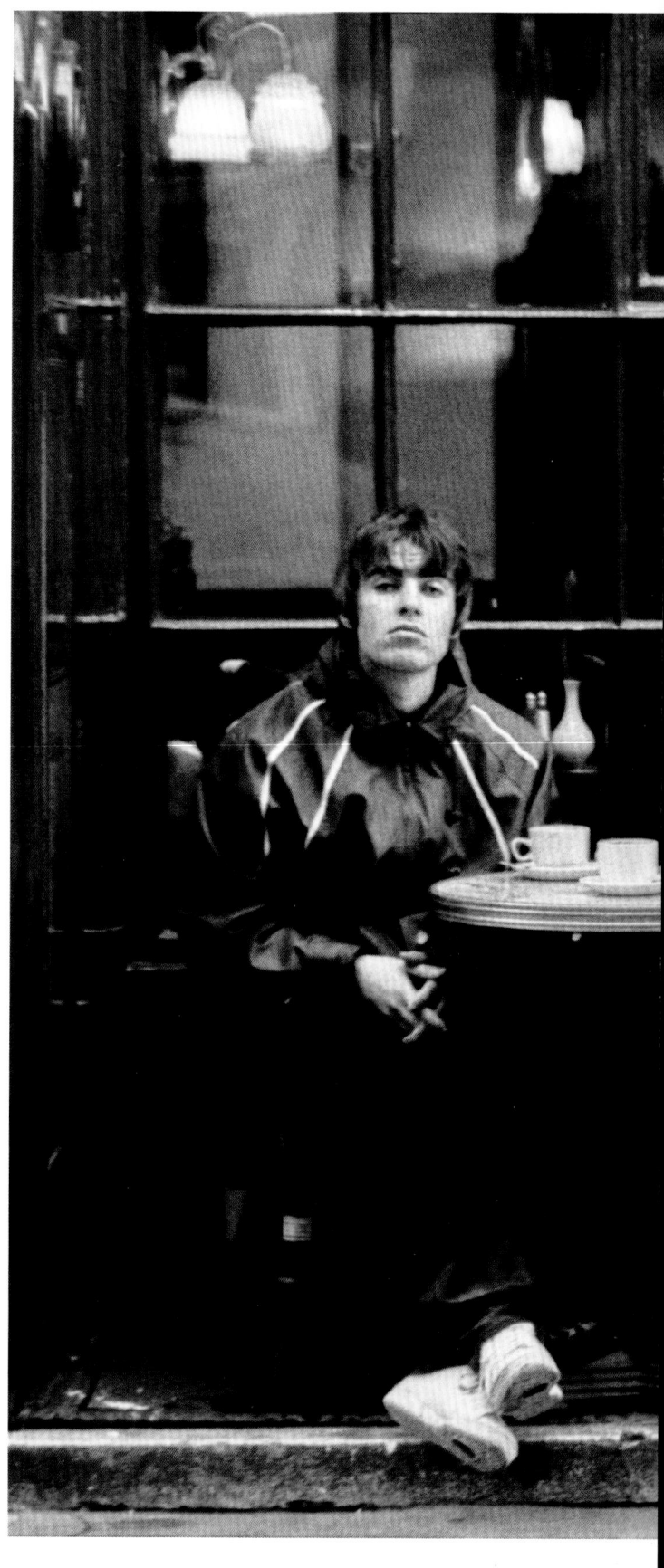

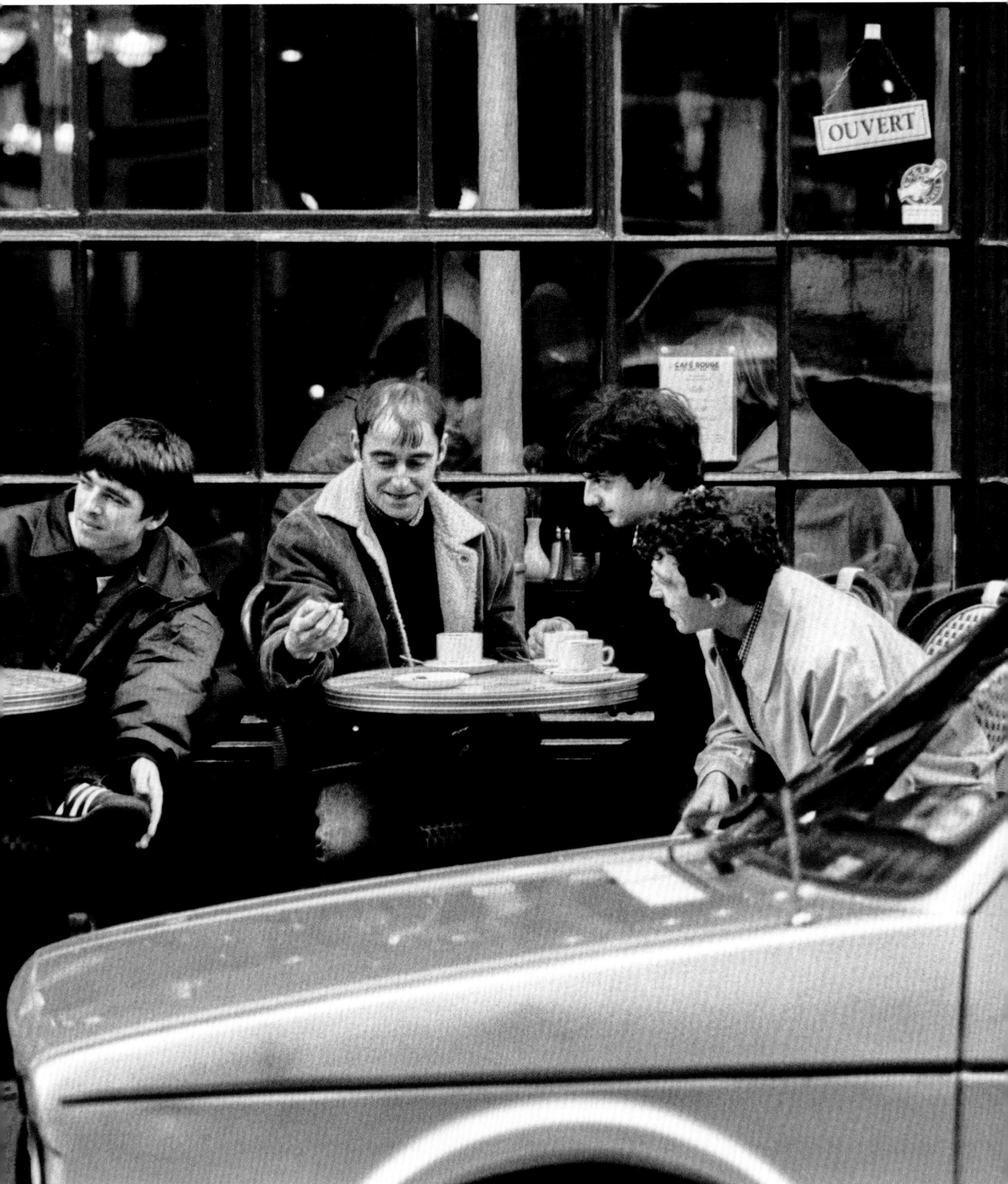

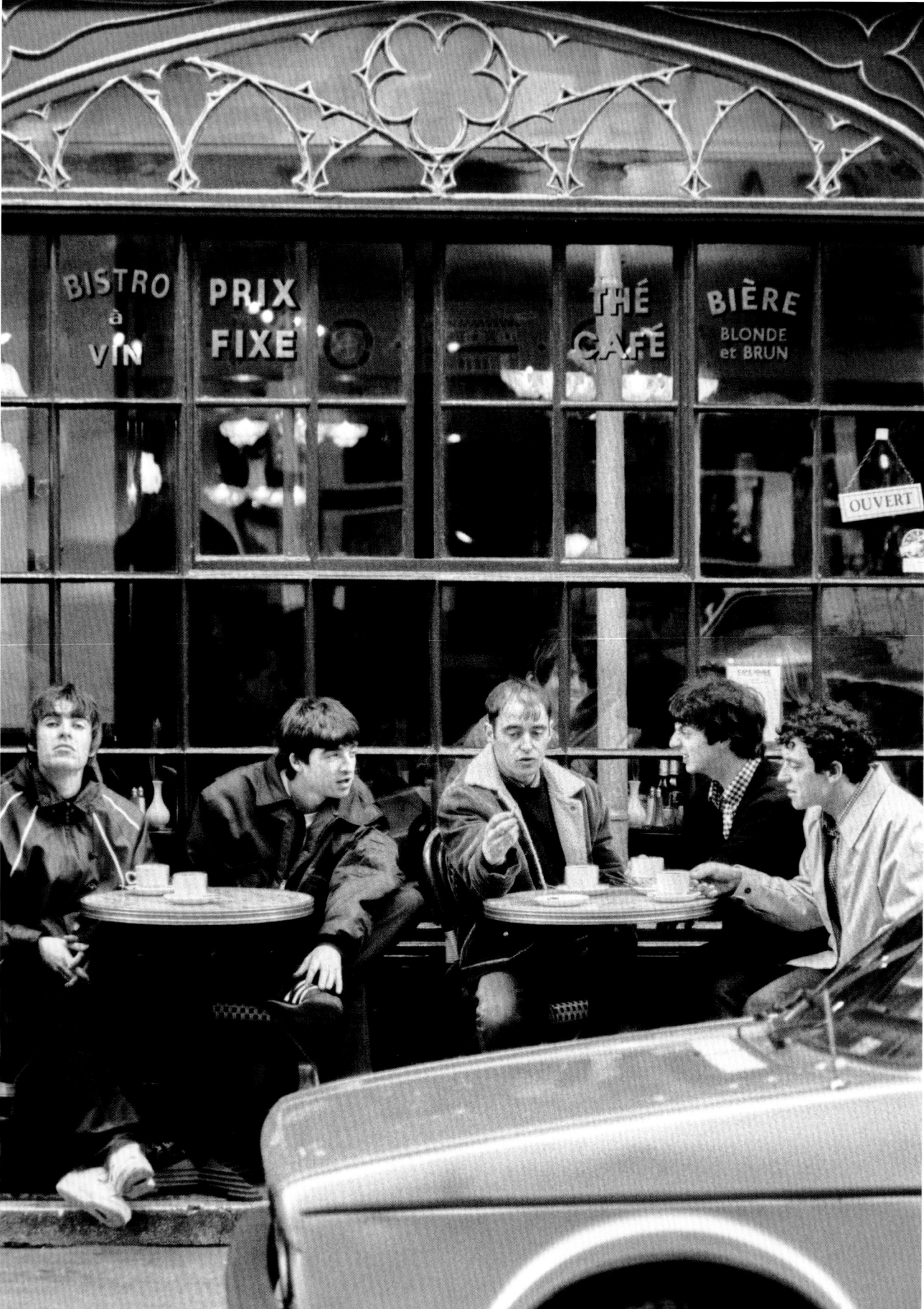

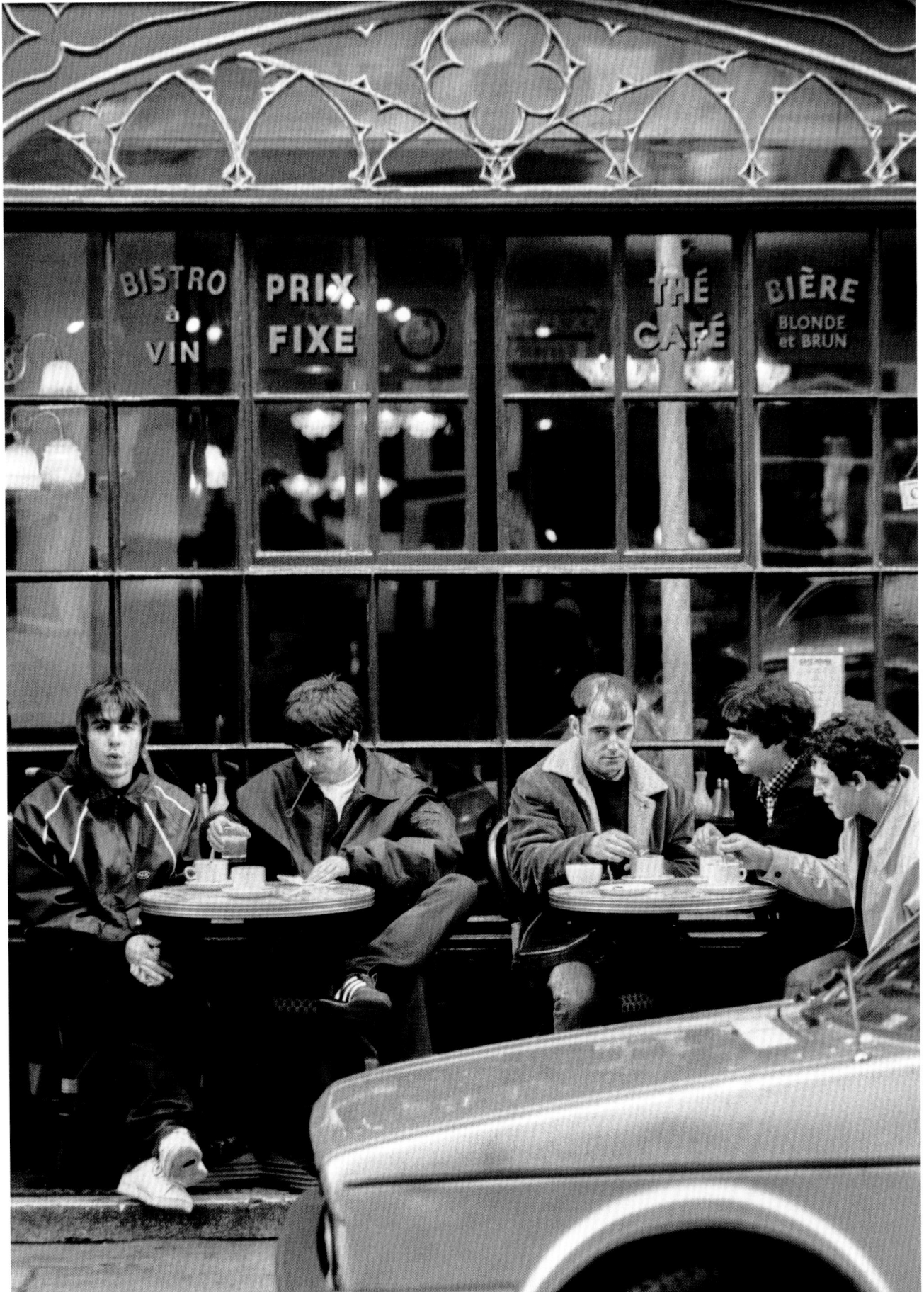

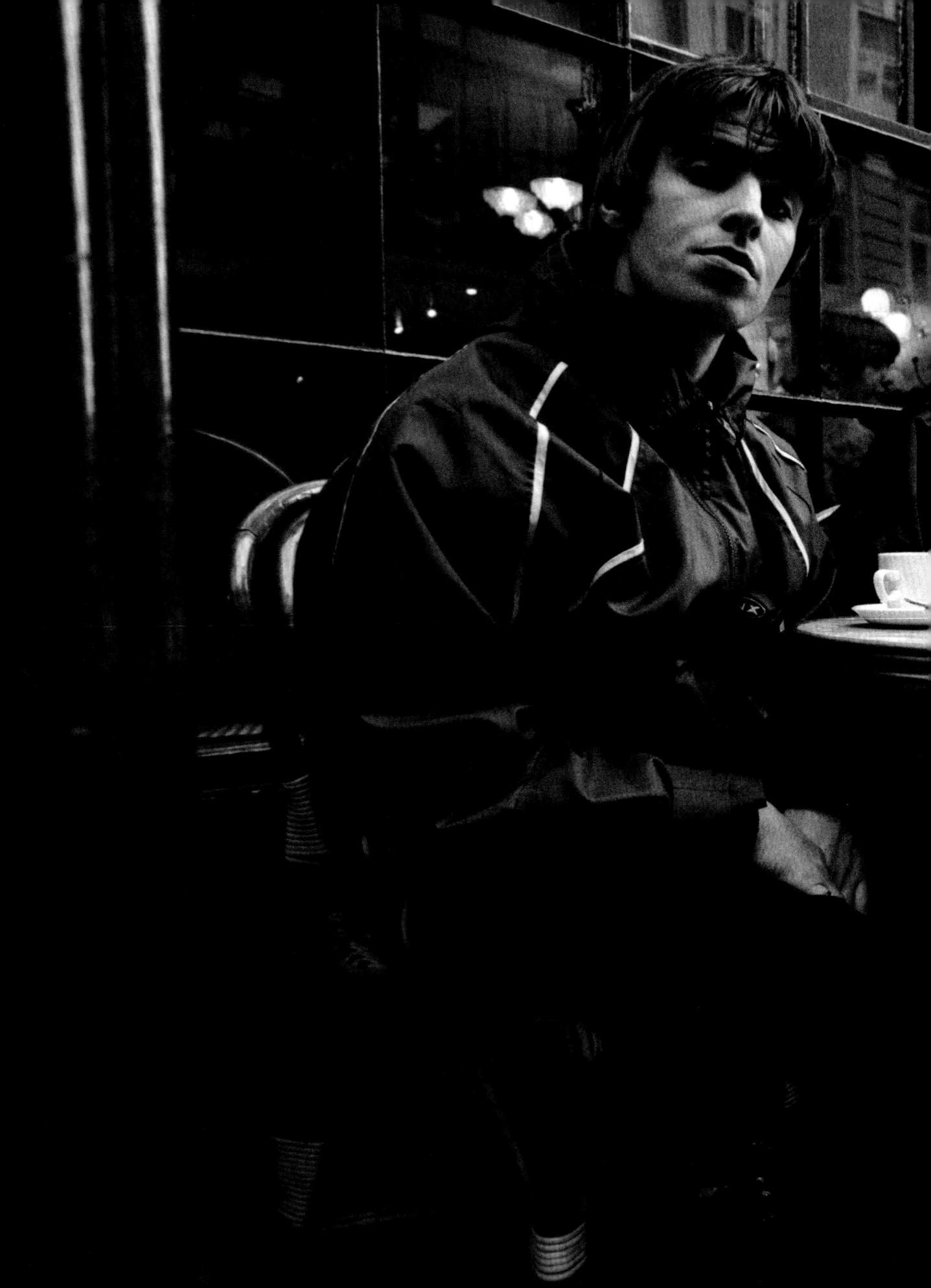

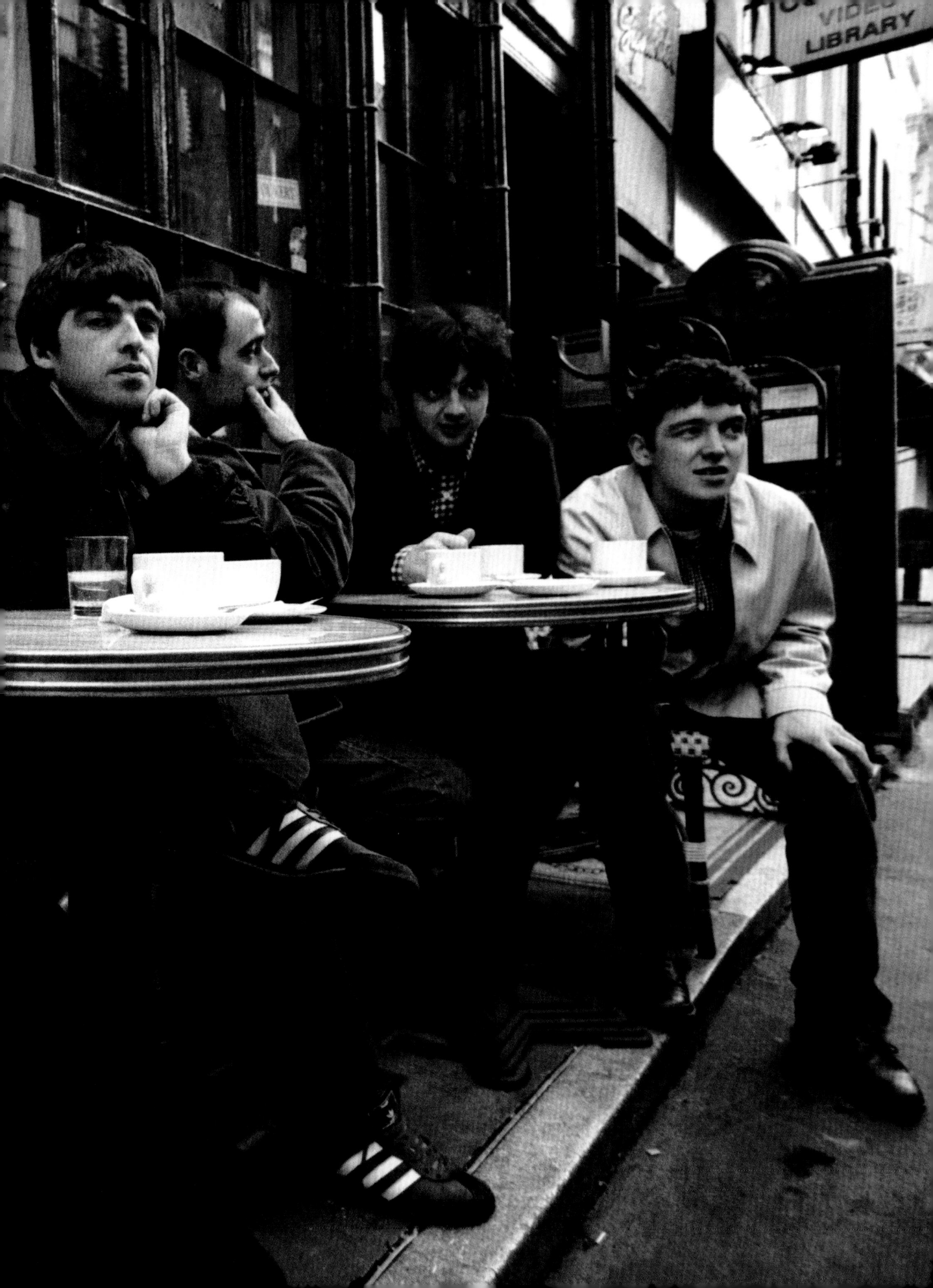

15 MARCH

OXFORD STREET, LONDON

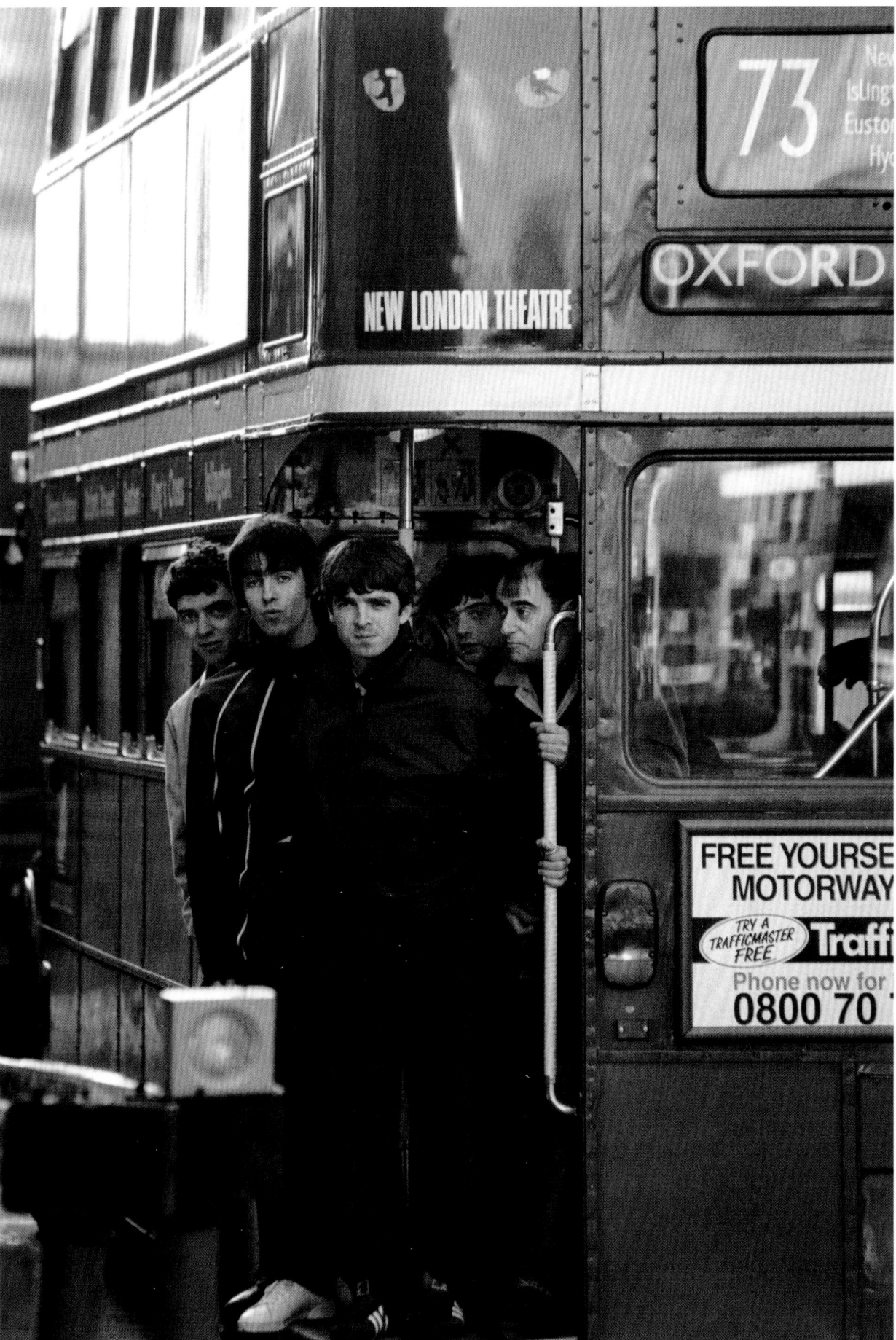

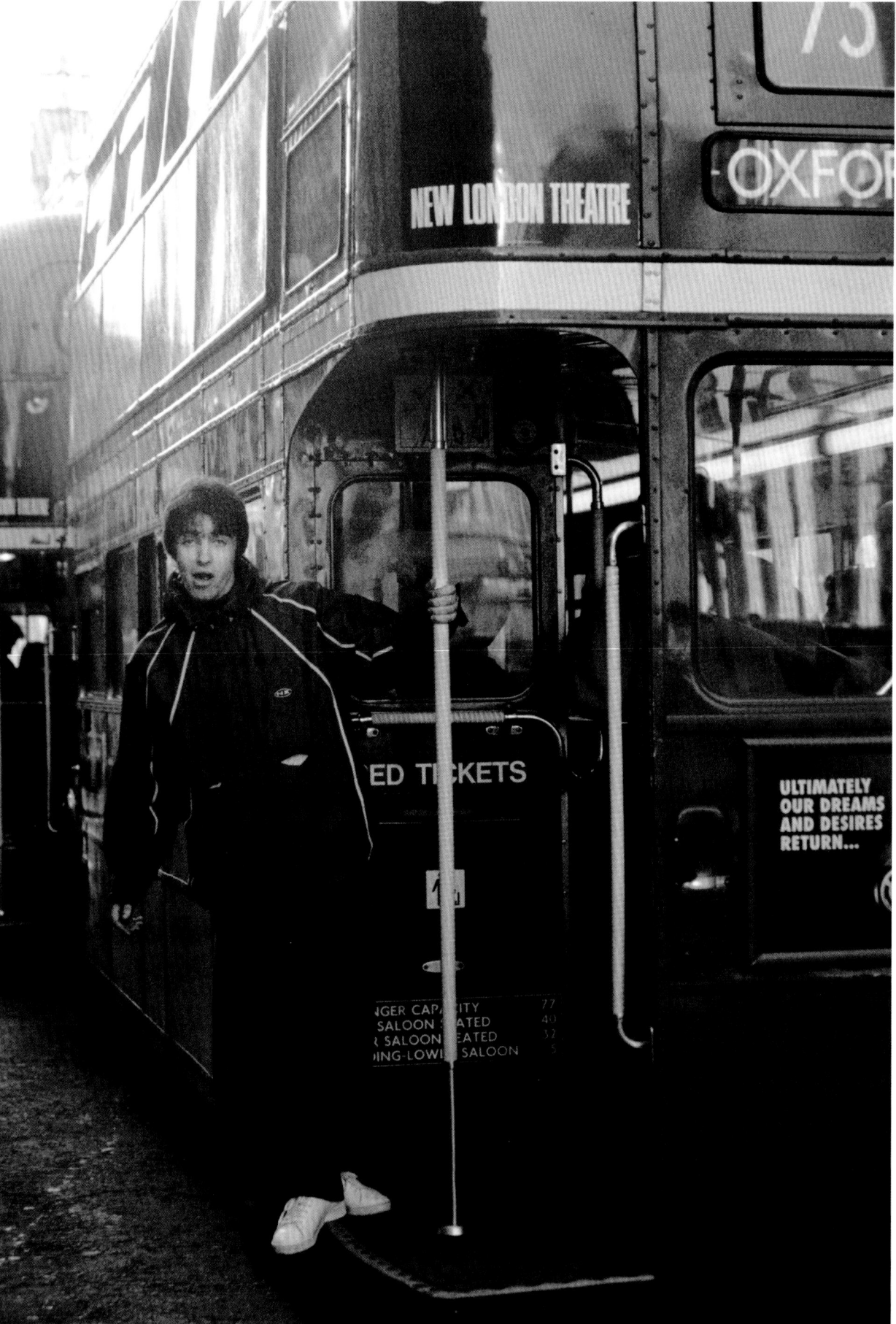

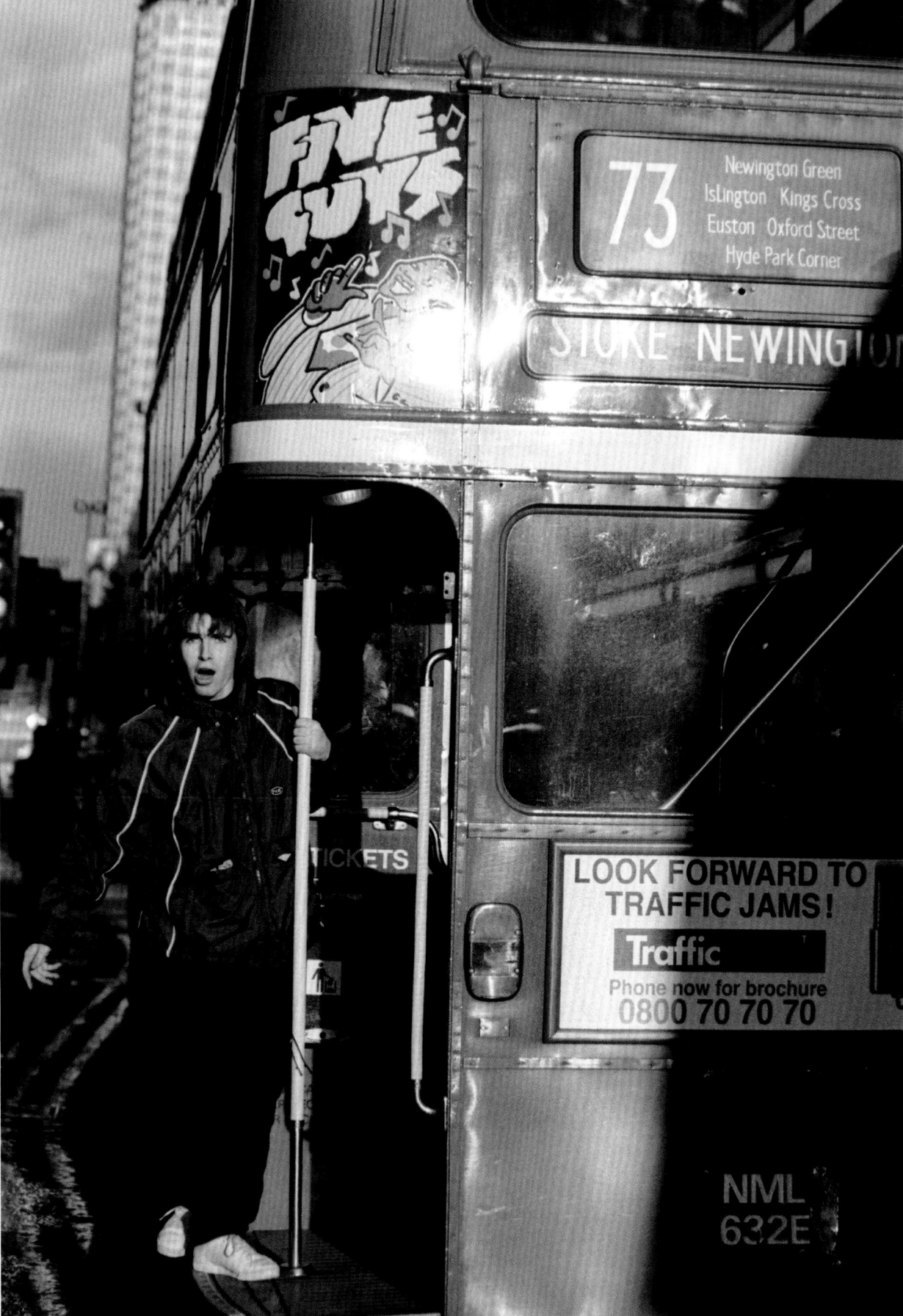

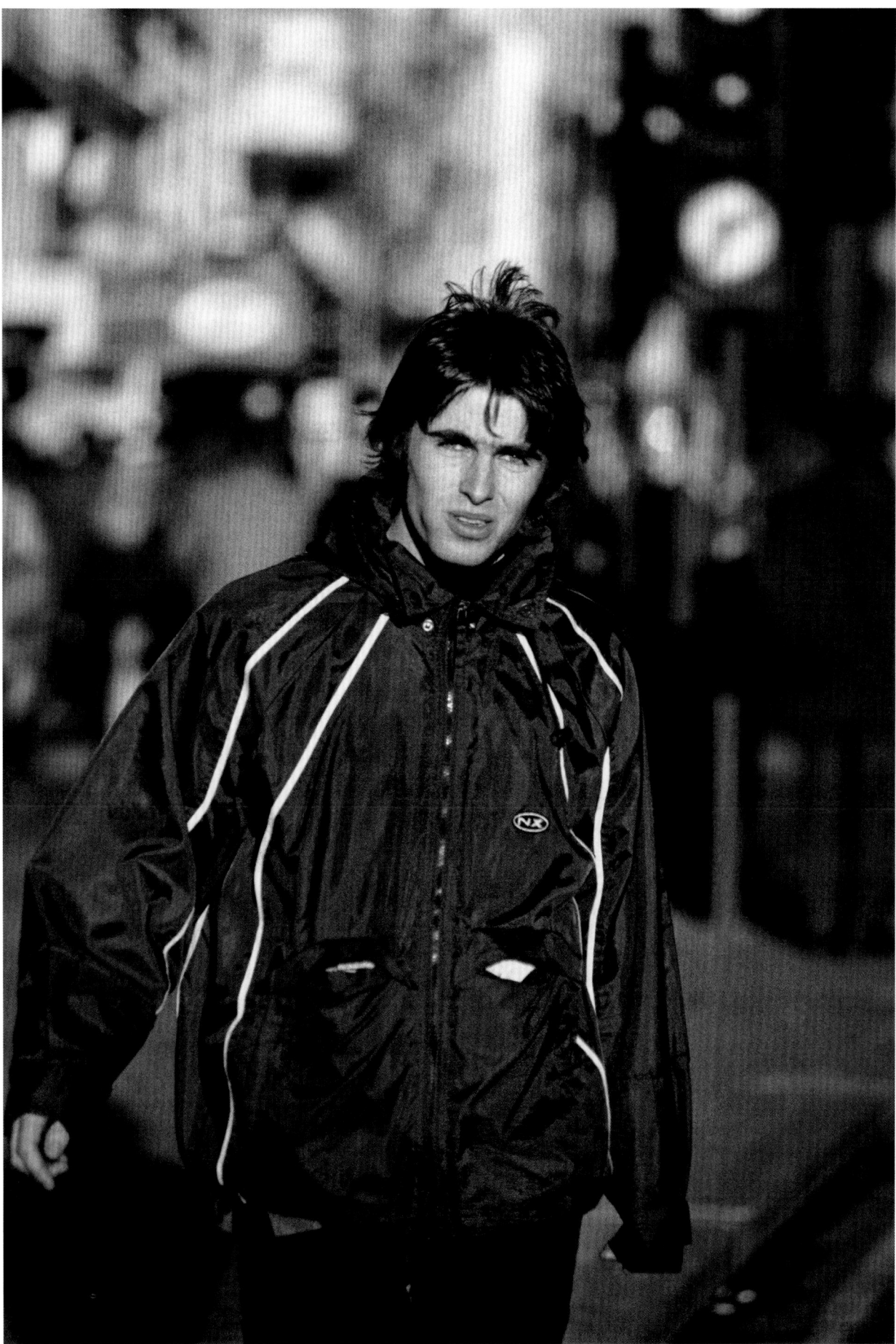

15 MARCH
FLITCROFT STREET, LONDON

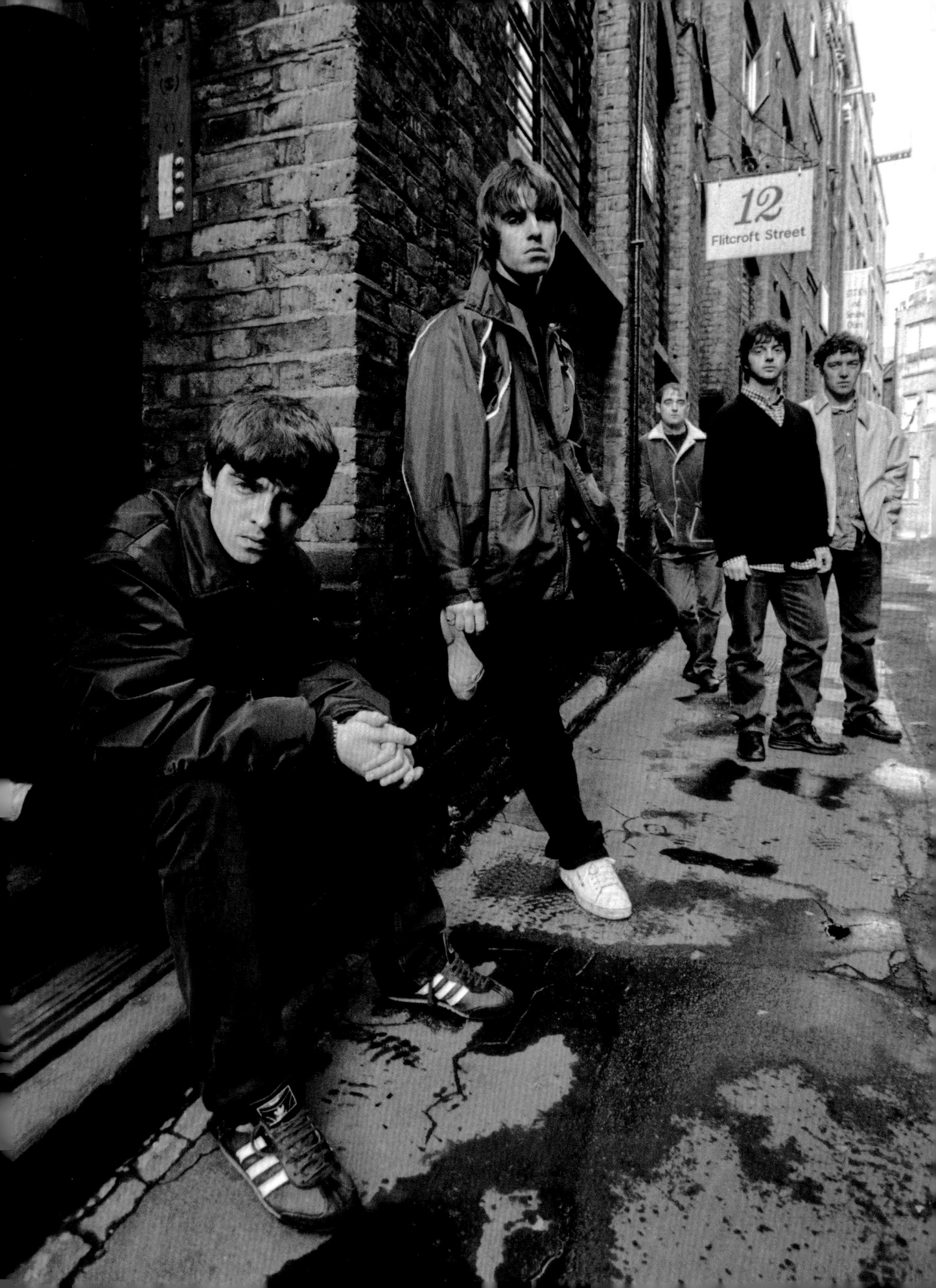

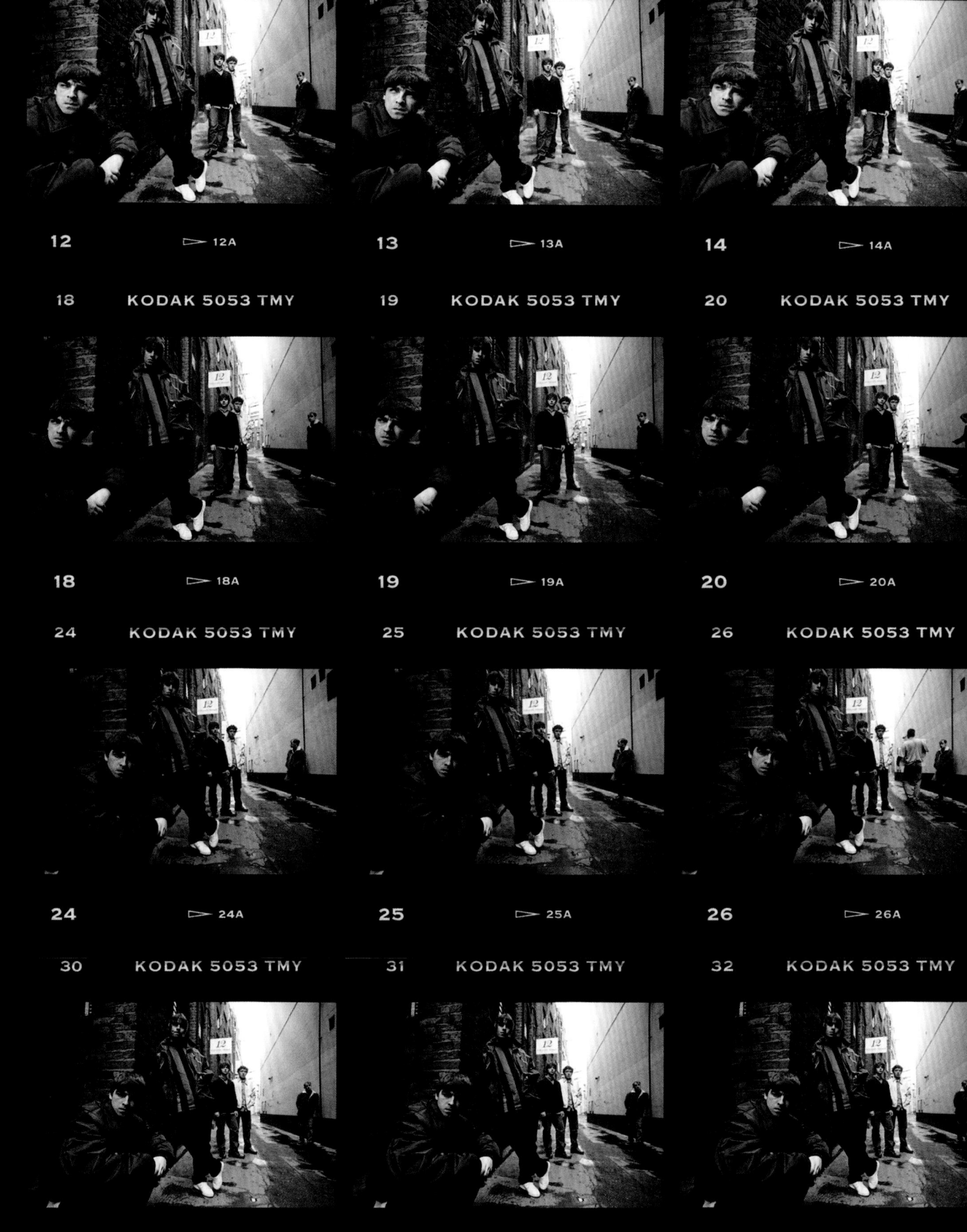

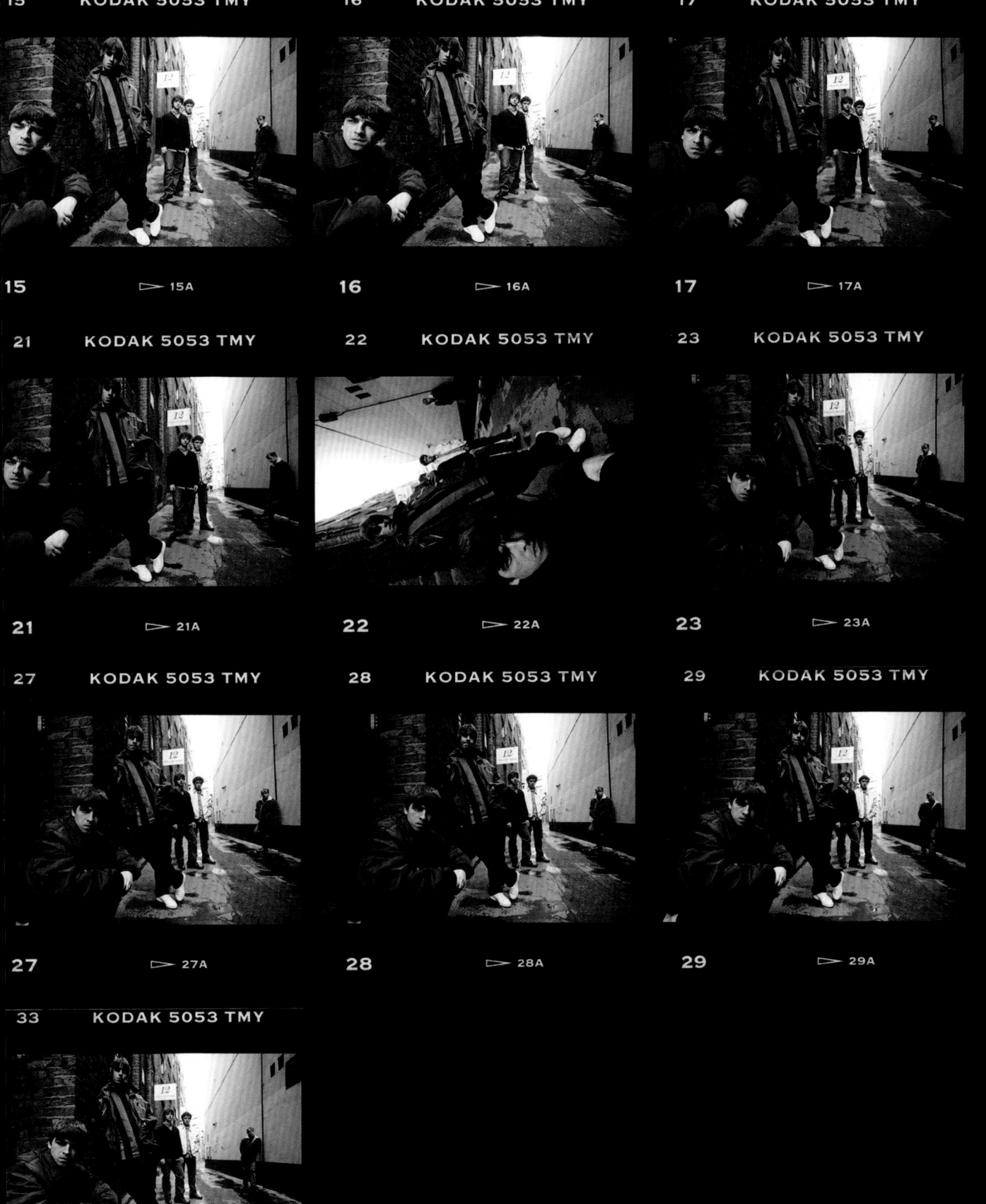

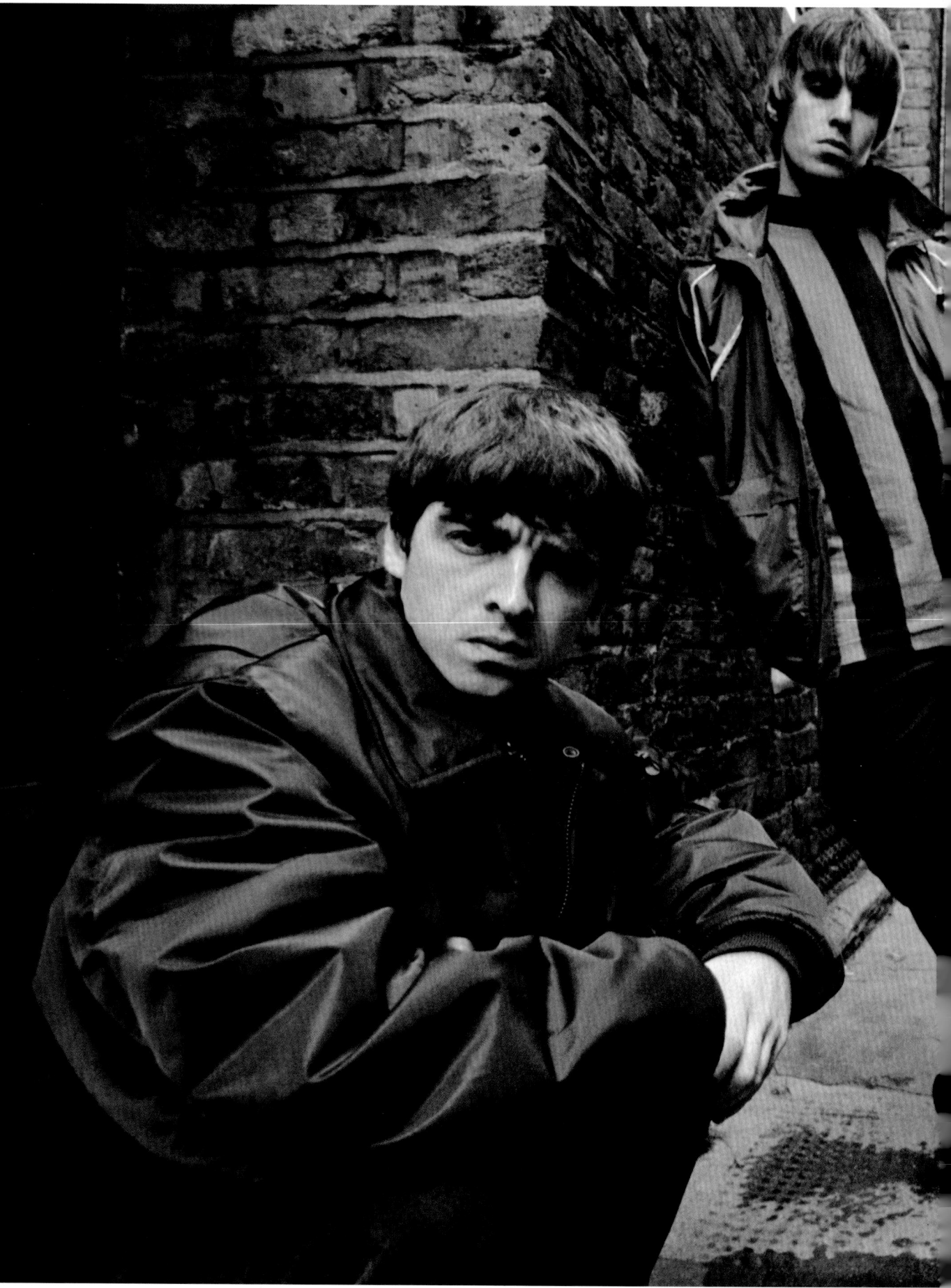

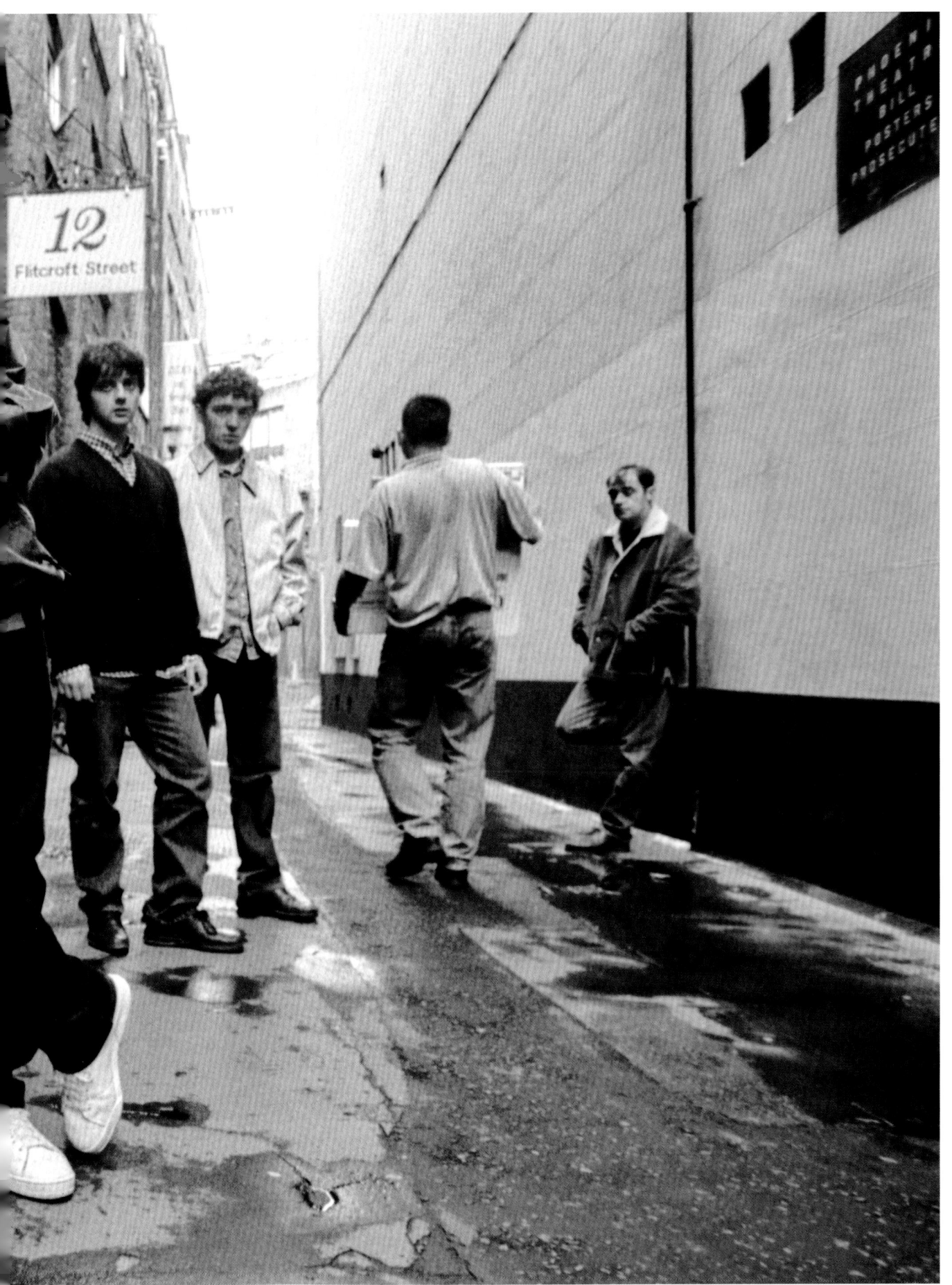

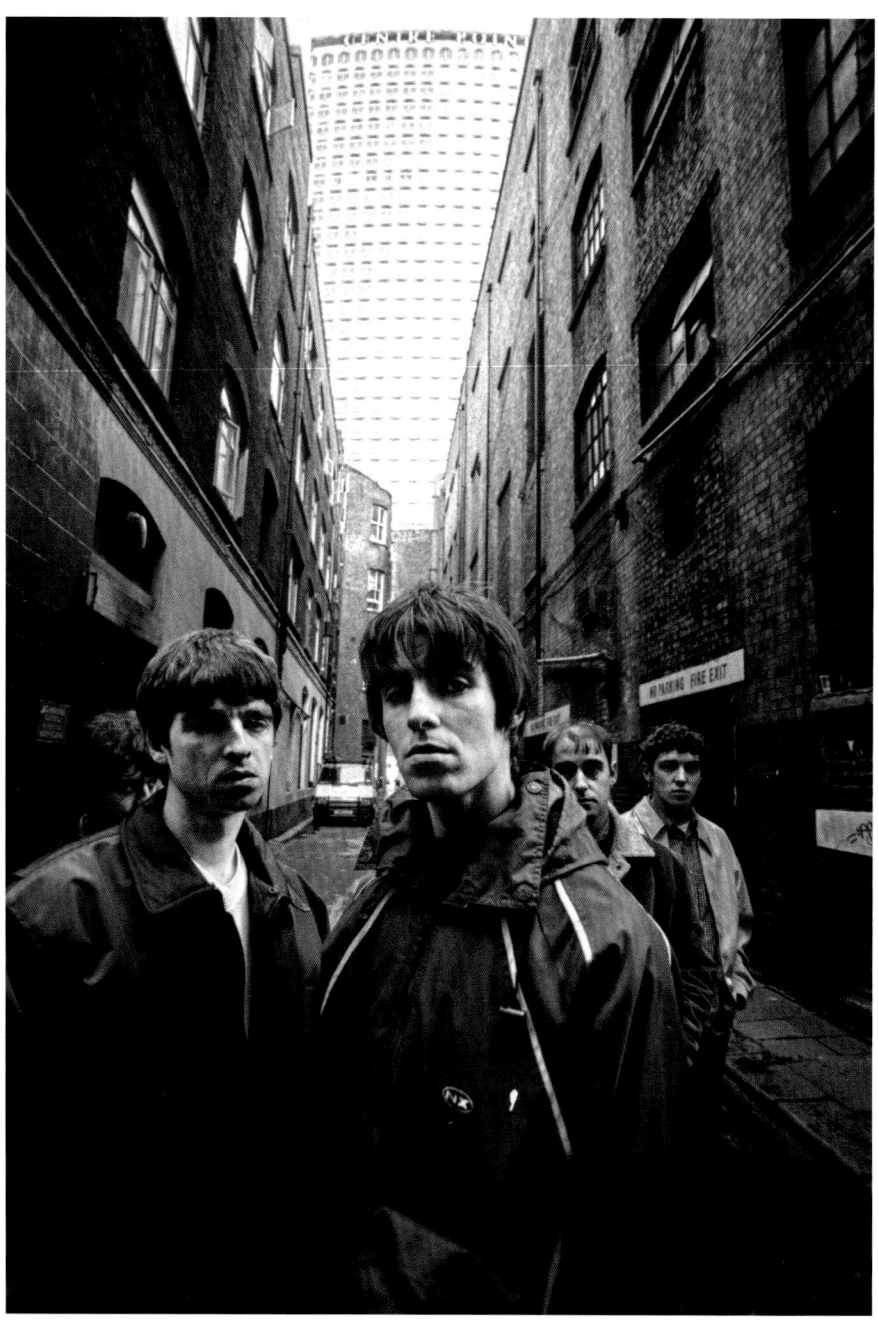

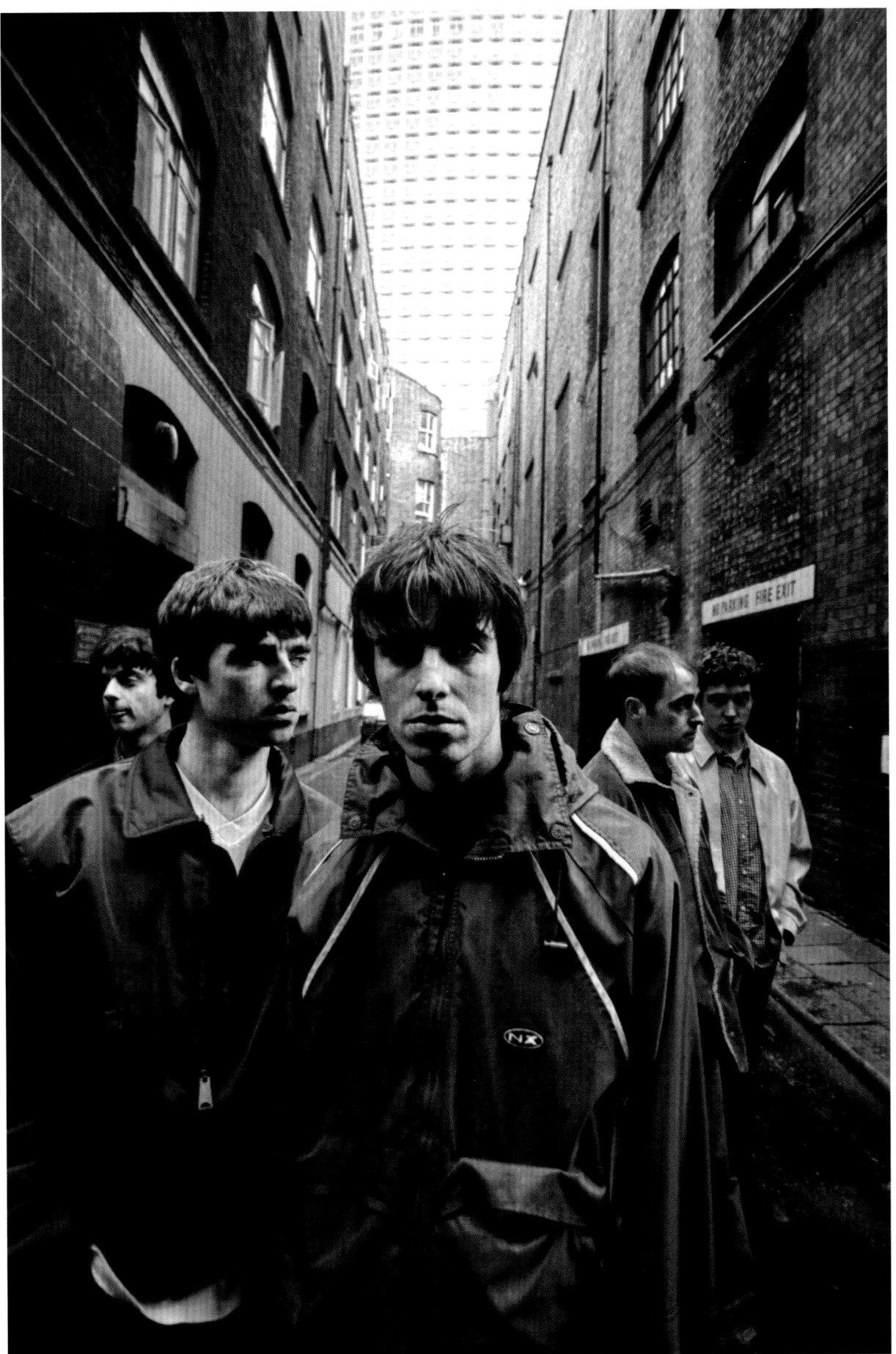

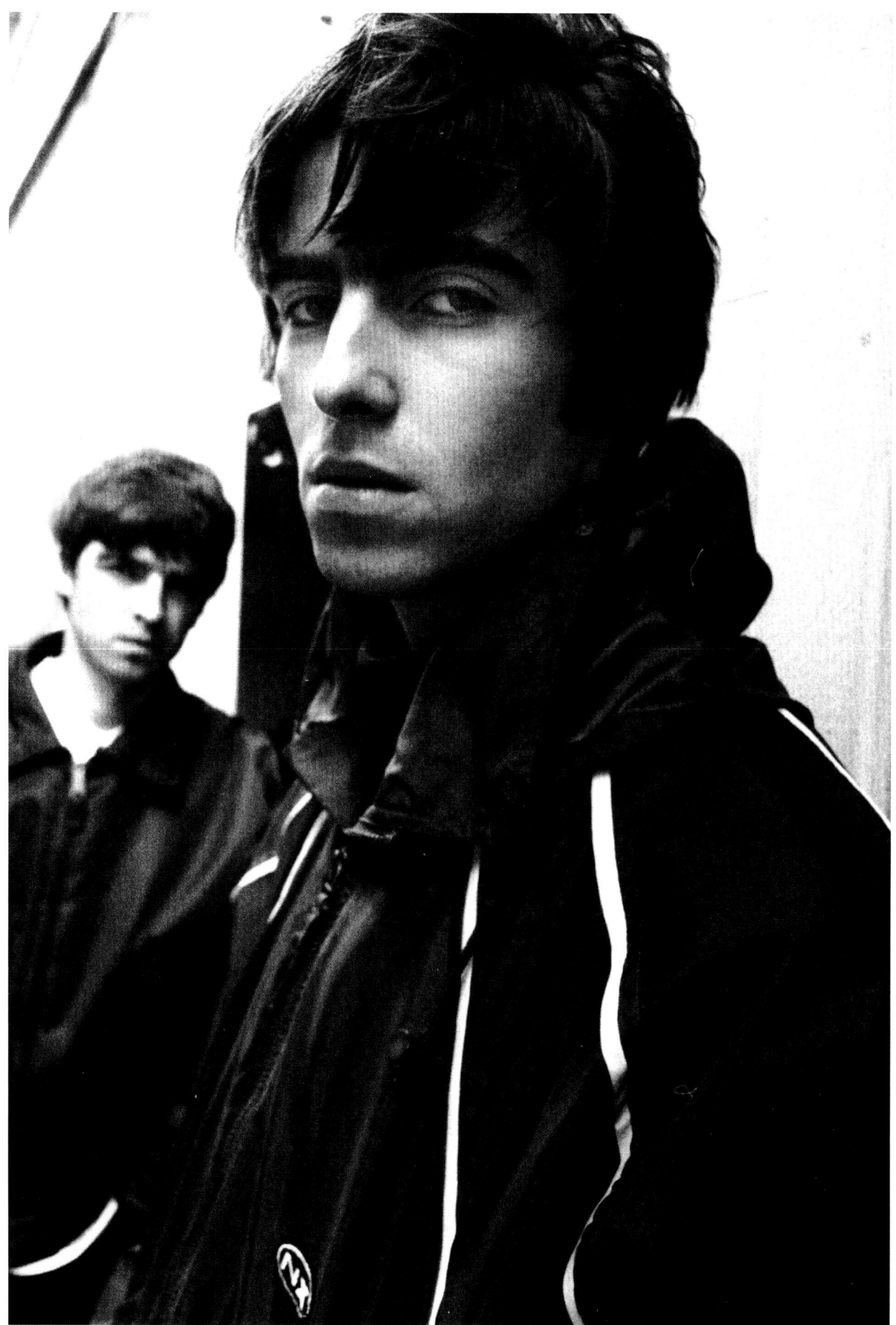

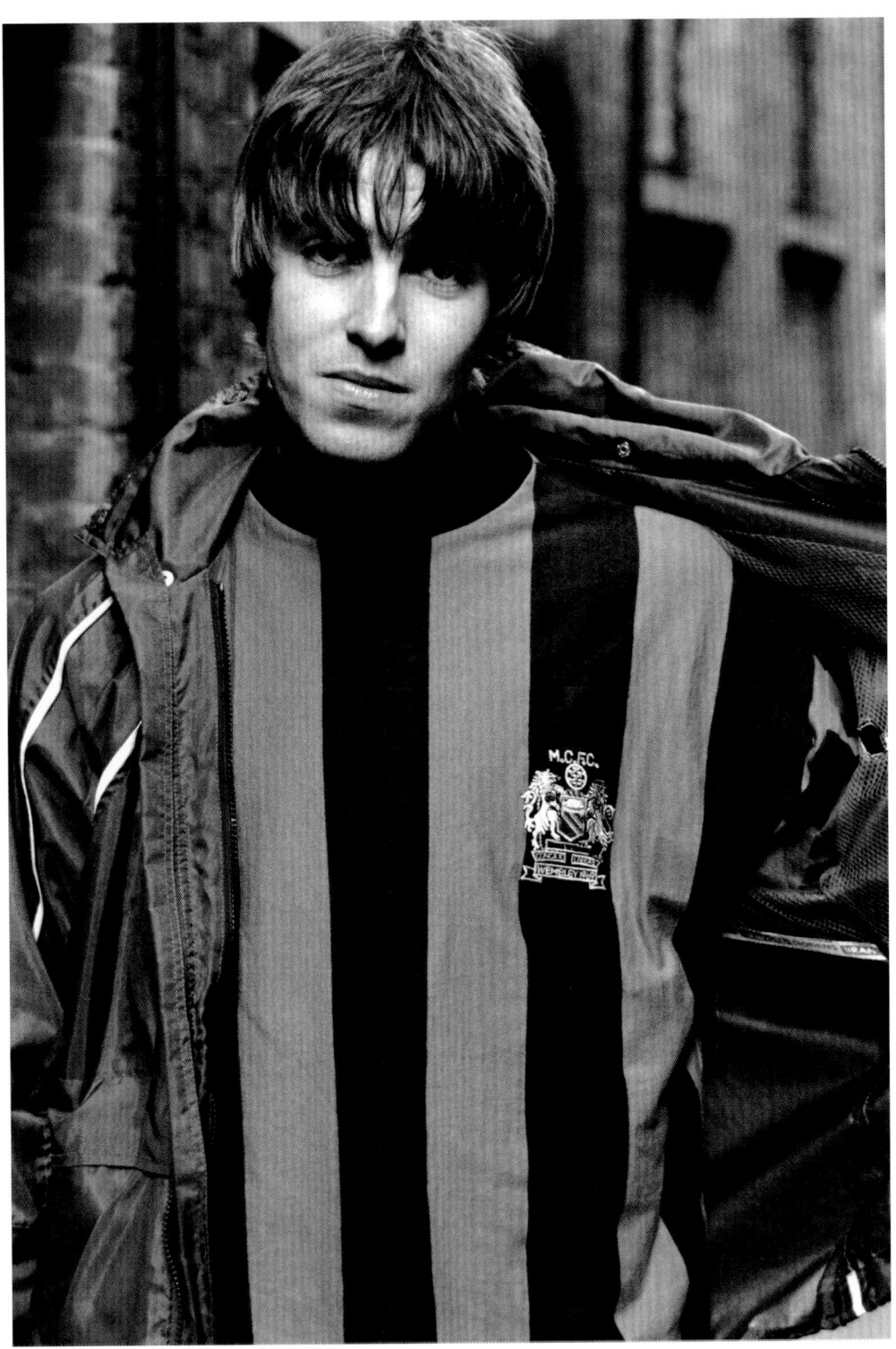

2 MAY
THE WEDGEWOOD ROOMS, PORTSMOUTH

"Playing small, intimate venues is totally different to a stadium. In many ways it's more nerve-wracking."
—*Noel Gallagher*

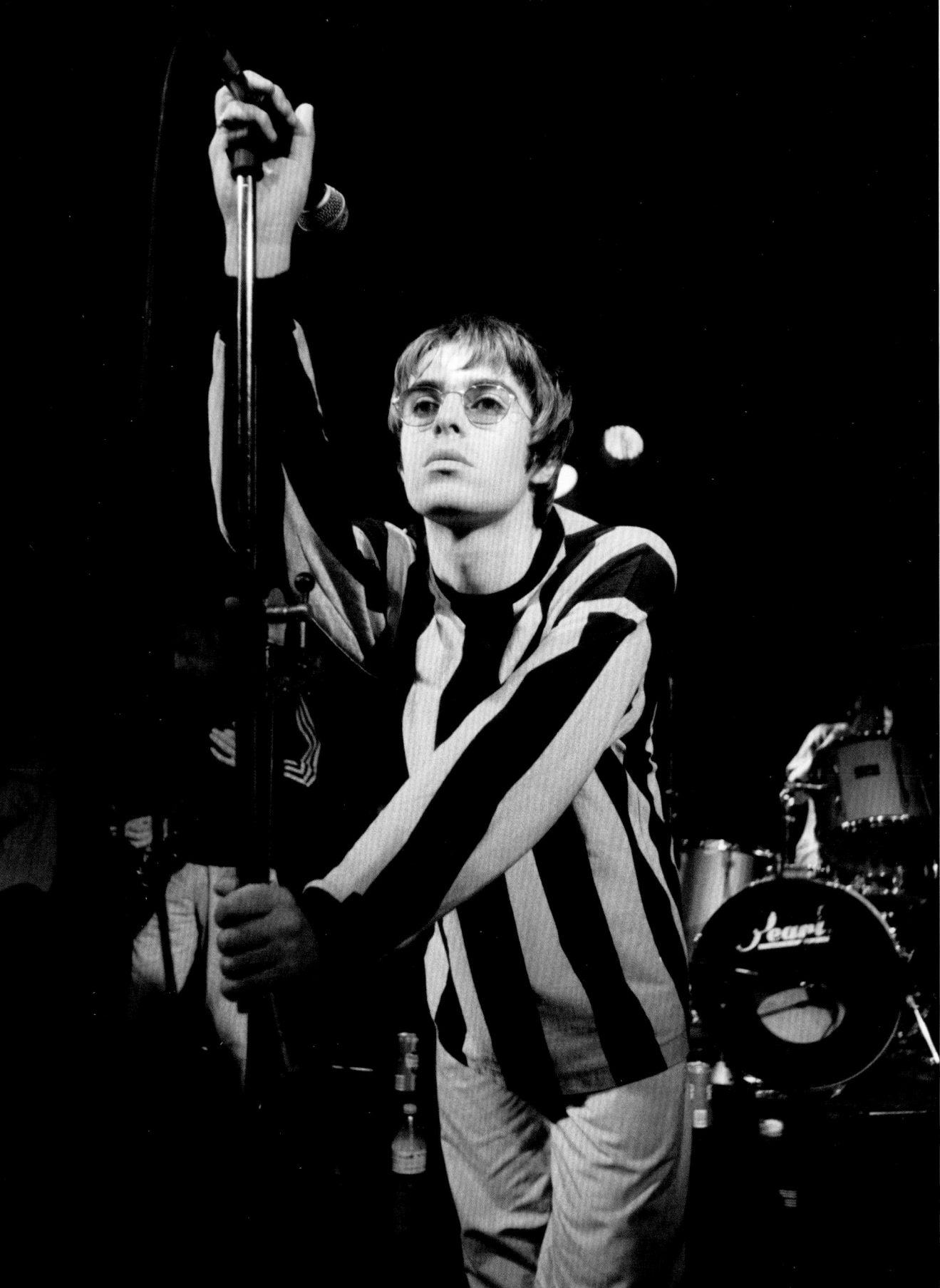

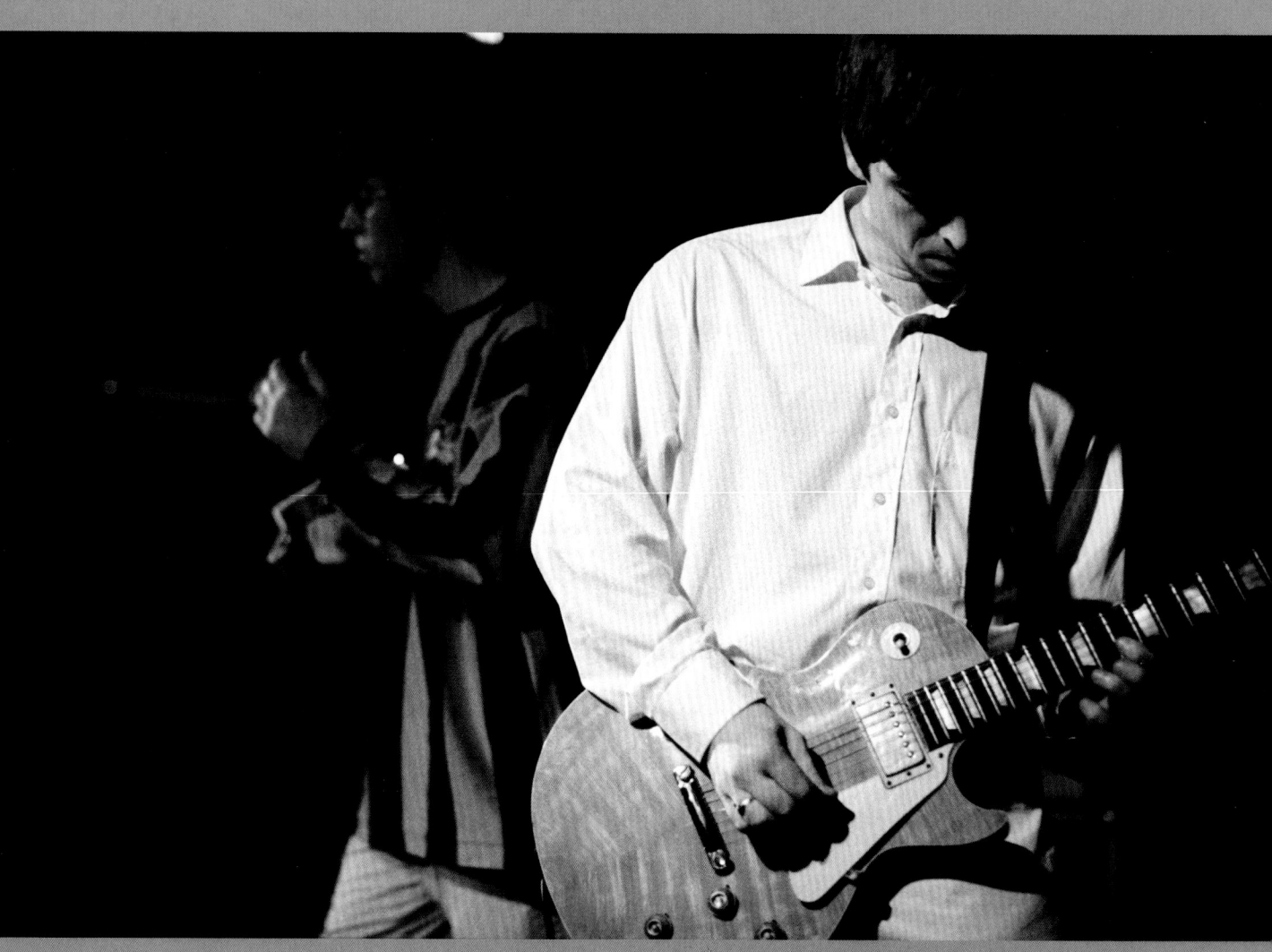

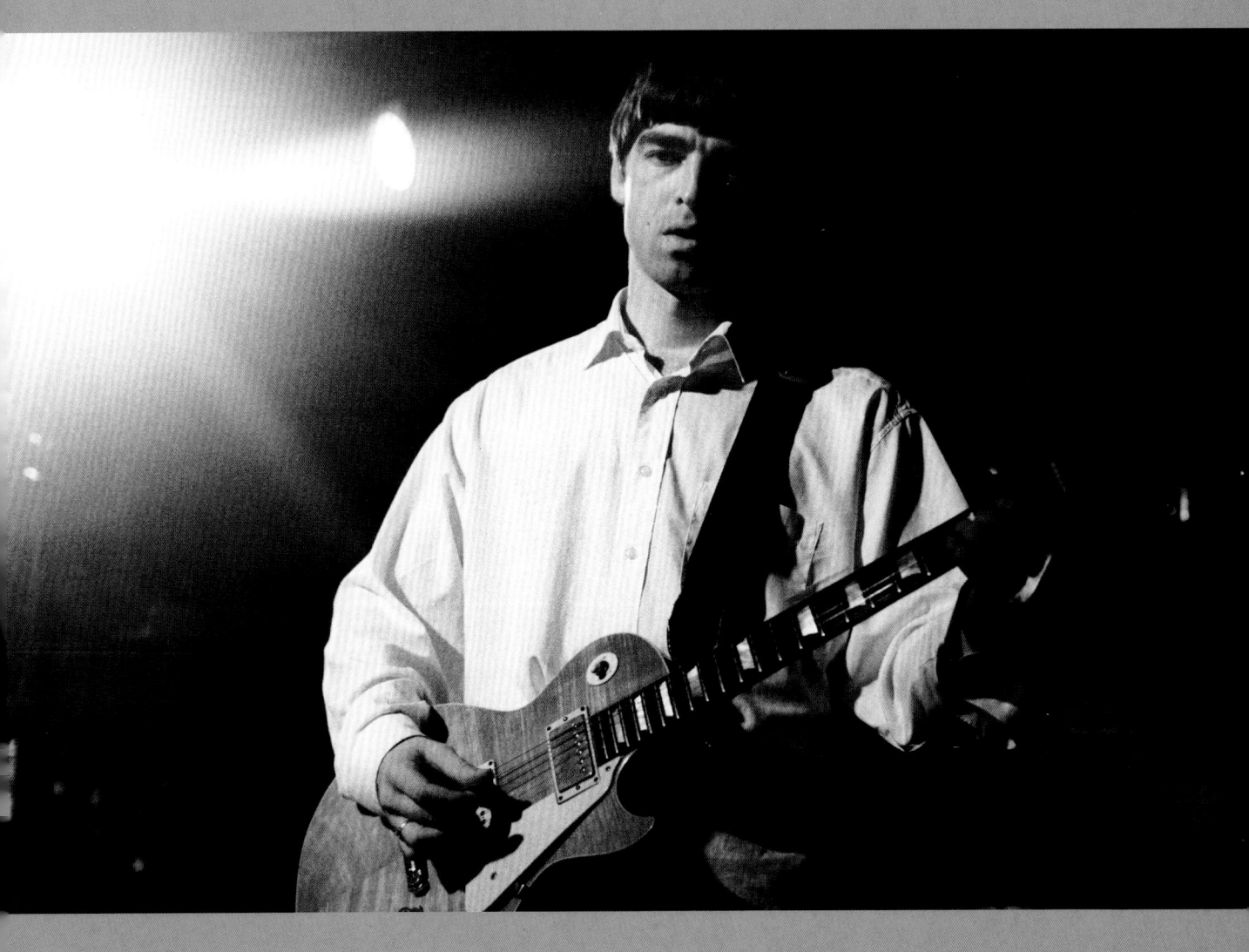

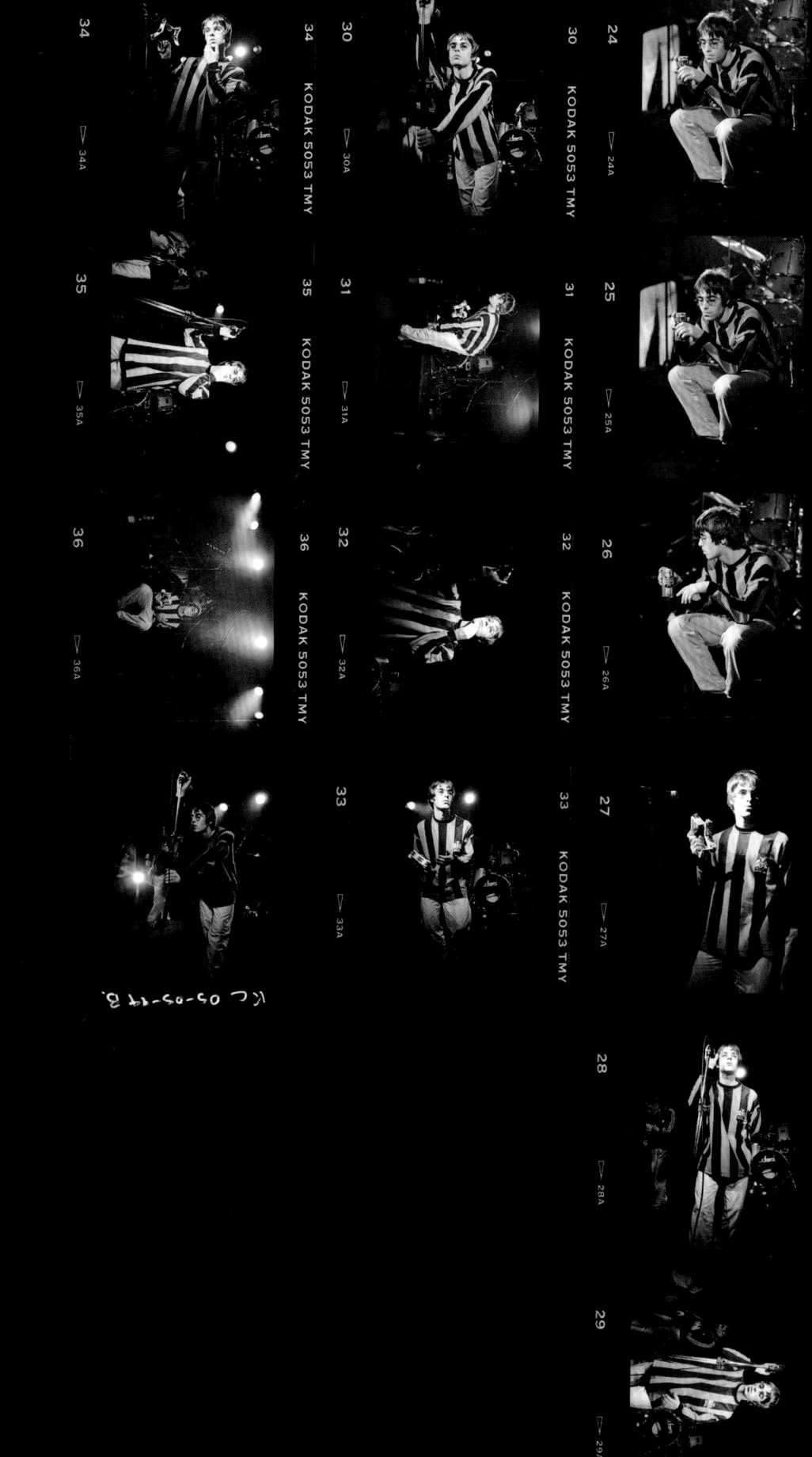

24 ▷ 24A

25 ▷ 25A

26 ▷ 26A

27 ▷ 27A

28 ▷ 28A

29 ▷ 29A

30 KODAK 5053 TMY 30A ▷

31 KODAK 5053 TMY 31A ▷

32 KODAK 5053 TMY 32A ▷

33 KODAK 5053 TMY 33A ▷

34 KODAK 5053 TMY 34A ▷

35 KODAK 5053 TMY 35A ▷

36 KODAK 5053 TMY 36A ▷

34 ▷ 34A

35 ▷ 35A

36 ▷ 36A

KC 05-05-97B.

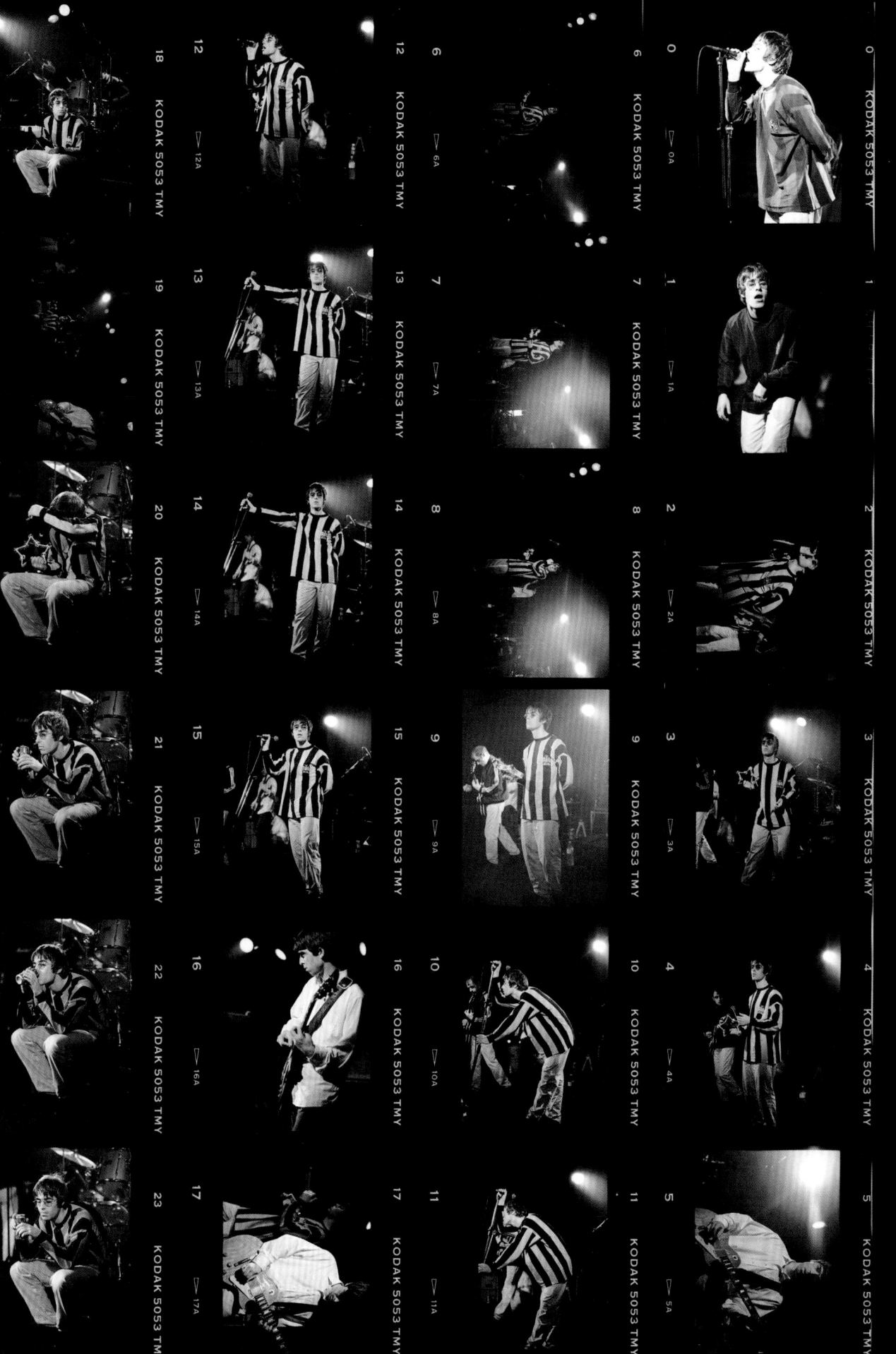

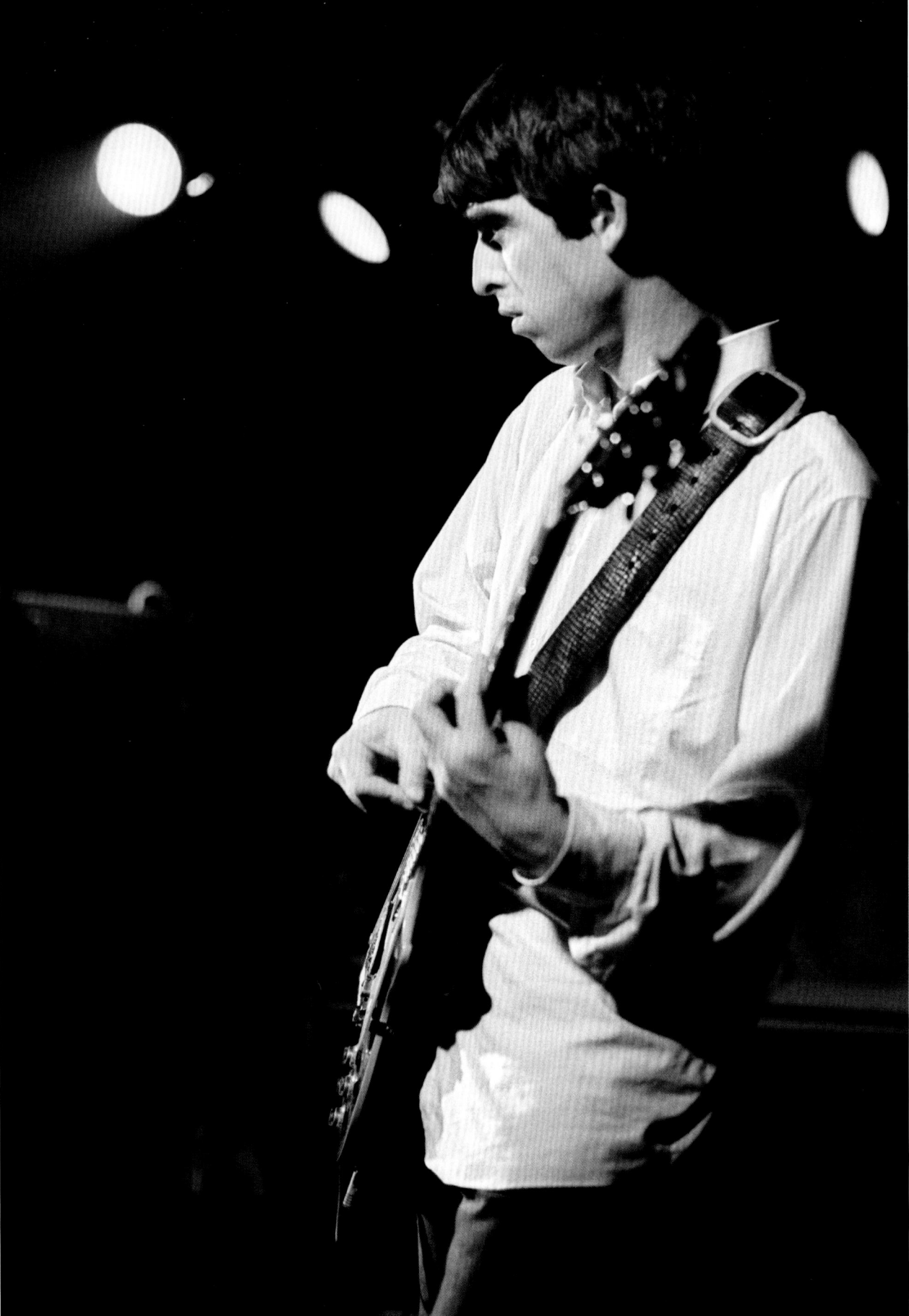

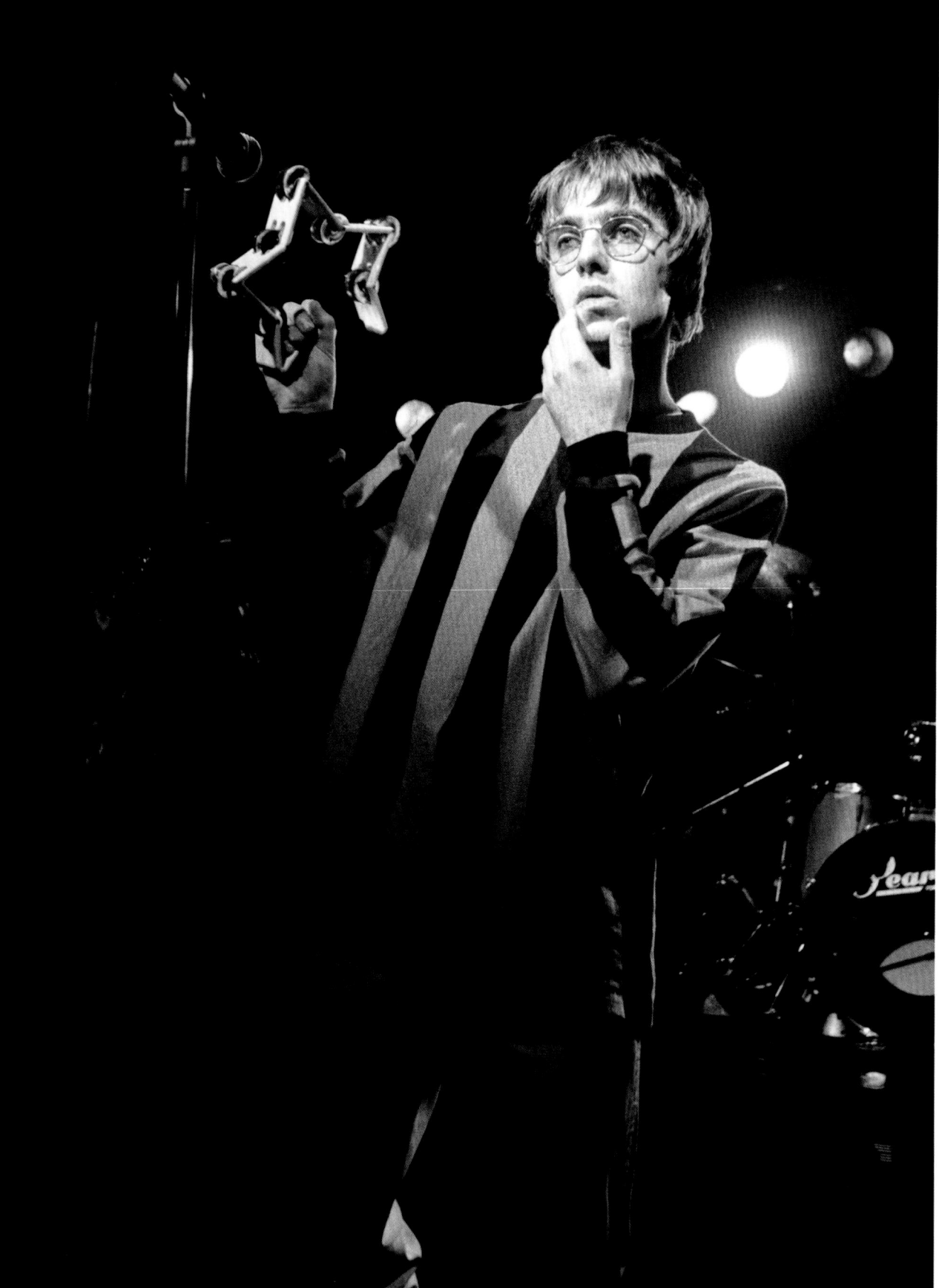

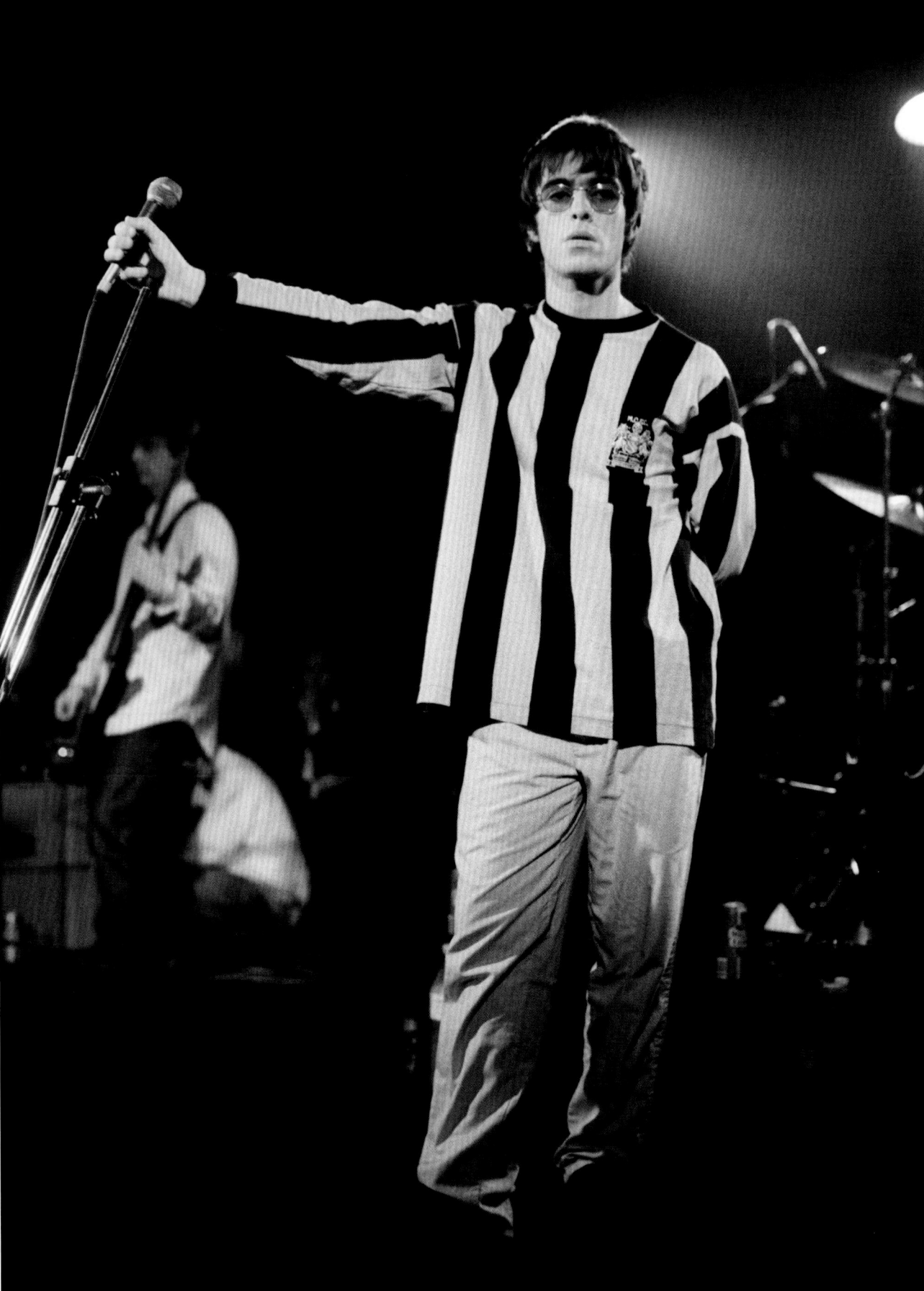

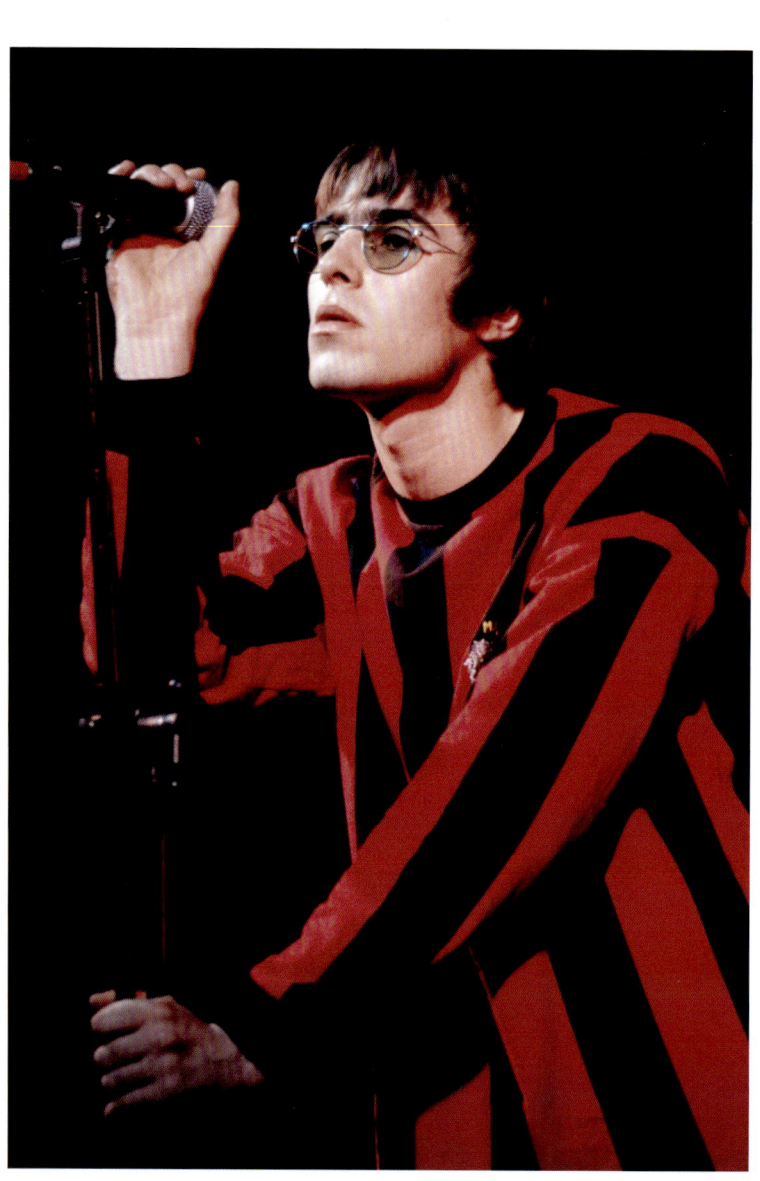

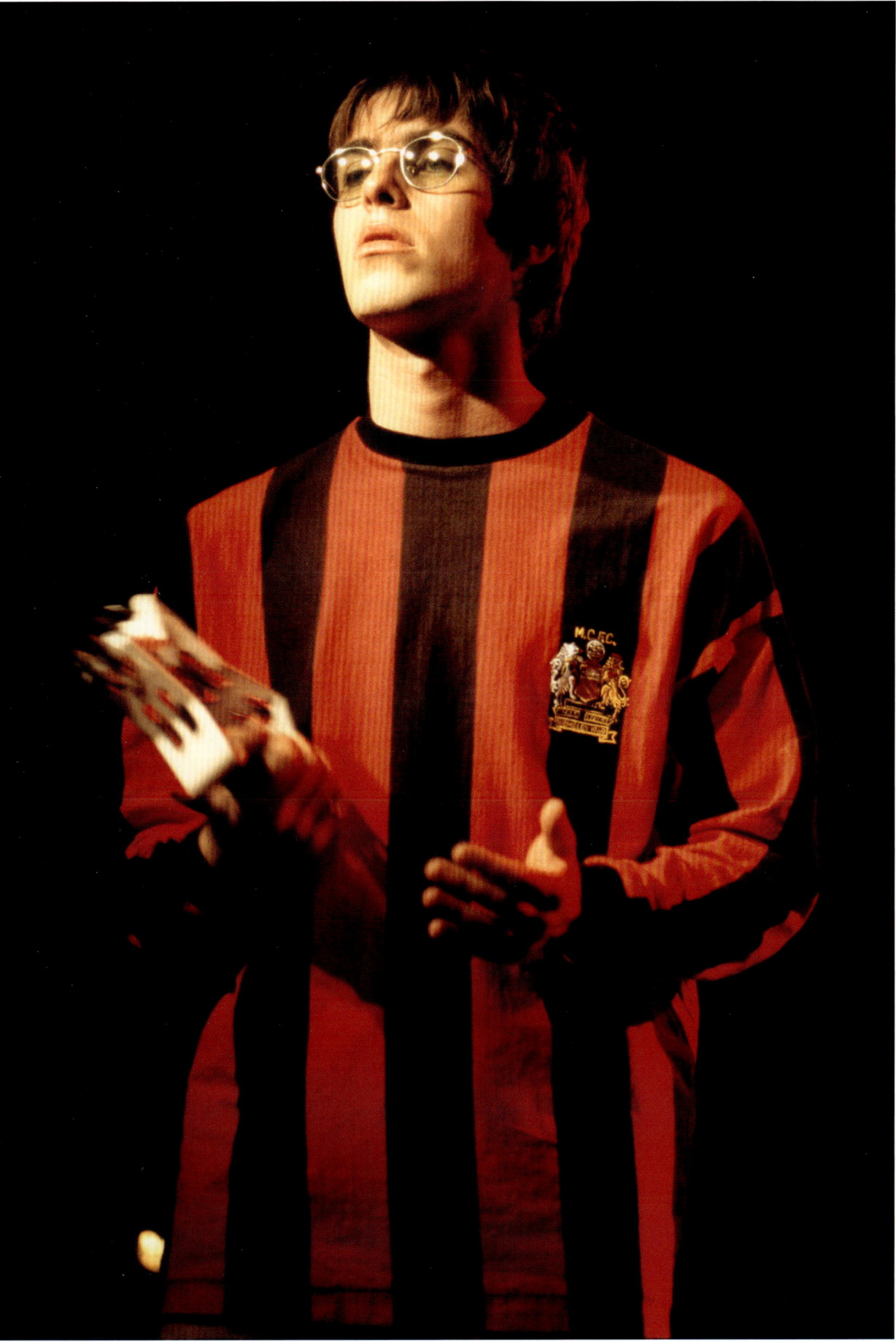

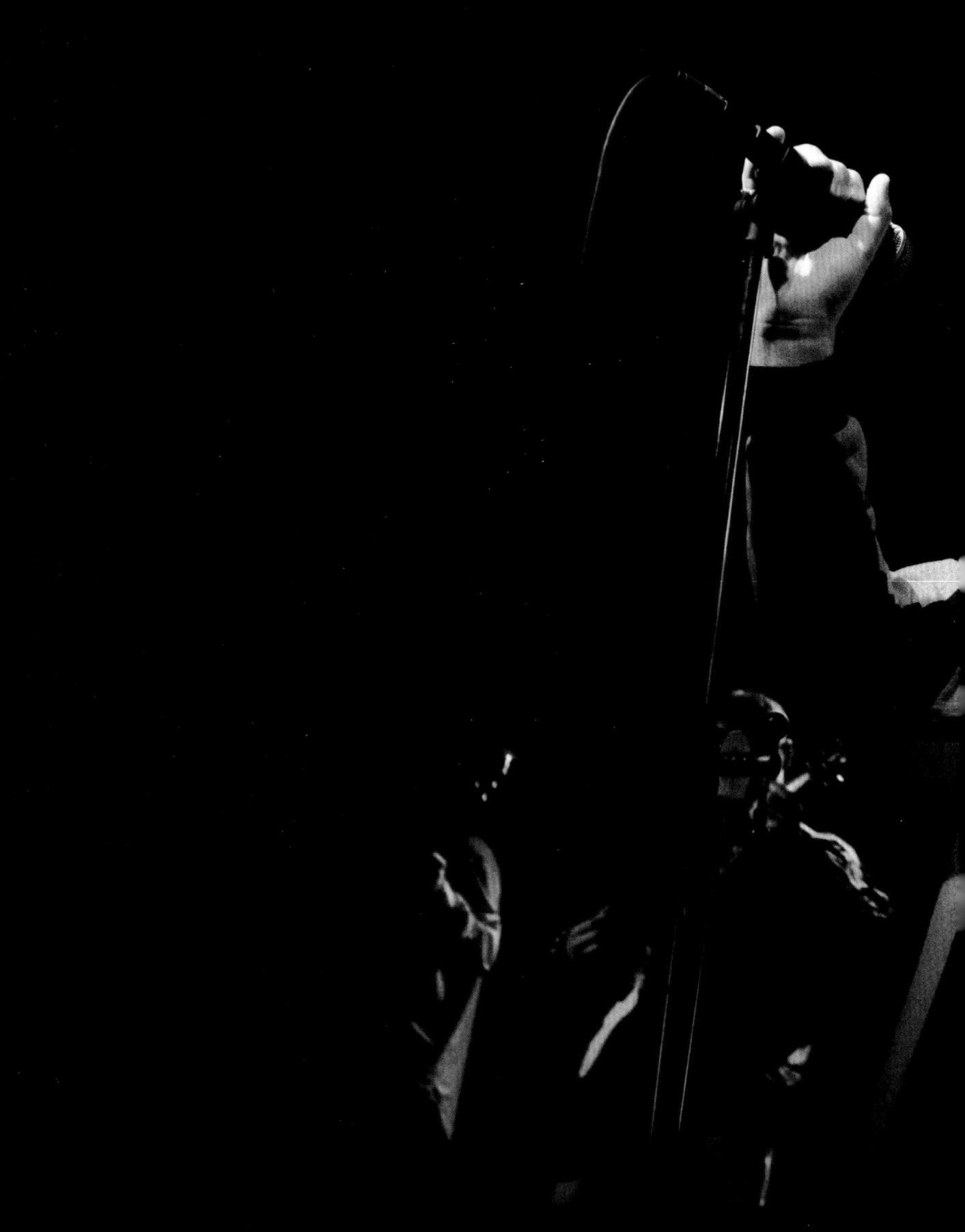

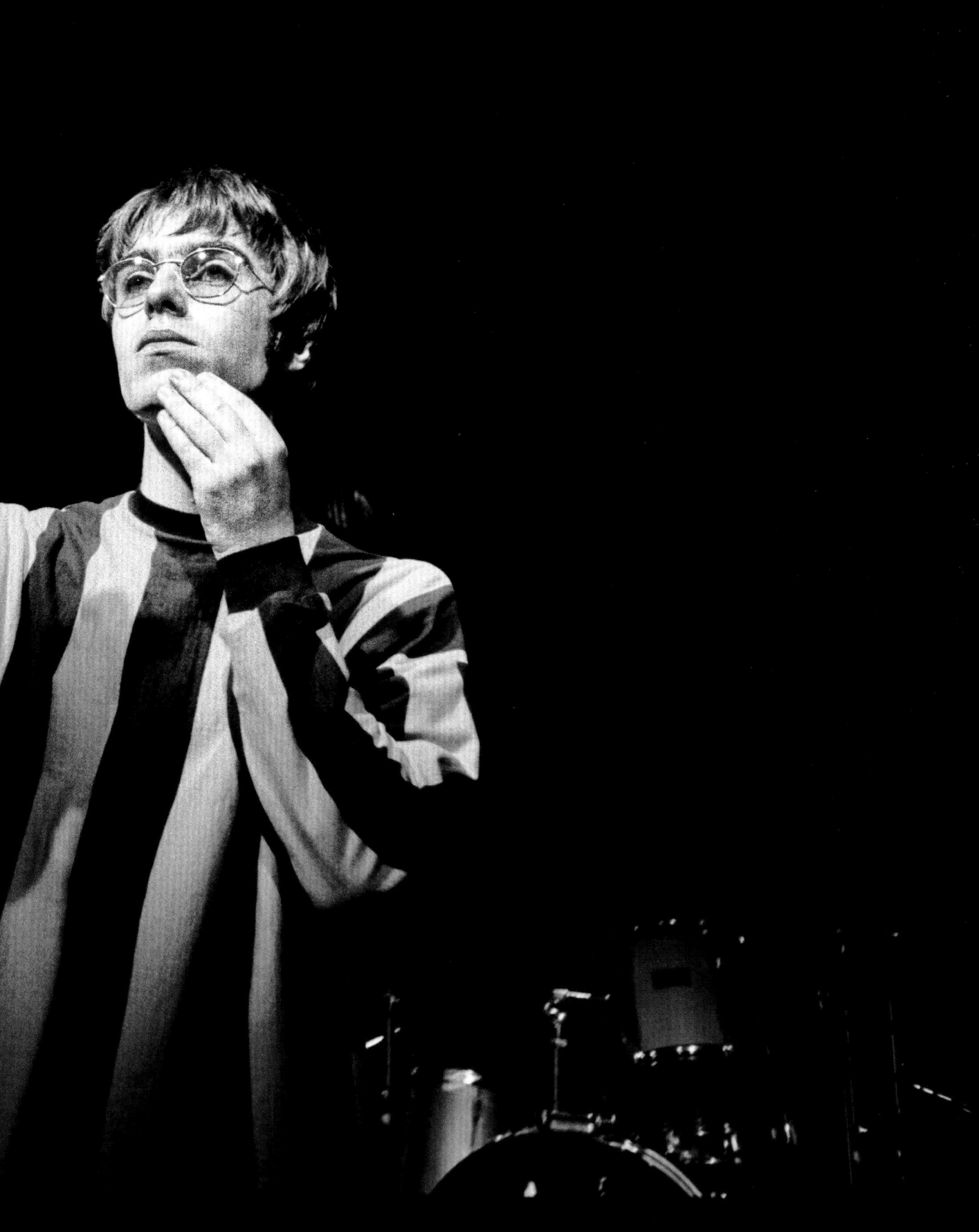

2 MAY
THE MARRIOTT HOTEL, PORTSMOUTH

In April 1994, I received a commission from the *NME* to shoot a cover feature with Oasis. It would be their first cover. Most bands are on their best behaviour when we deem them fit for the cover. Not Oasis.

The interest in the band had exploded in just a few months and they were already too big for the venues they were playing on this tour. I managed to get a few photos during the sound check prior to the doors opening. Then, within seconds, the 400-capacity Wedgewood Rooms was packed, hot and sweaty. The stage was far too small. It was absolute chaos. I had to shoot from the stage as there was no room anywhere else, then half the punters thought they should be on stage too.

I was amazed and relieved when we finally got out of the building and back to the calm of the Marriott Hotel in Portsmouth Harbour – how wrong could I be? East 17 were having a quiet drink in the bar when we arrived. They saw 21 Mancunians and disappeared quickly. Well, at least we had the bar to ourselves.

Whoever designed the interior of the hotel hadn't considered the fact that rock bands might stay there. If they had, they would not have put the bar on the ground floor next to the swimming pool. Liam, still honing his bad boy rock 'n' roll persona, proceeded to throw all the plastic tables and chairs into the pool.

Noel, quite reasonably, pointed out to him that we now had nowhere to sit and have a drink. He then told his younger brother to get in the pool and put all the furniture back in position. Liam did as he was told, then tried to kick off with Noel. The road crew stood around taking no notice of this regular performance. Finally, they hugged, and we all sat down. The barman was looking increasingly worried. He told us it was last orders. Noel then ordered six drinks each for all twenty-one of us. The barman decided it made more commercial sense to stay open, but he needed the toilet. By the time he had come back, someone had already served everyone a range of drinks from his bar. It was going to be a long night.

Many drinks and tall stories later, at around 5am, one of the crew, remembering that we soon had to drive to Newport in South Wales, decided to wrap things up. Someone must have signed the five-hour bar bill to Brian Harvey's room because, as we were leaving, I remember hearing the barman say, "Goodnight Mr Harvey," to one of our party.

I still wonder if the East 17 frontman paid it for us. If so, thanks Bri. I owe you for 15 G&Ts.

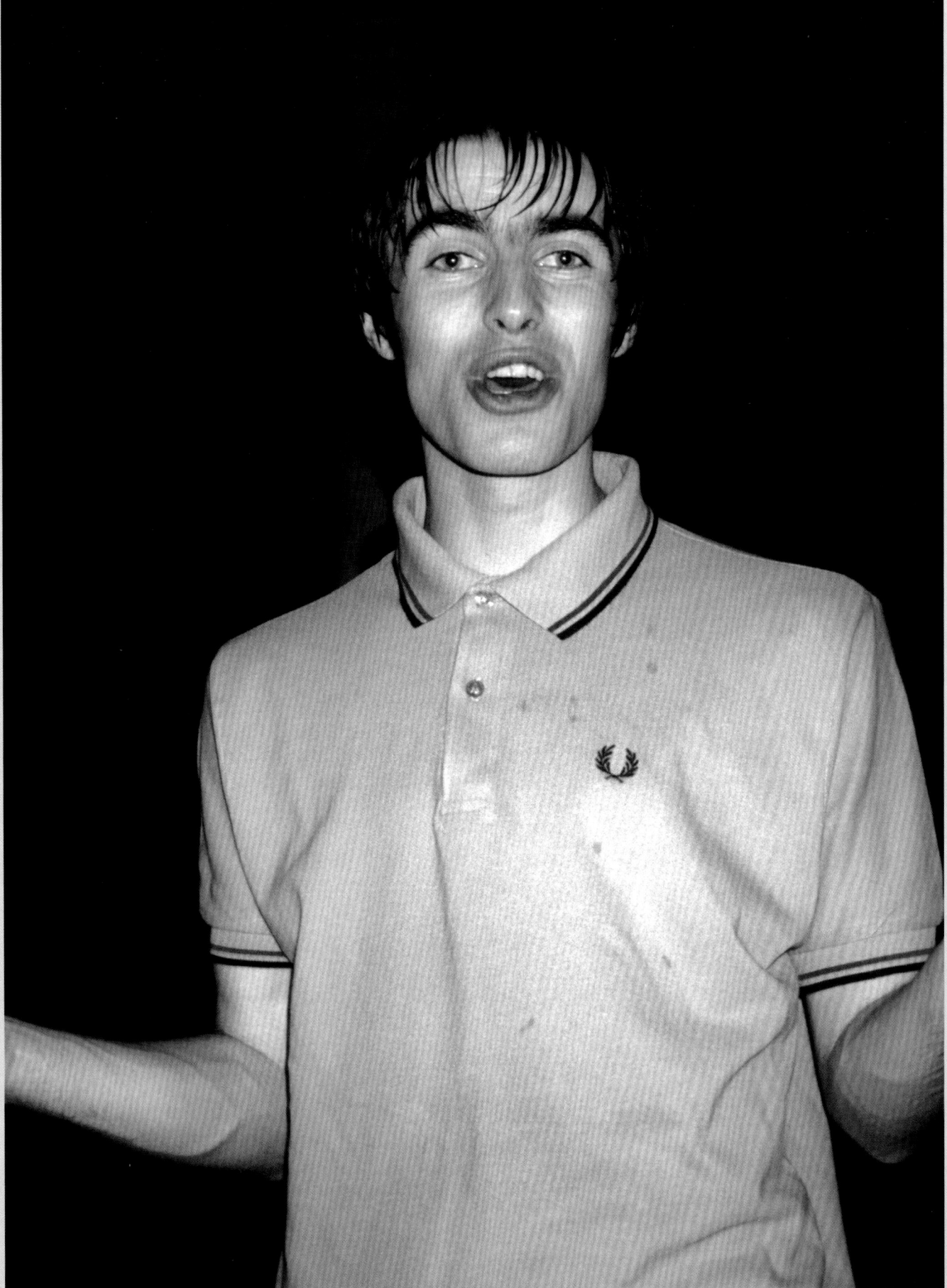

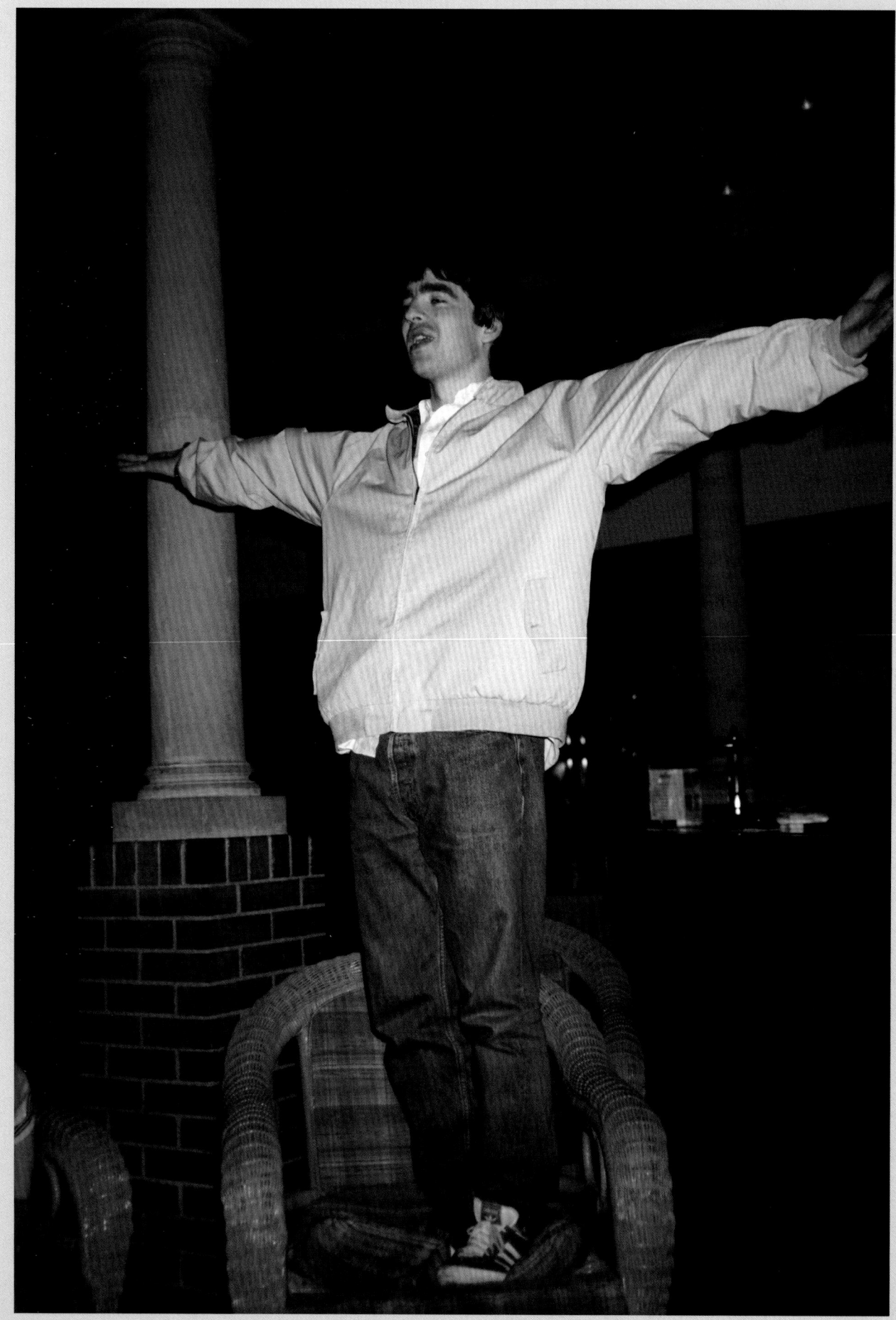

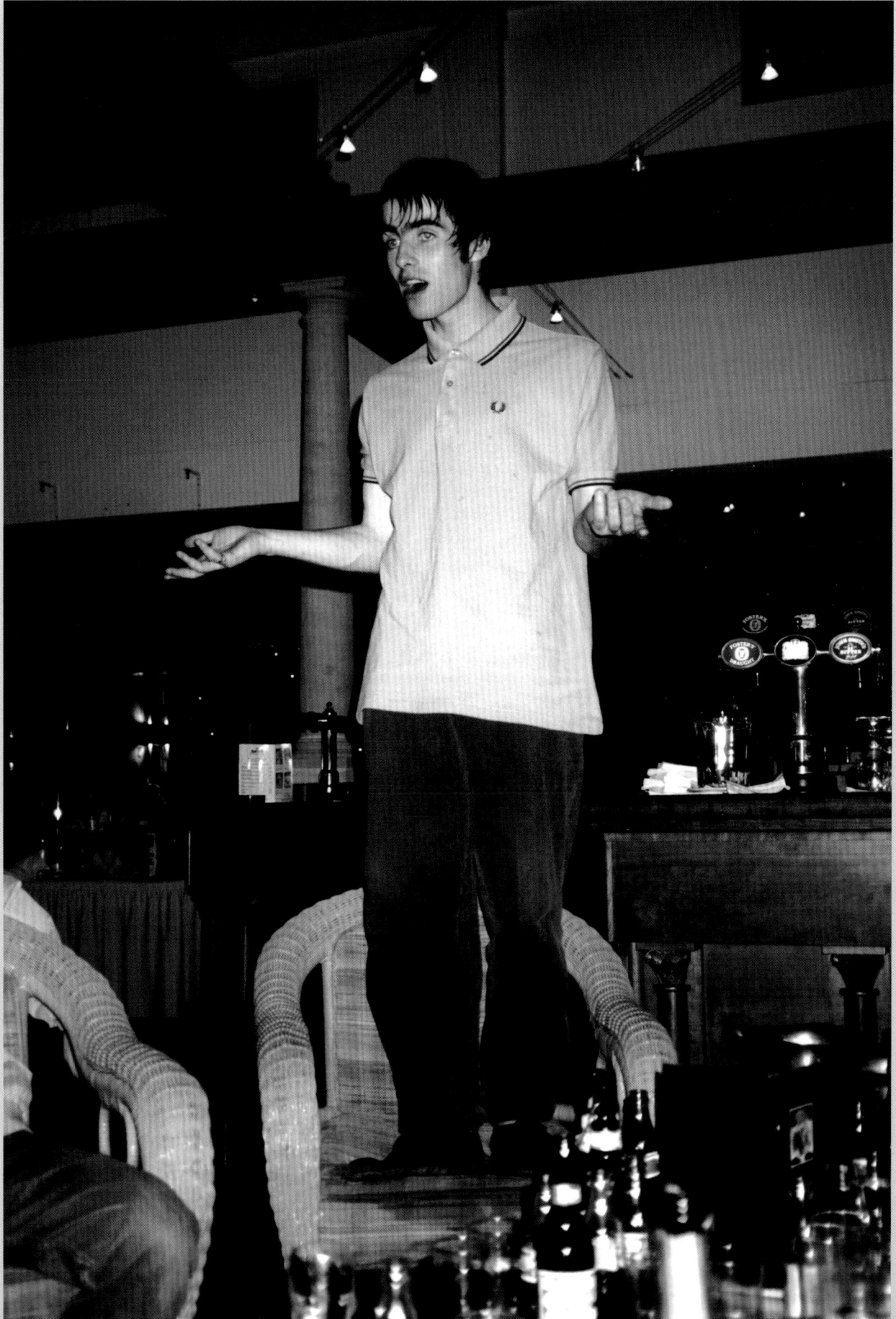

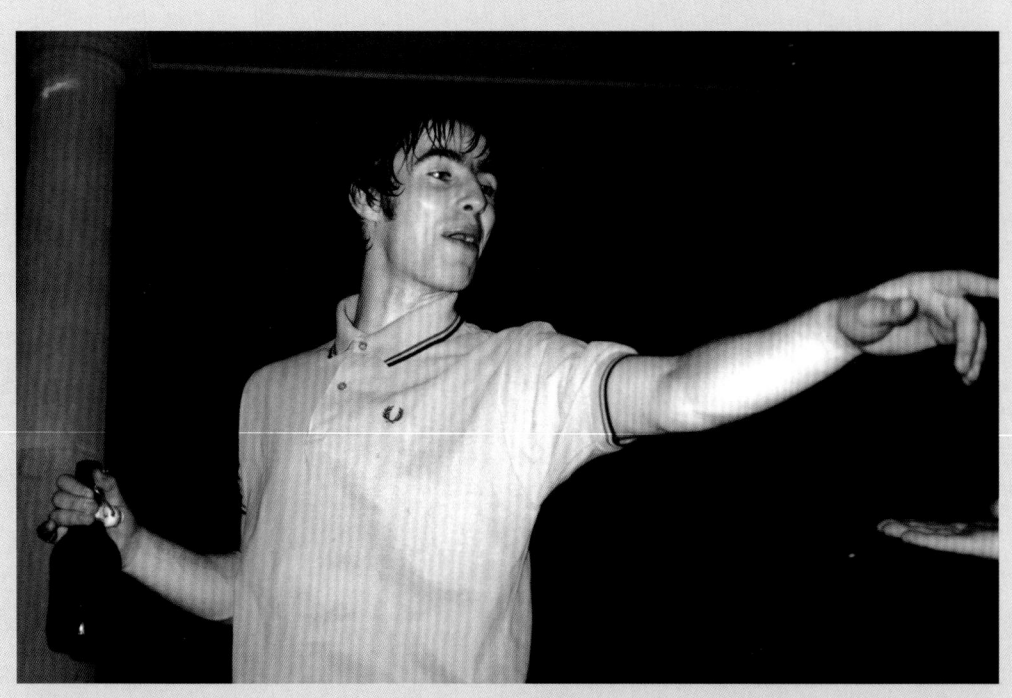
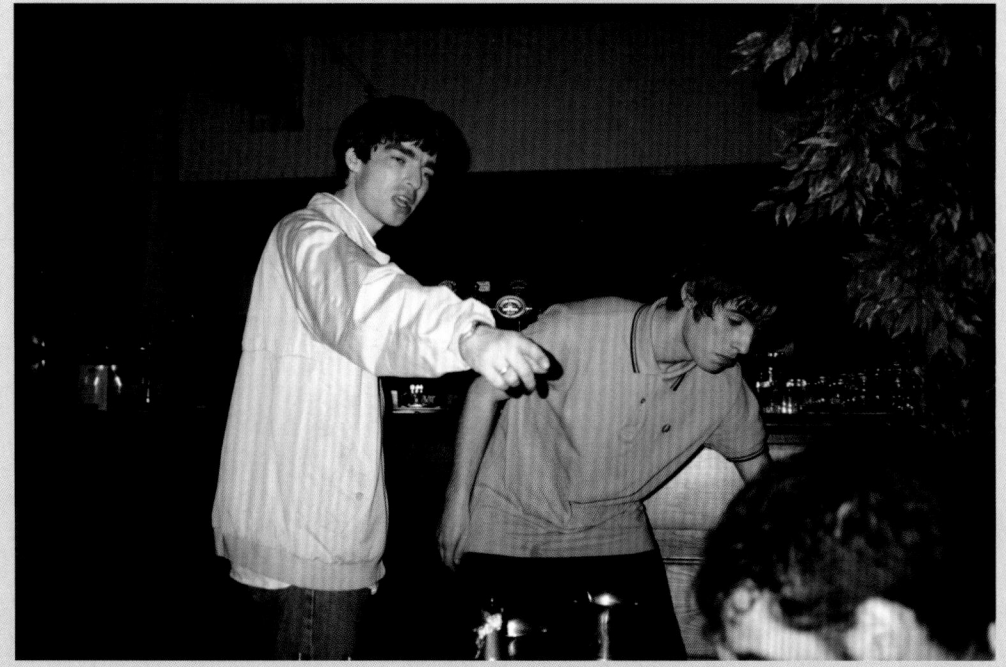

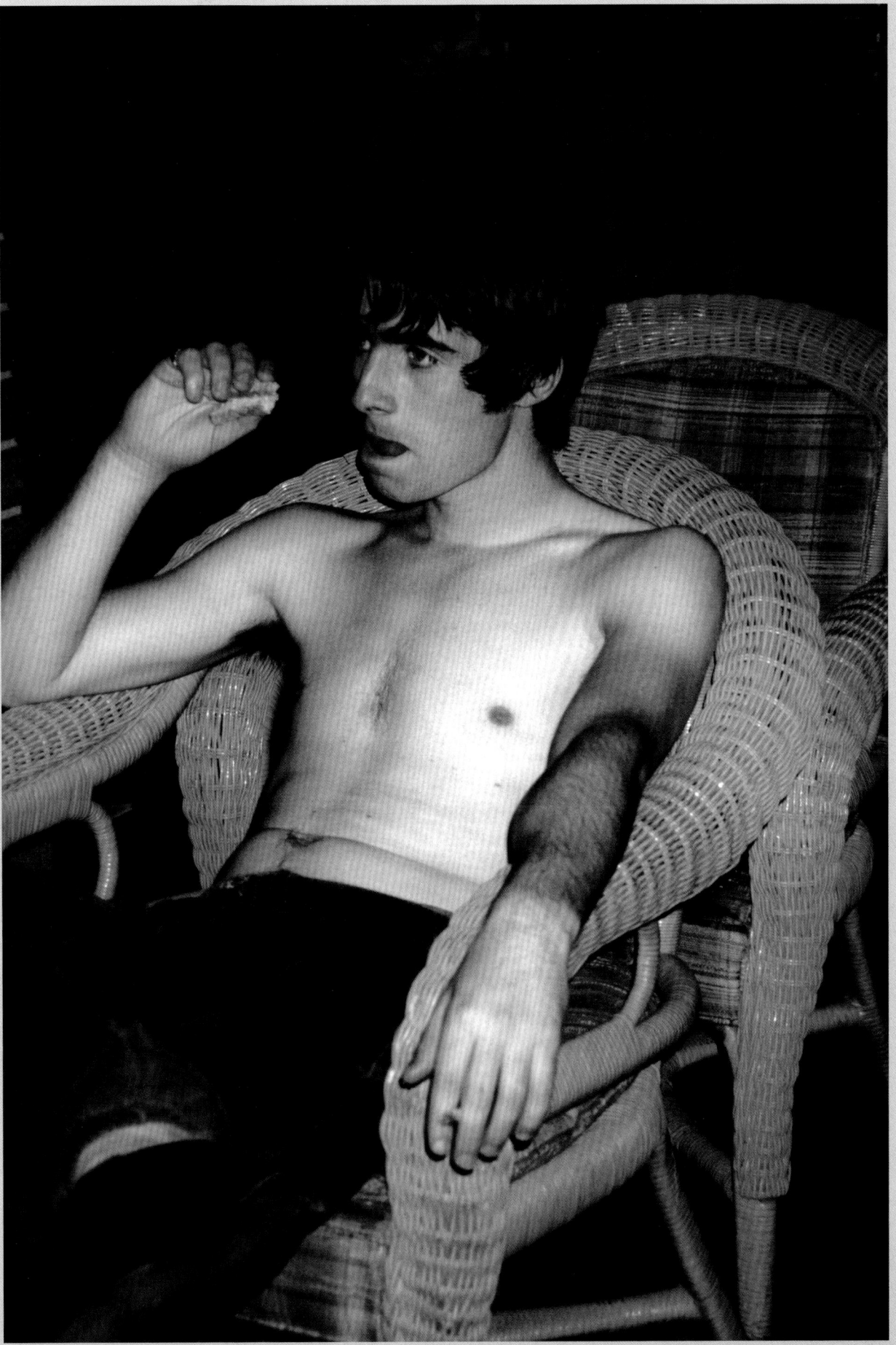

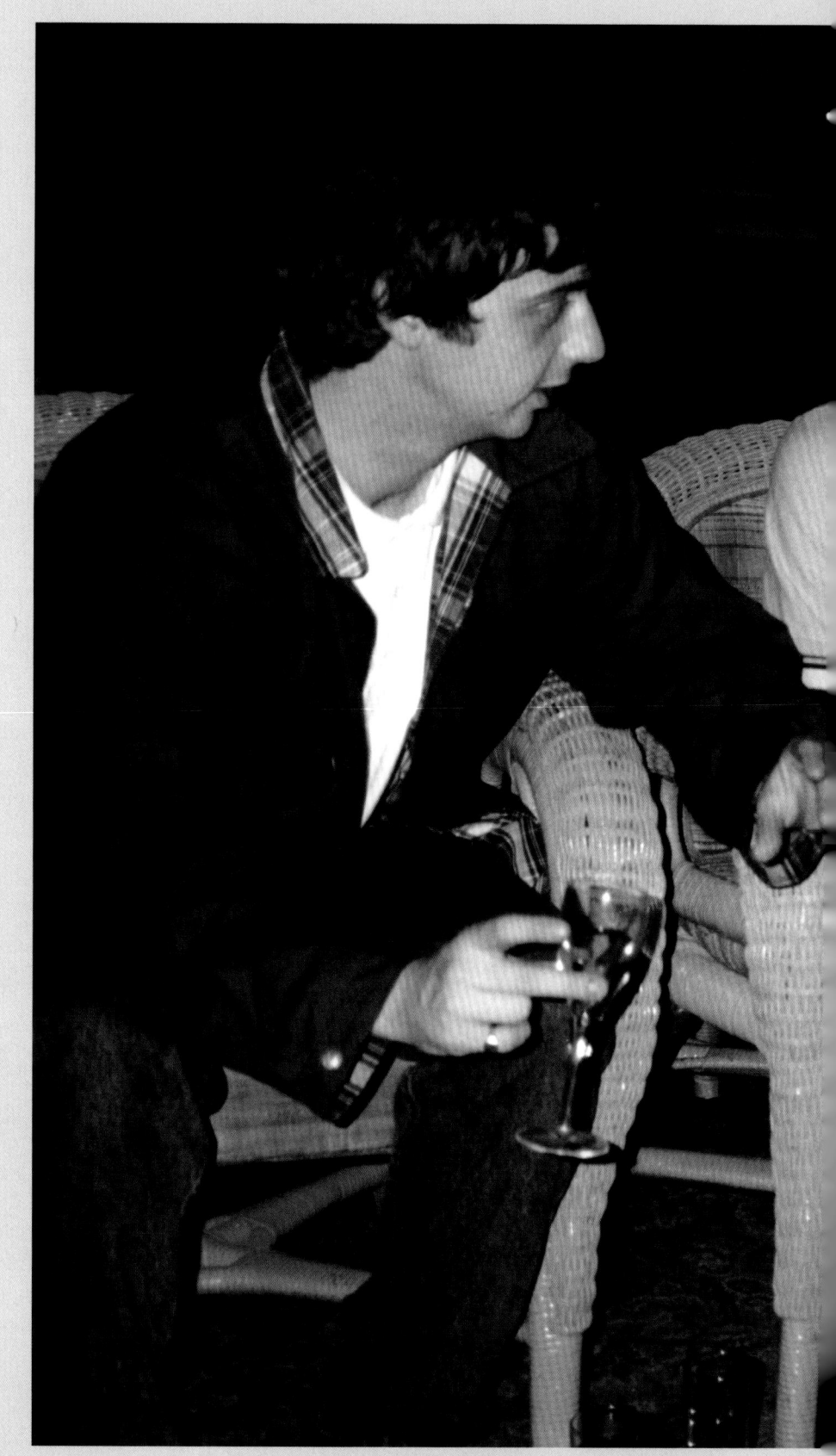

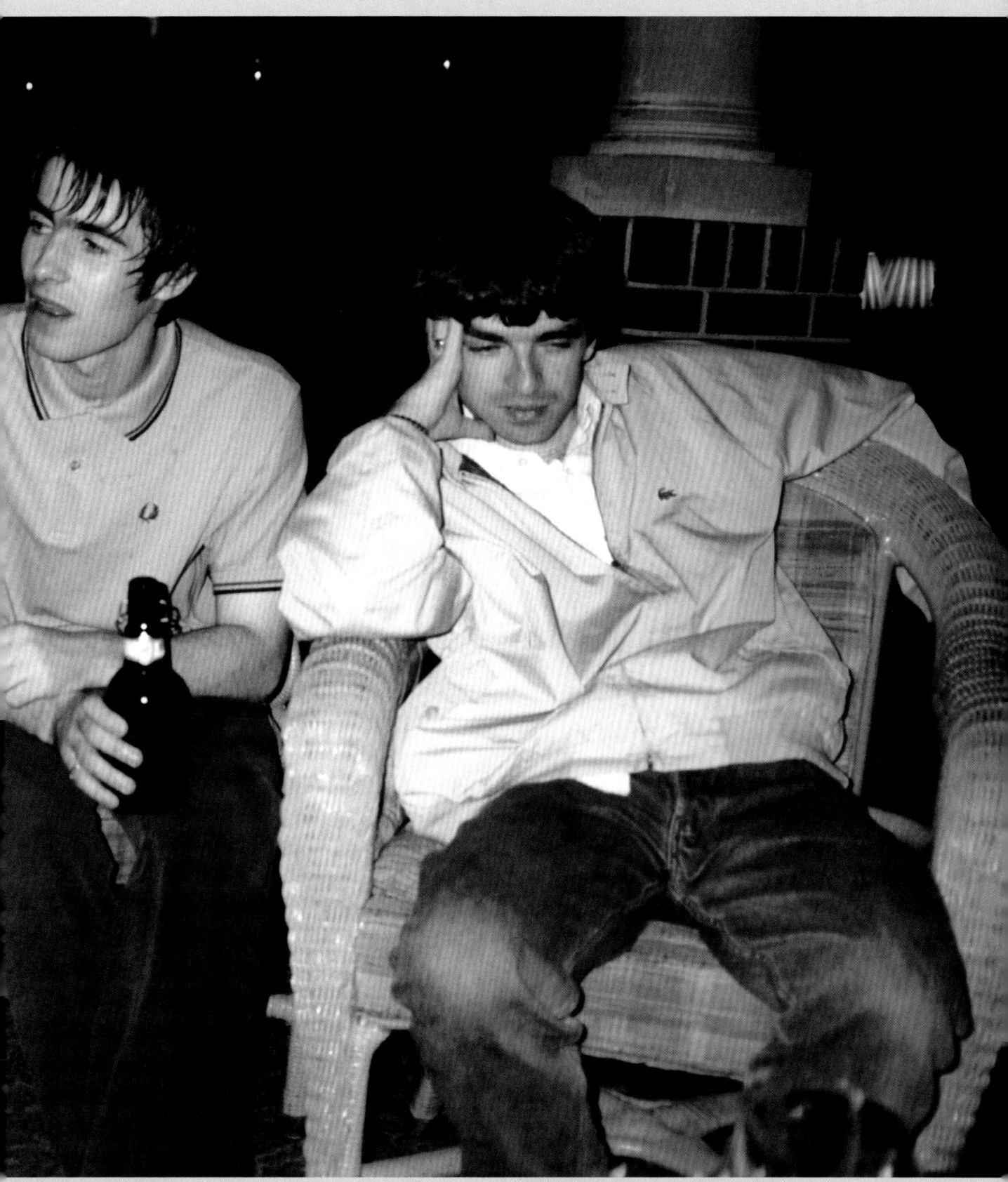

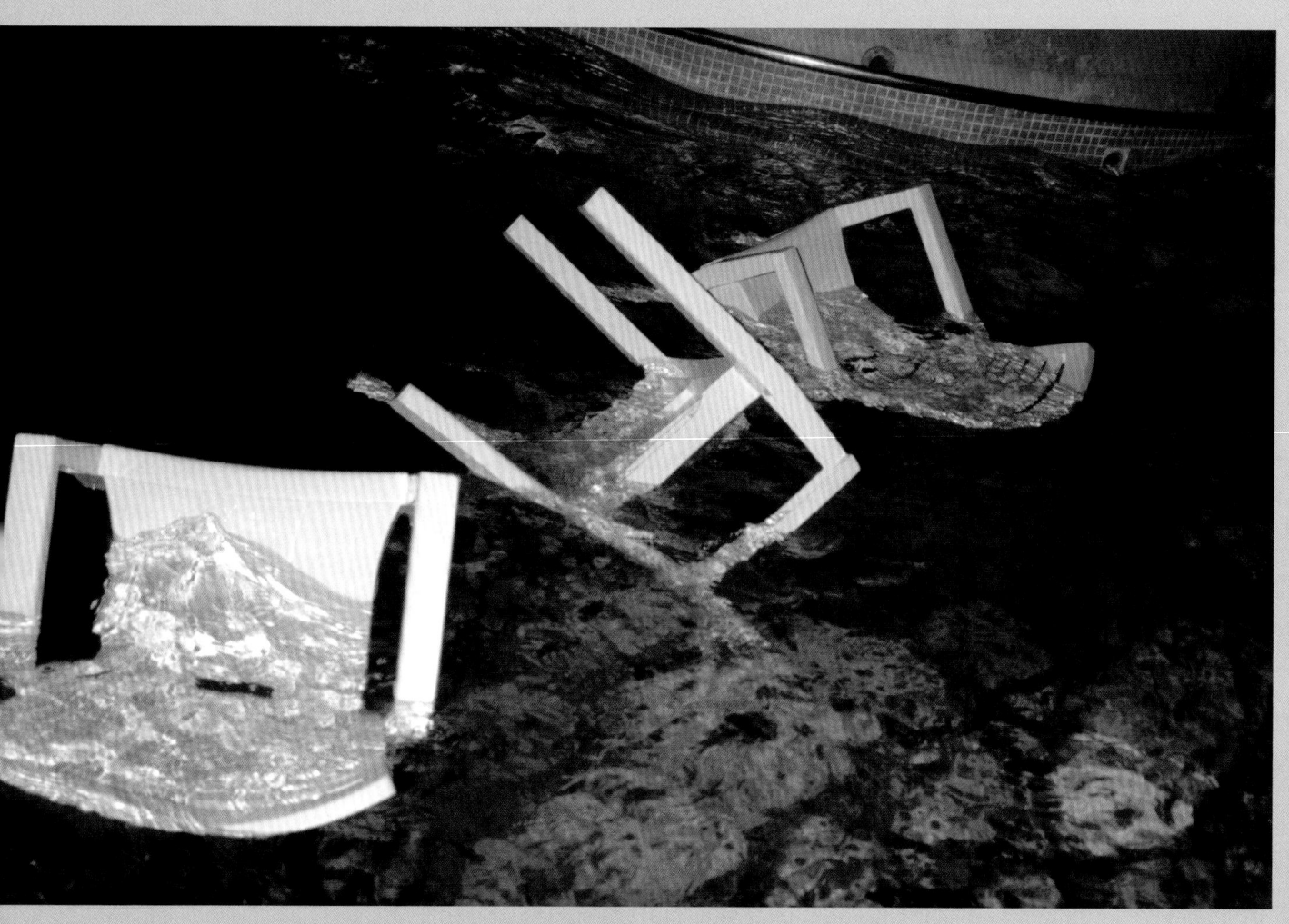

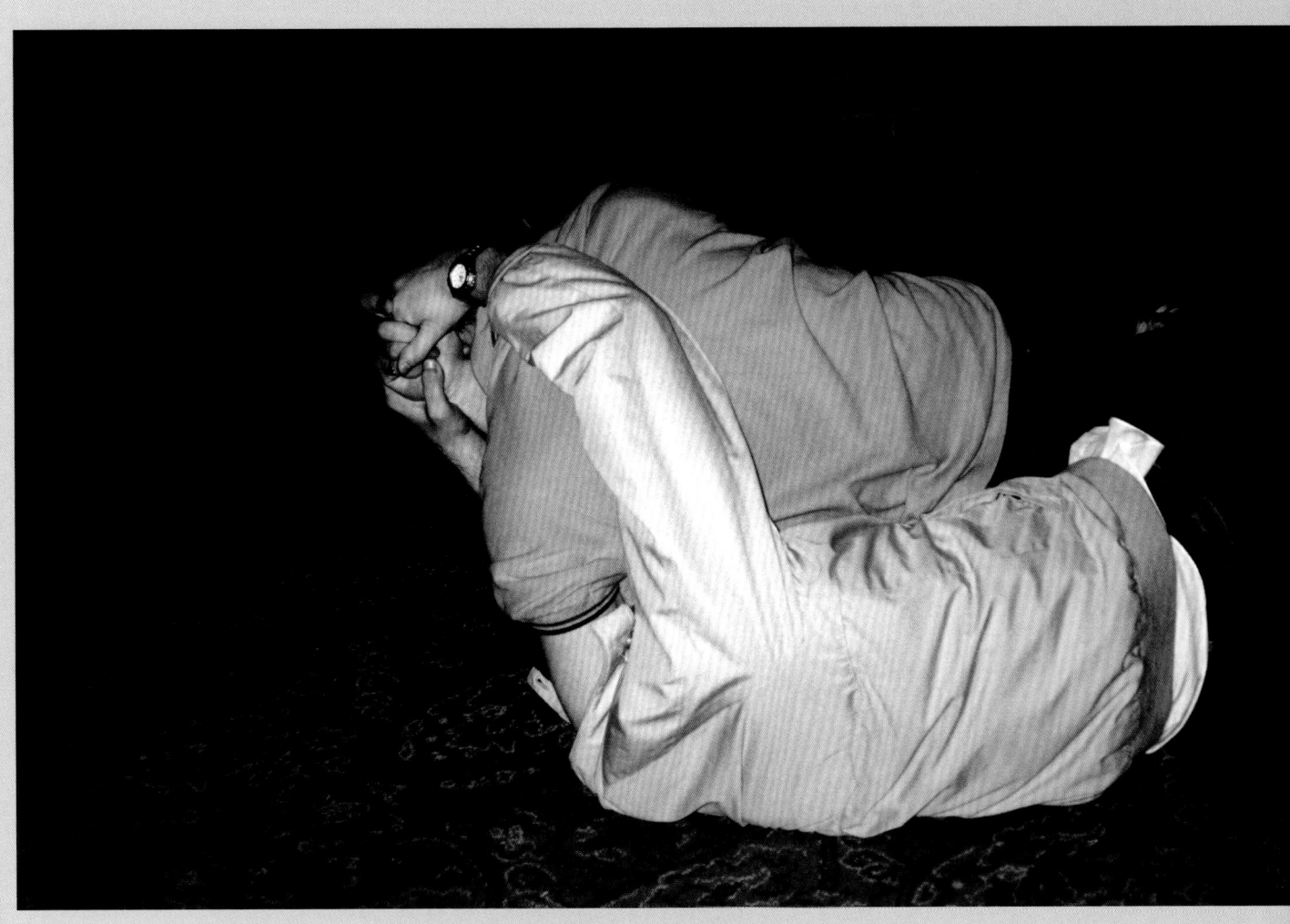

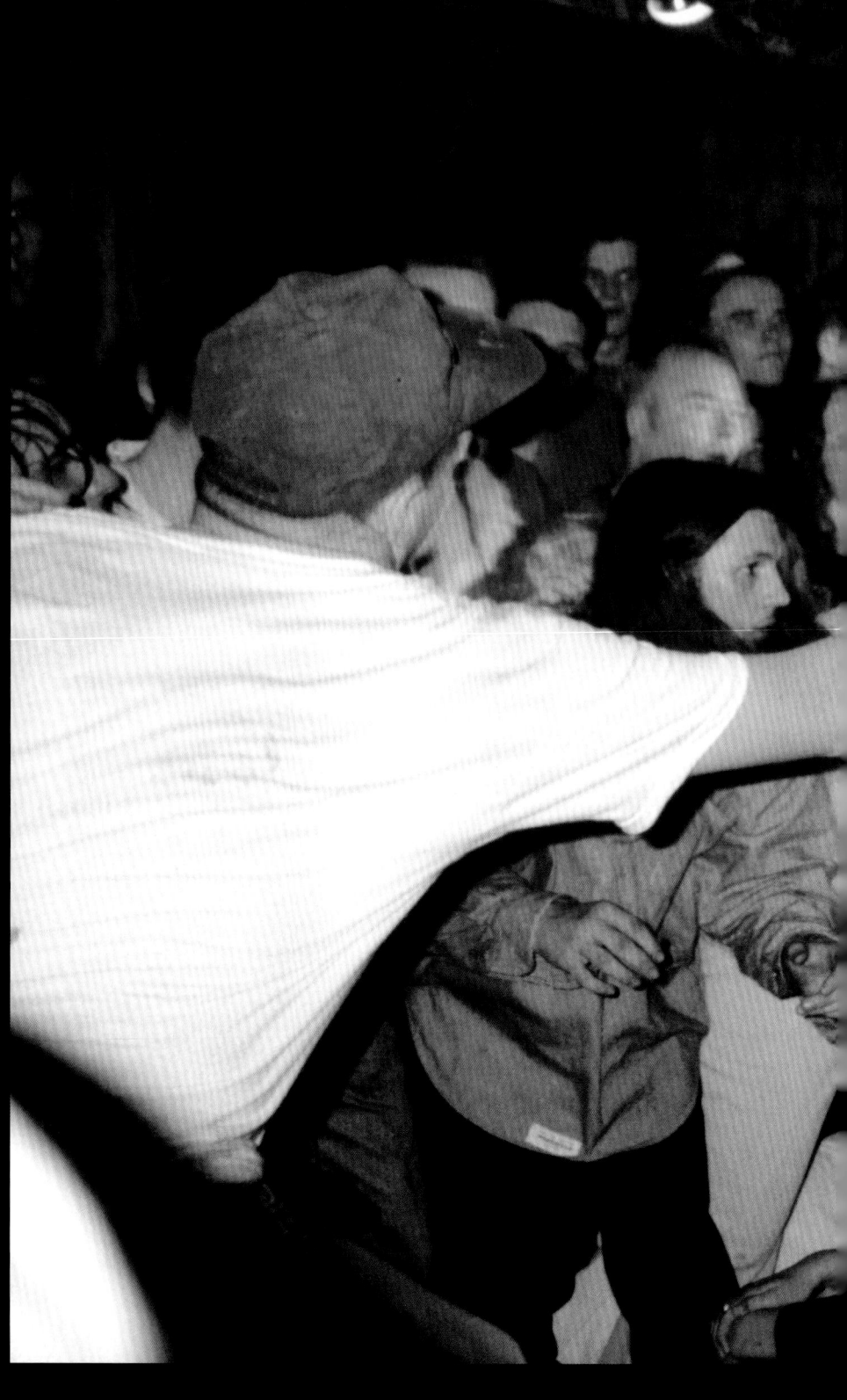

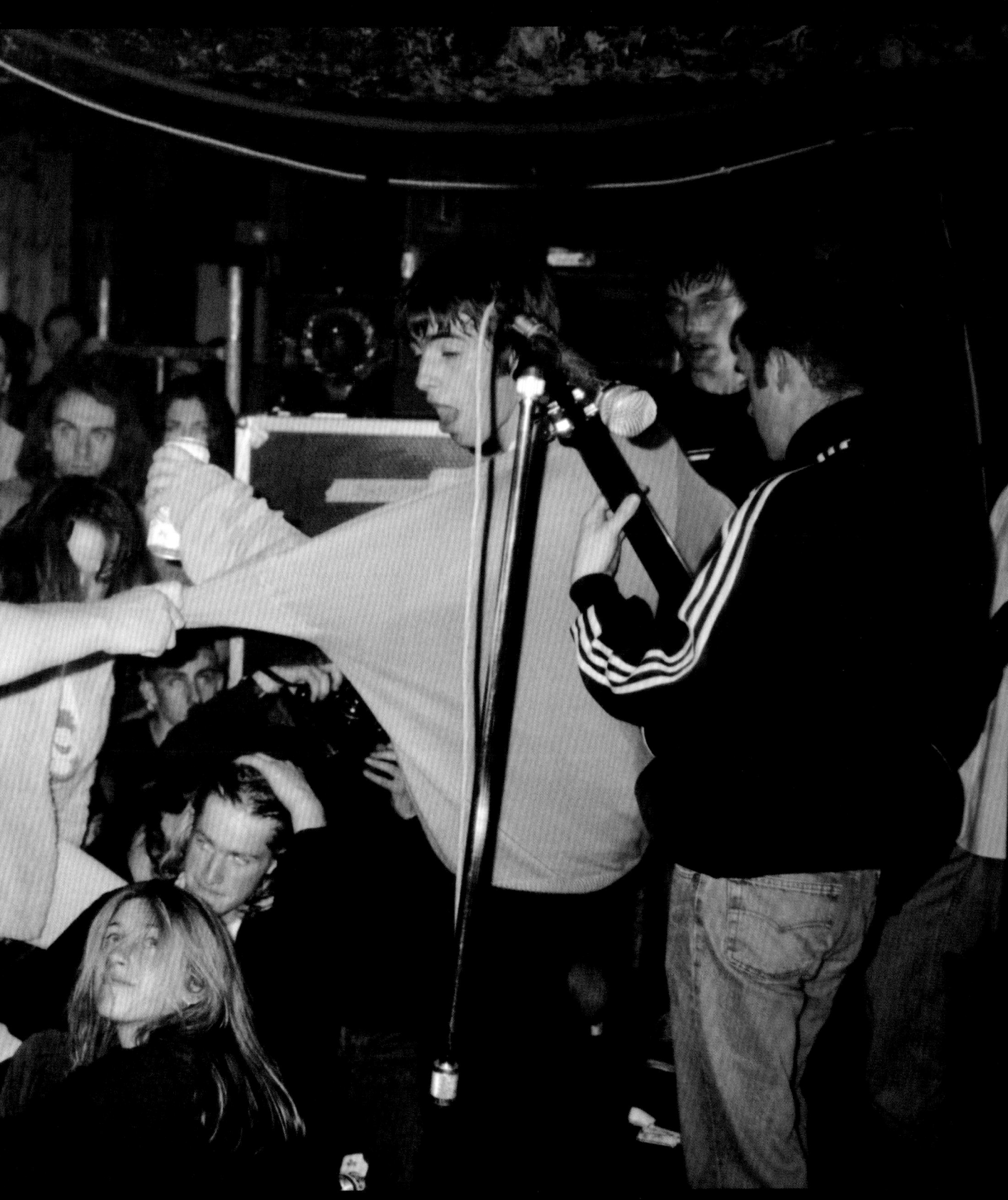

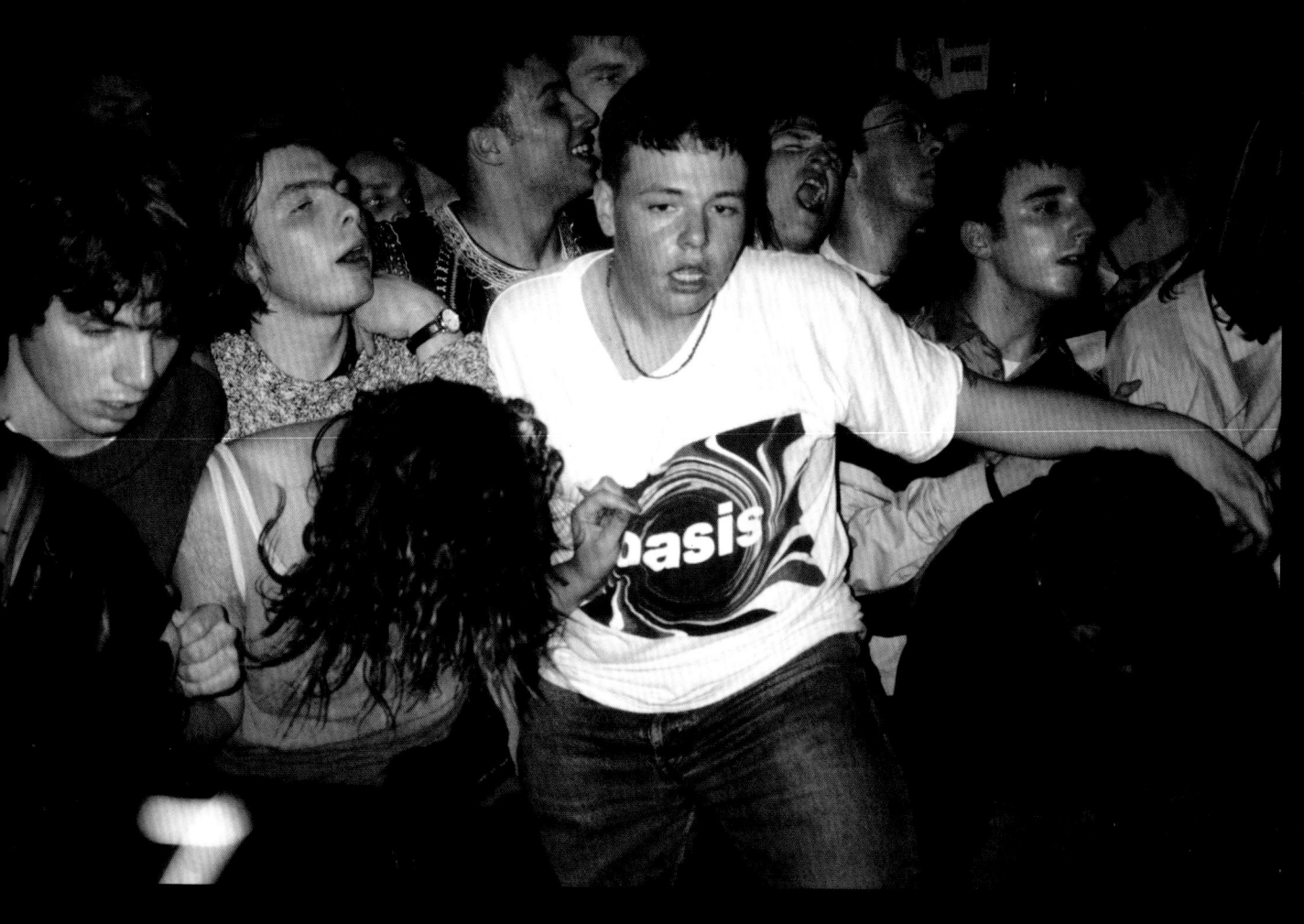

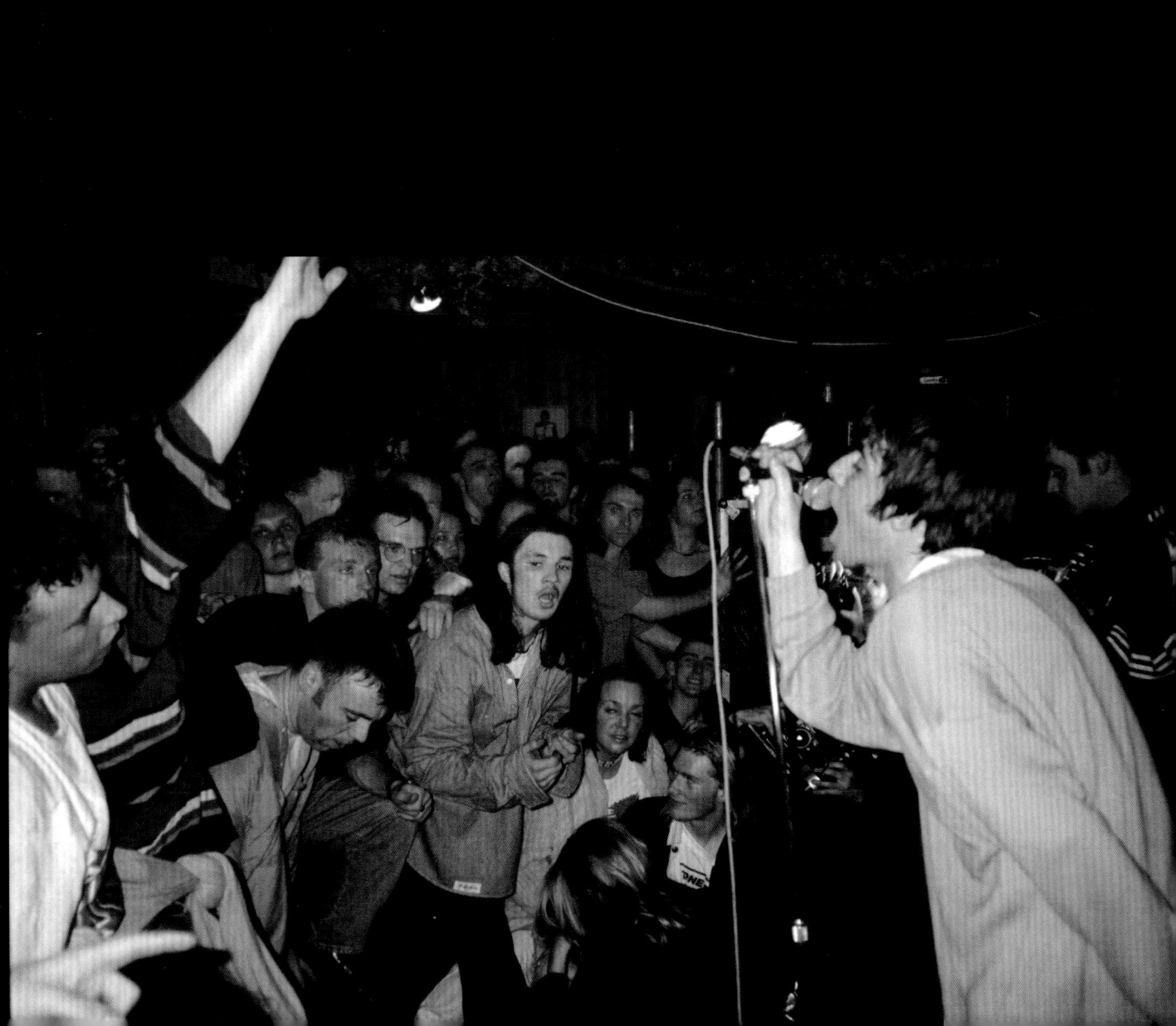

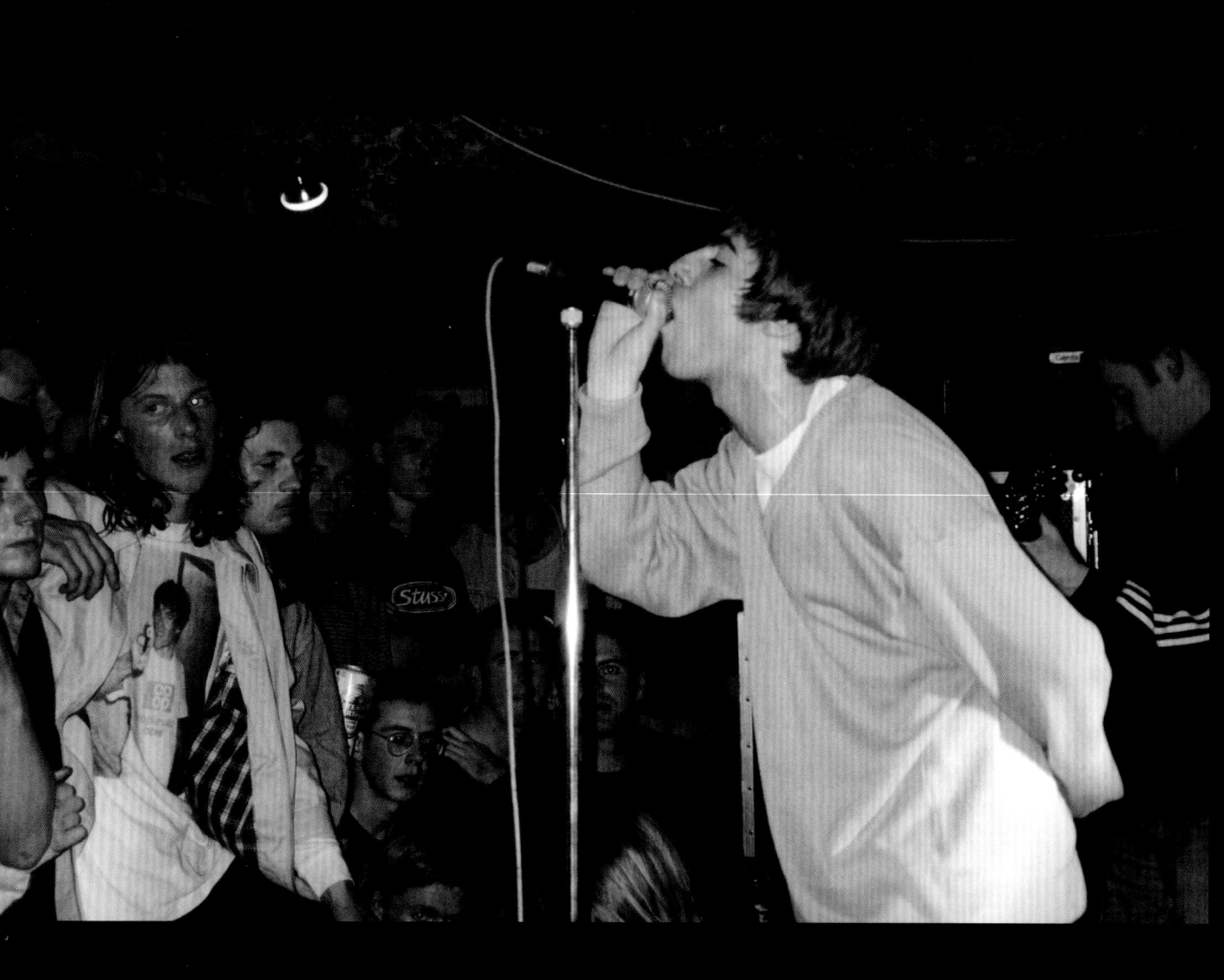

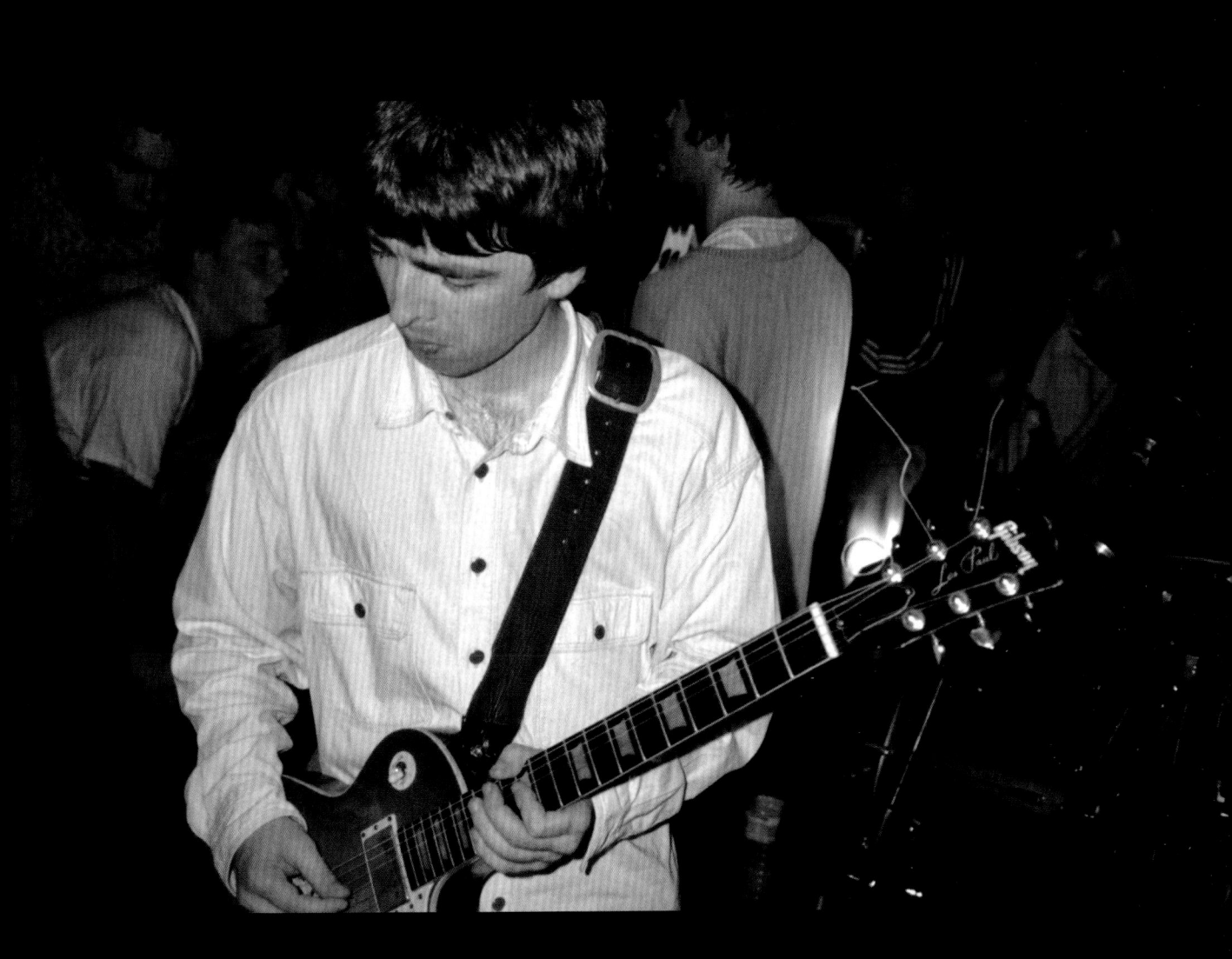

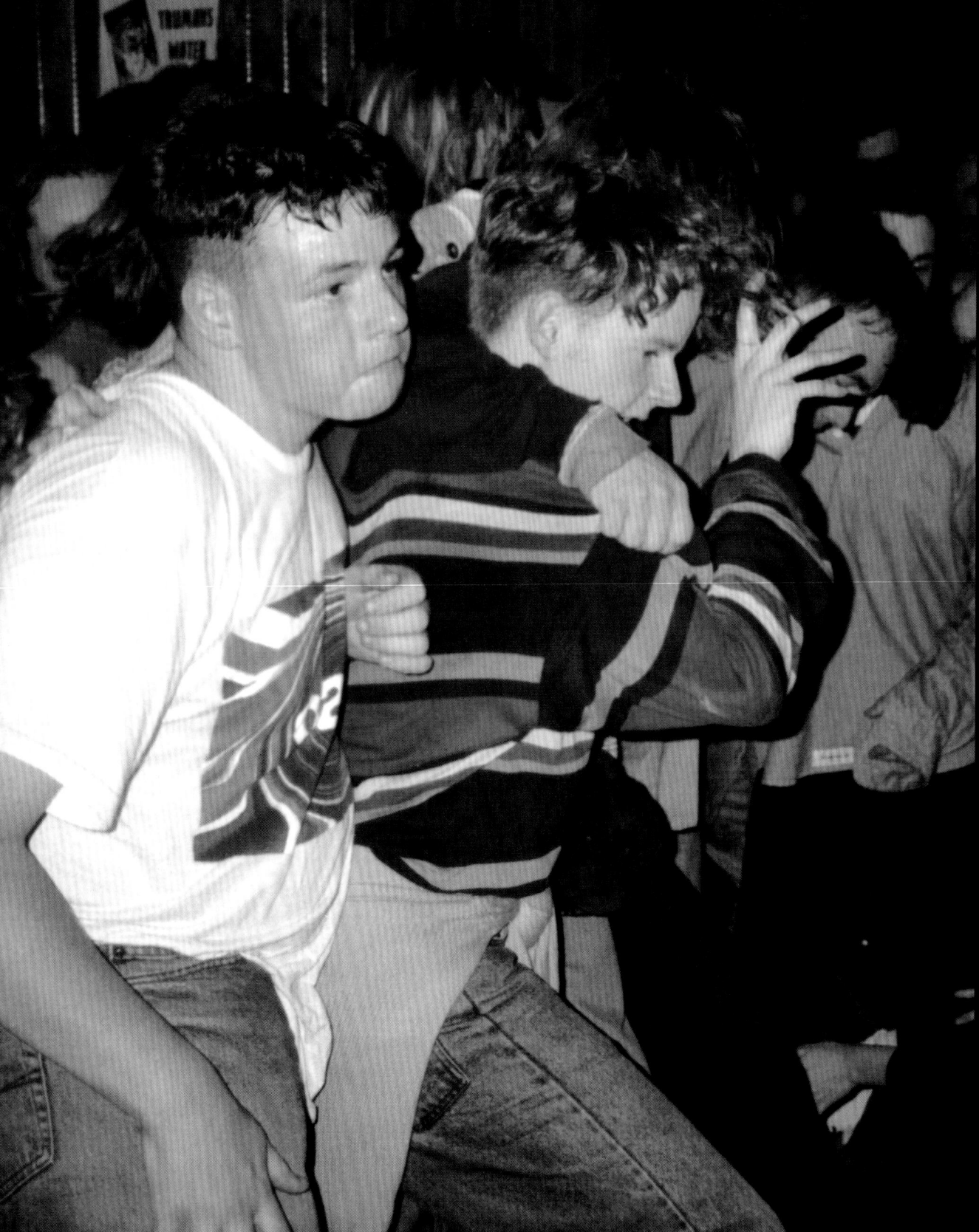

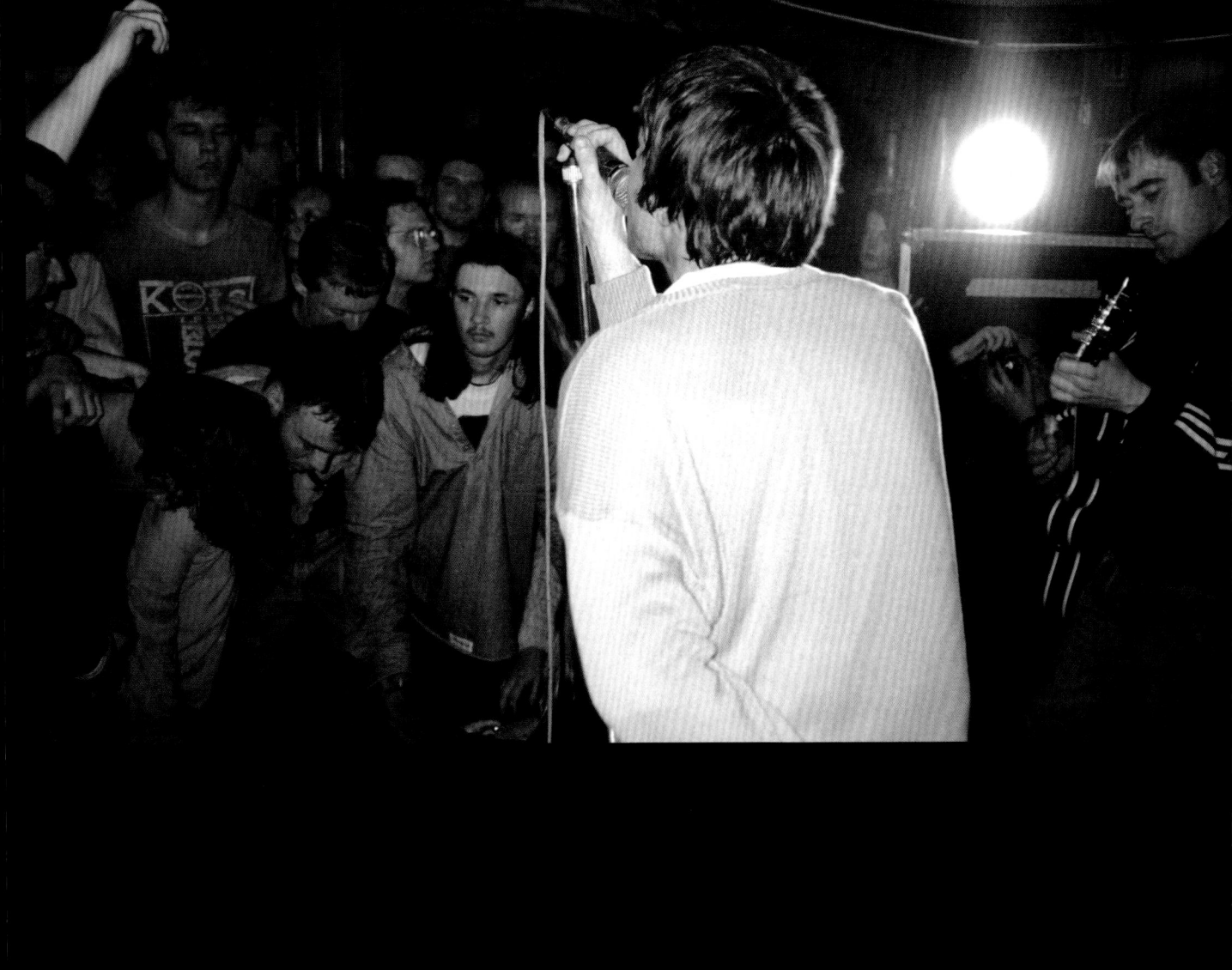

4 MAY

THE KING'S HEAD HOTEL, NEWPORT, GWENT

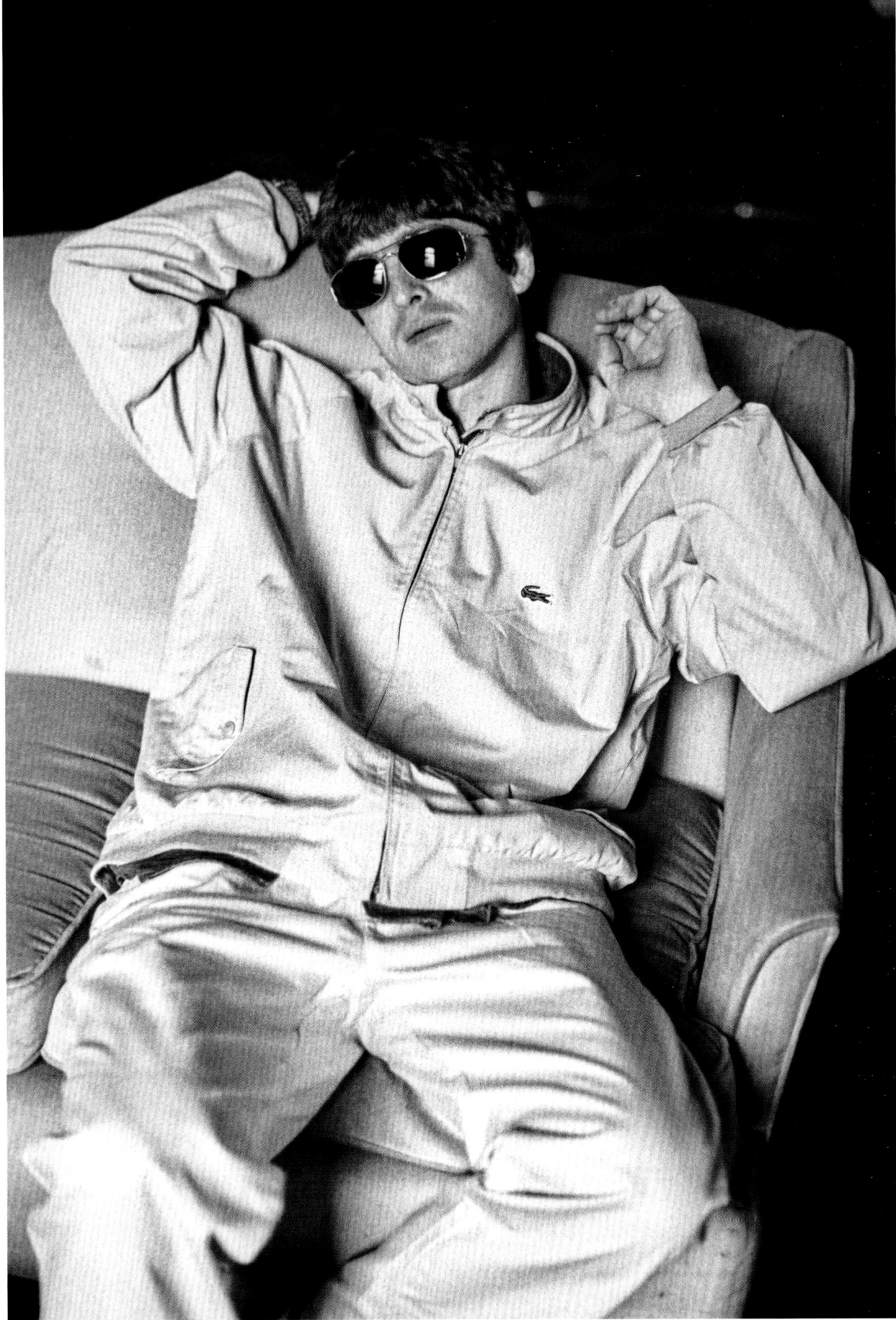

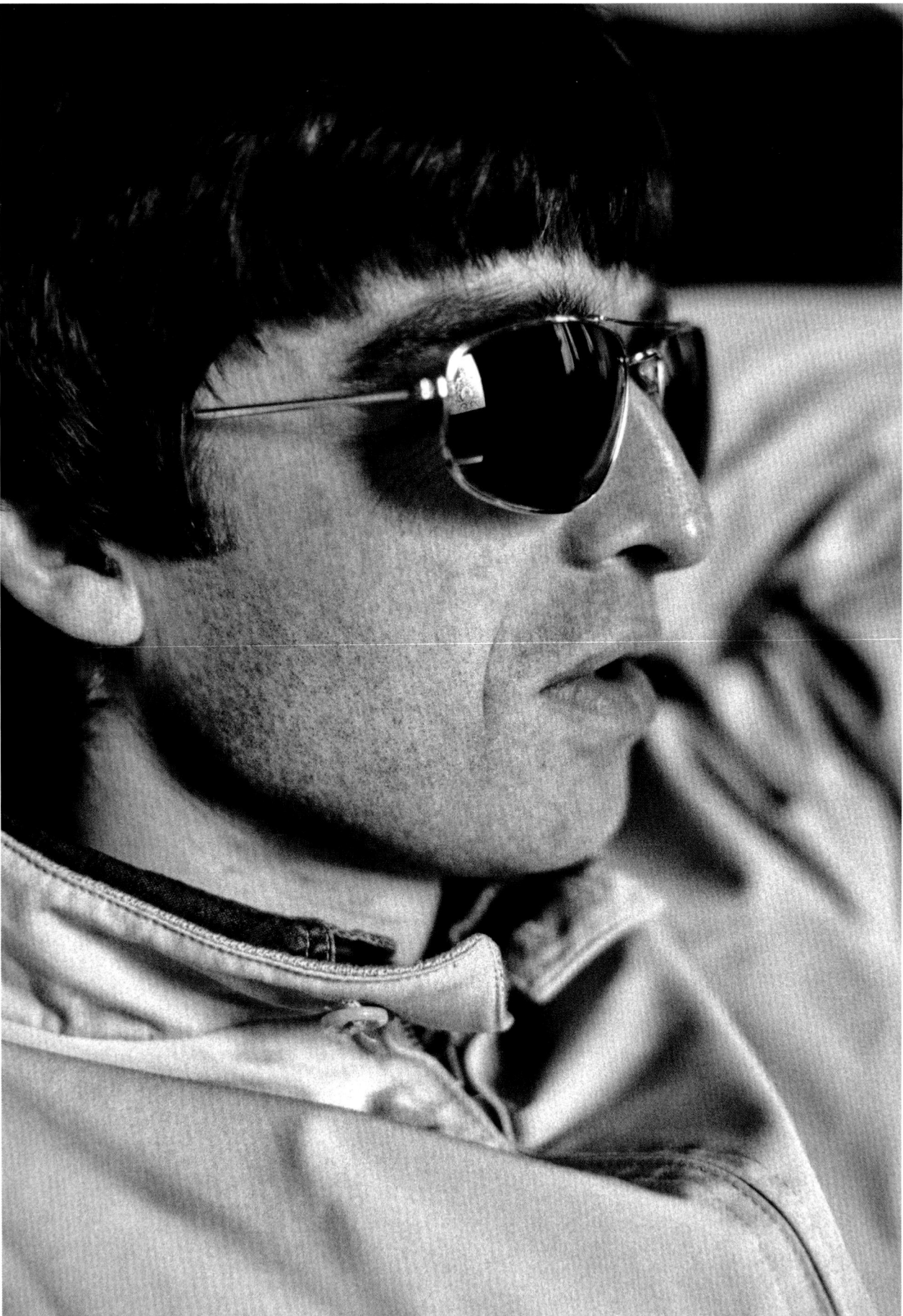

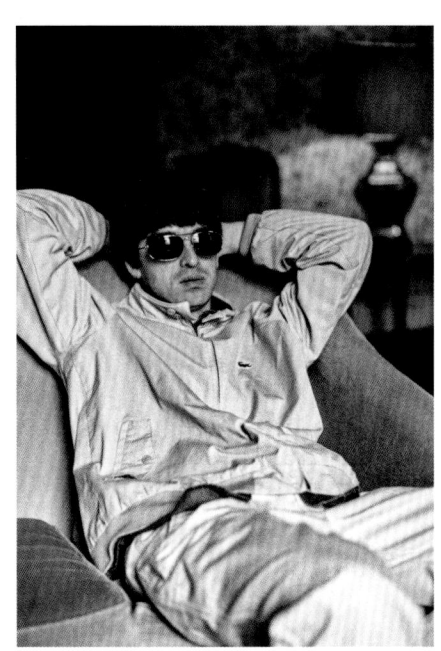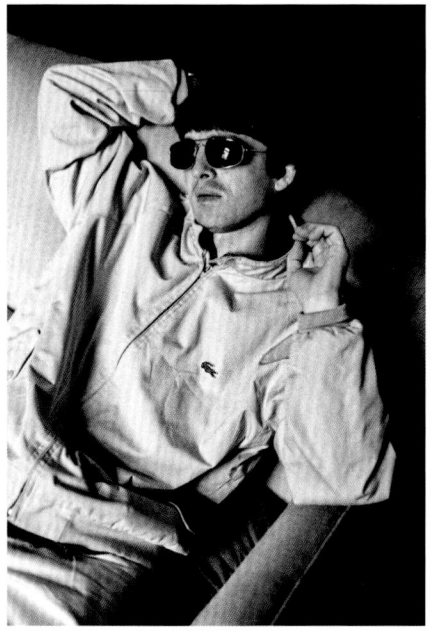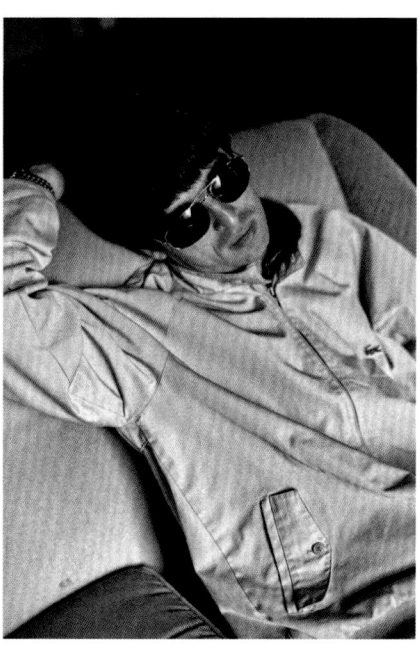

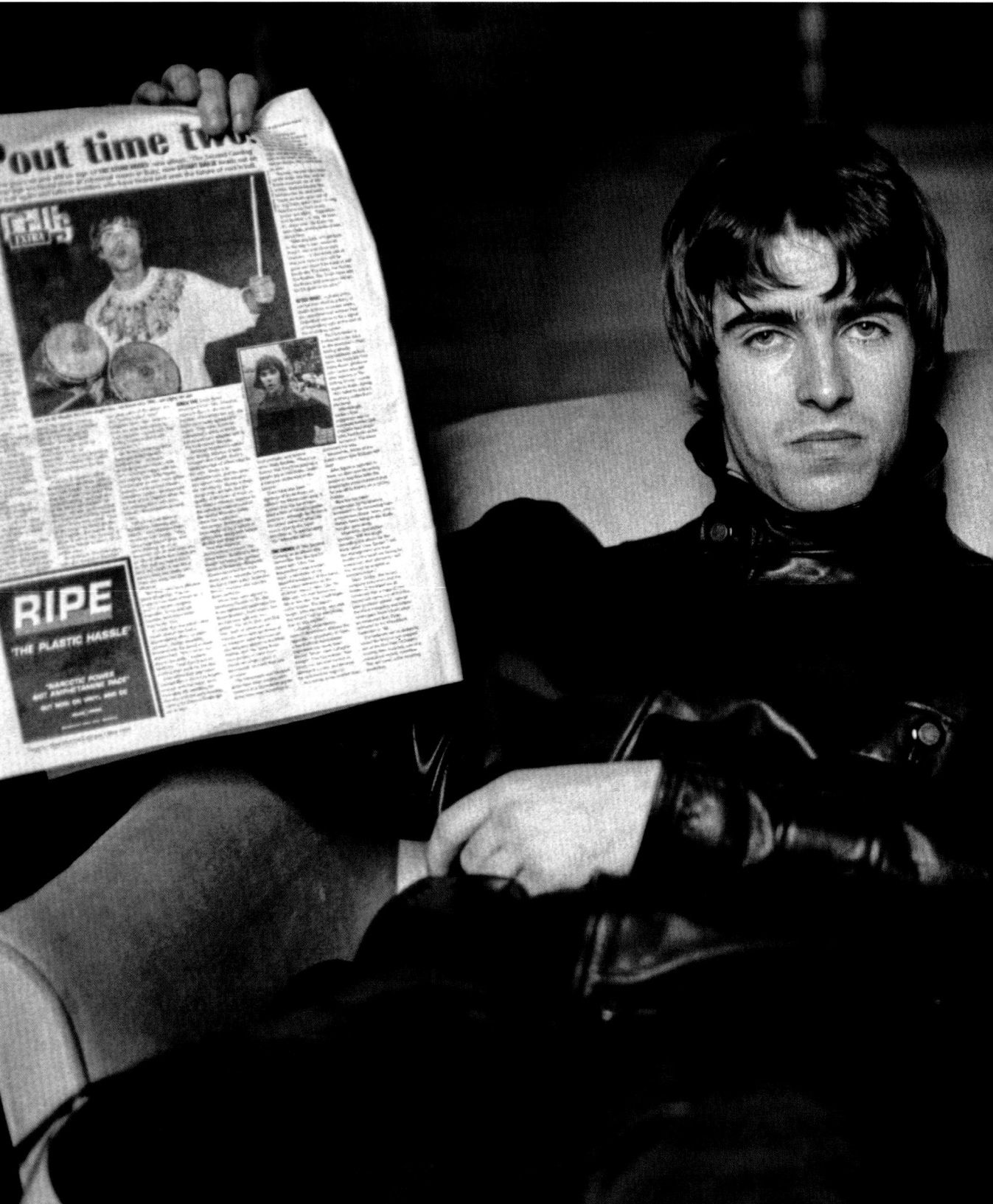

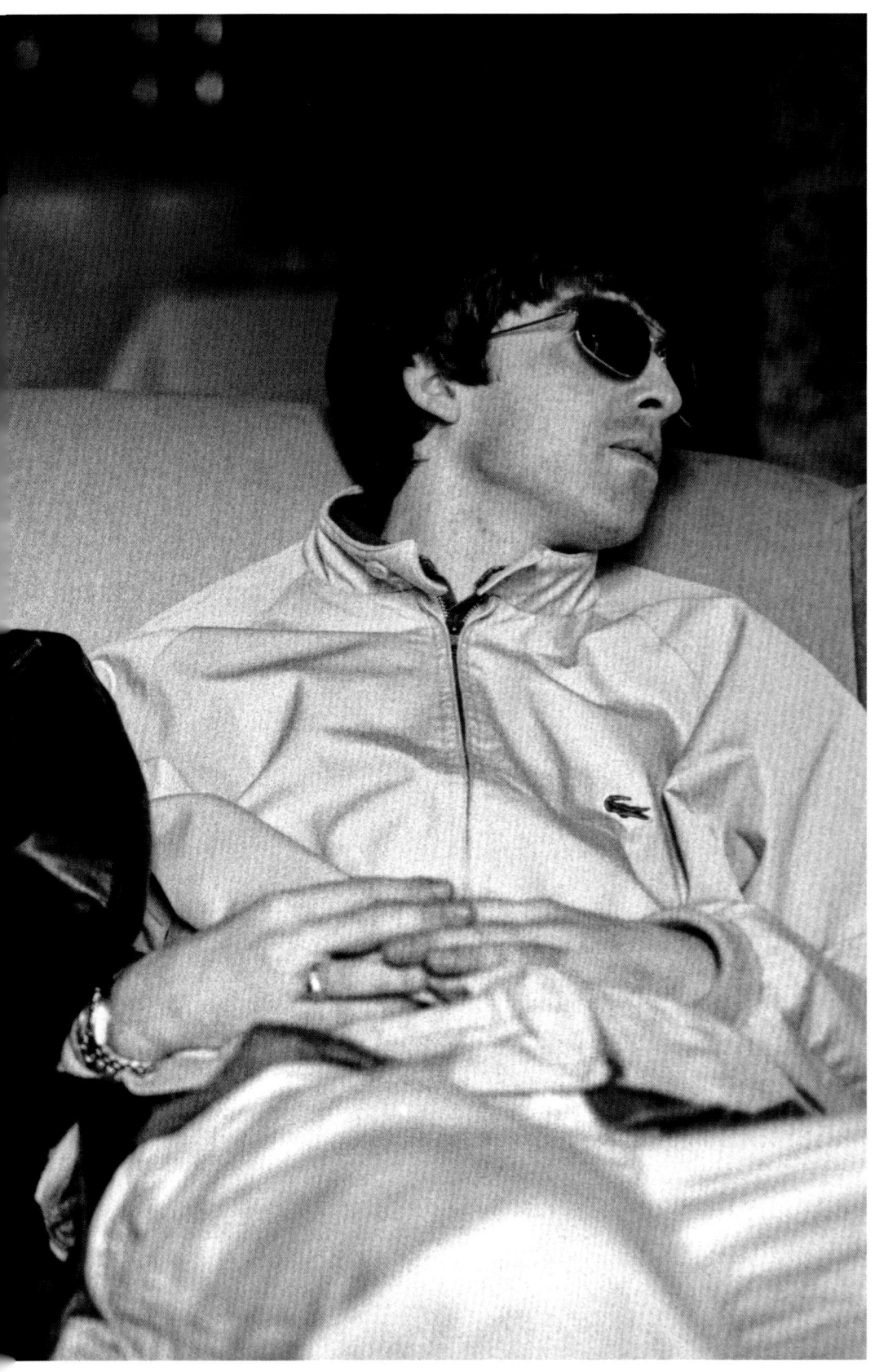

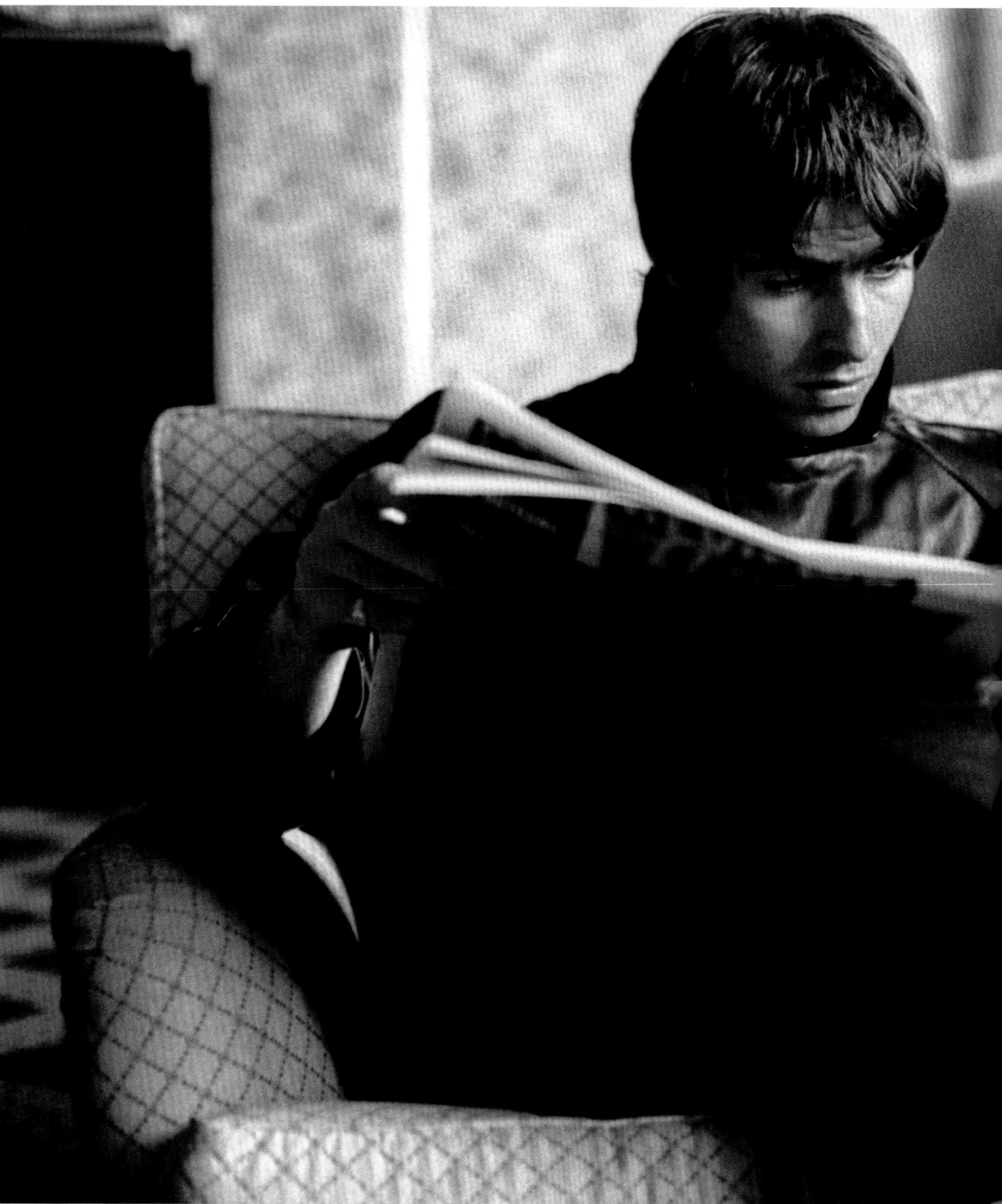

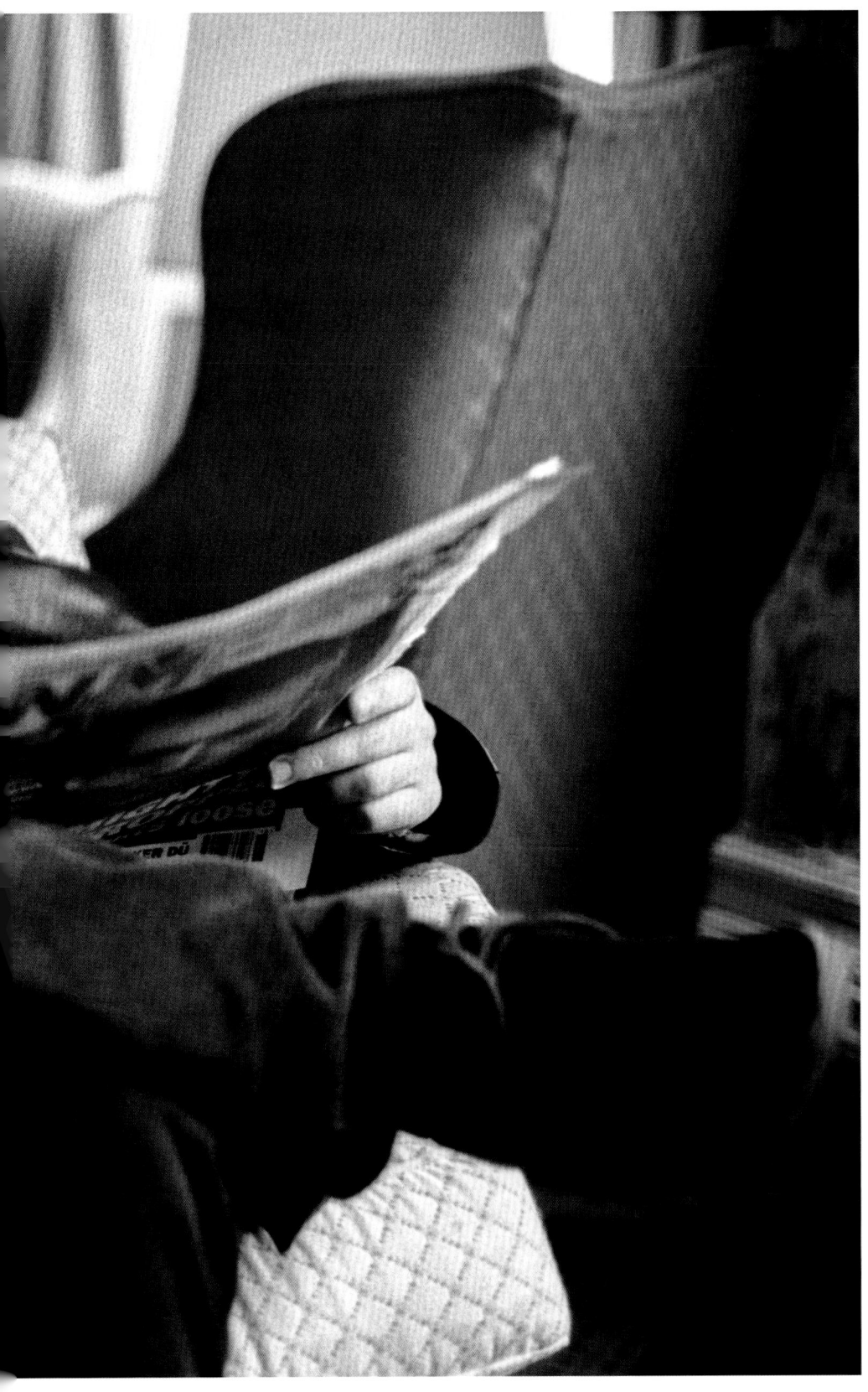

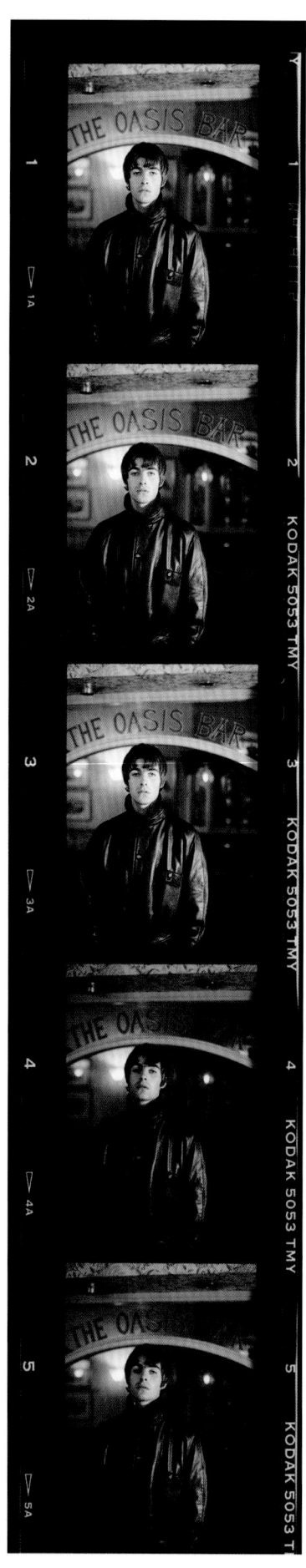

"That cover shot was great, though.
Fun night too!"
—*Noel Gallagher*

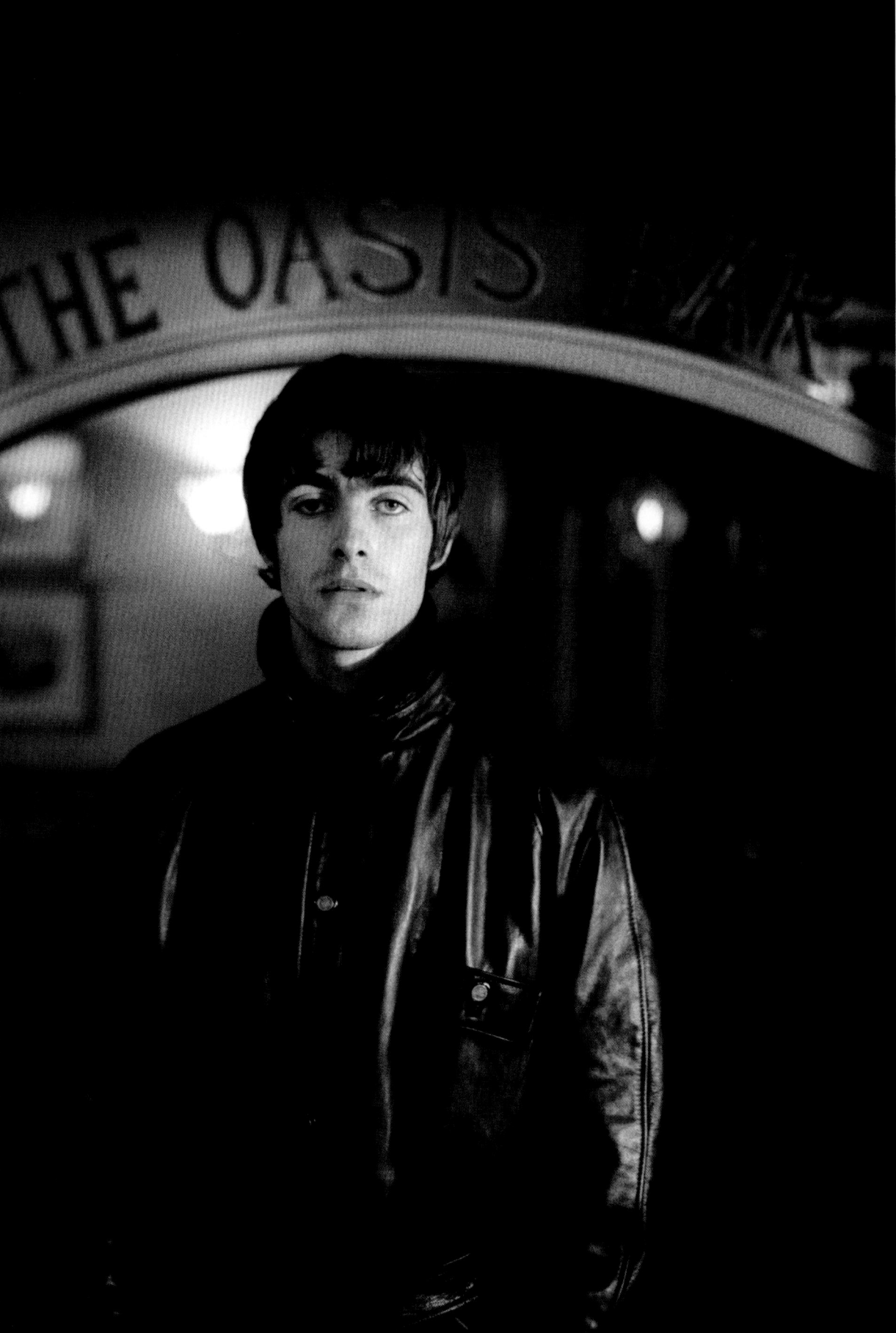

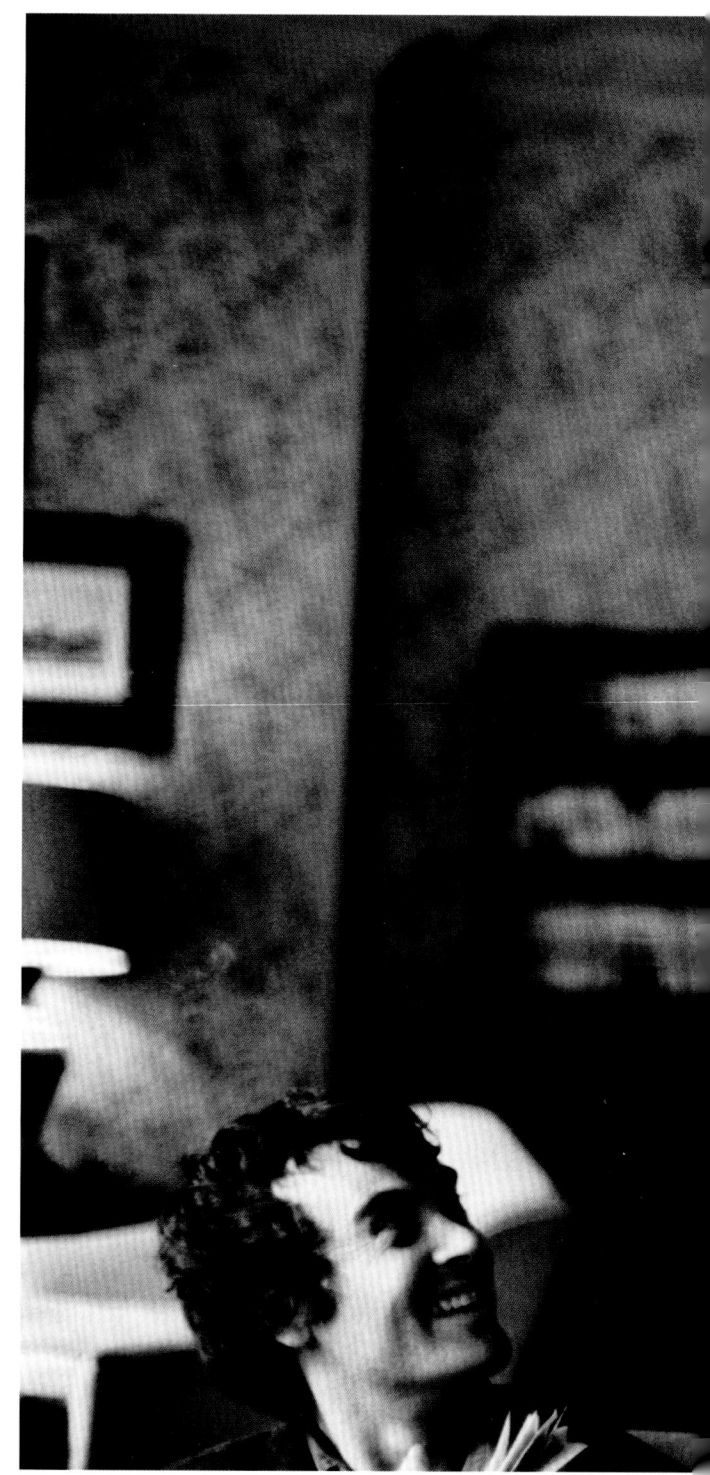

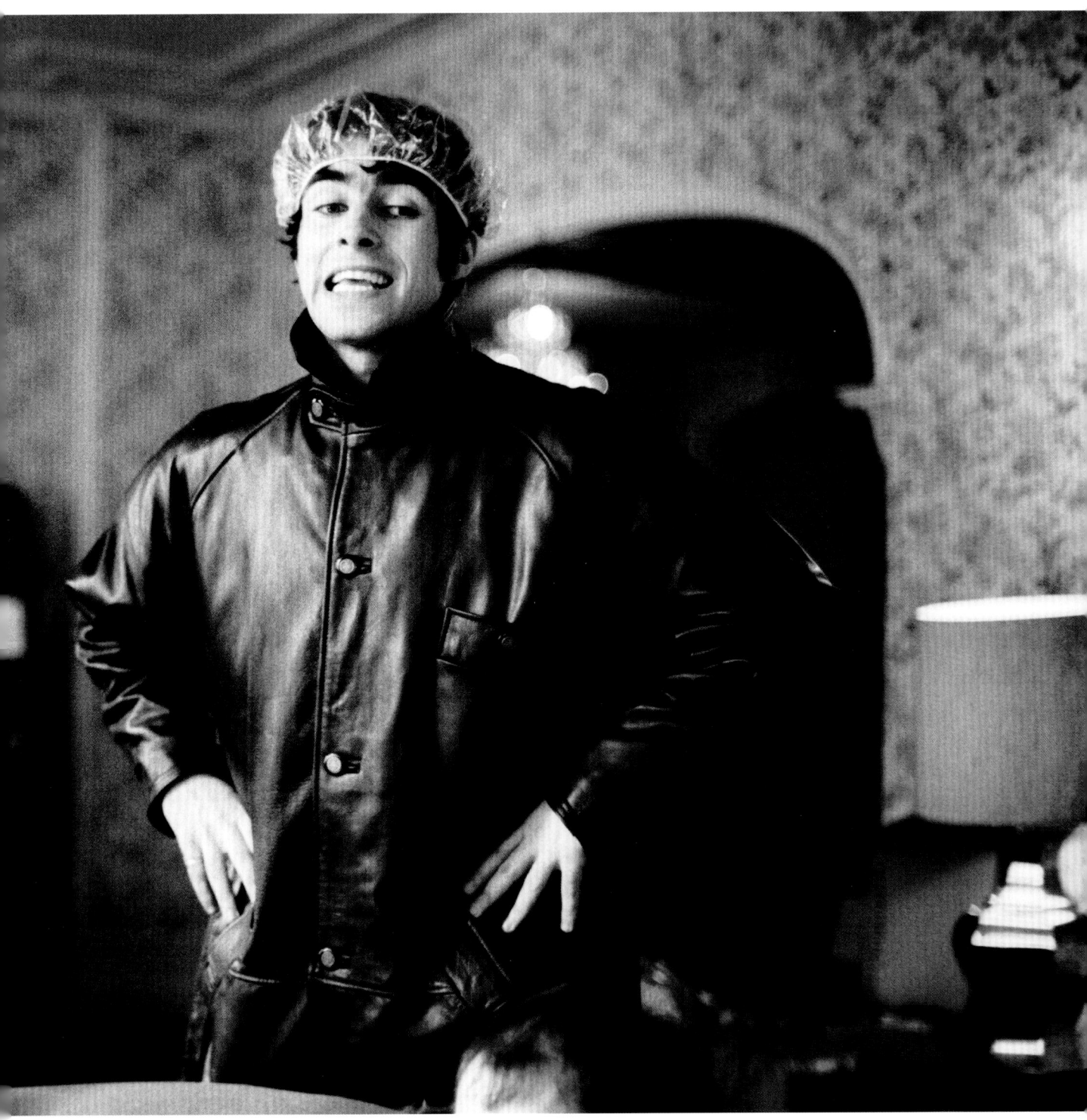

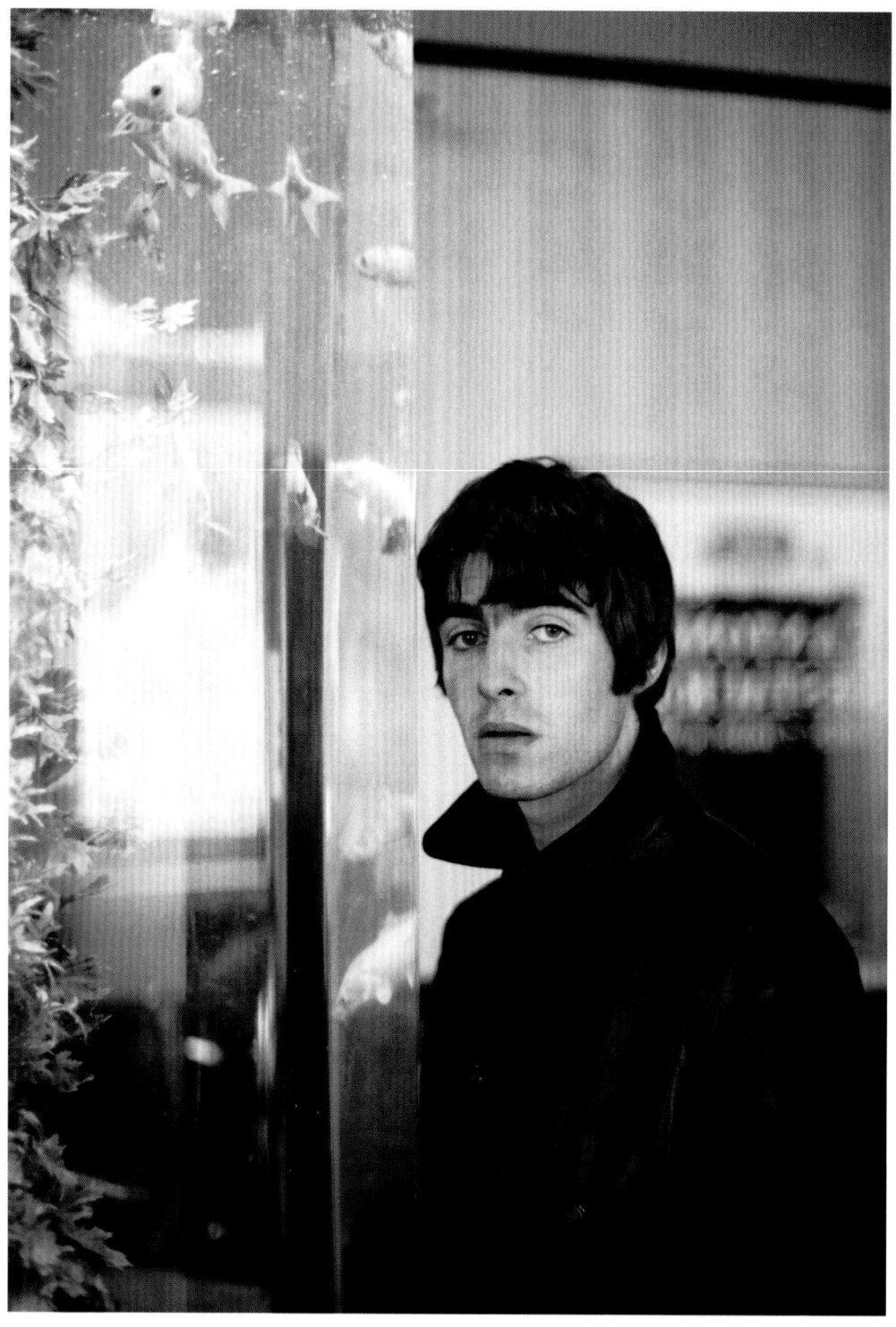

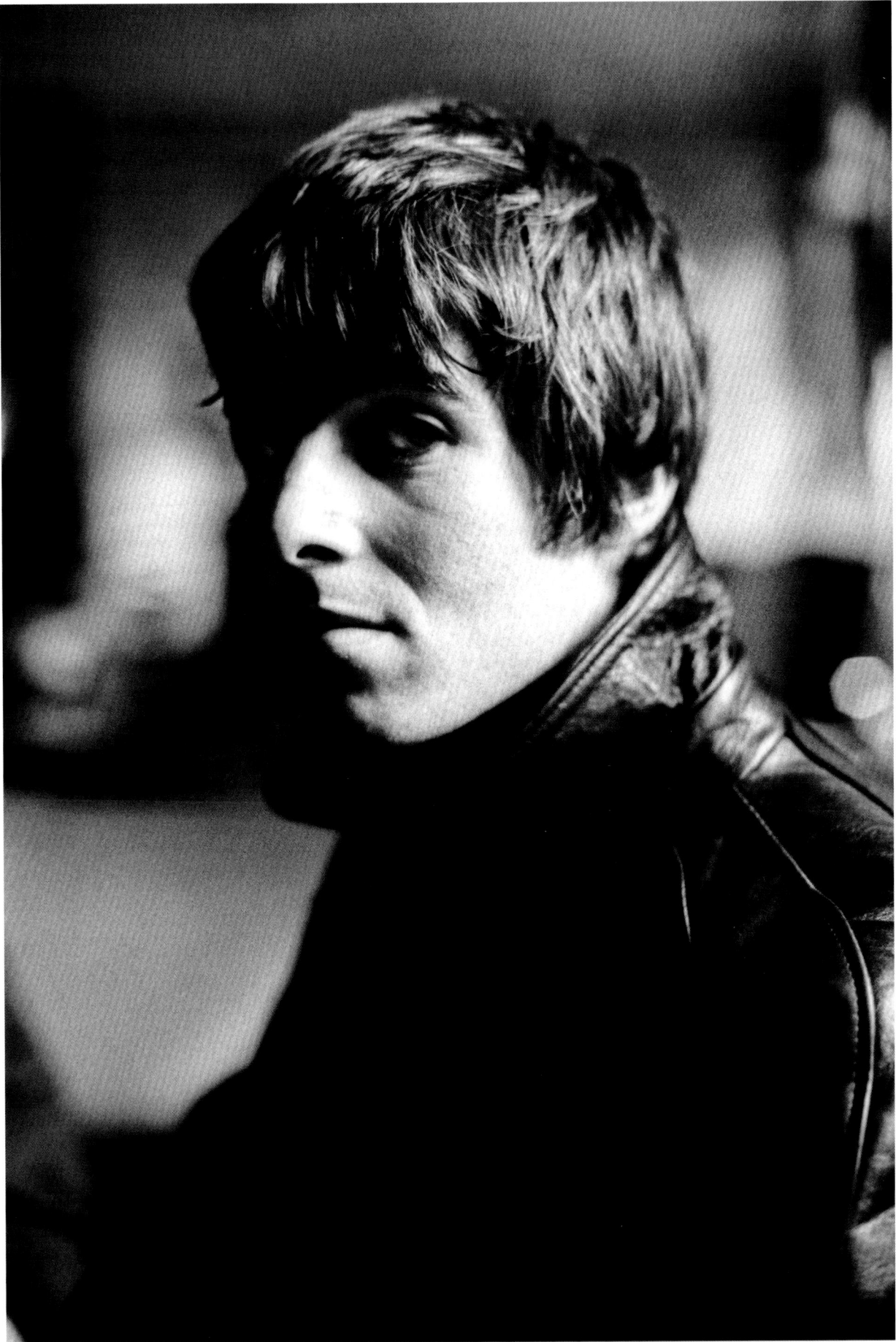

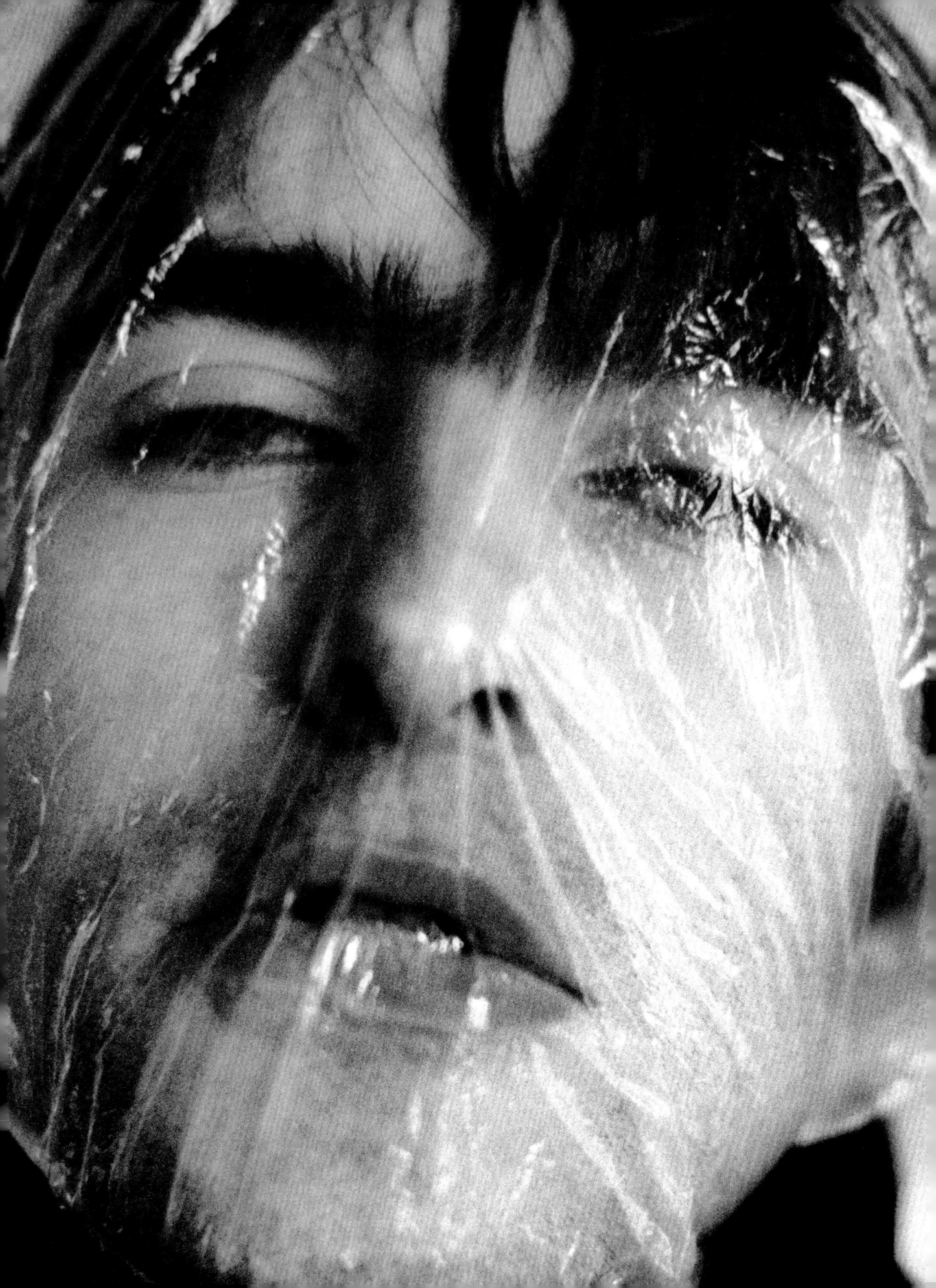

9 MAY

SLY STREET STUDIO, LONDON

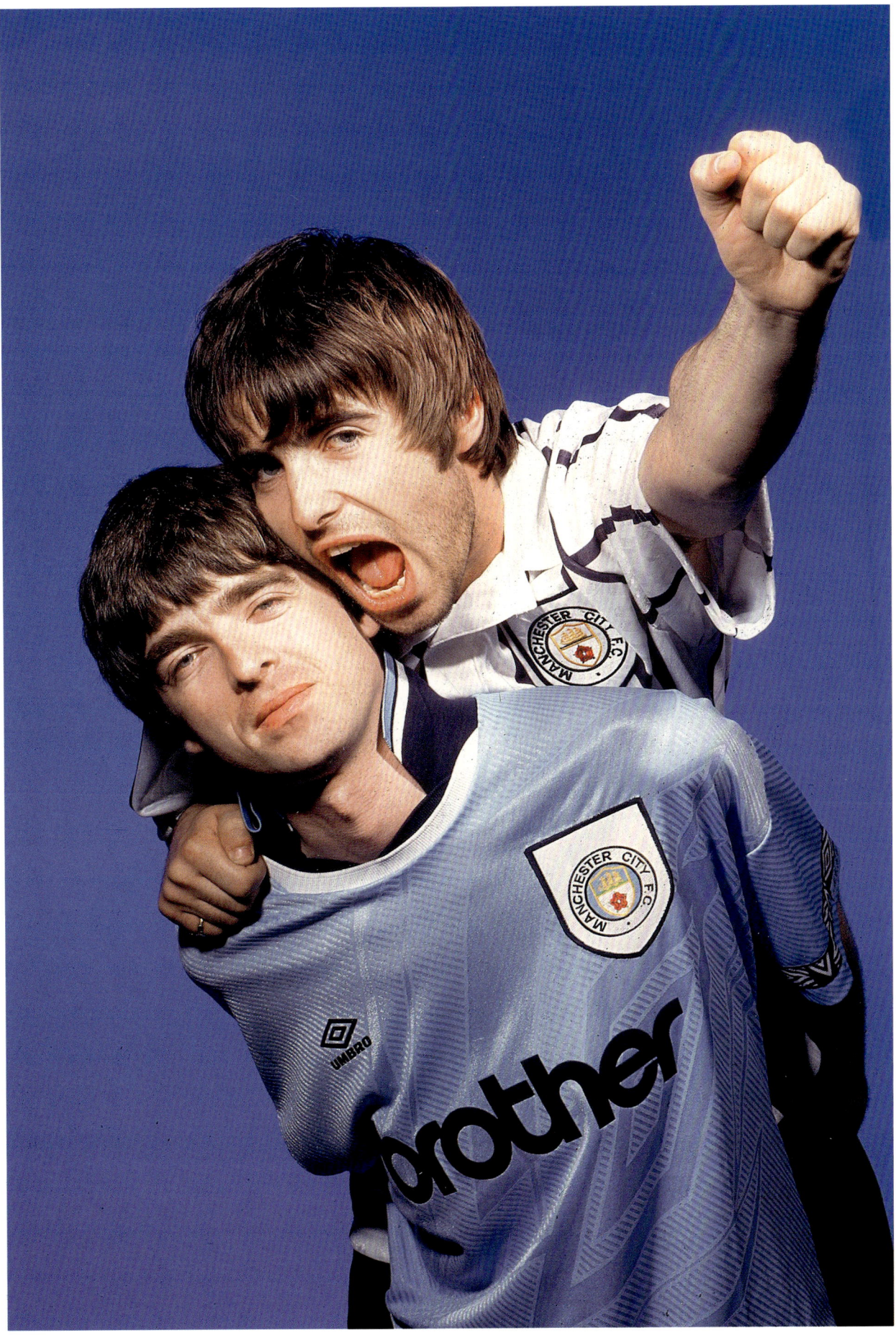

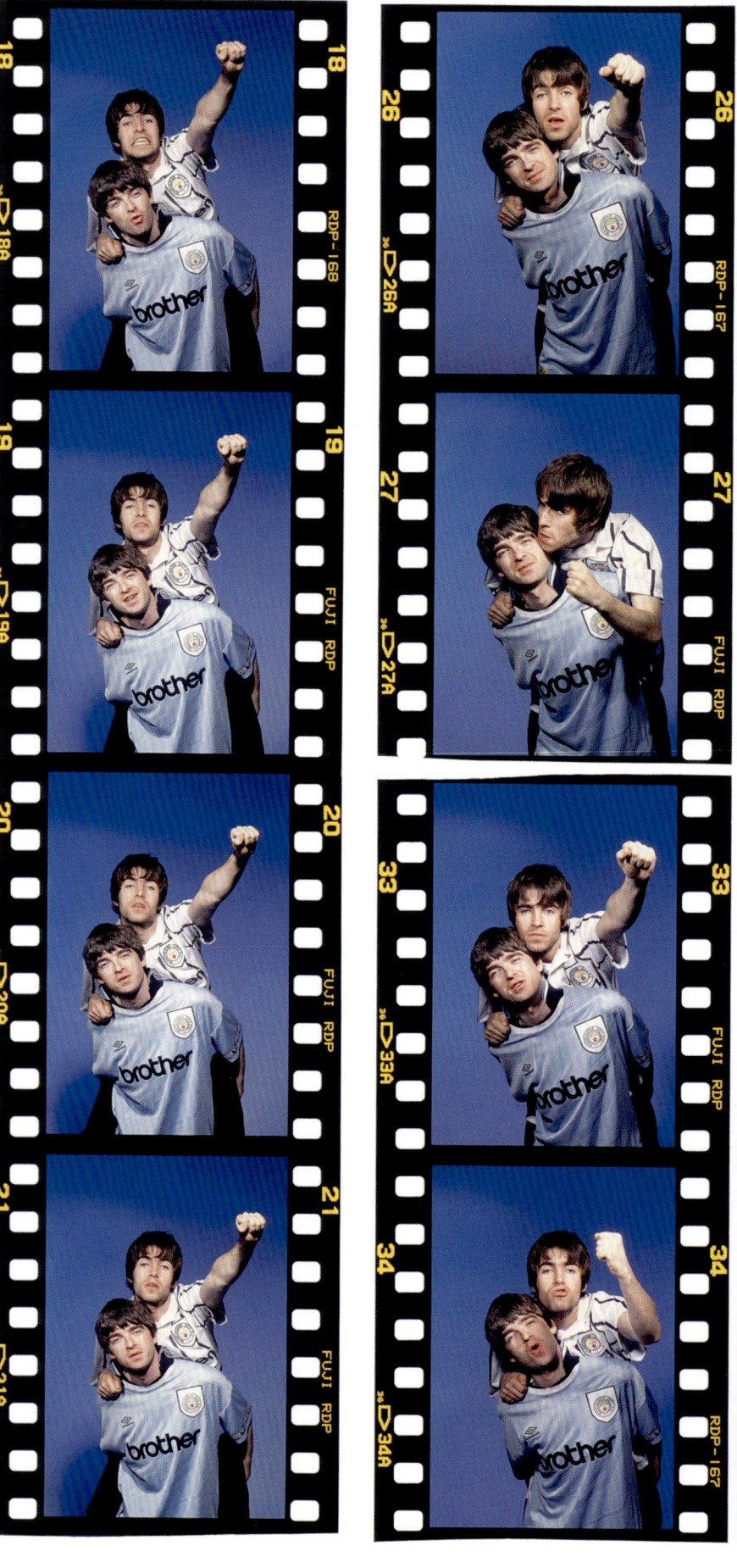

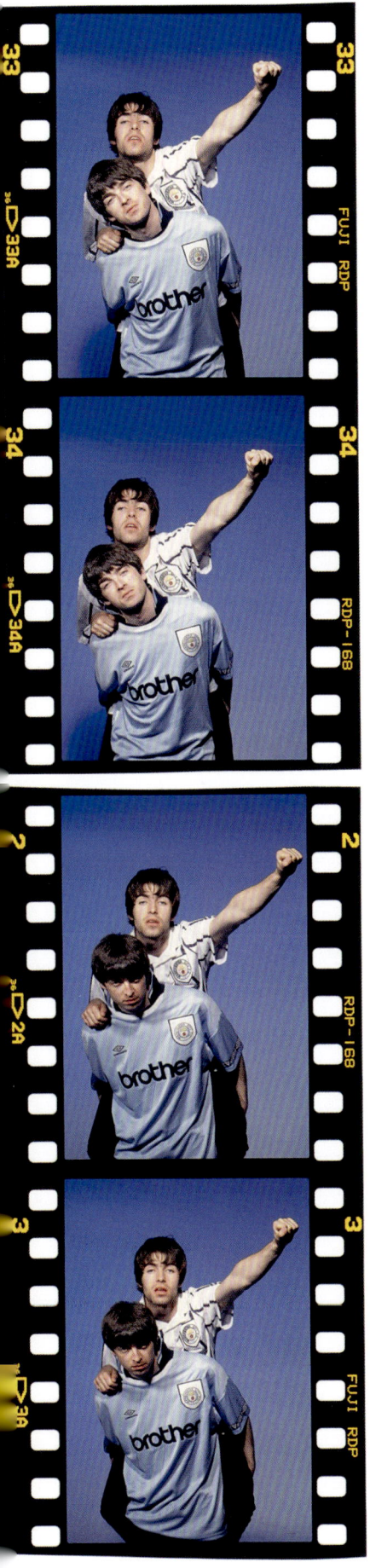
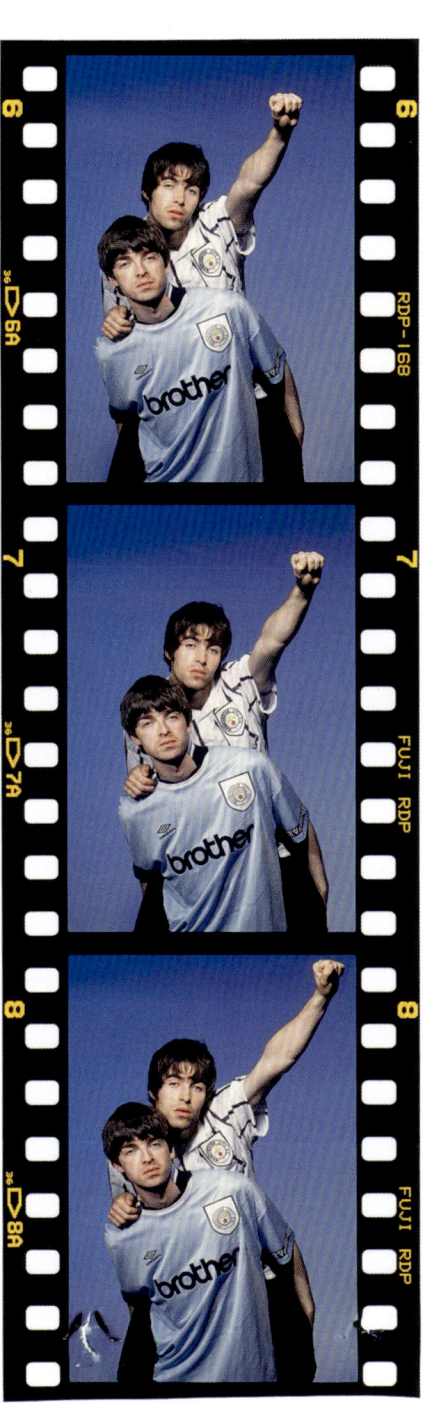
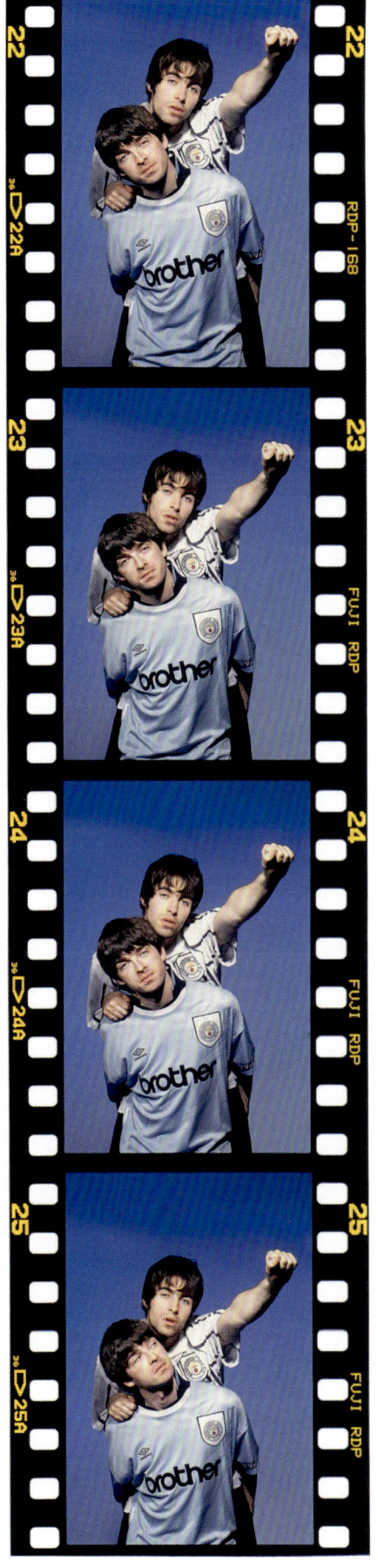

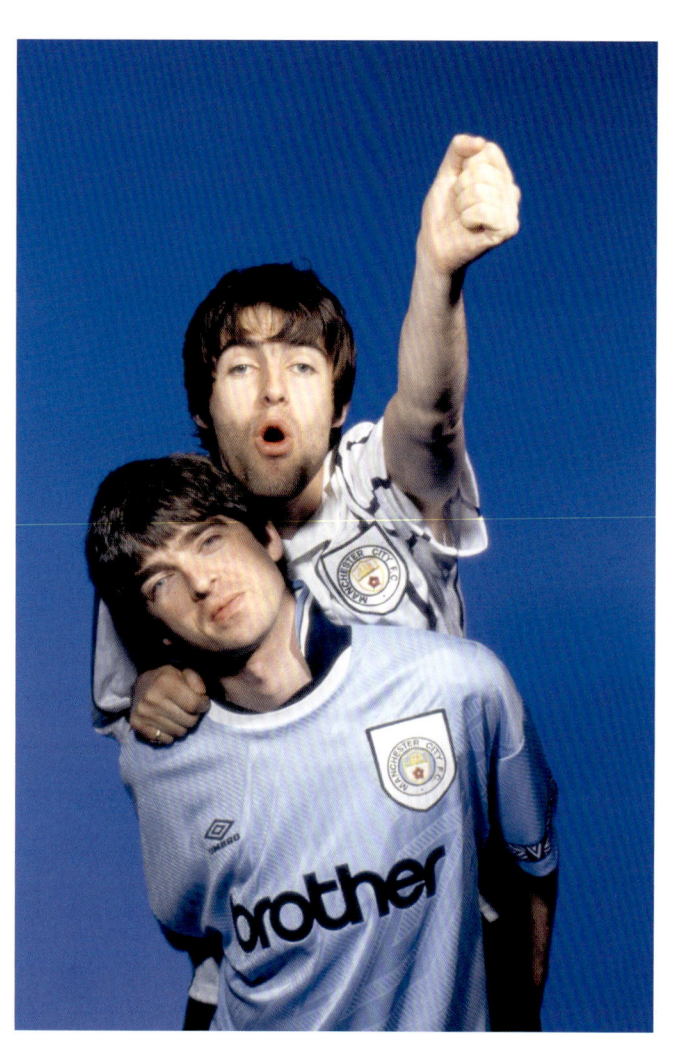
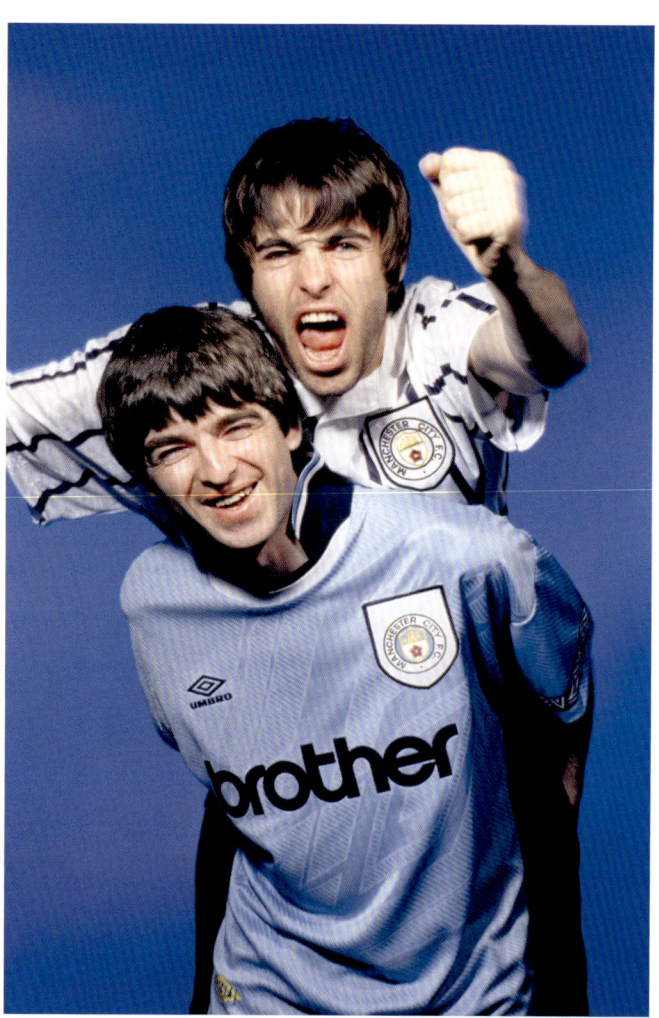

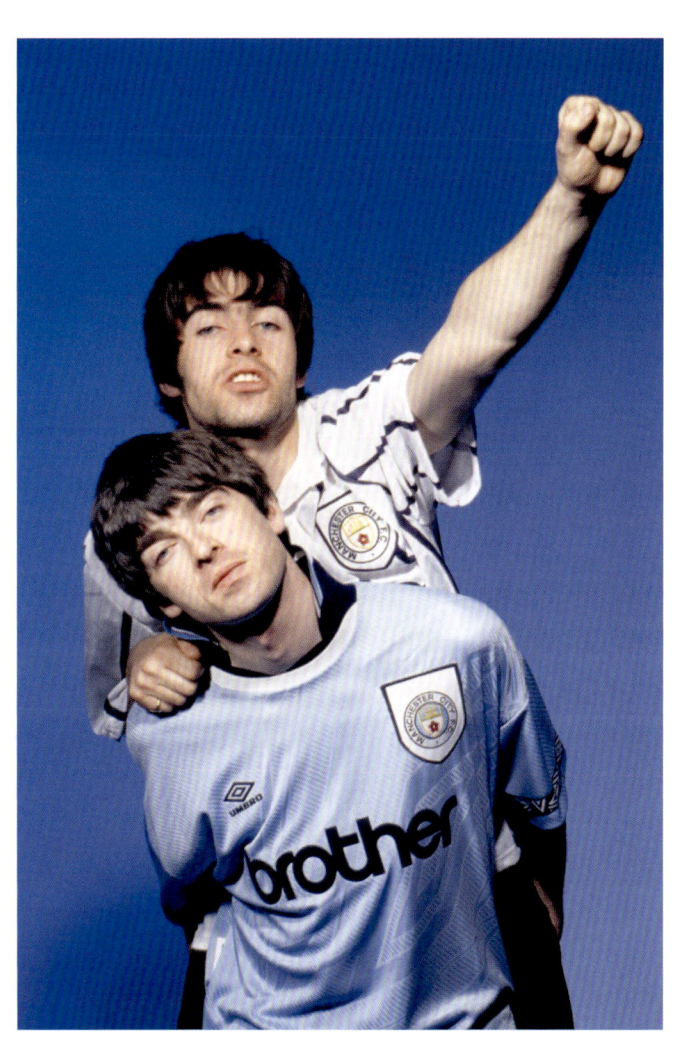
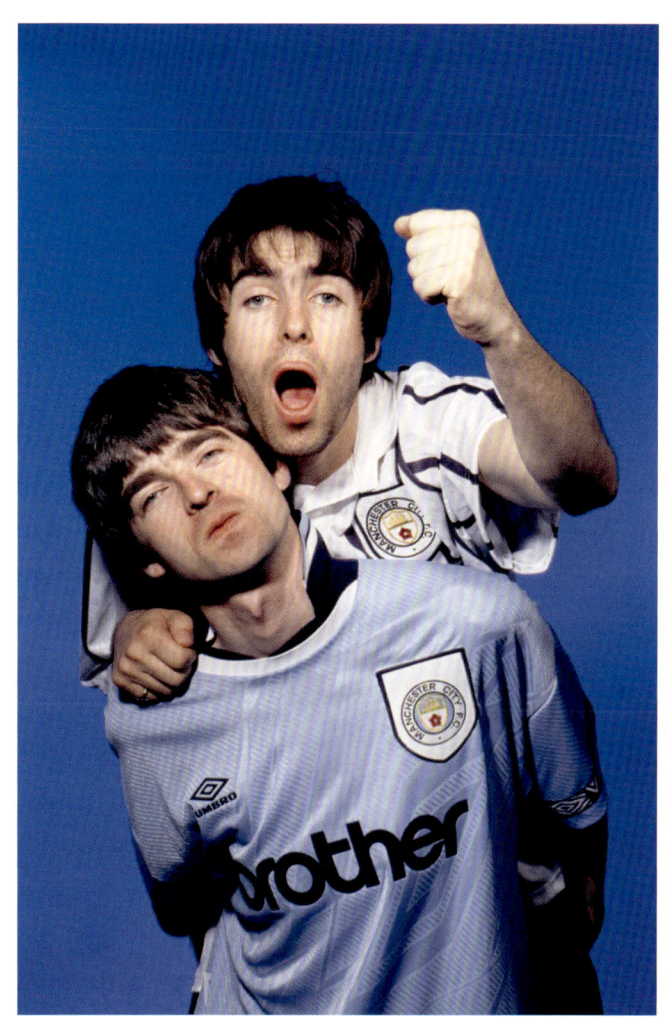

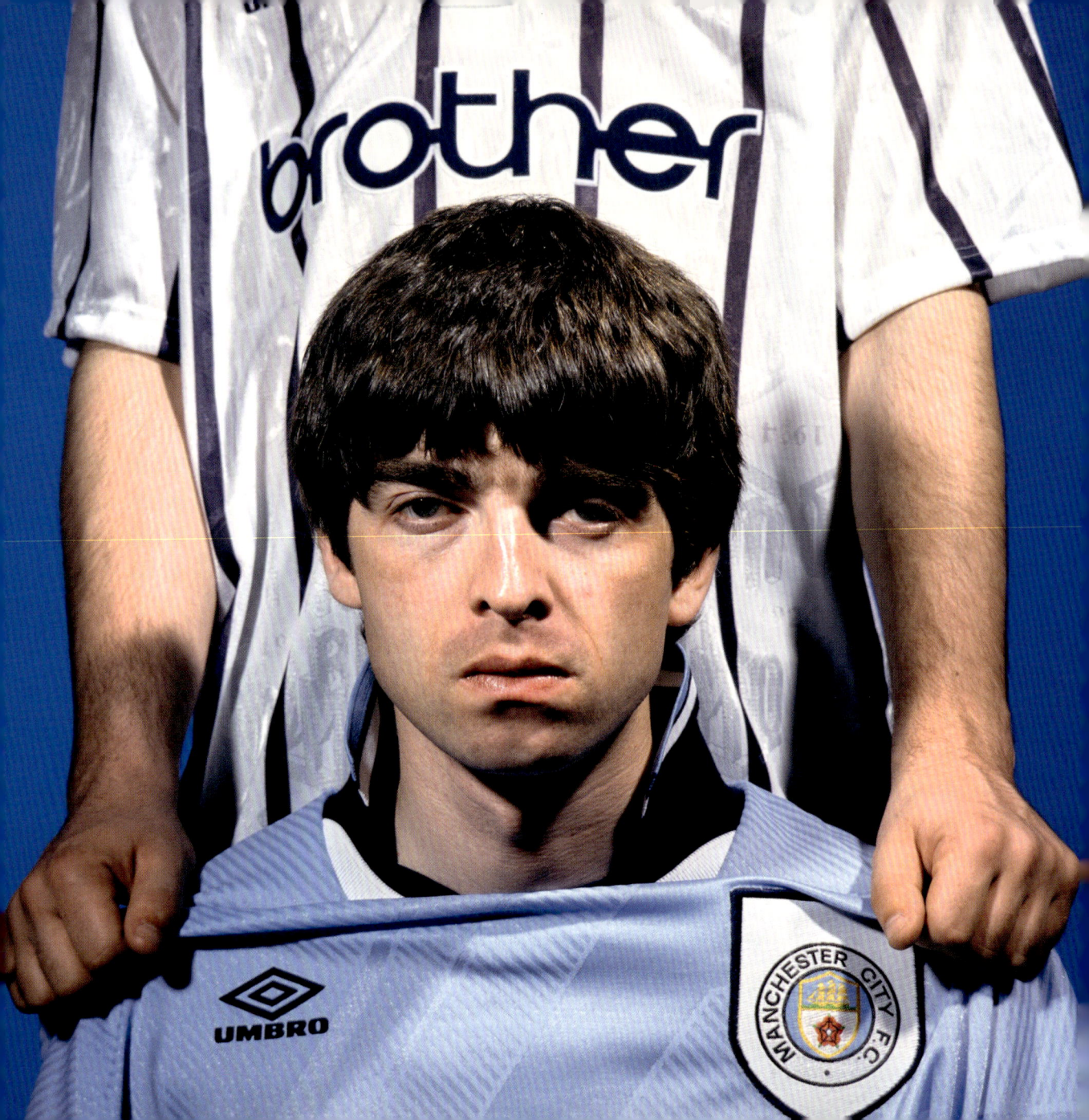

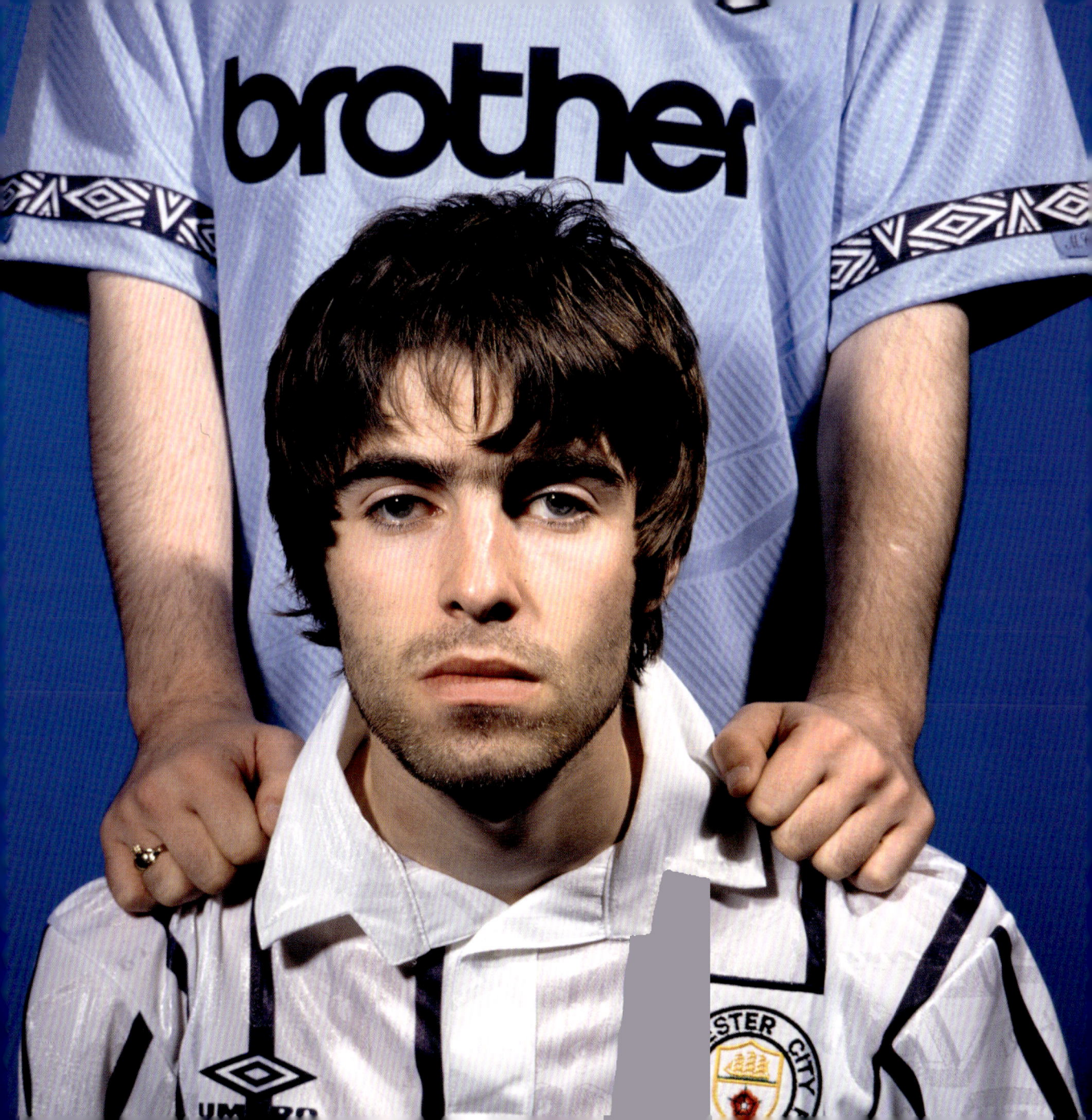

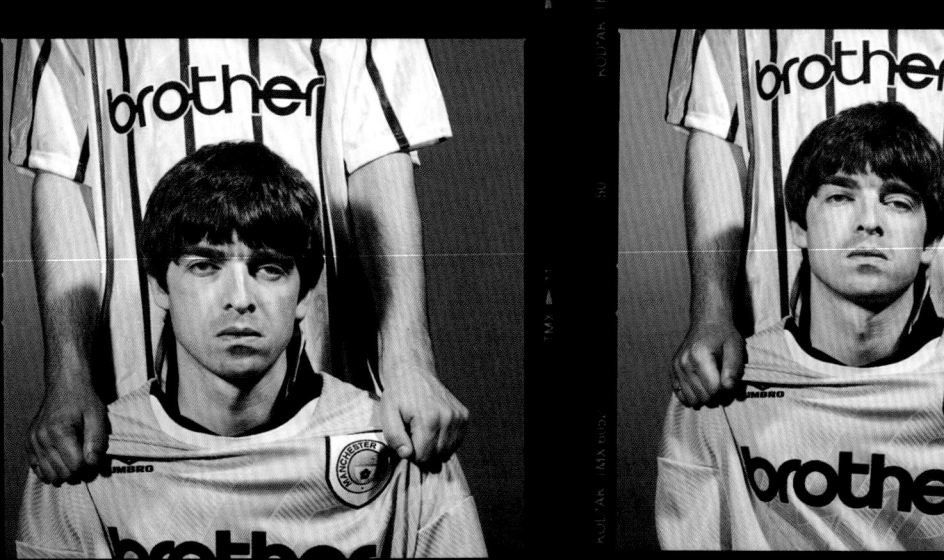
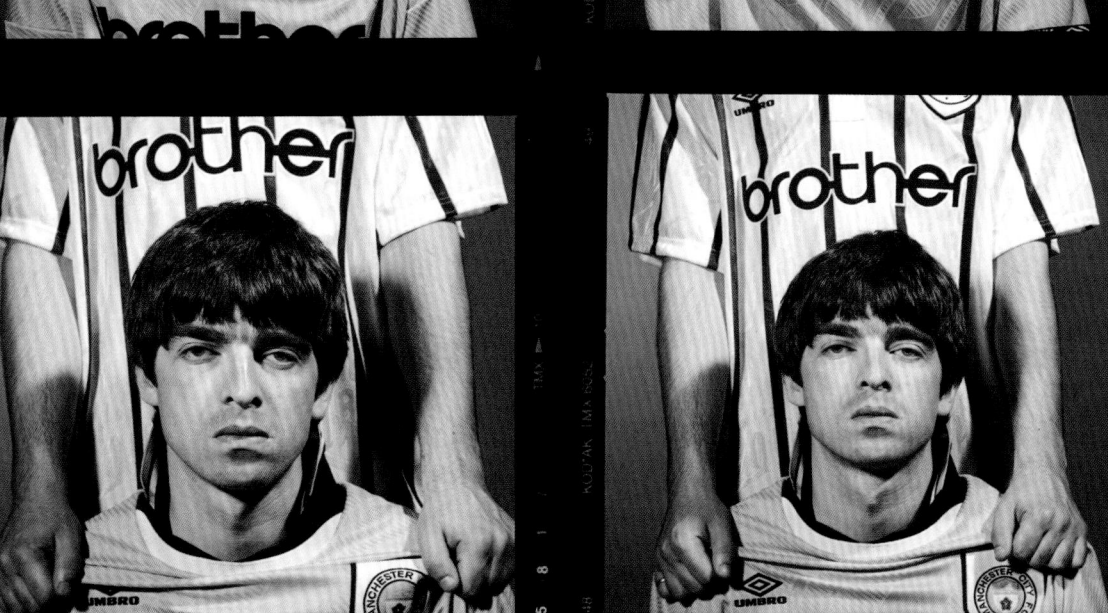

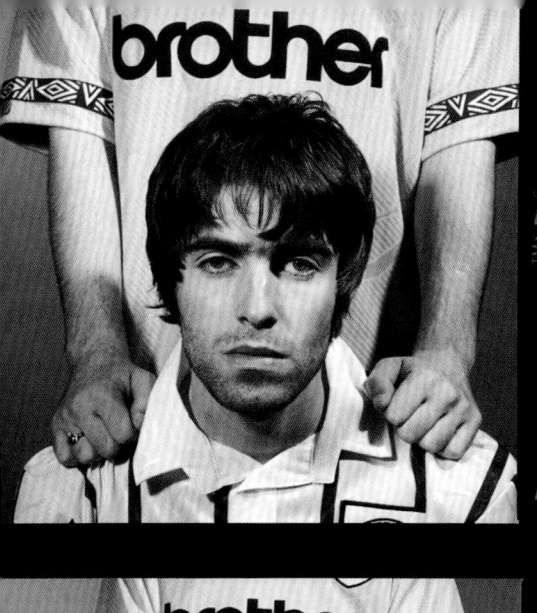
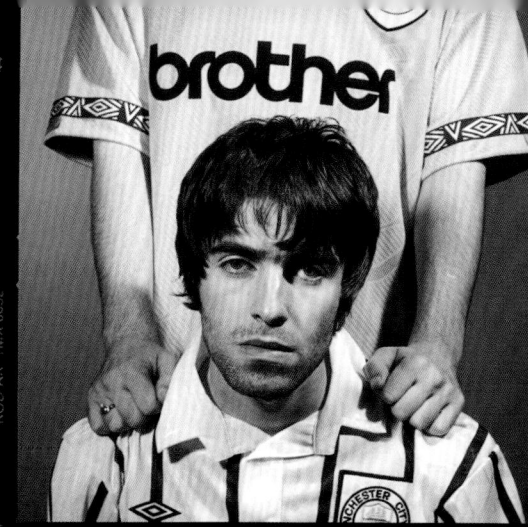
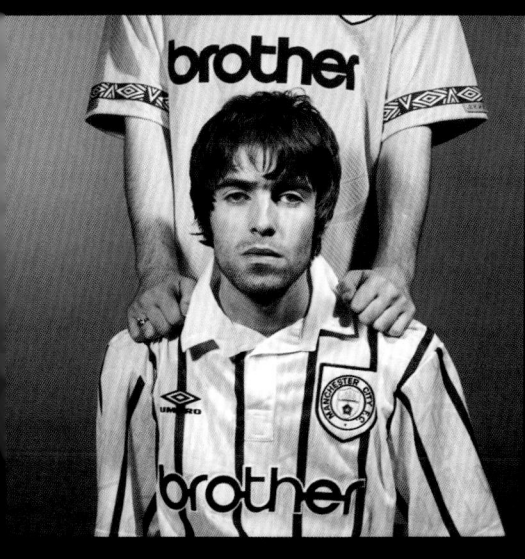
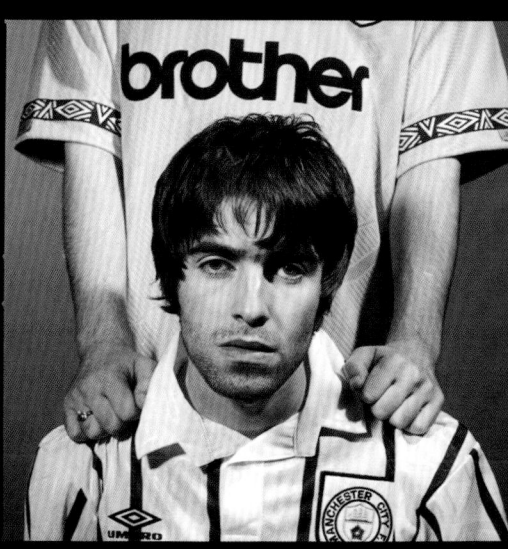
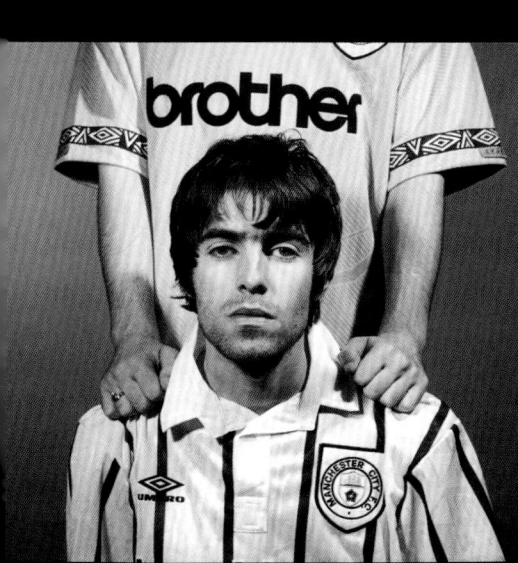
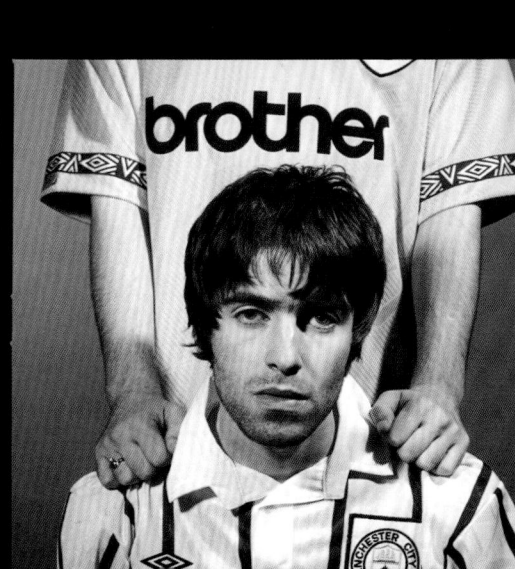

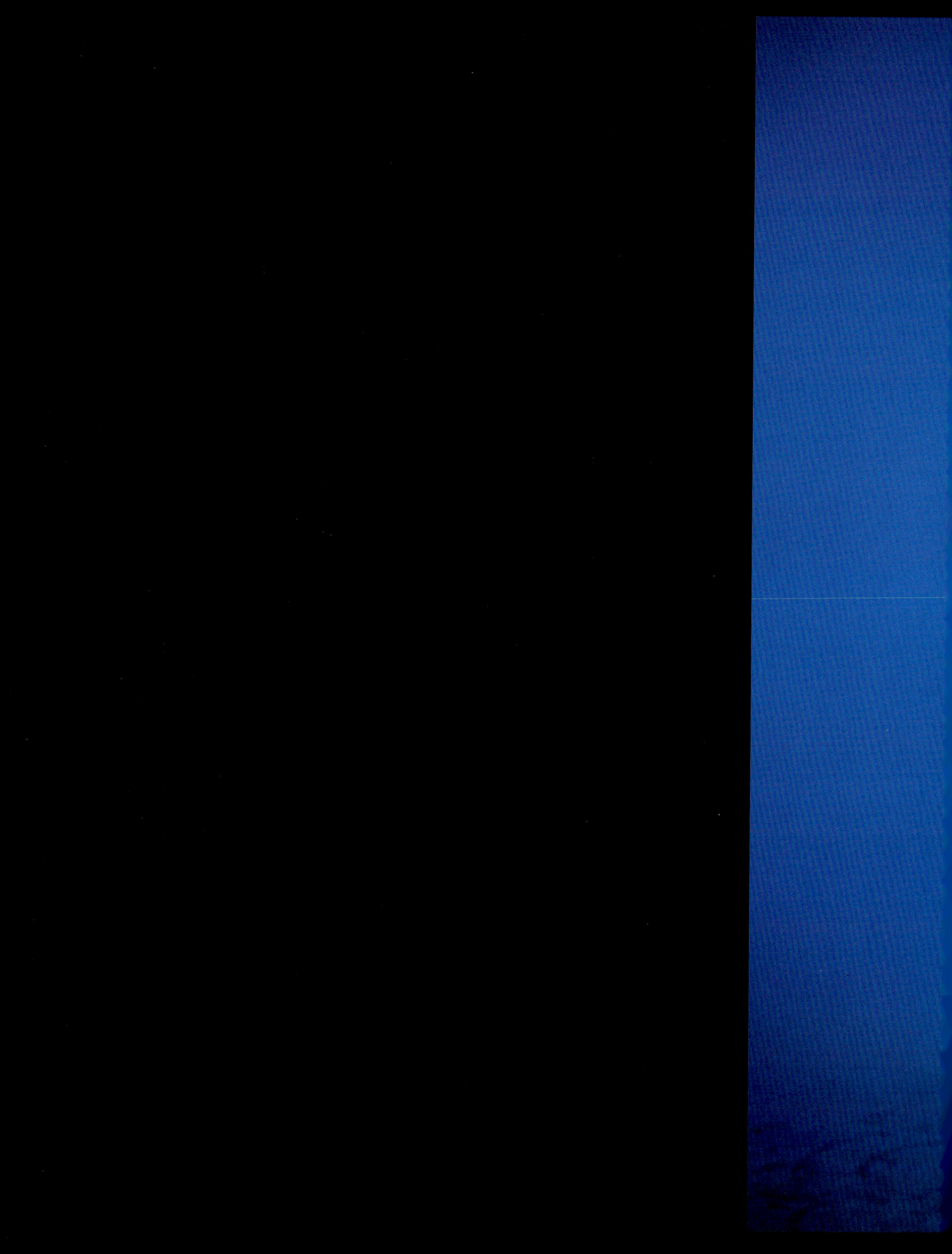

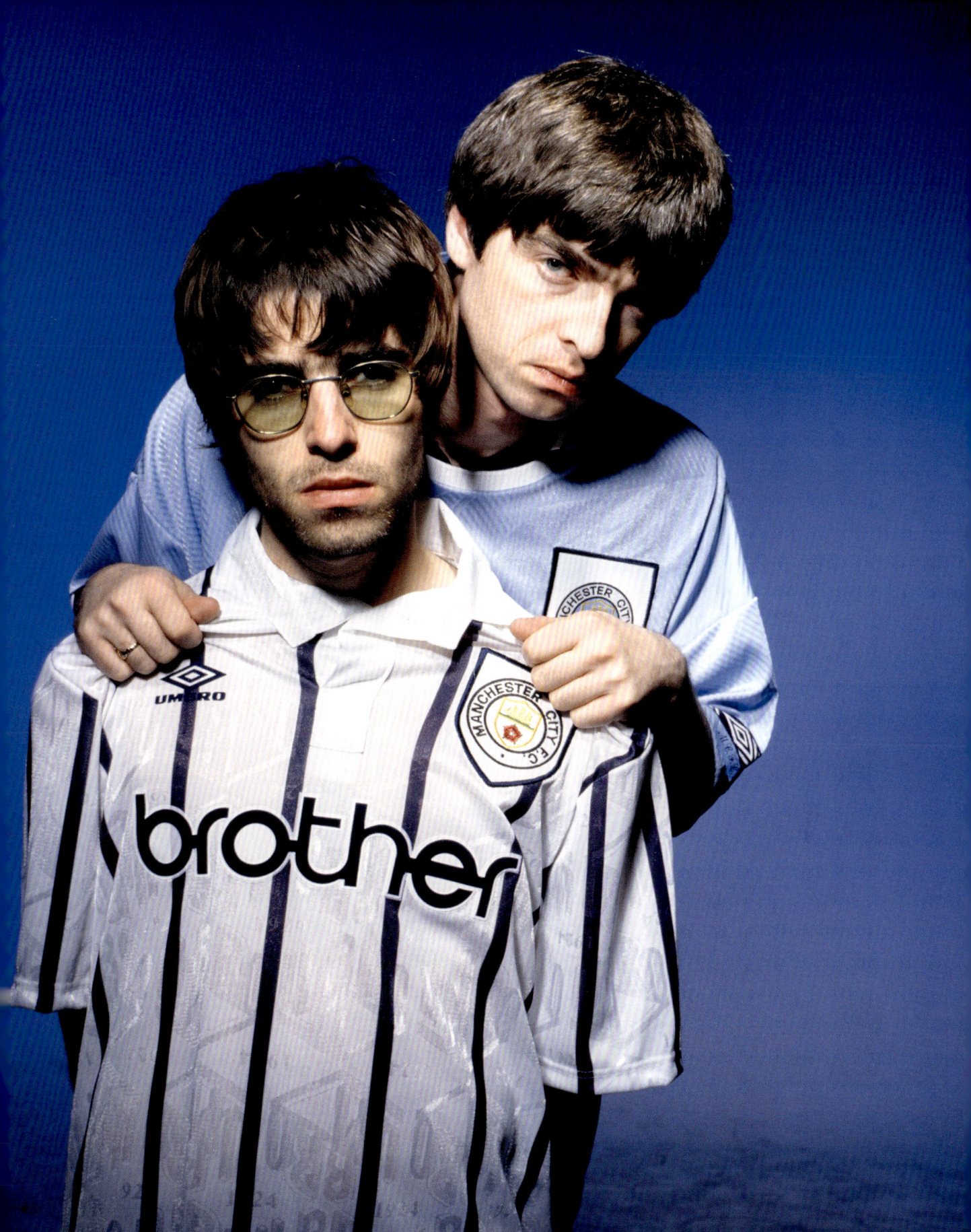

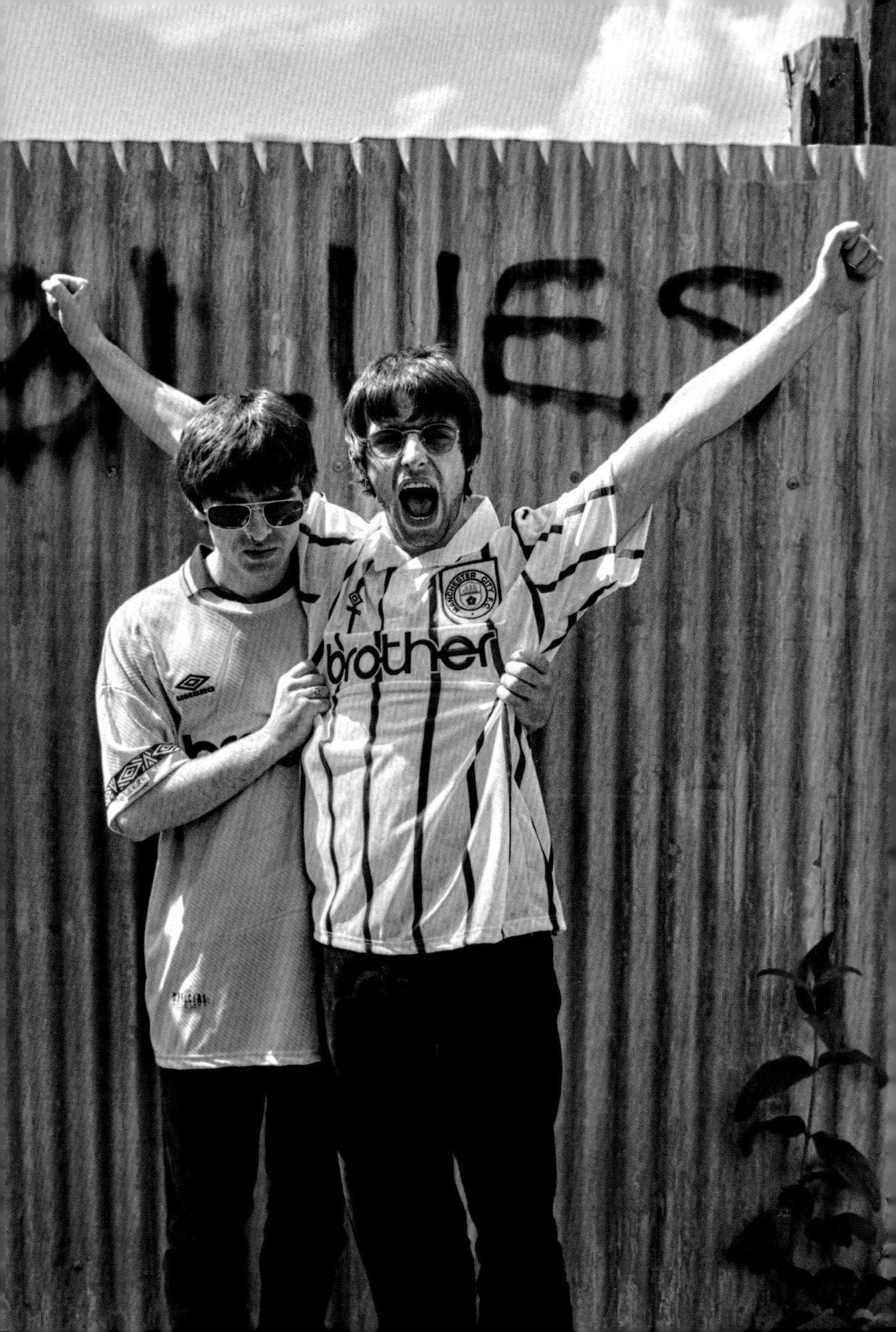

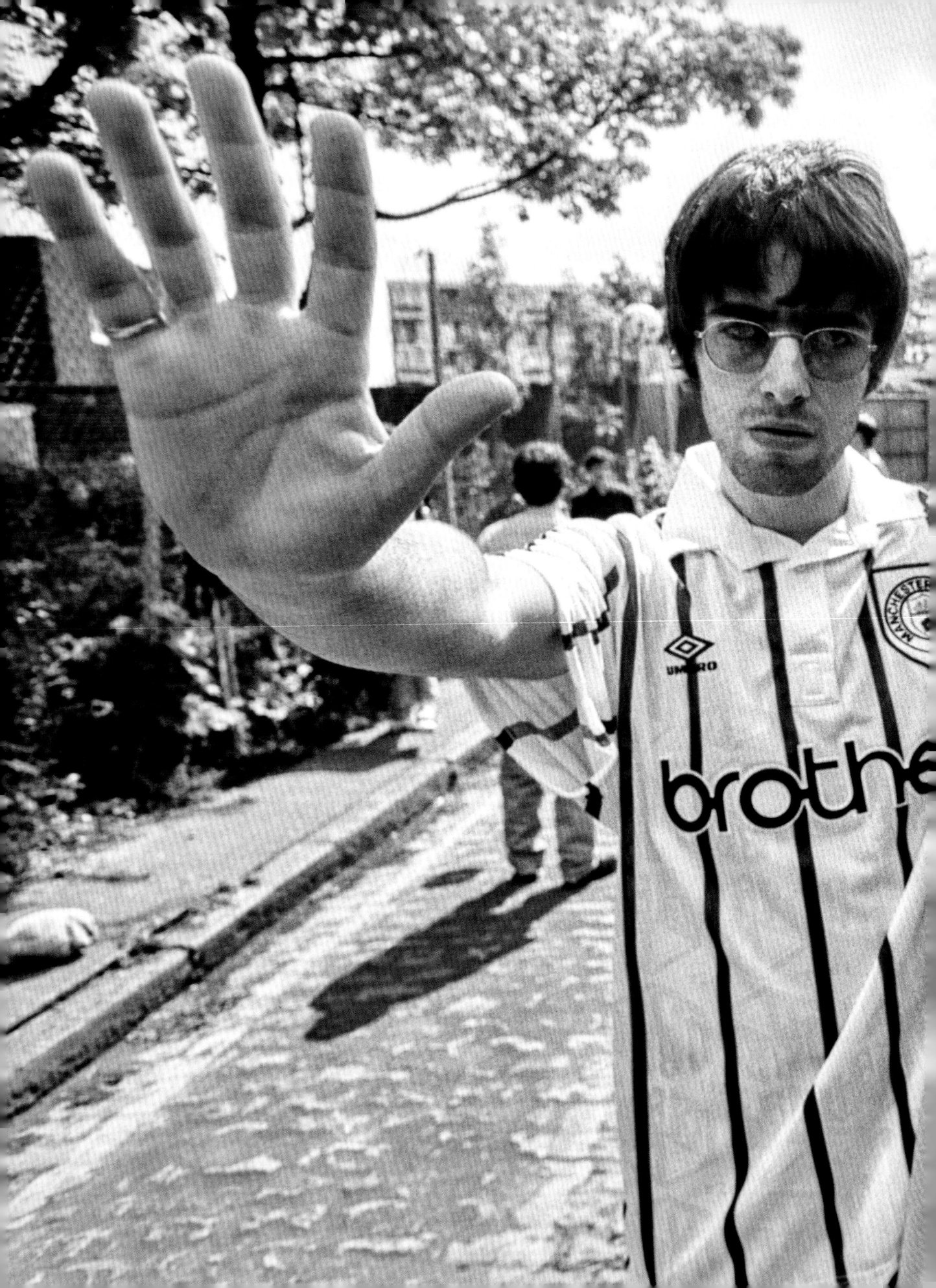

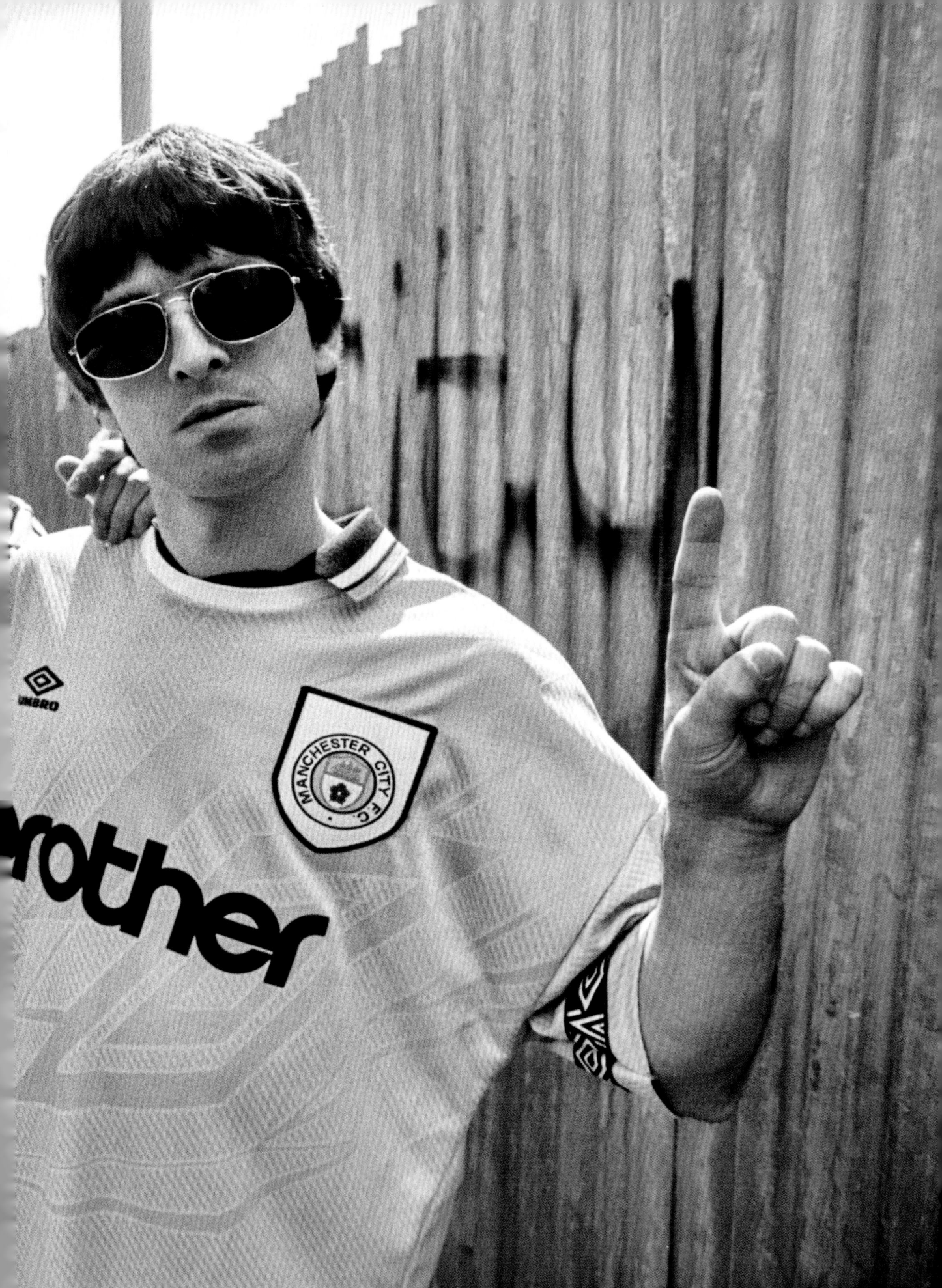

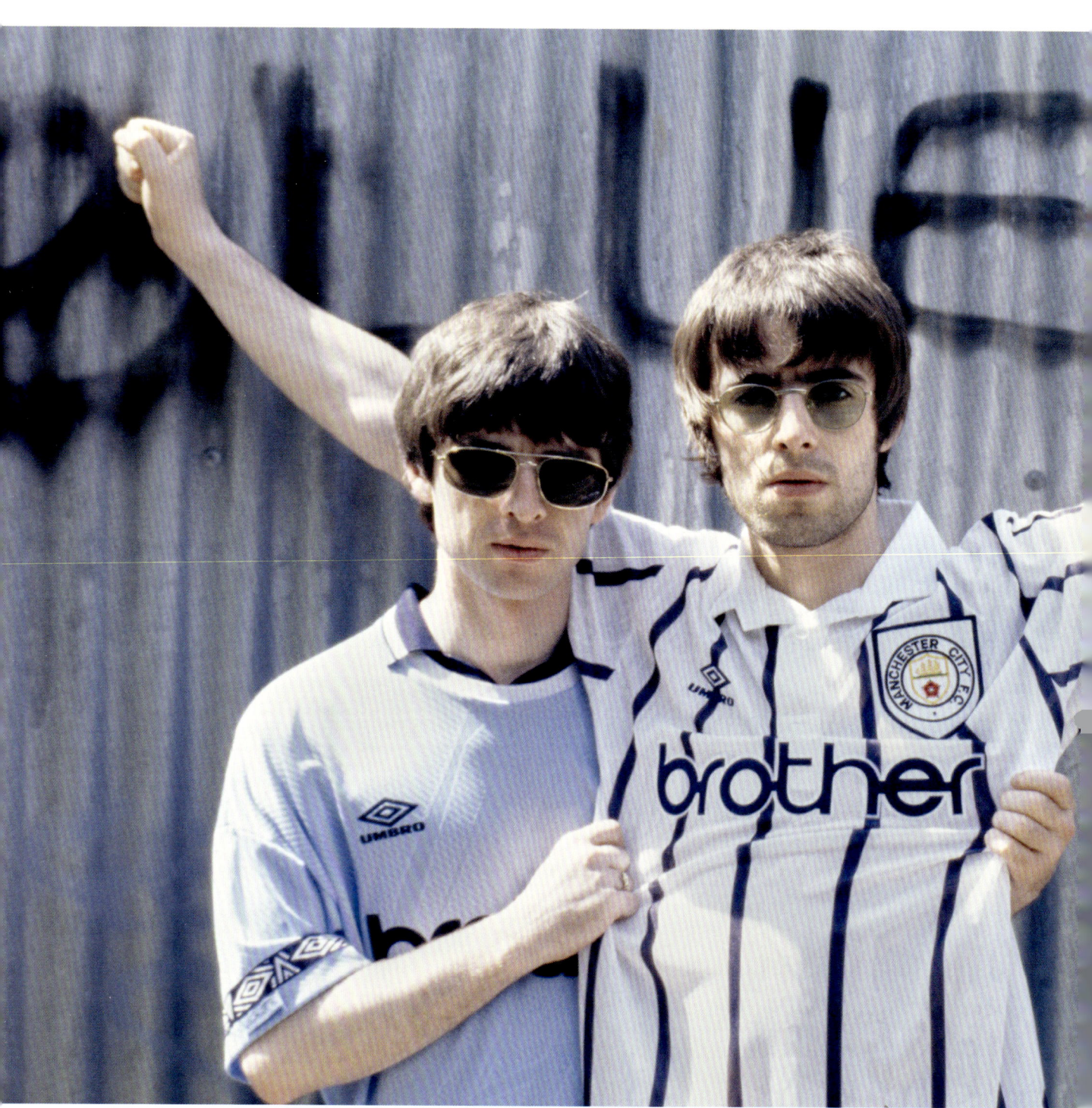

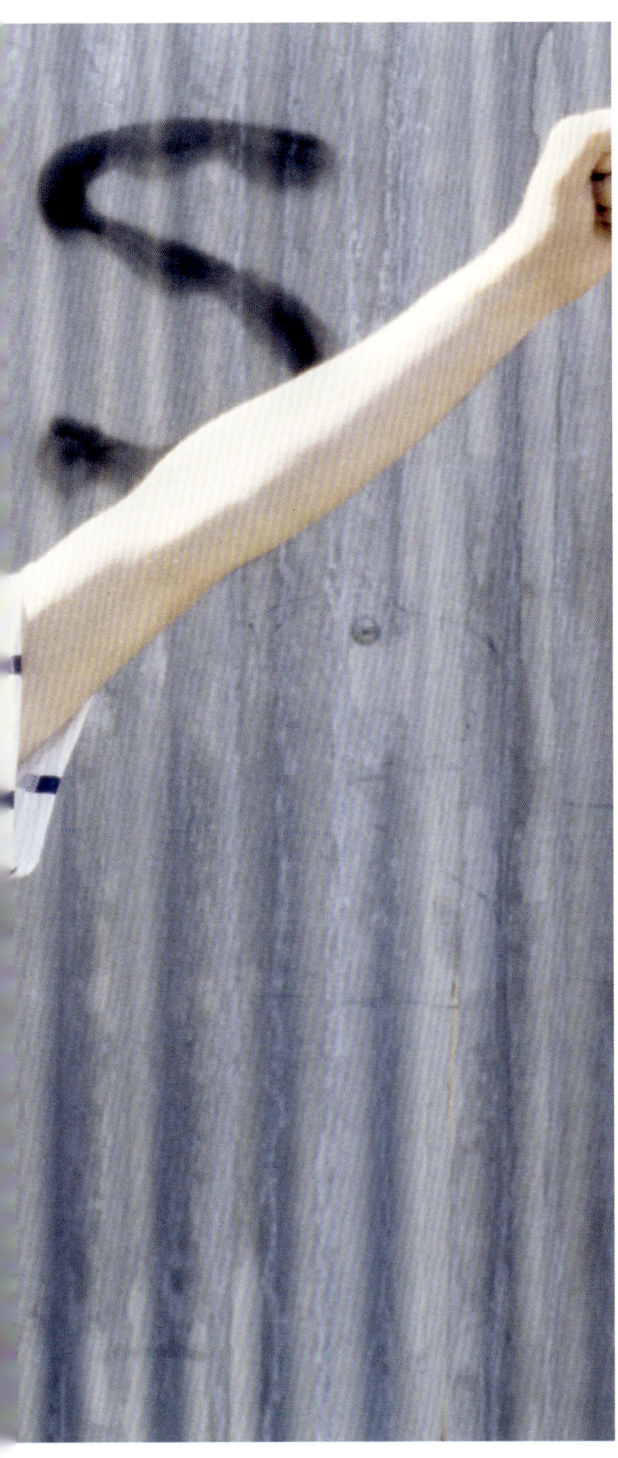

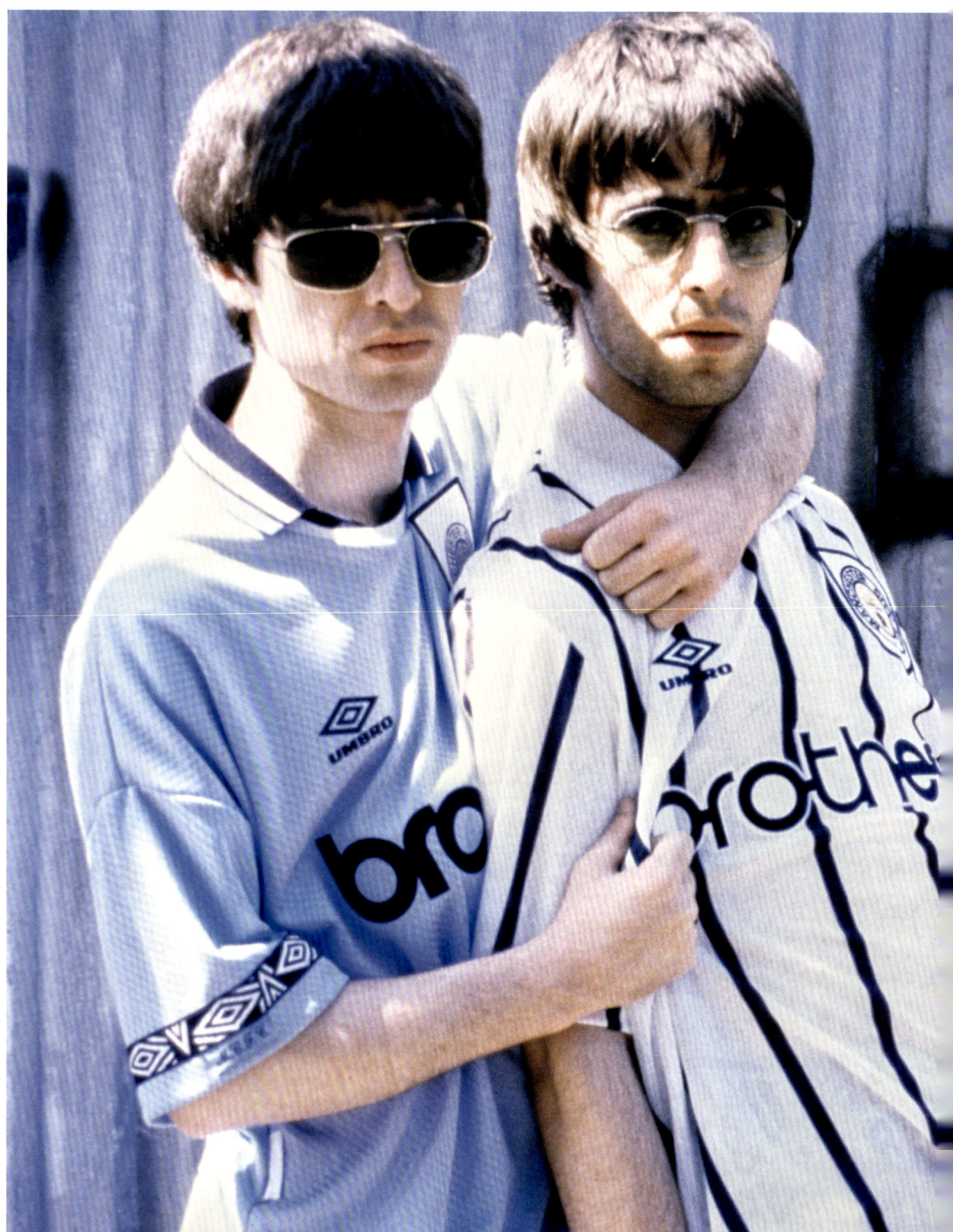

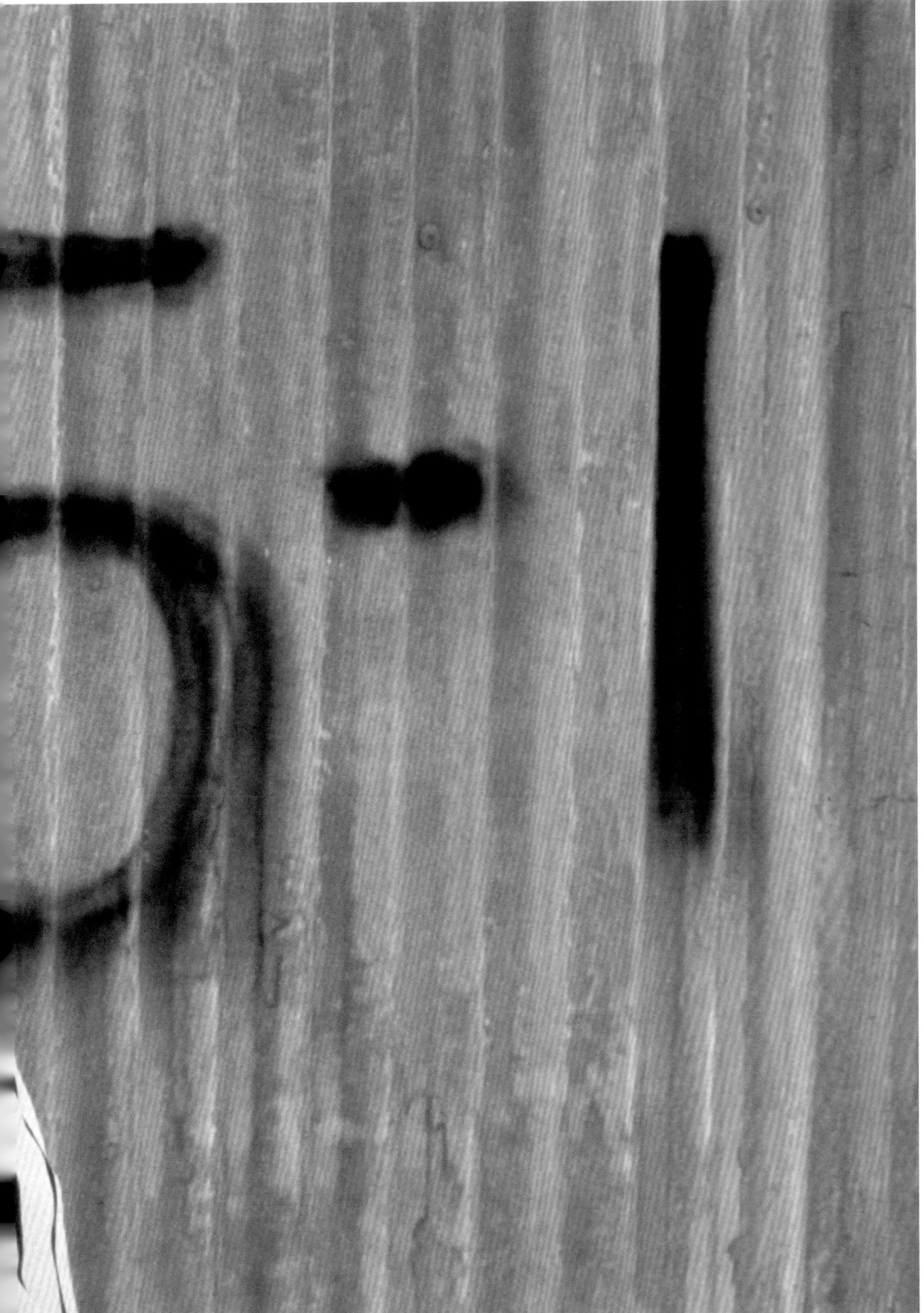

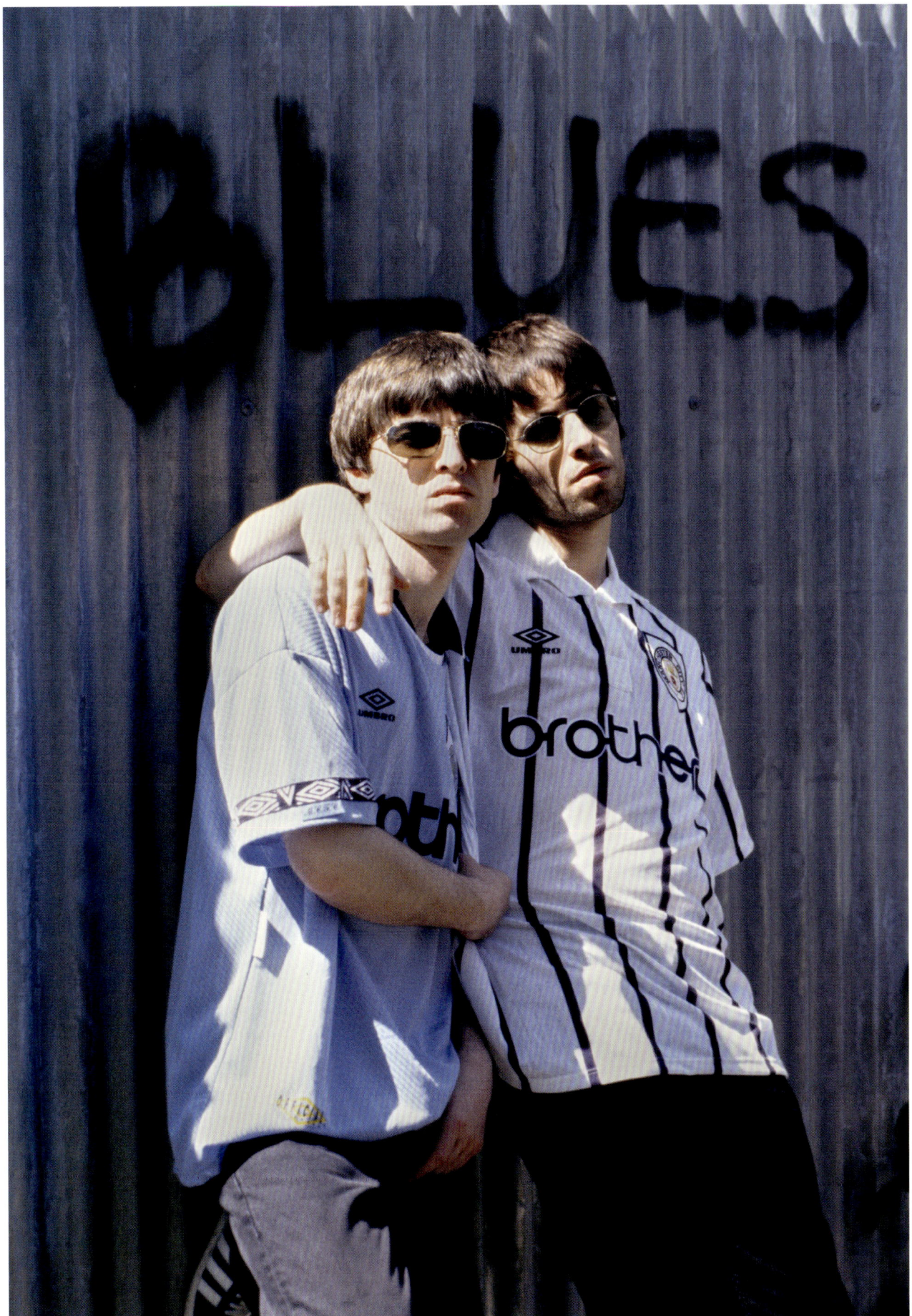

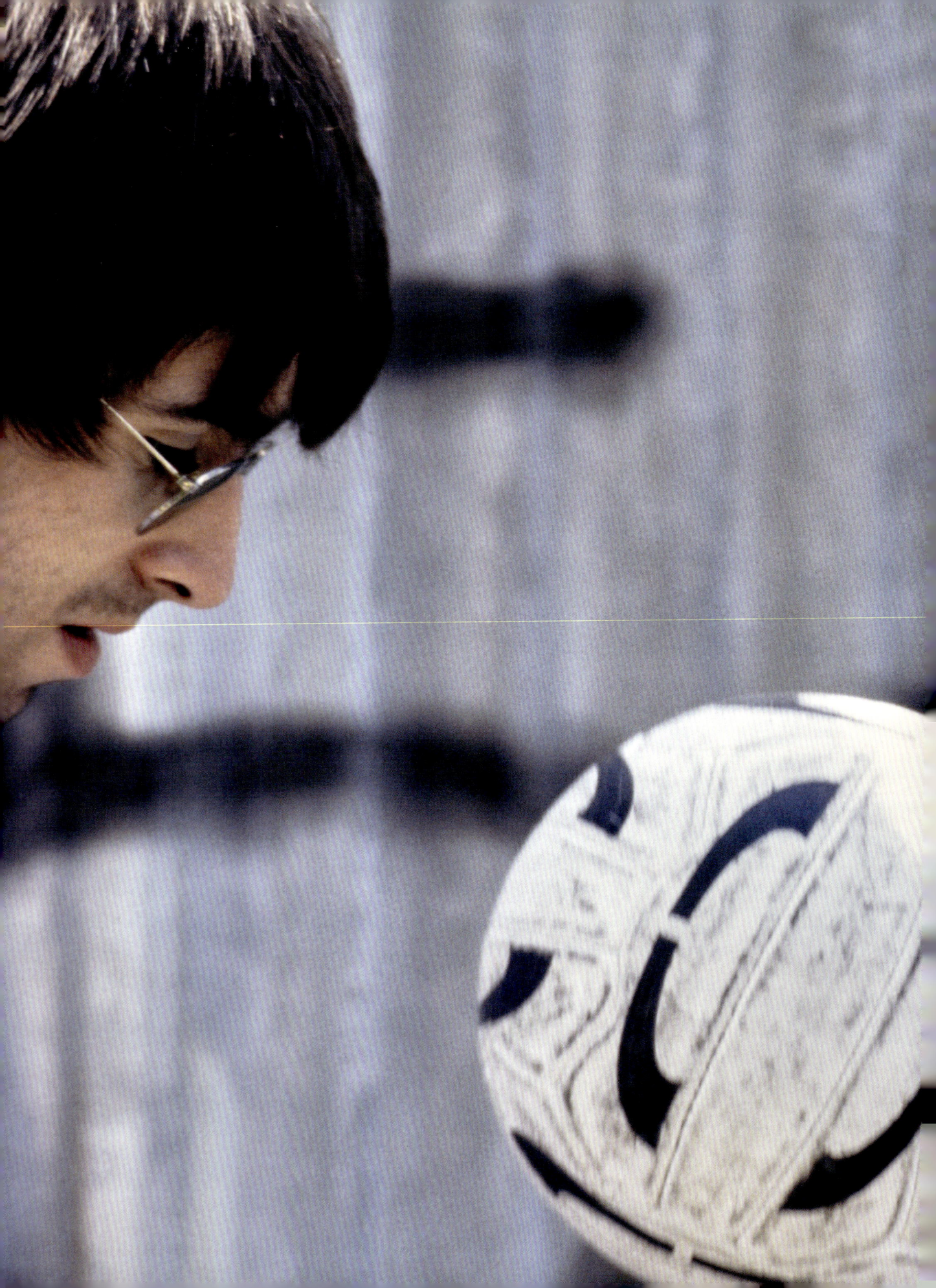

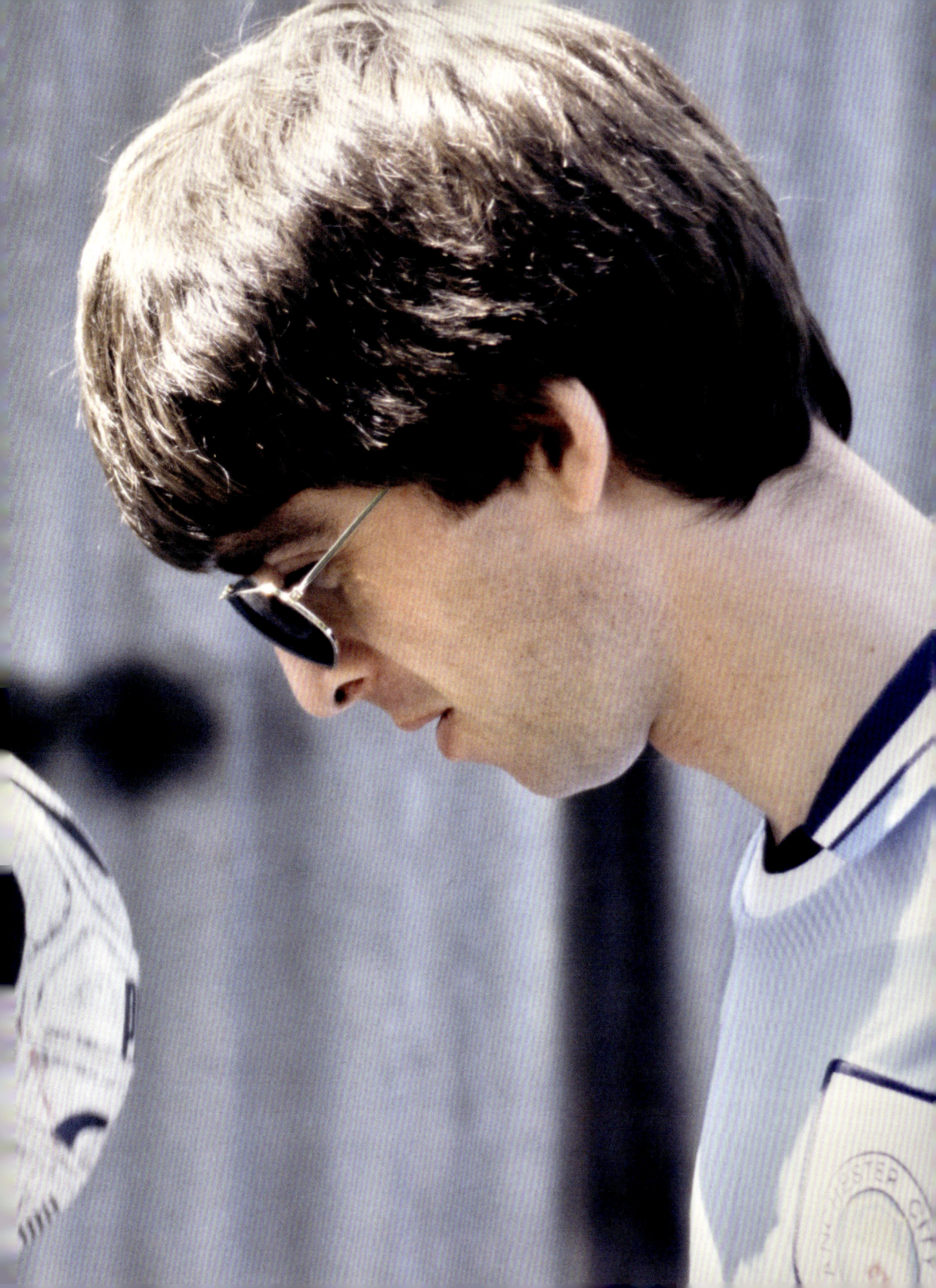

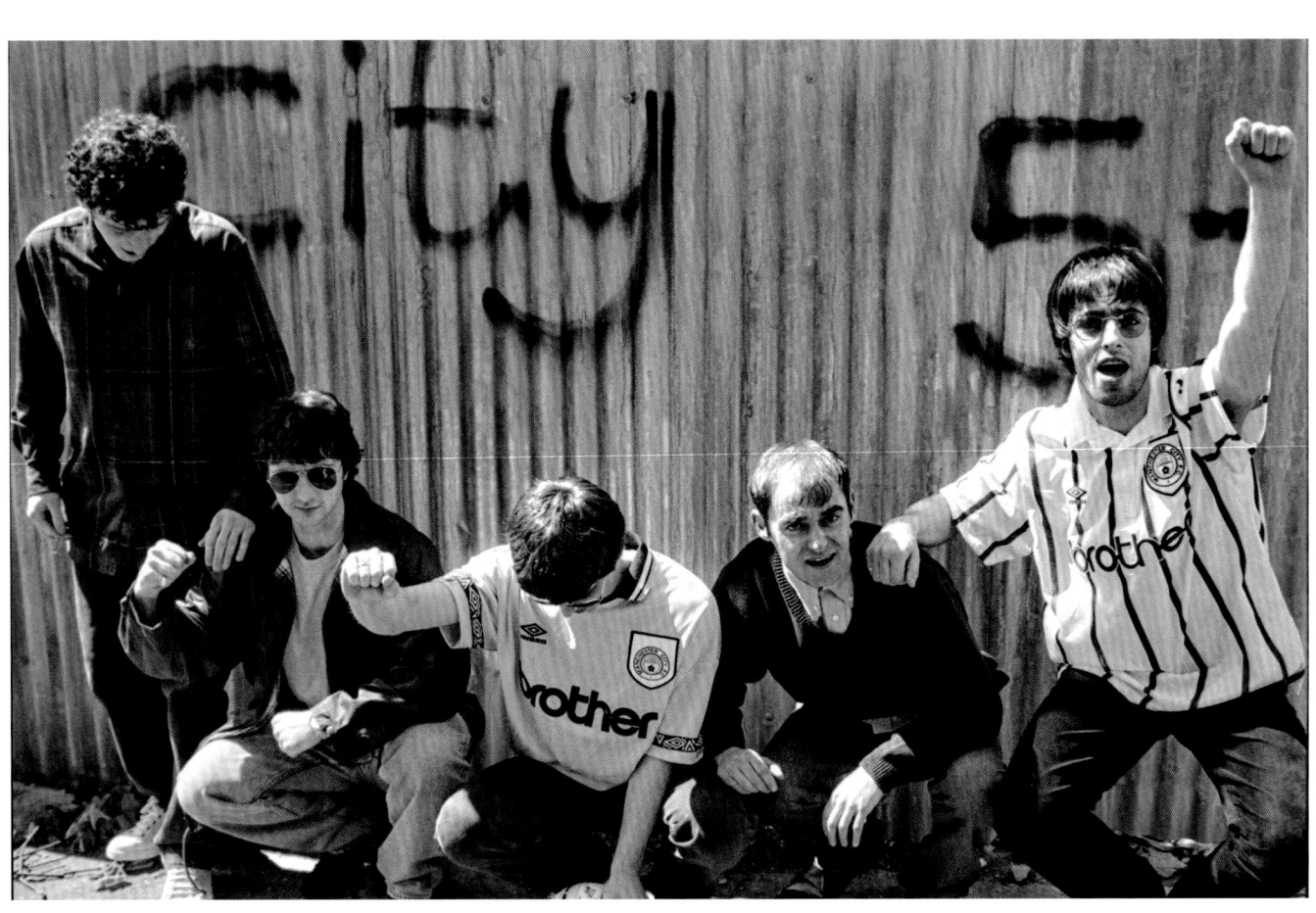

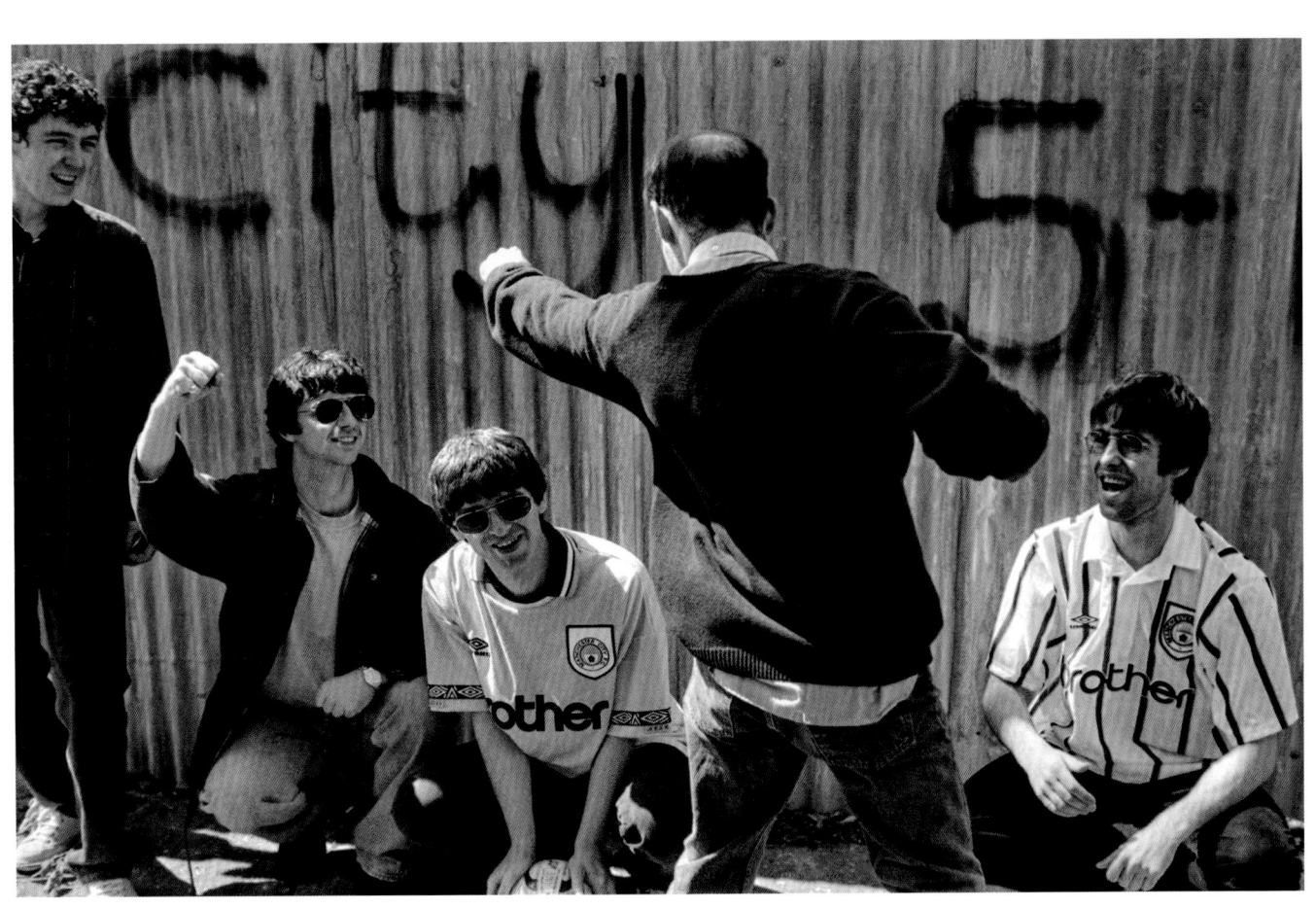

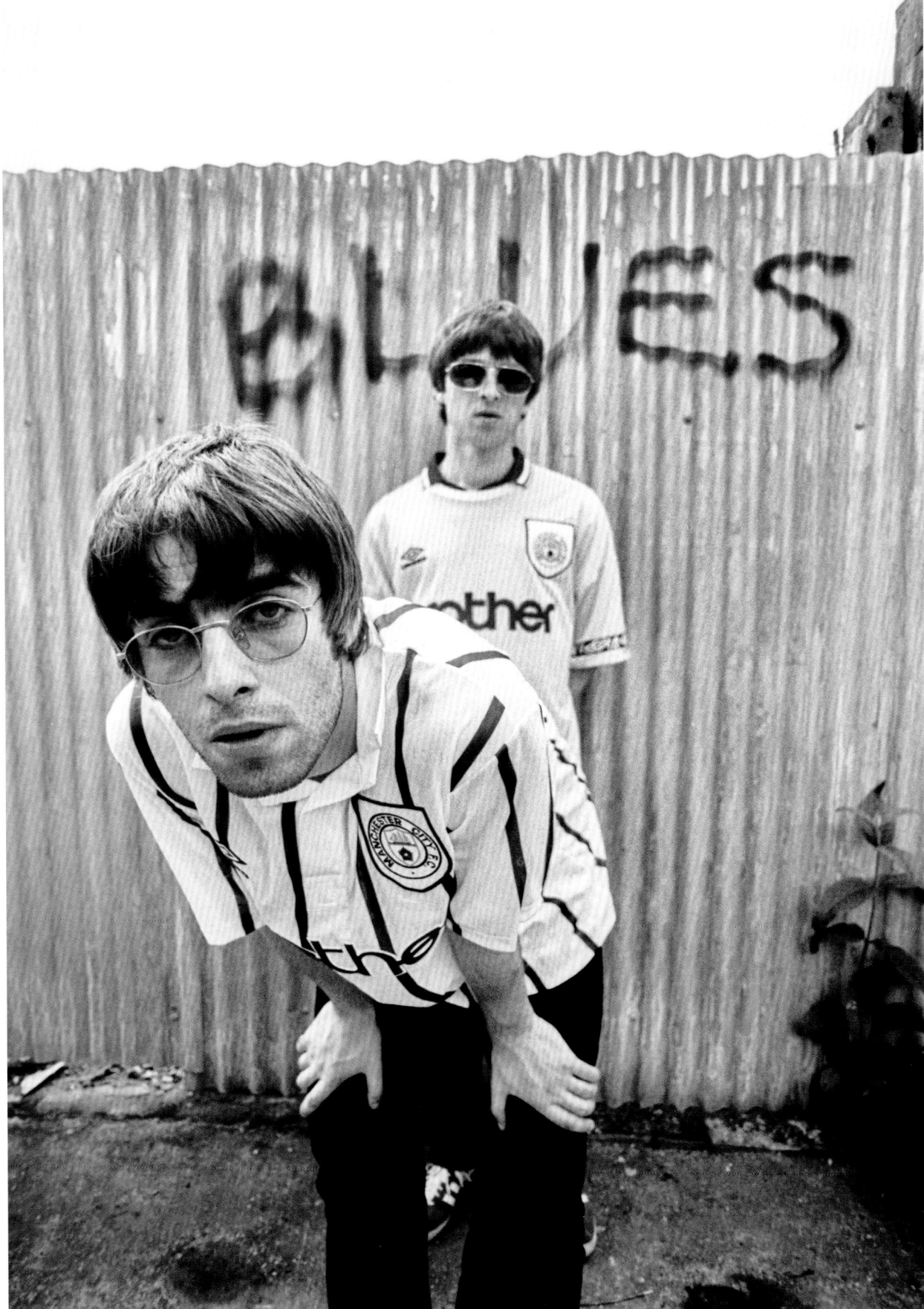

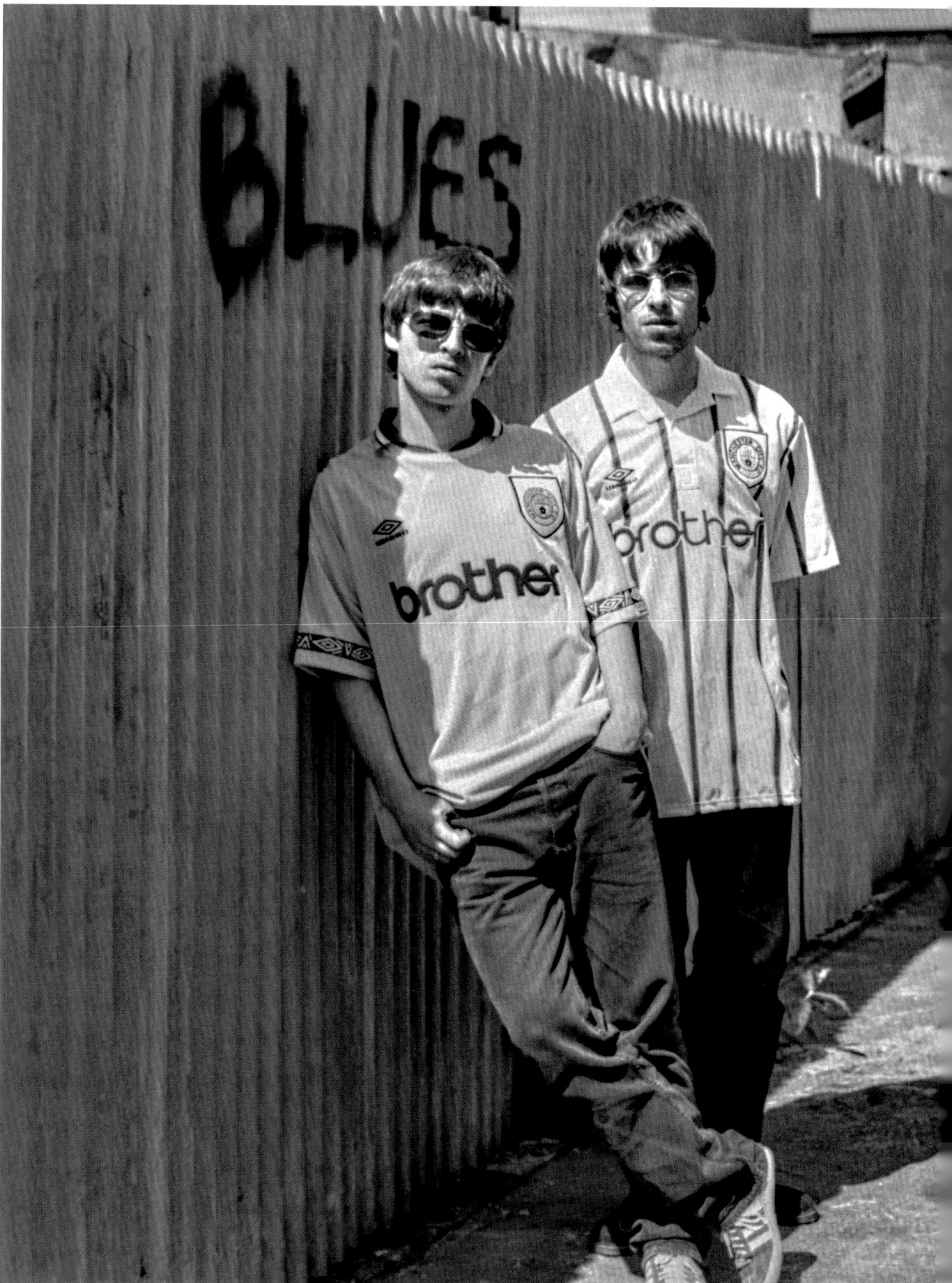

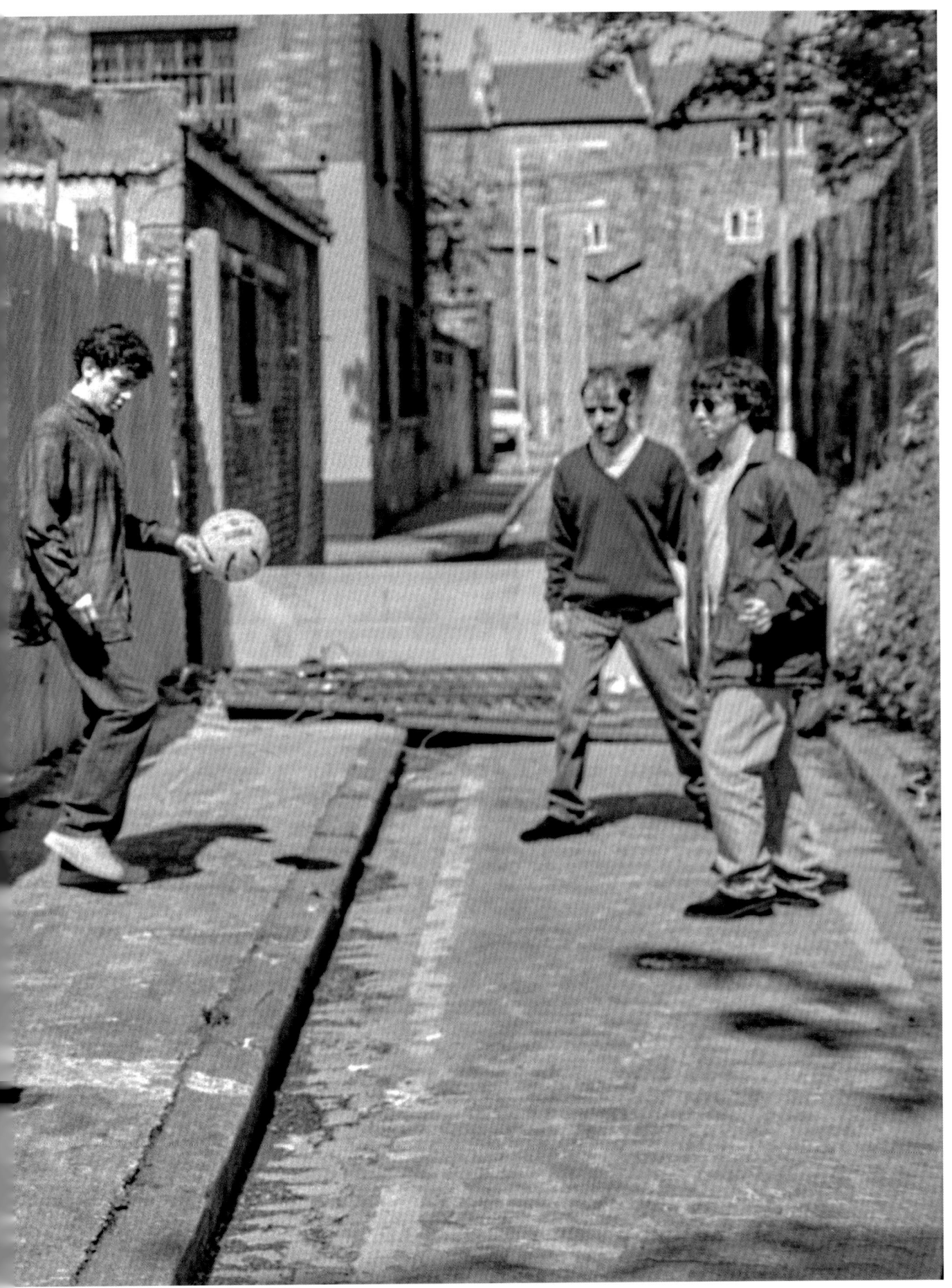

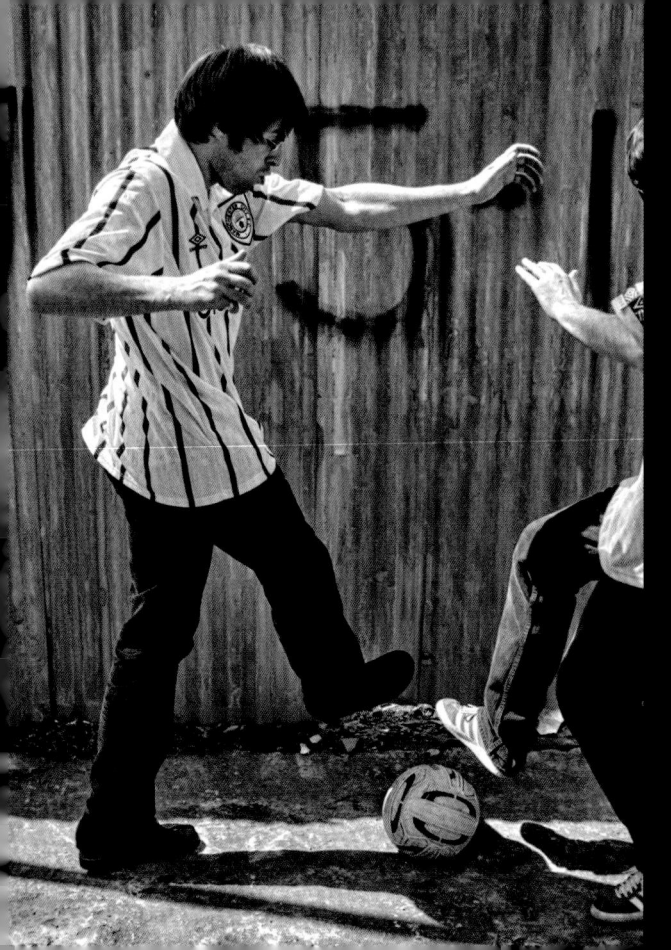

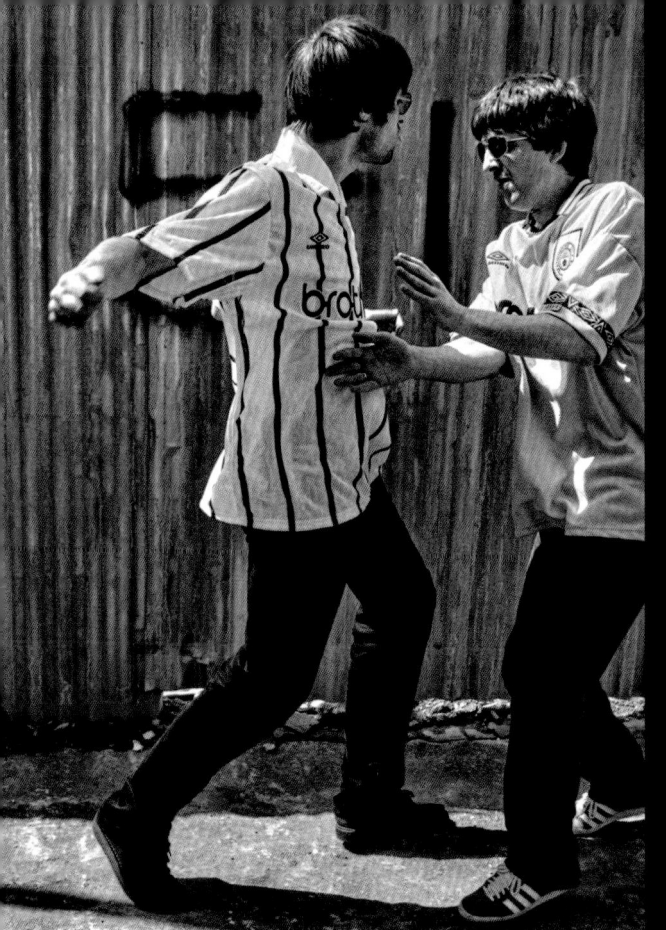

MAY

KING'S REACH TOWER, LONDON
NME EVENT

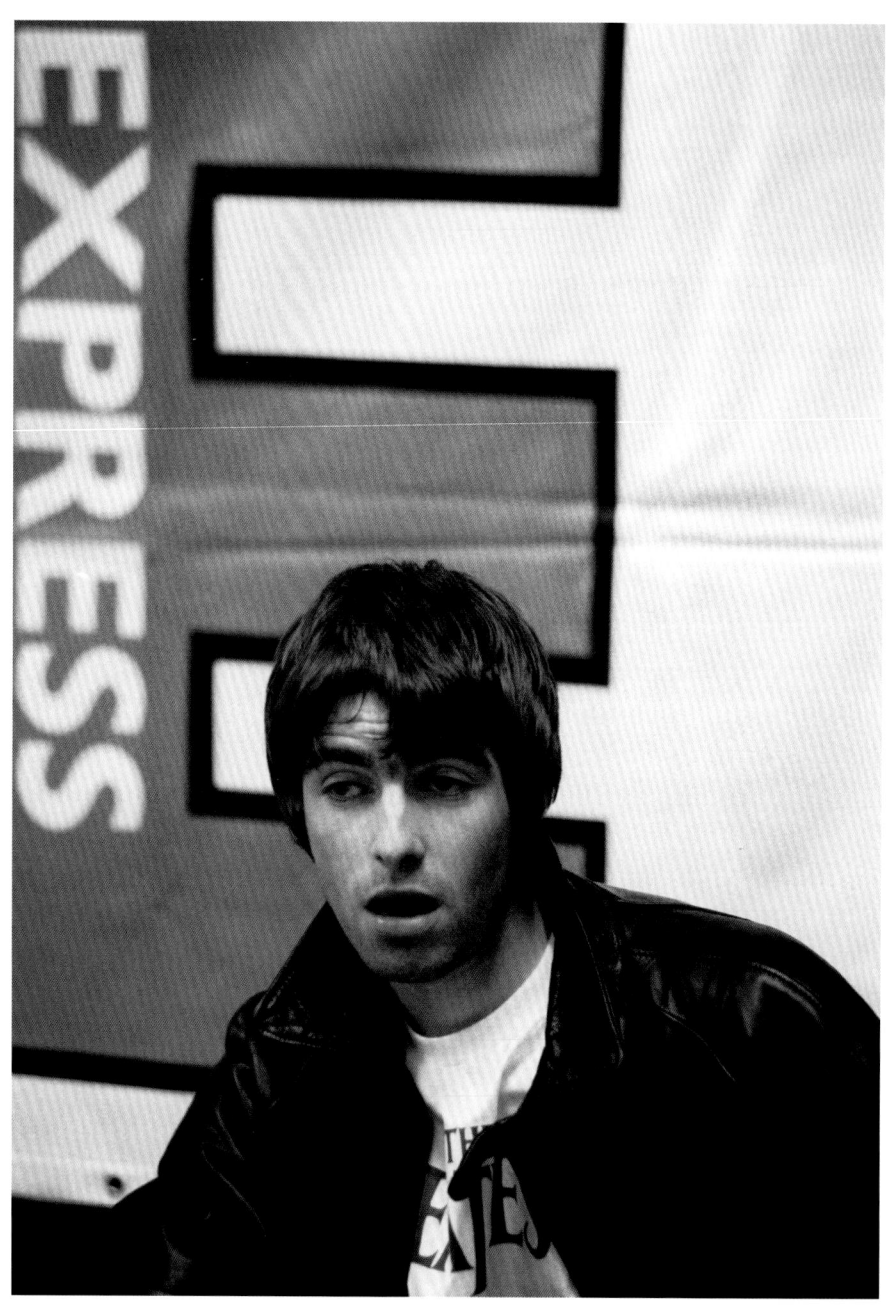

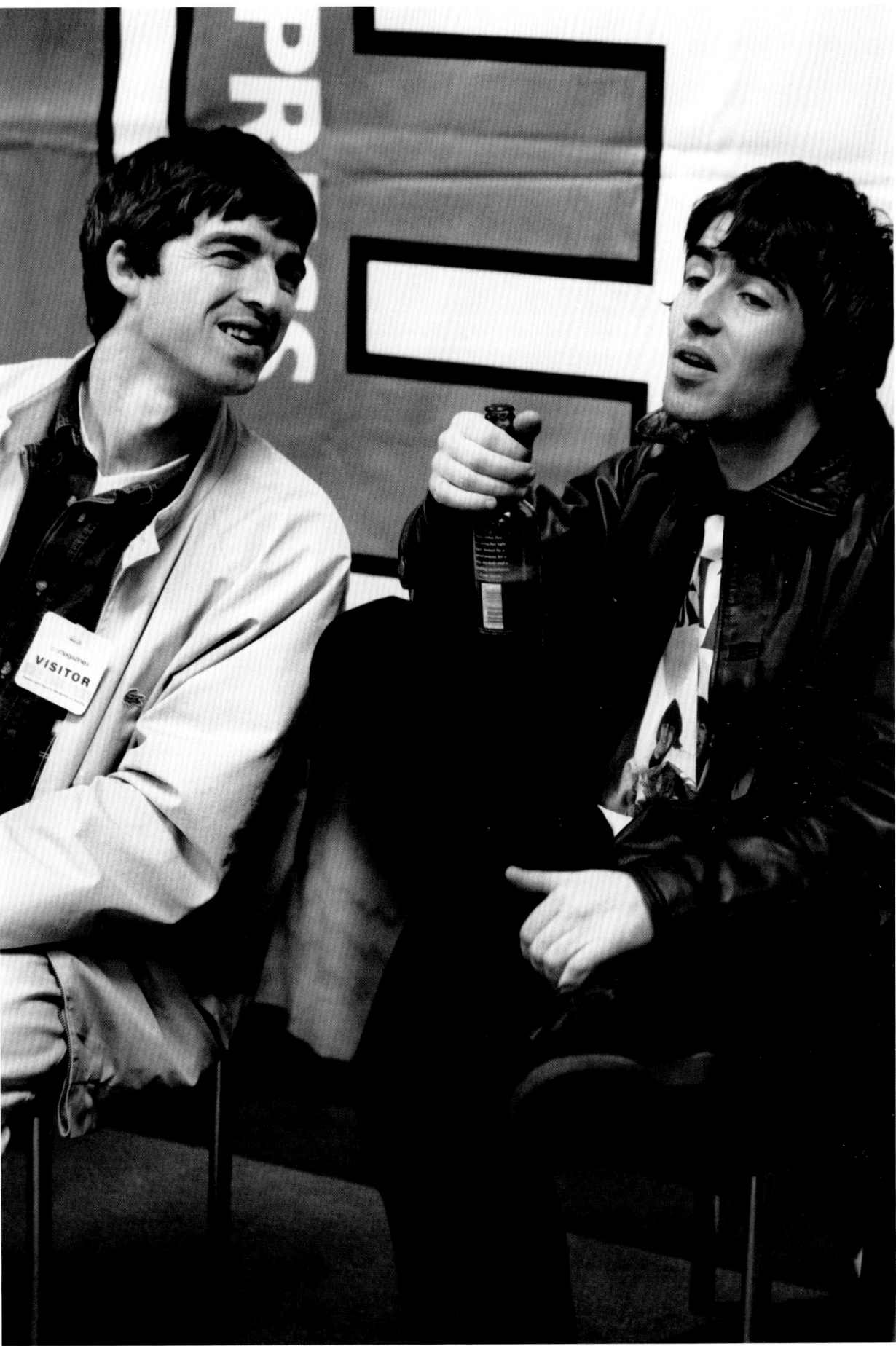

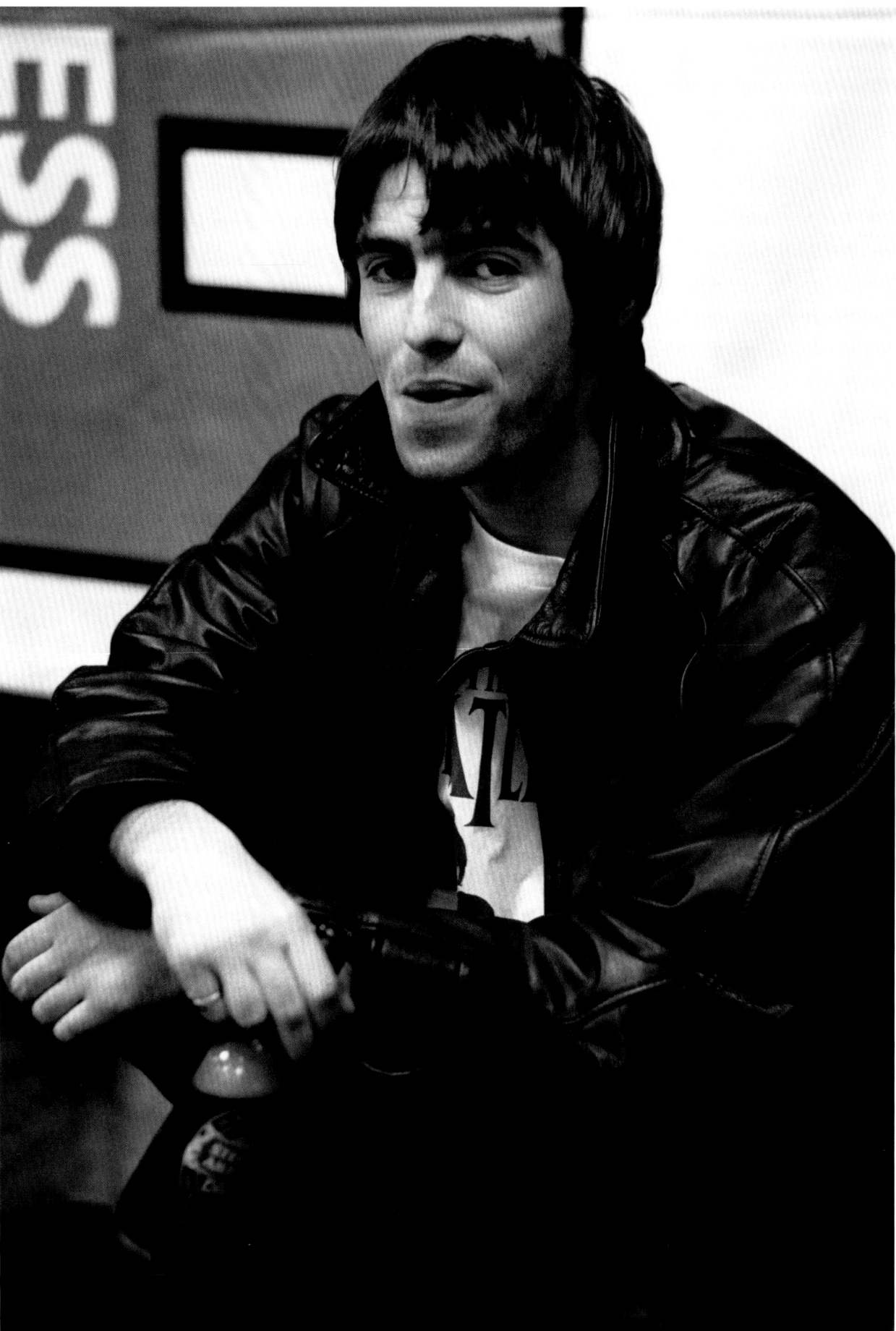

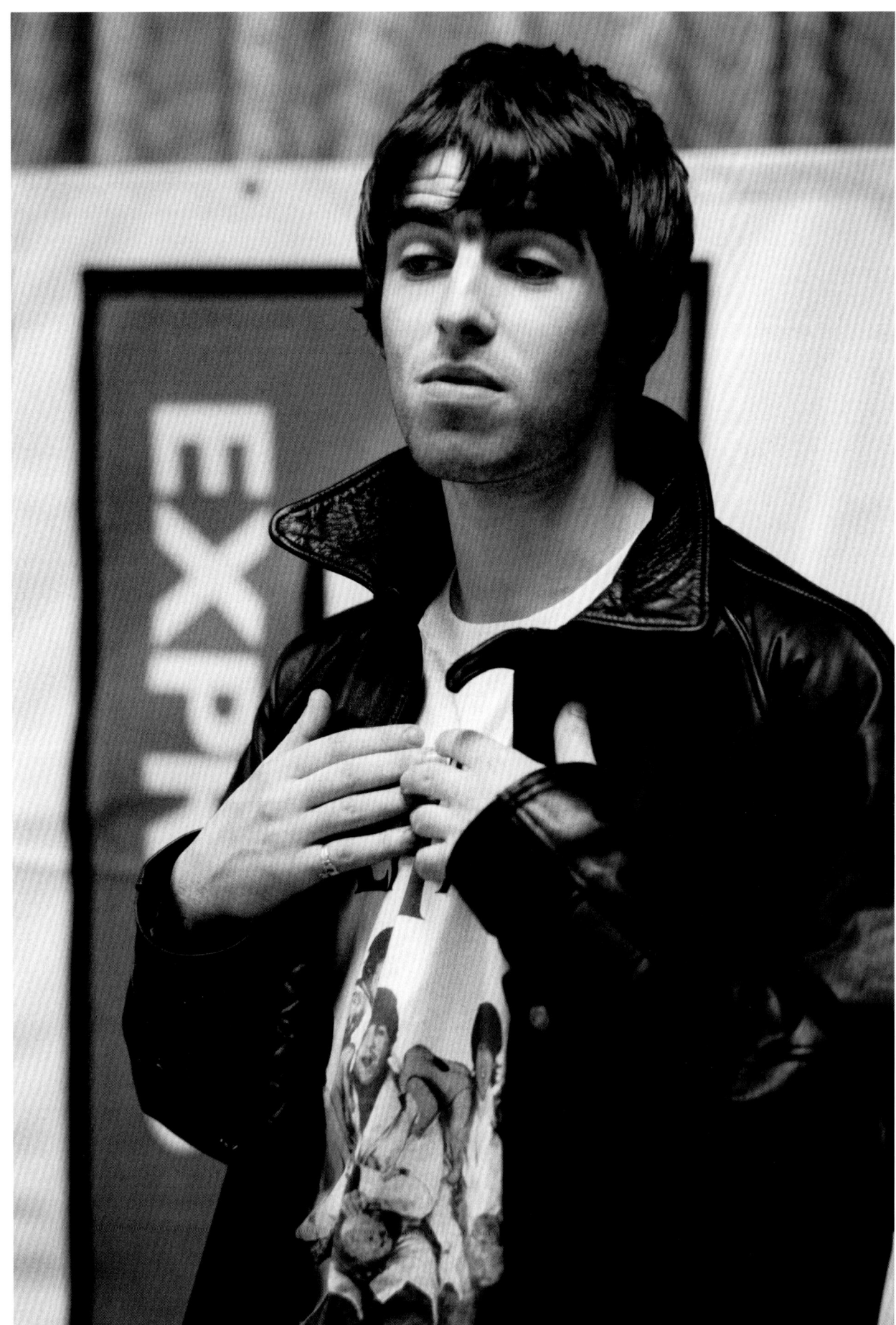

29 JULY

ARNDALE CENTRE, MANCHESTER

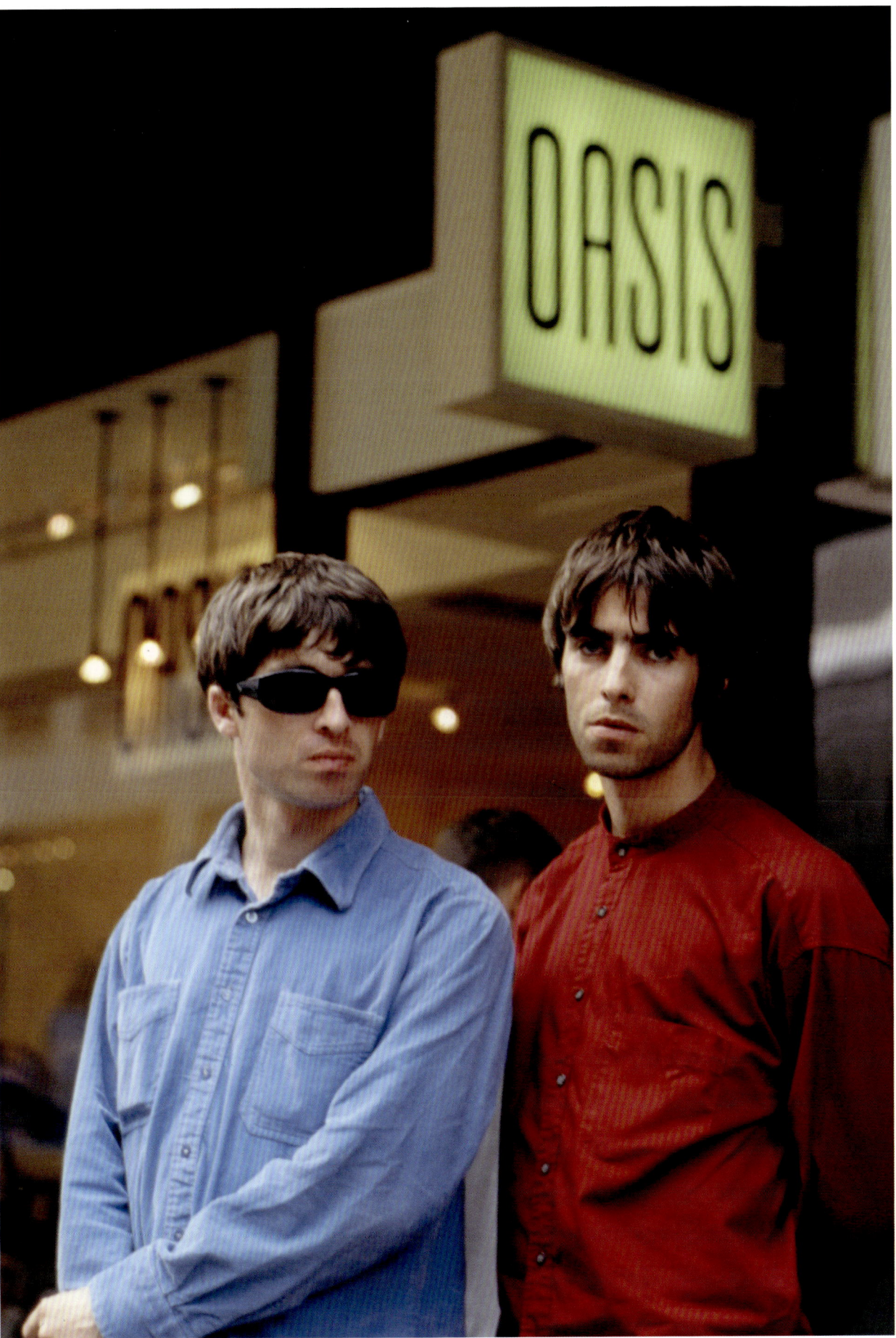

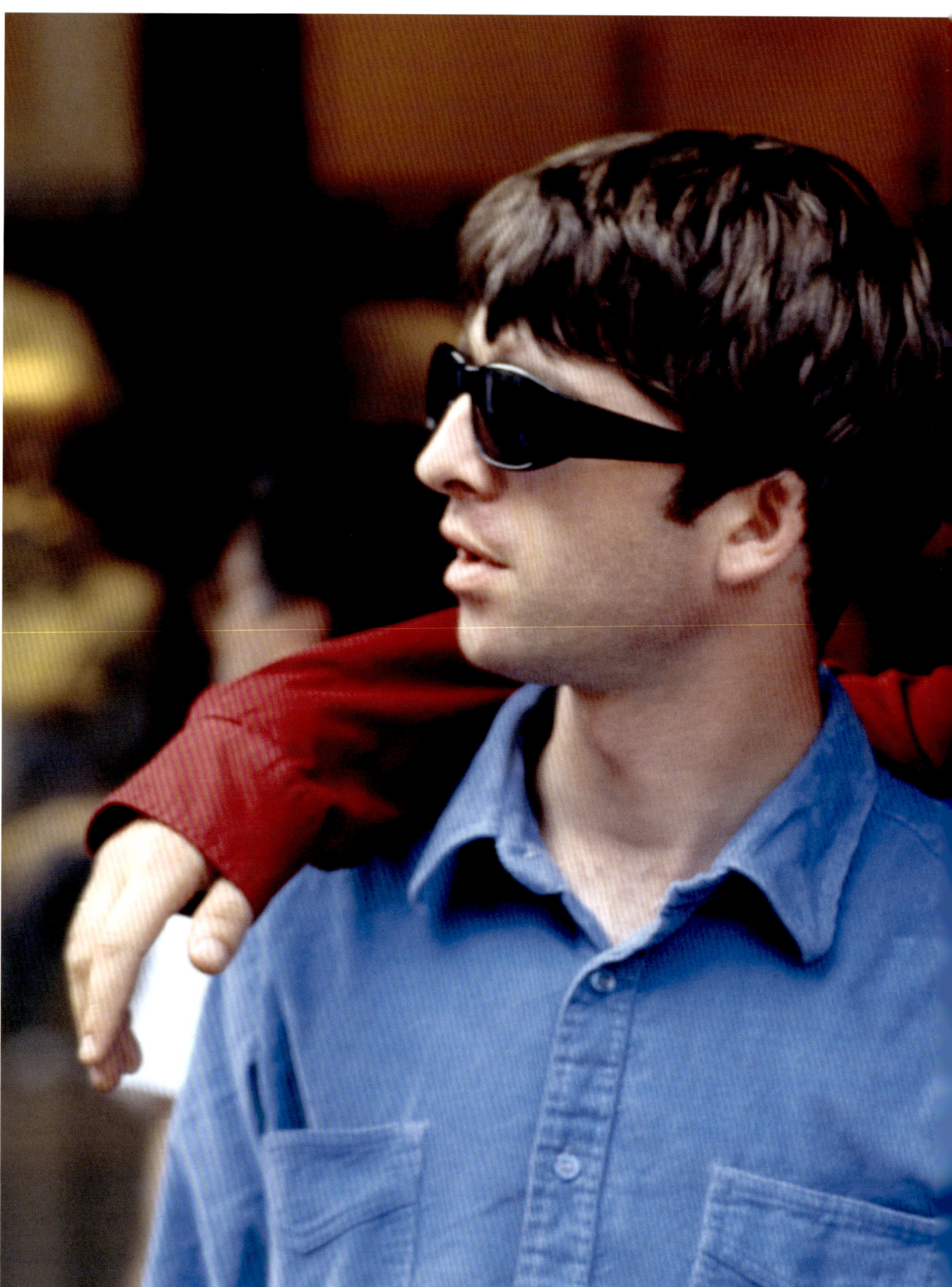

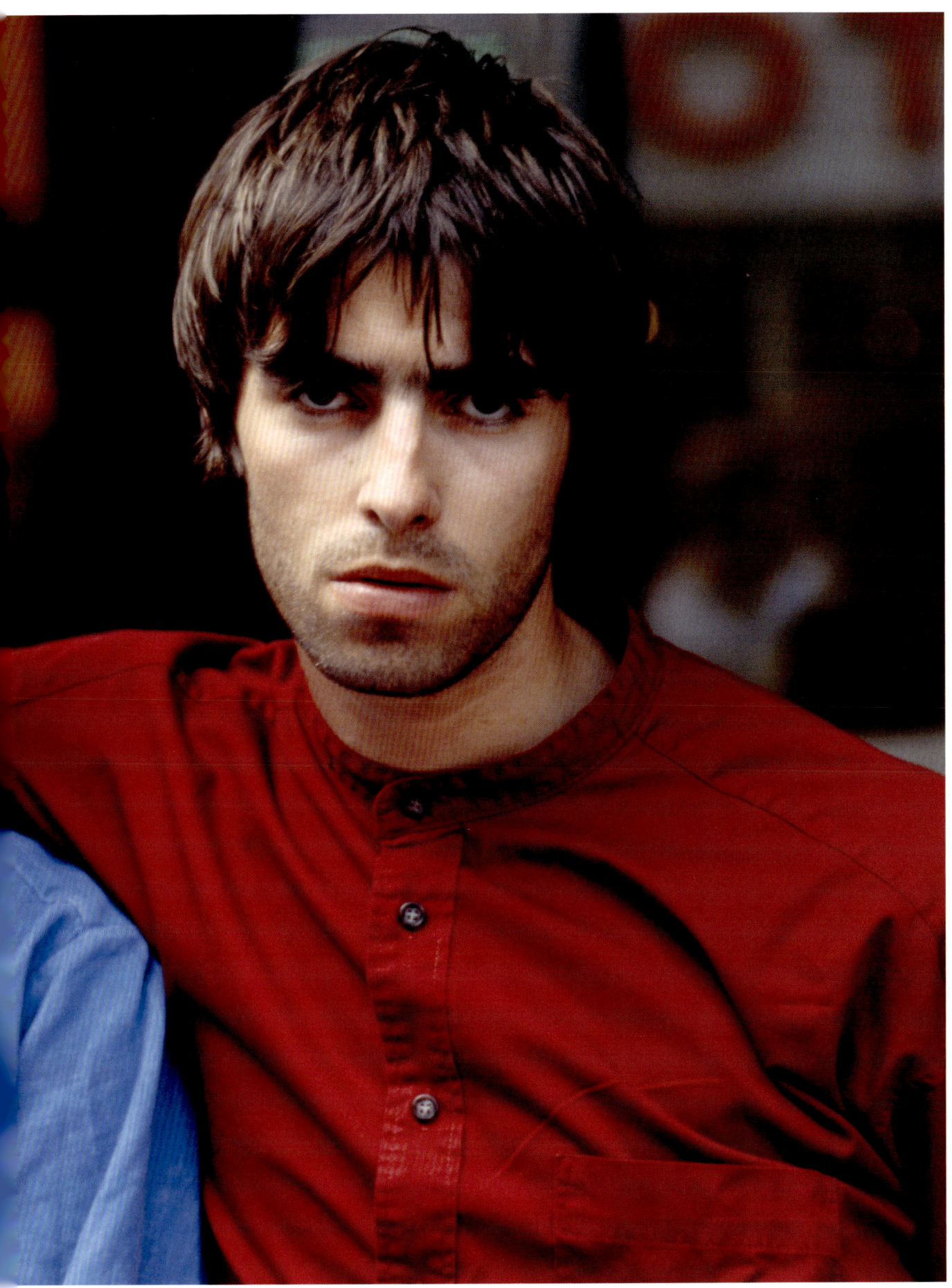

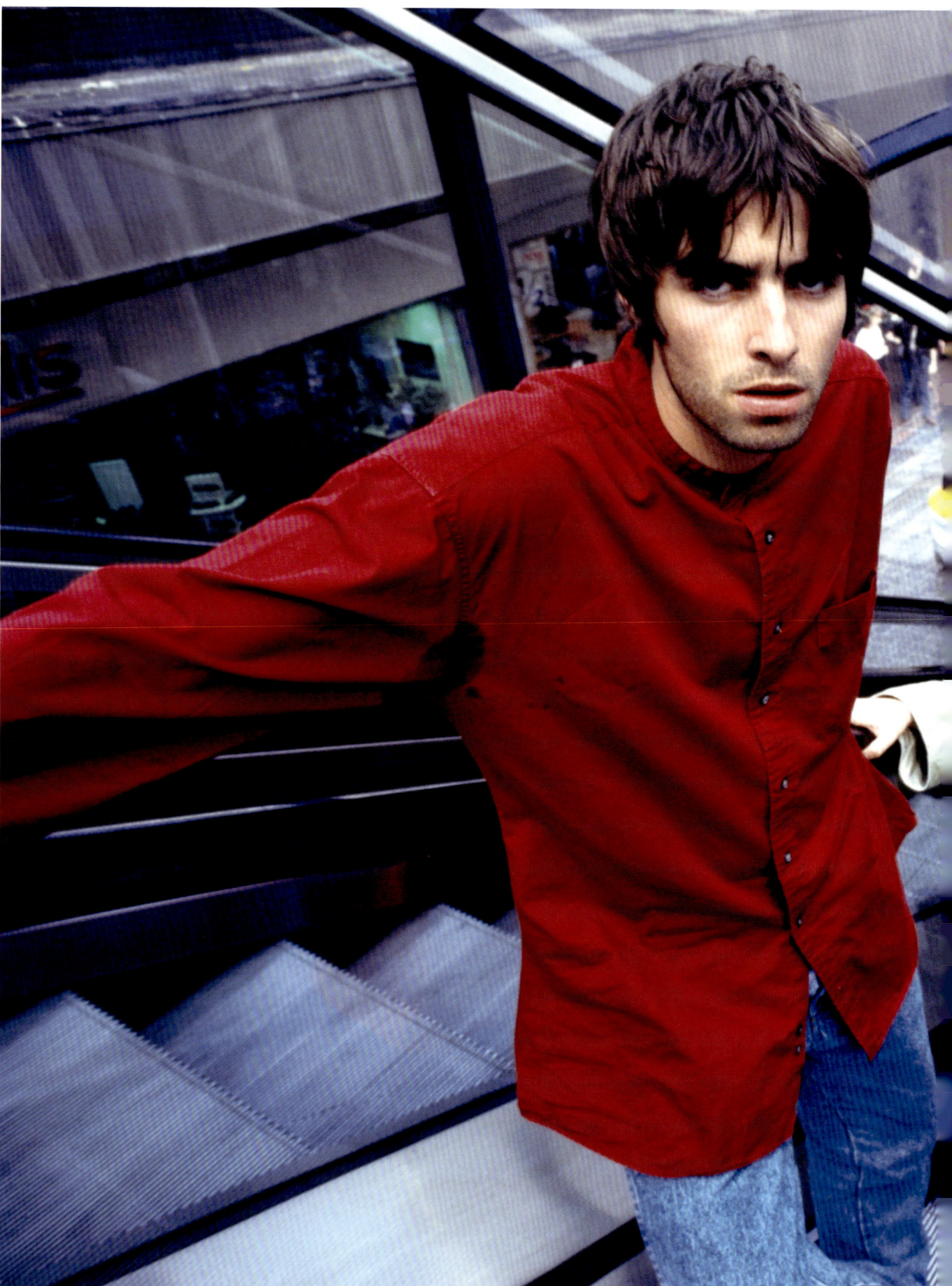

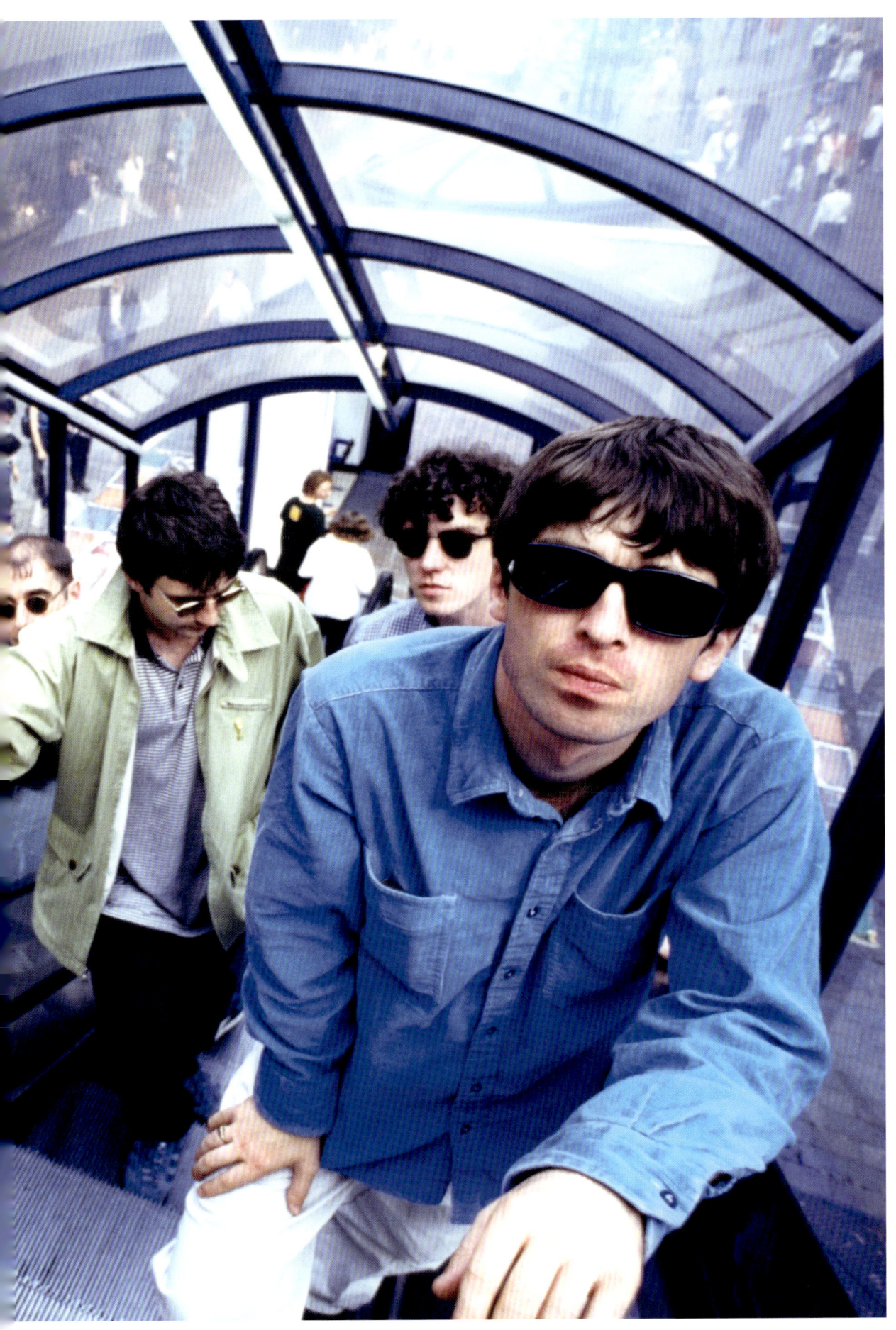

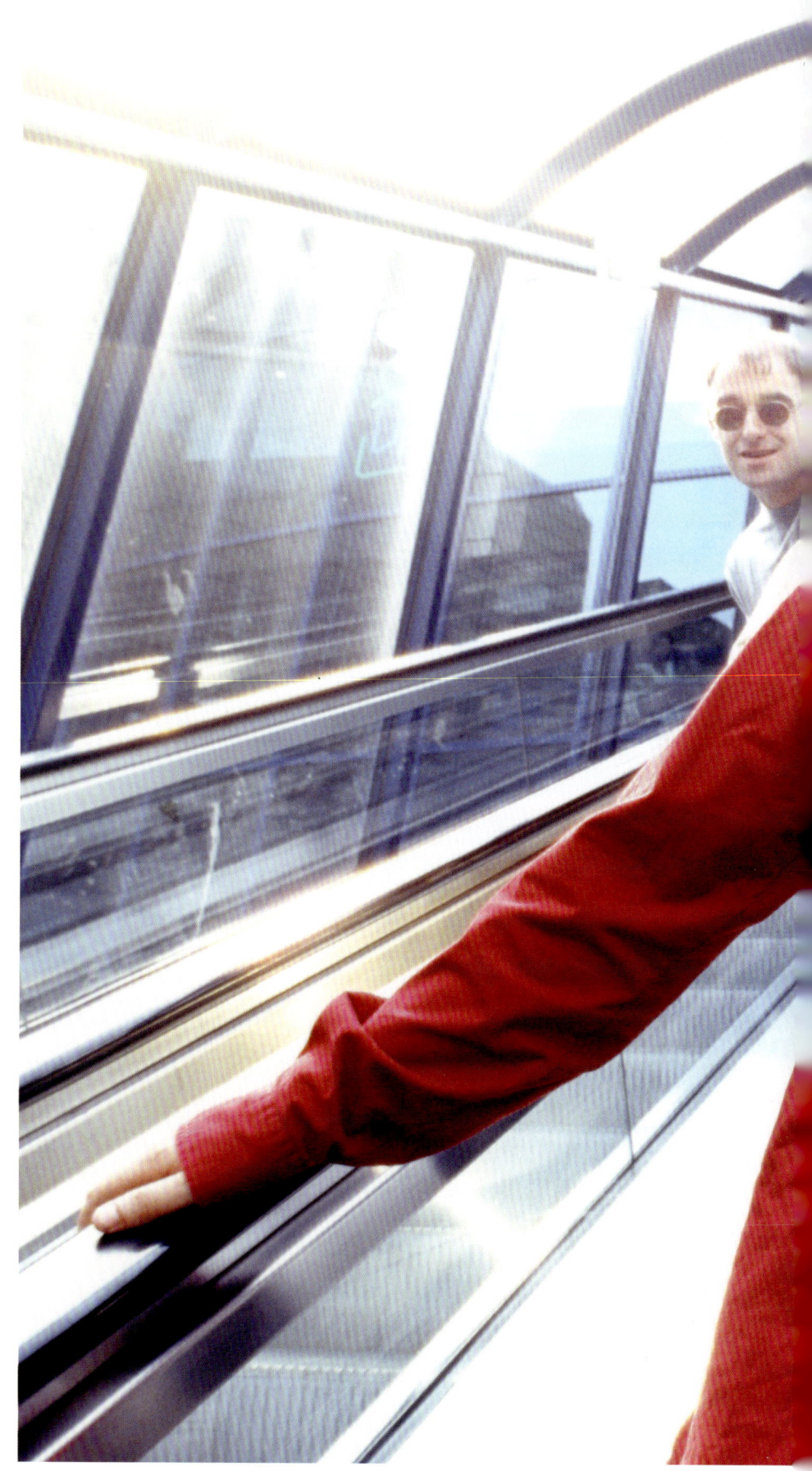

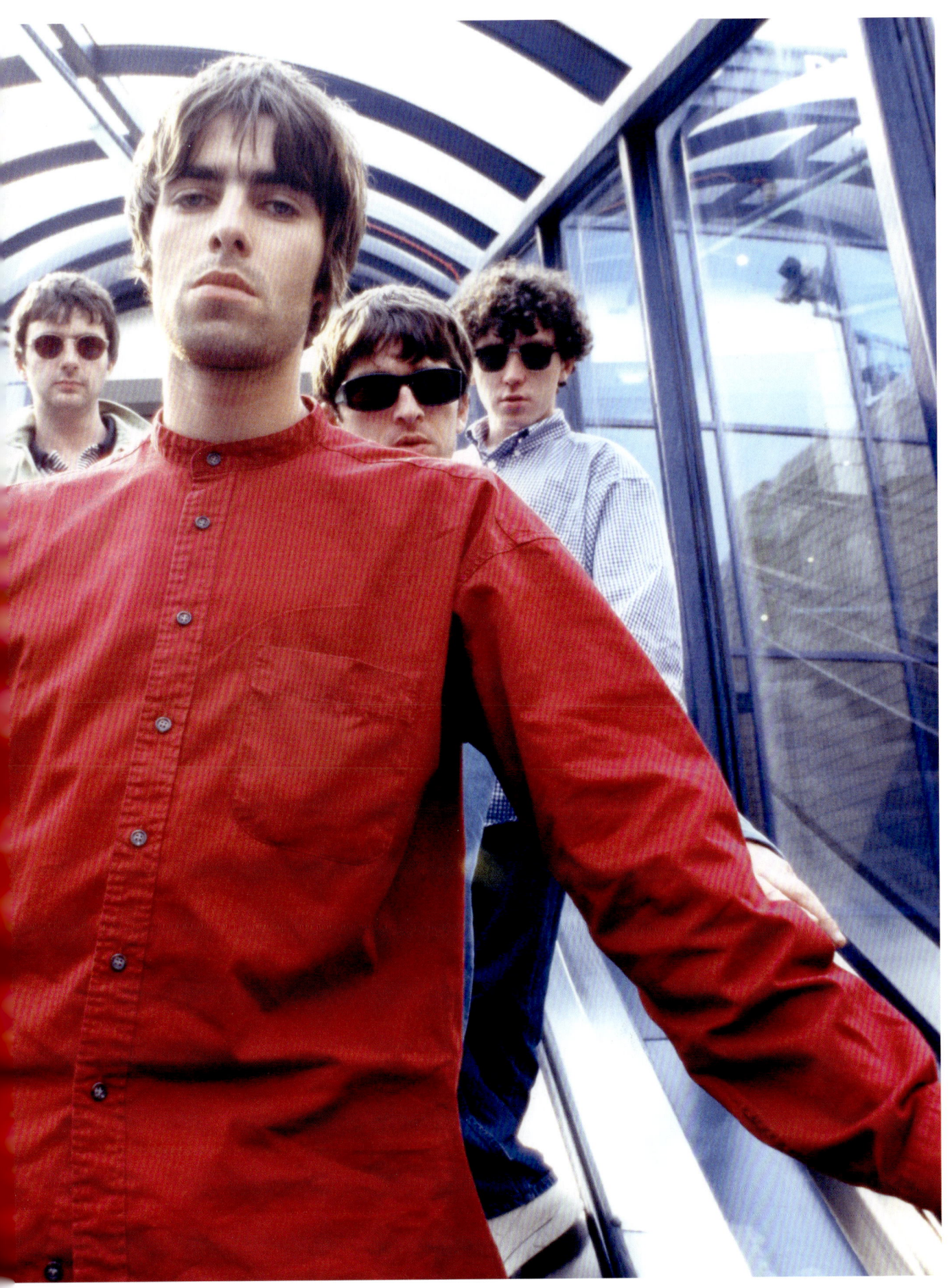

29 JULY

PICCADILLY GARDENS, MANCHESTER

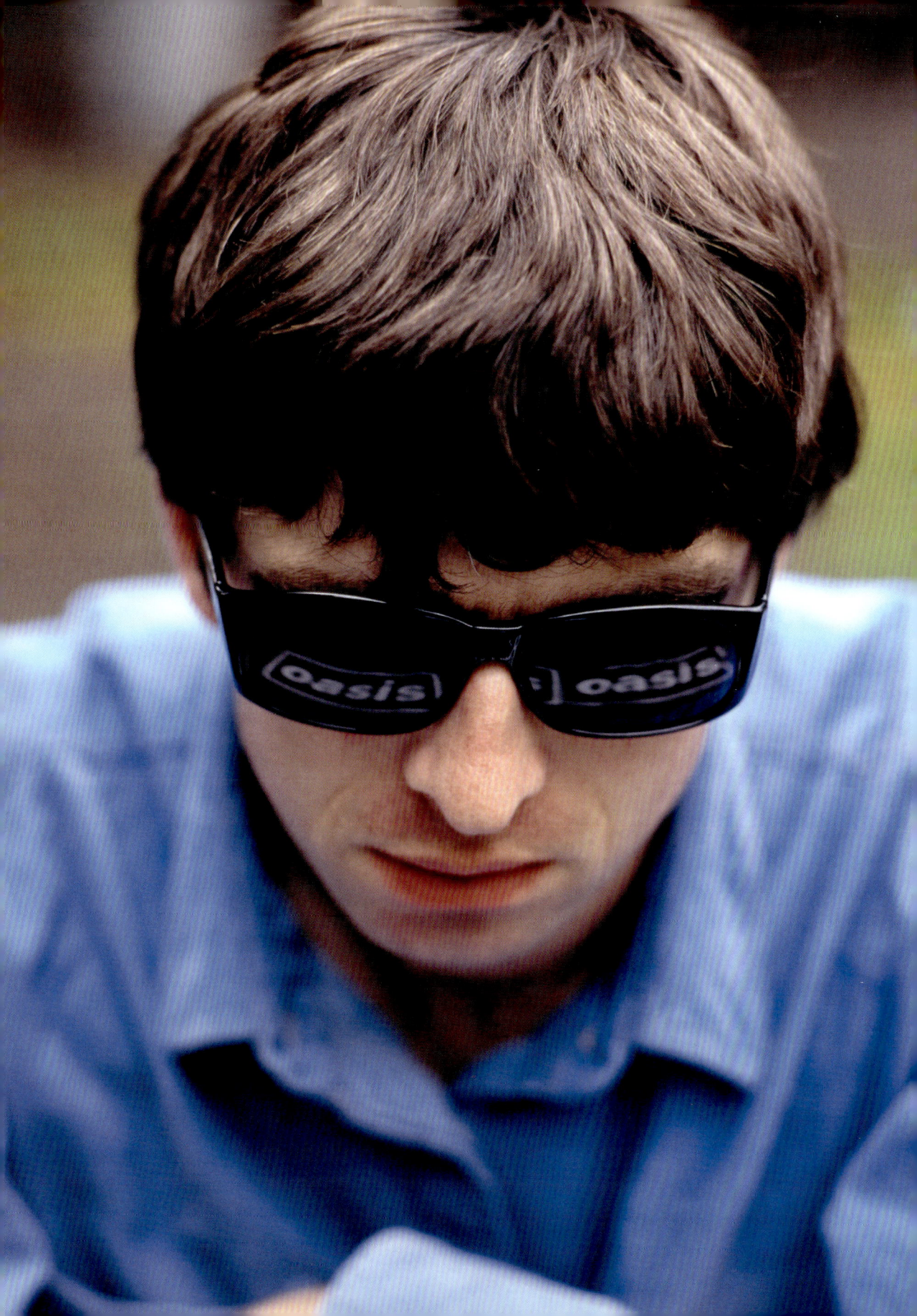

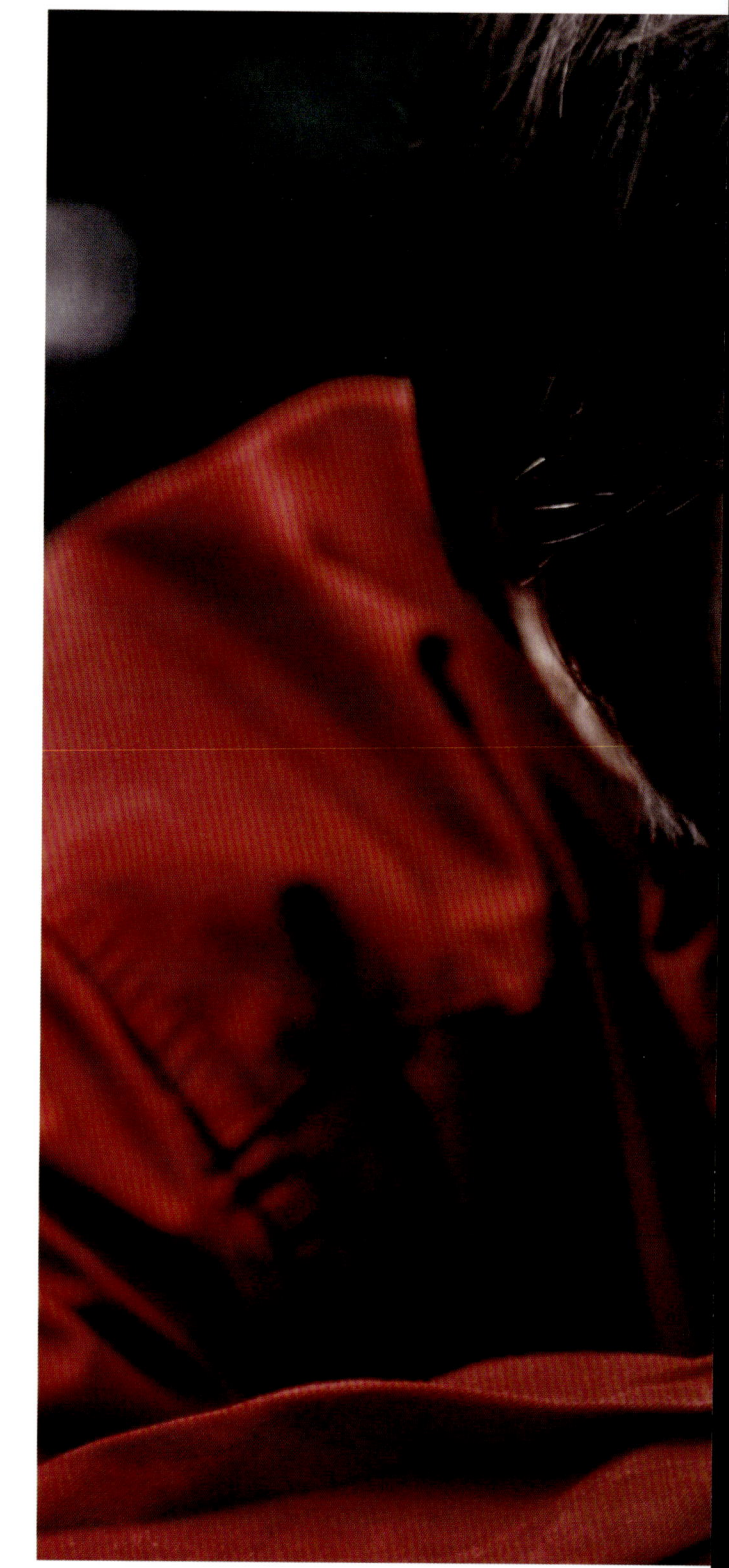

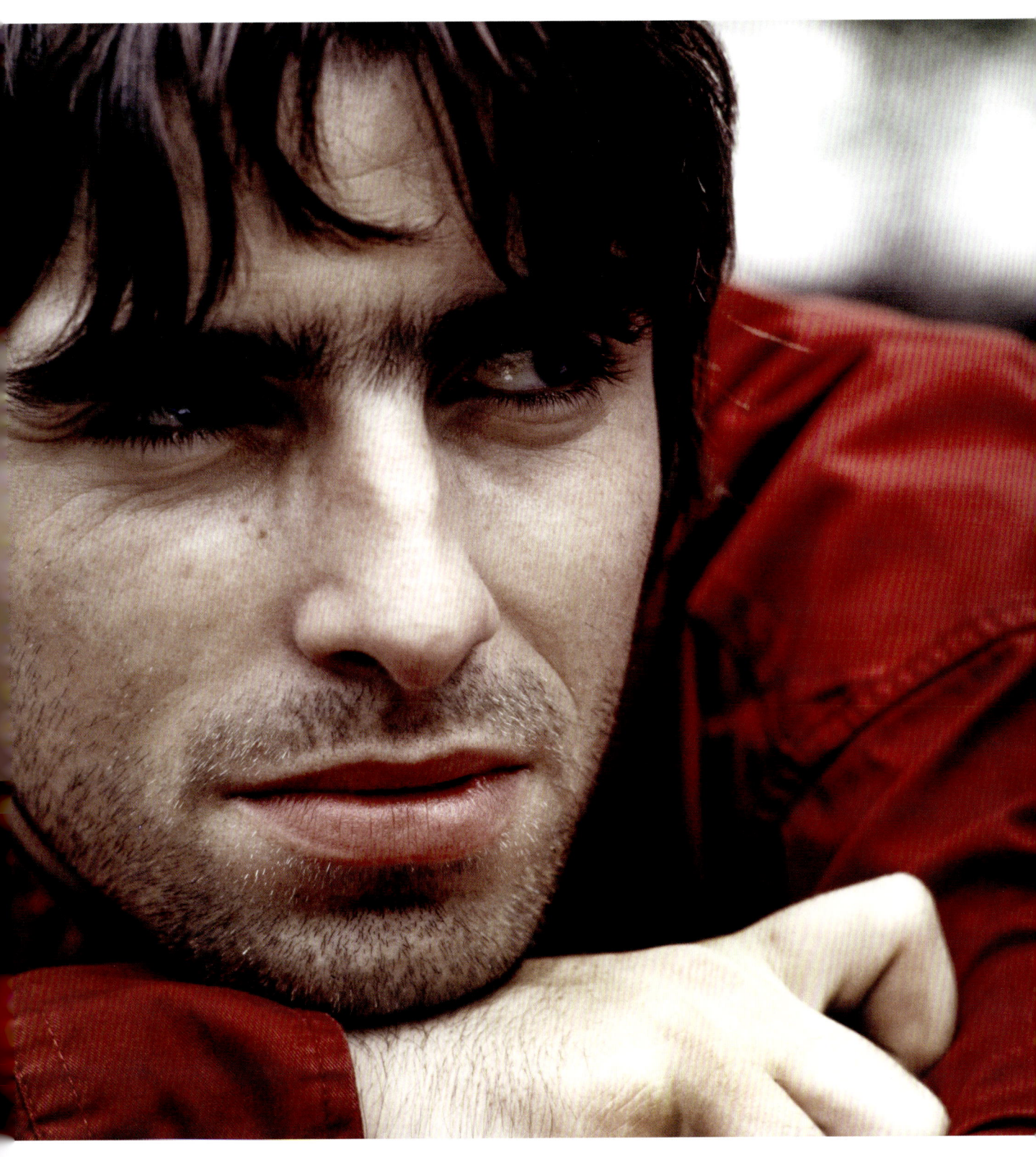

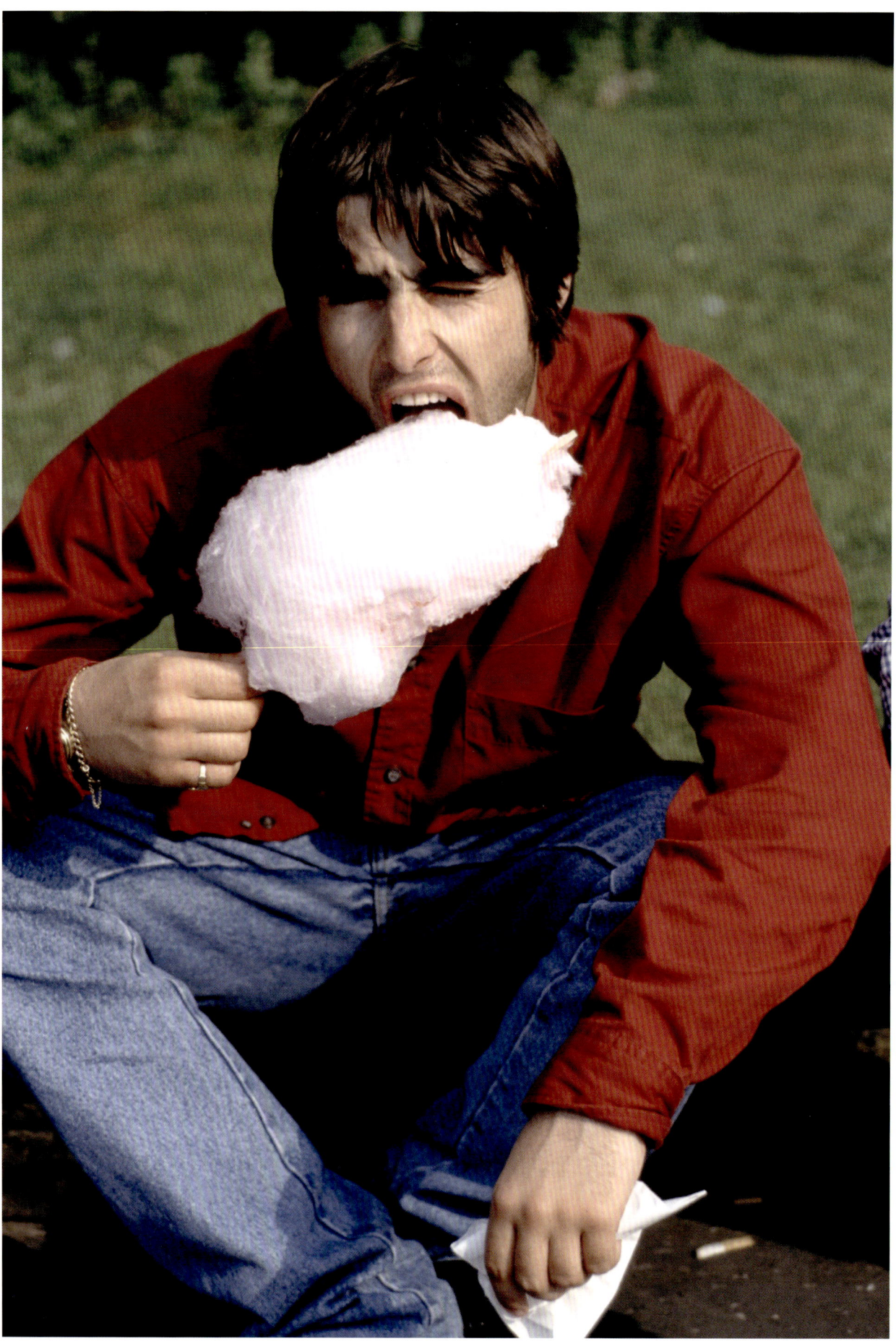

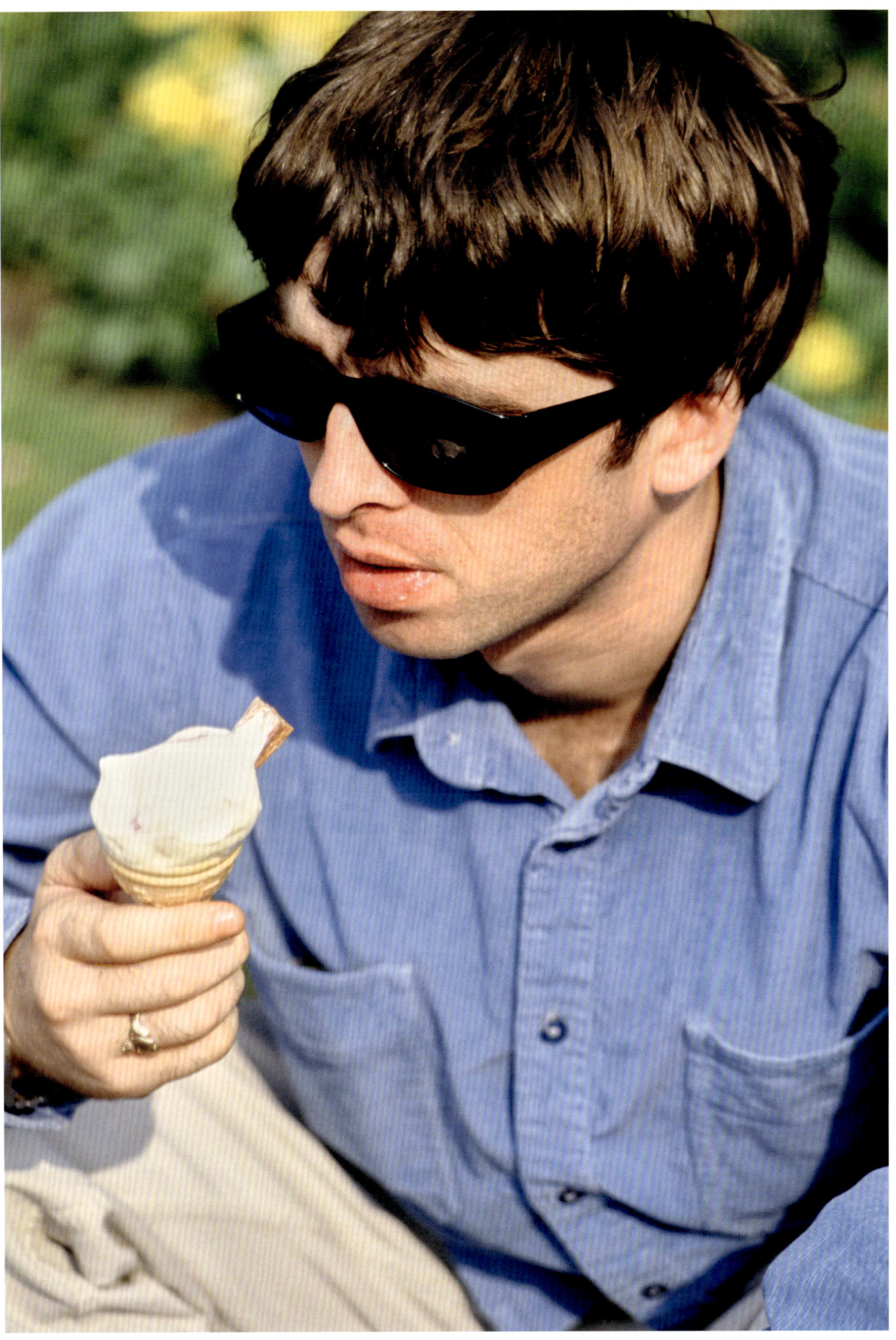

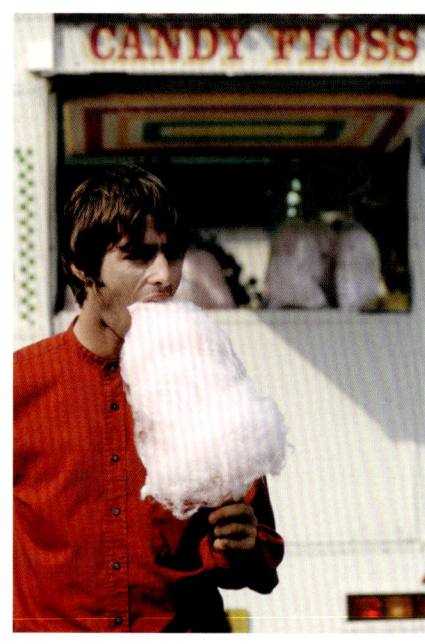
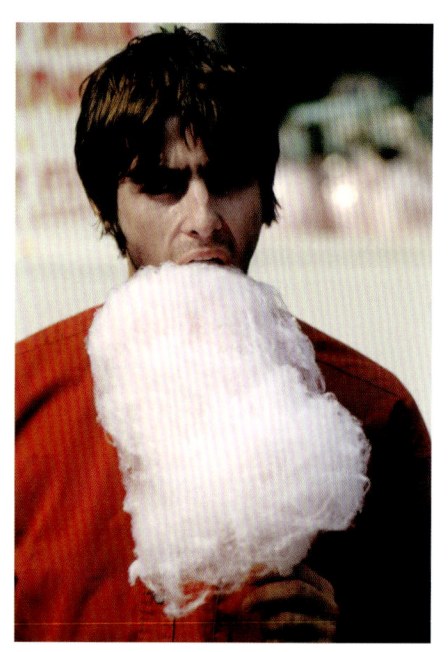
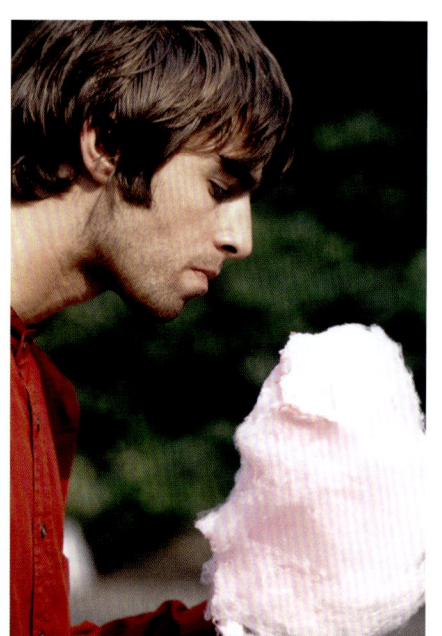
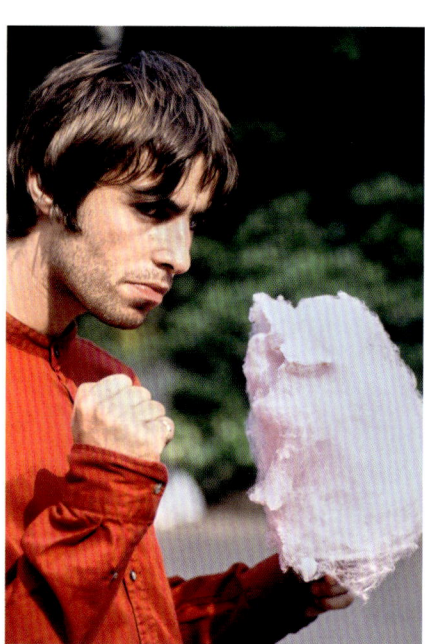

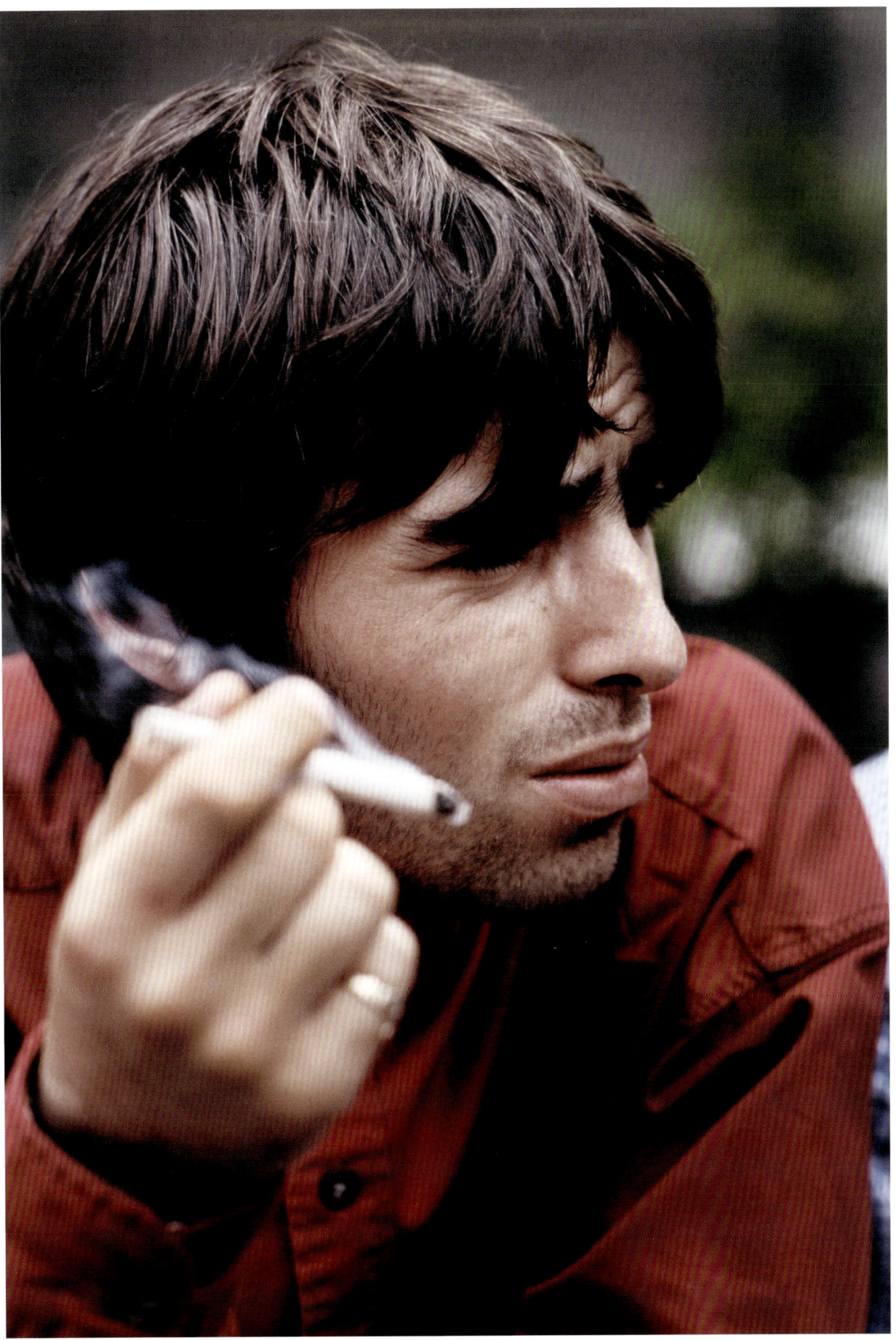

29 JULY
BACK GEORGE STREET, MANCHESTER

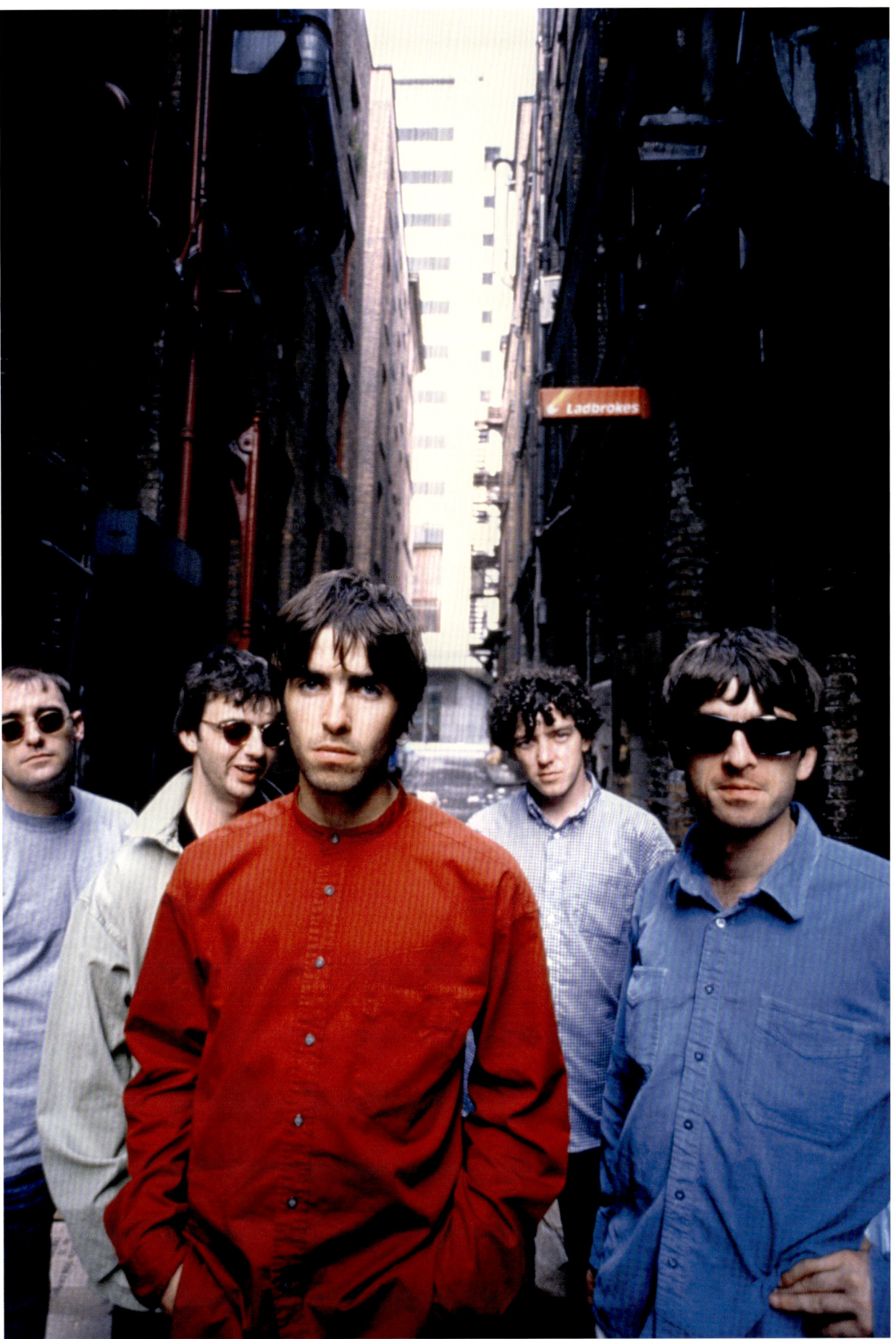

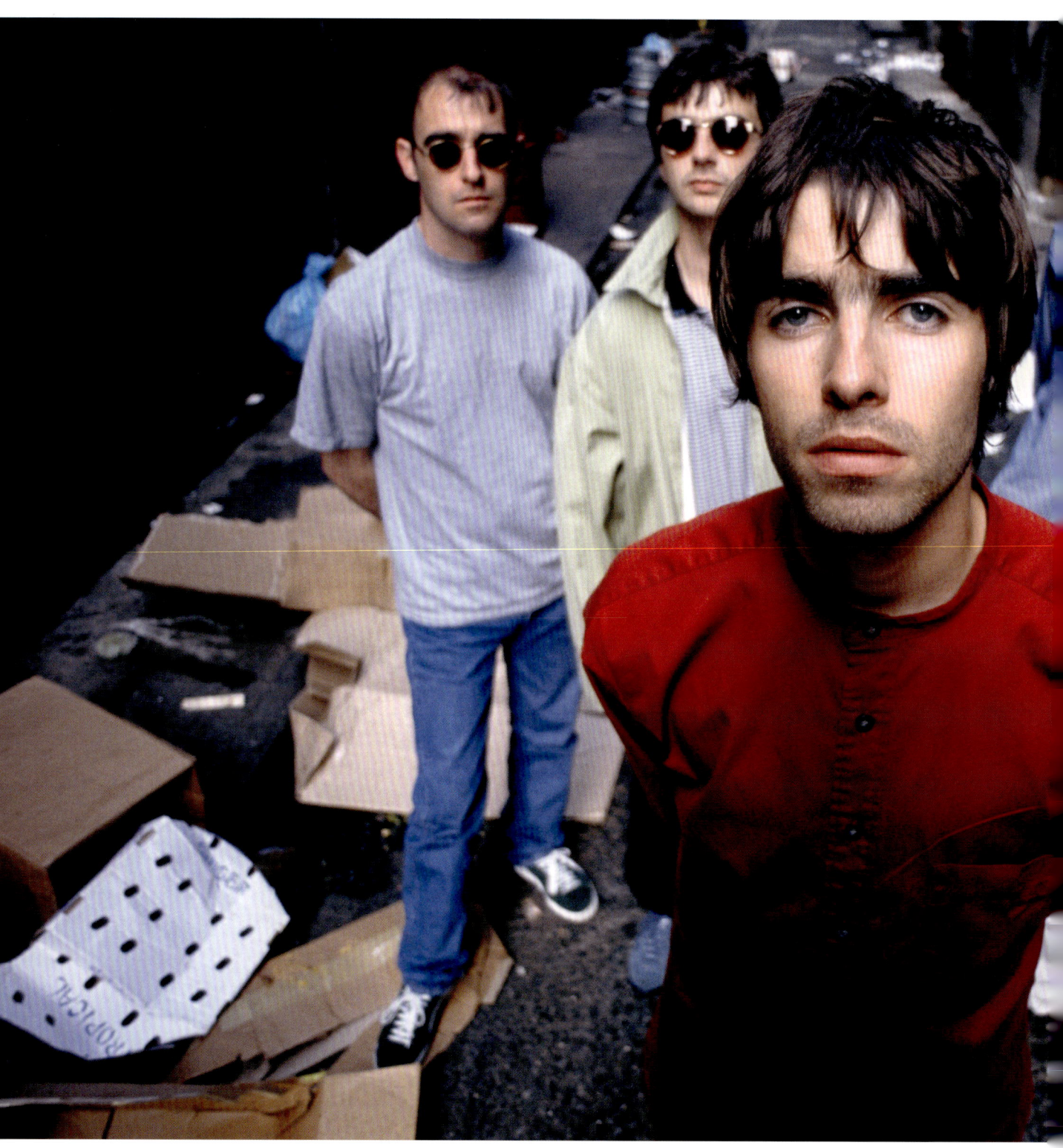

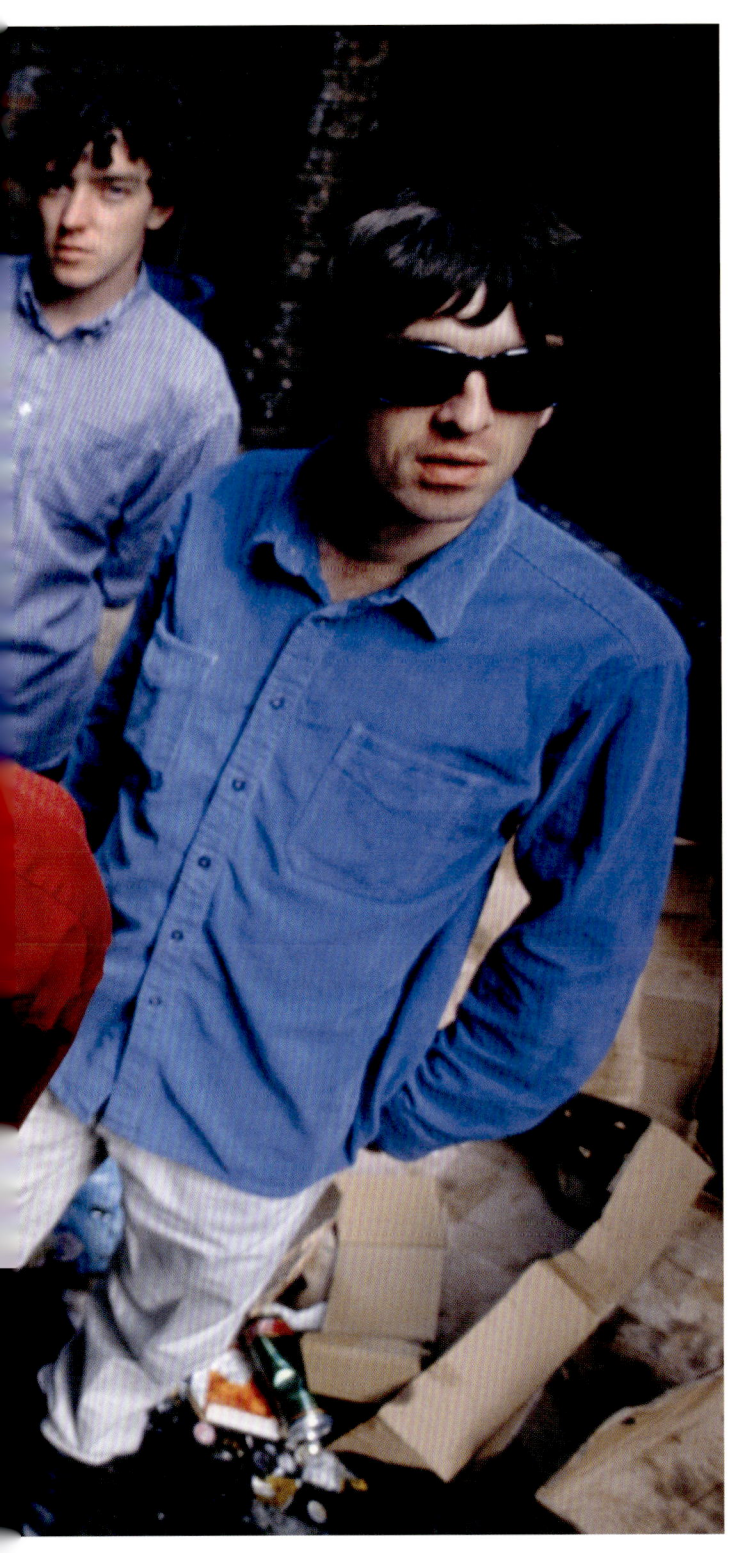

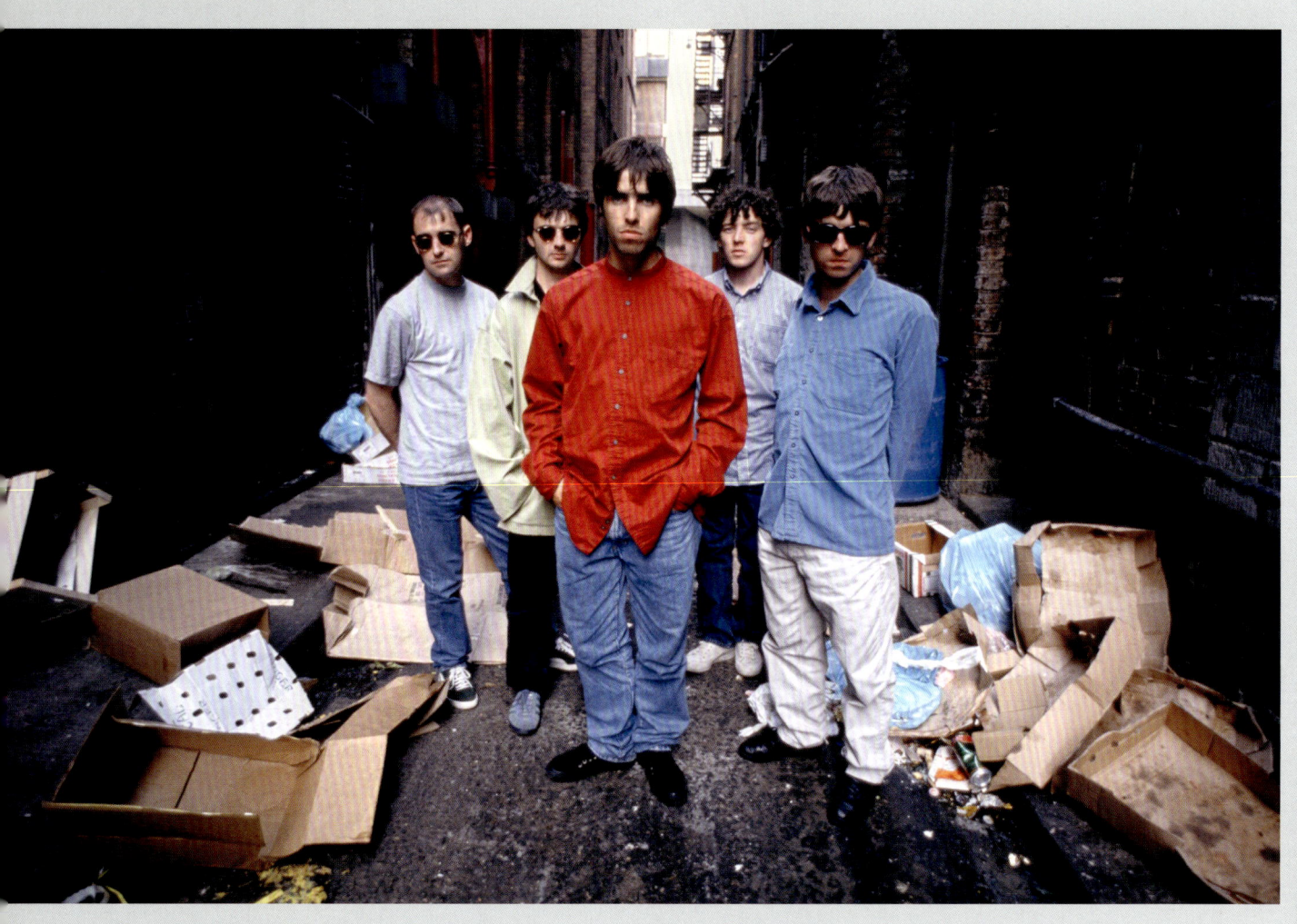

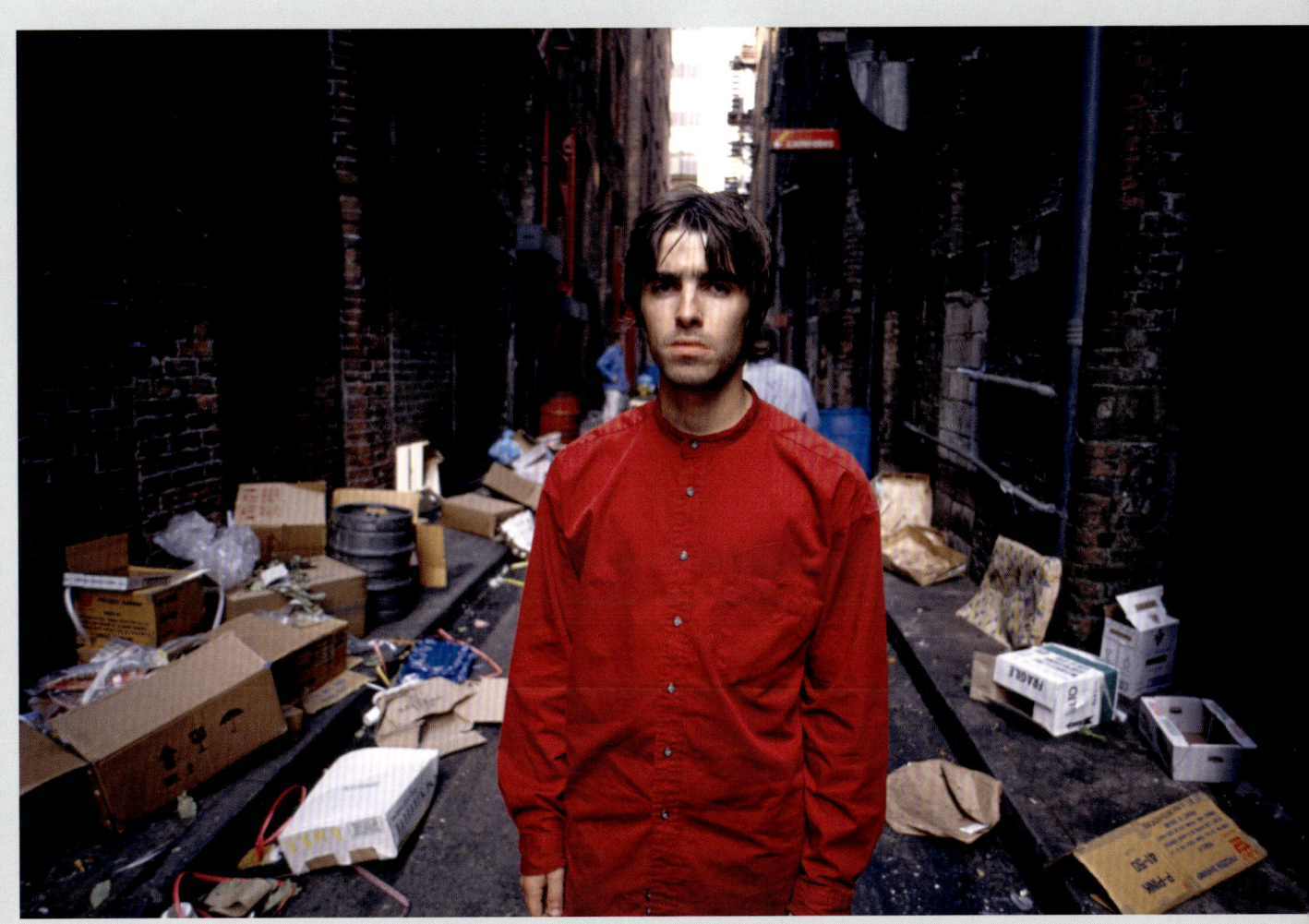

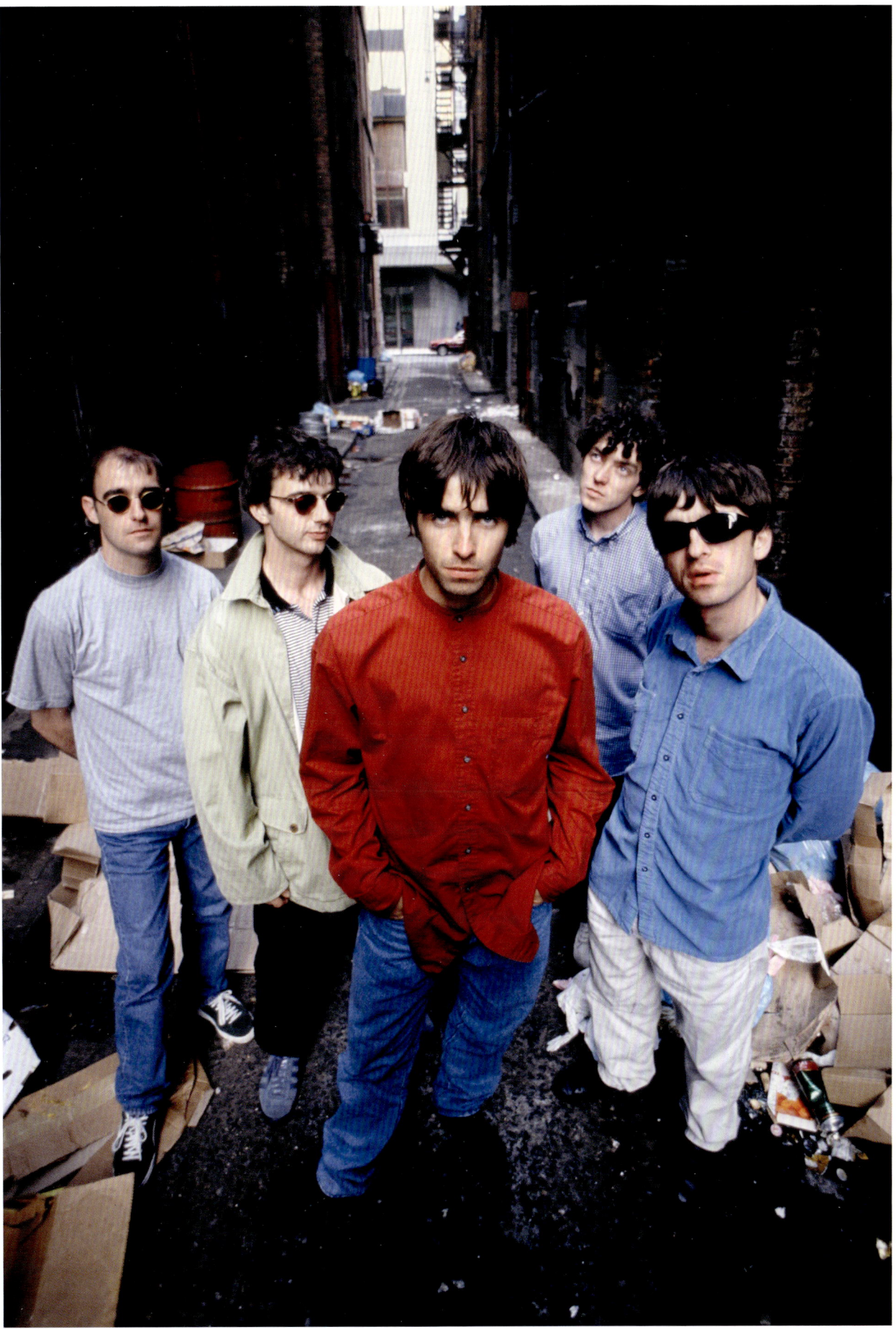

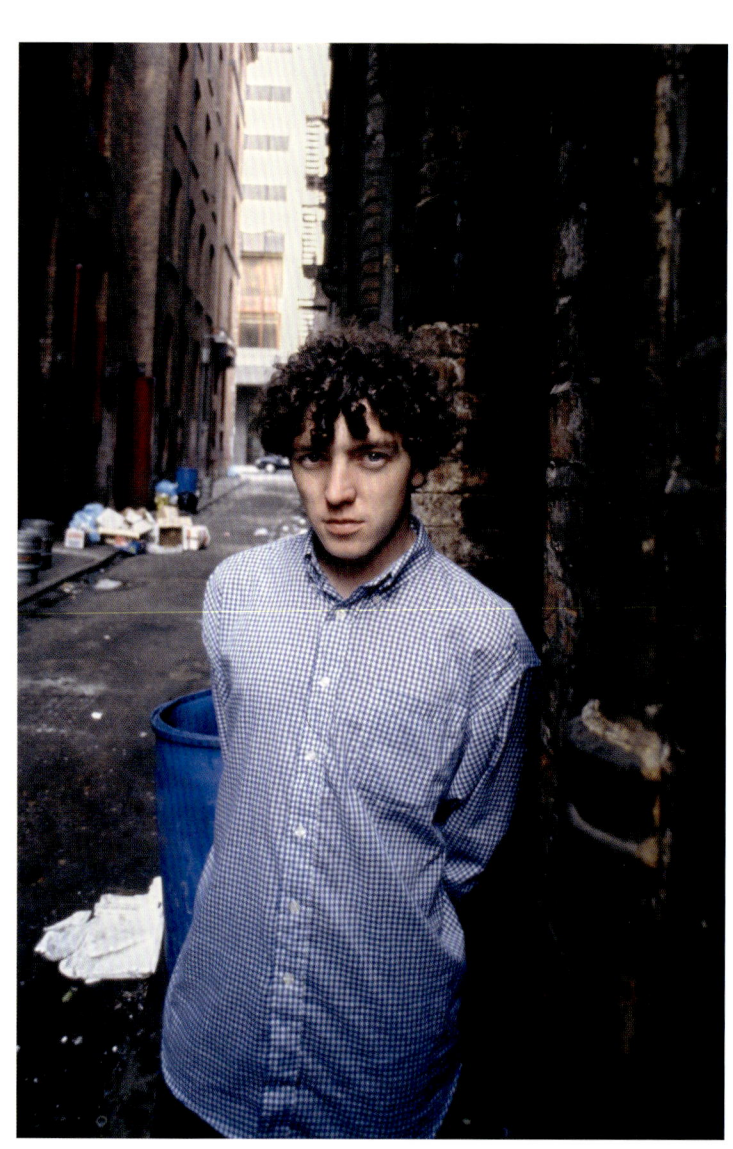

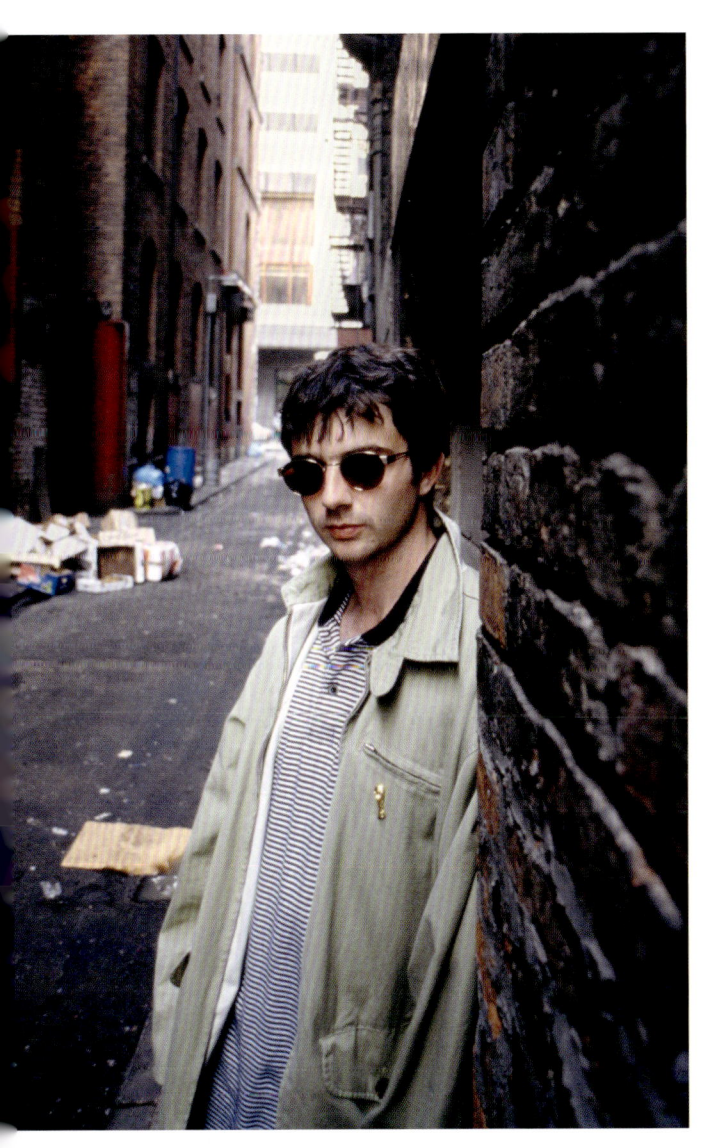
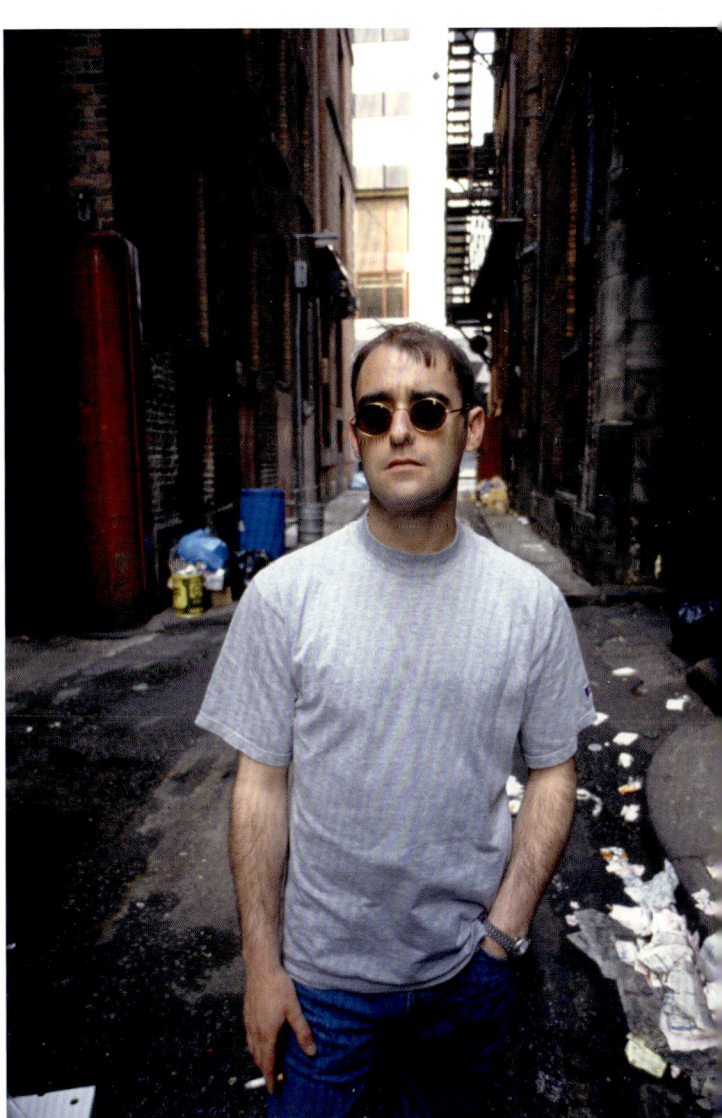

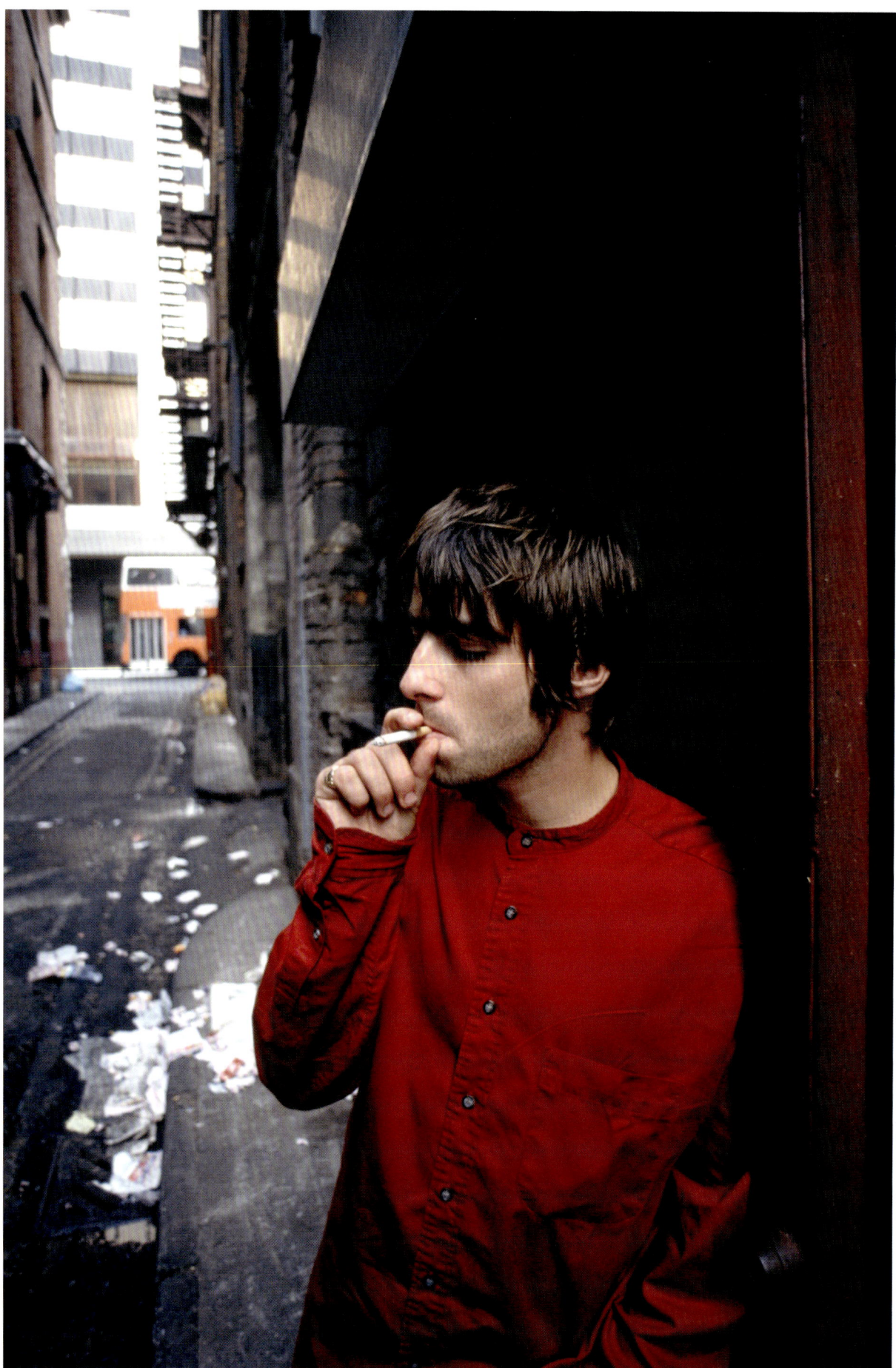

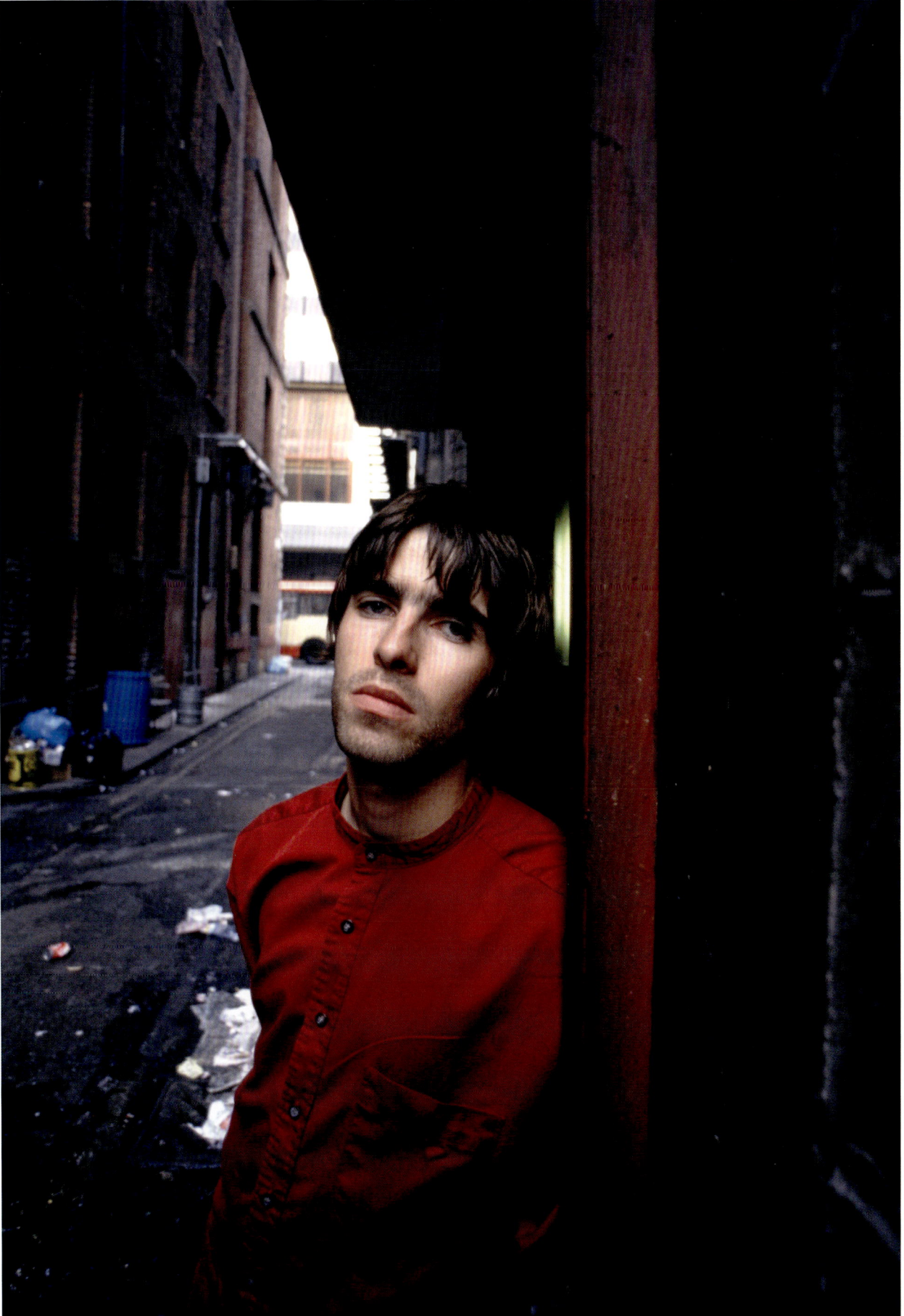

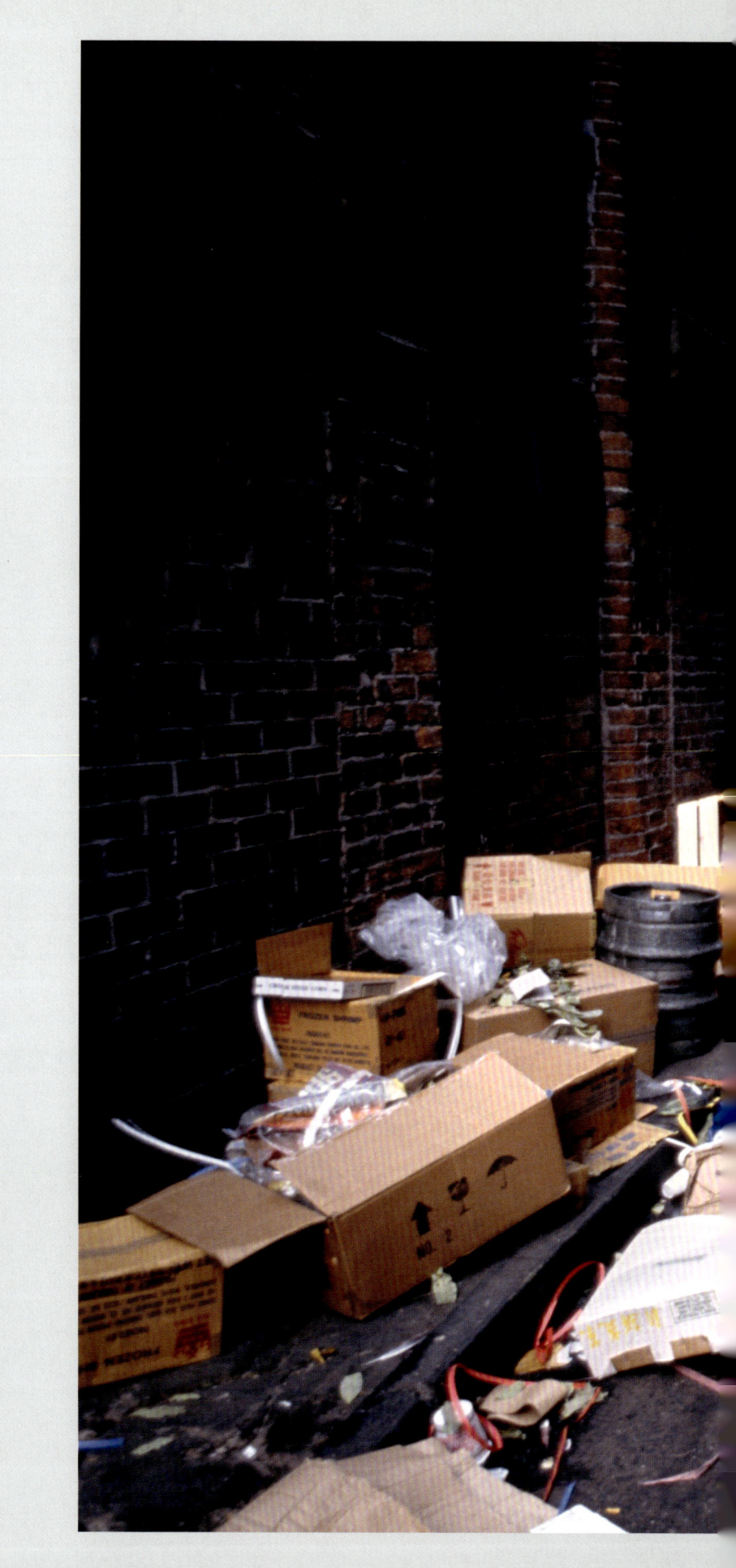

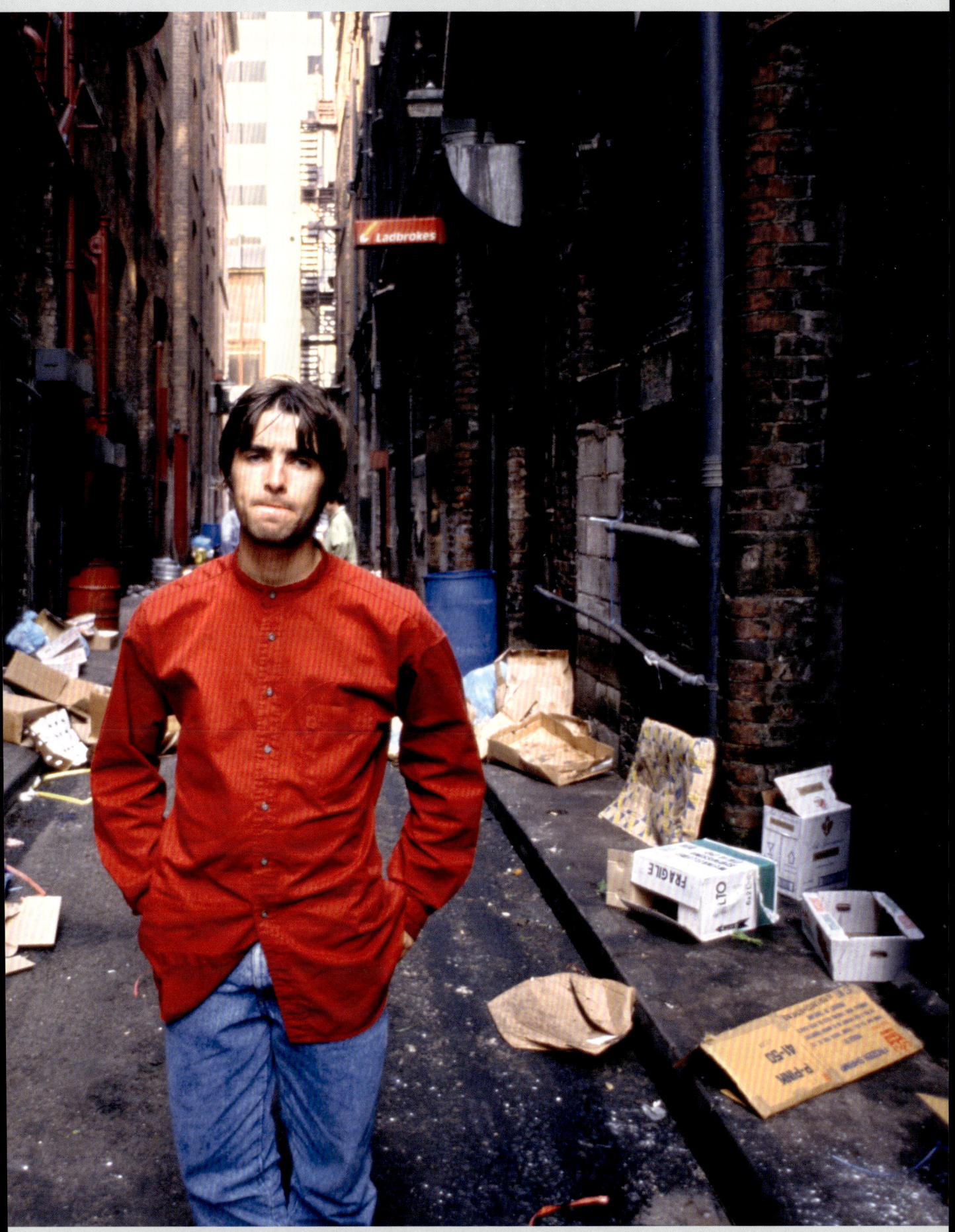

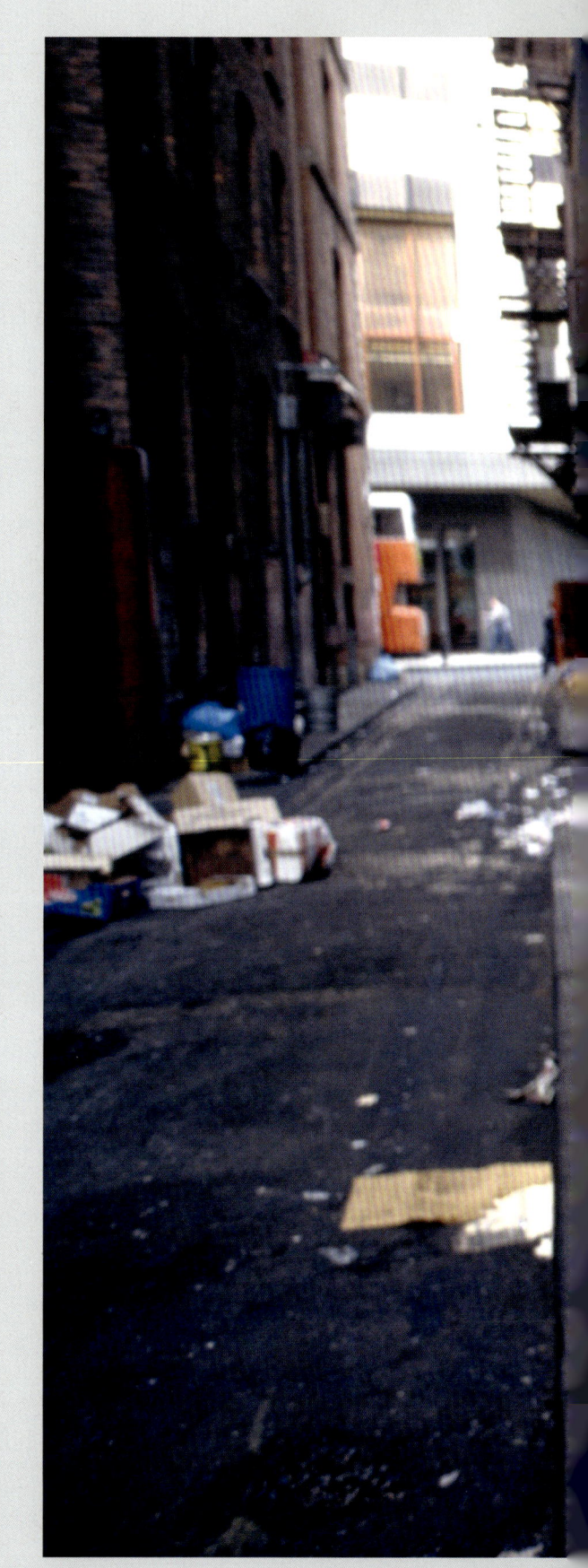

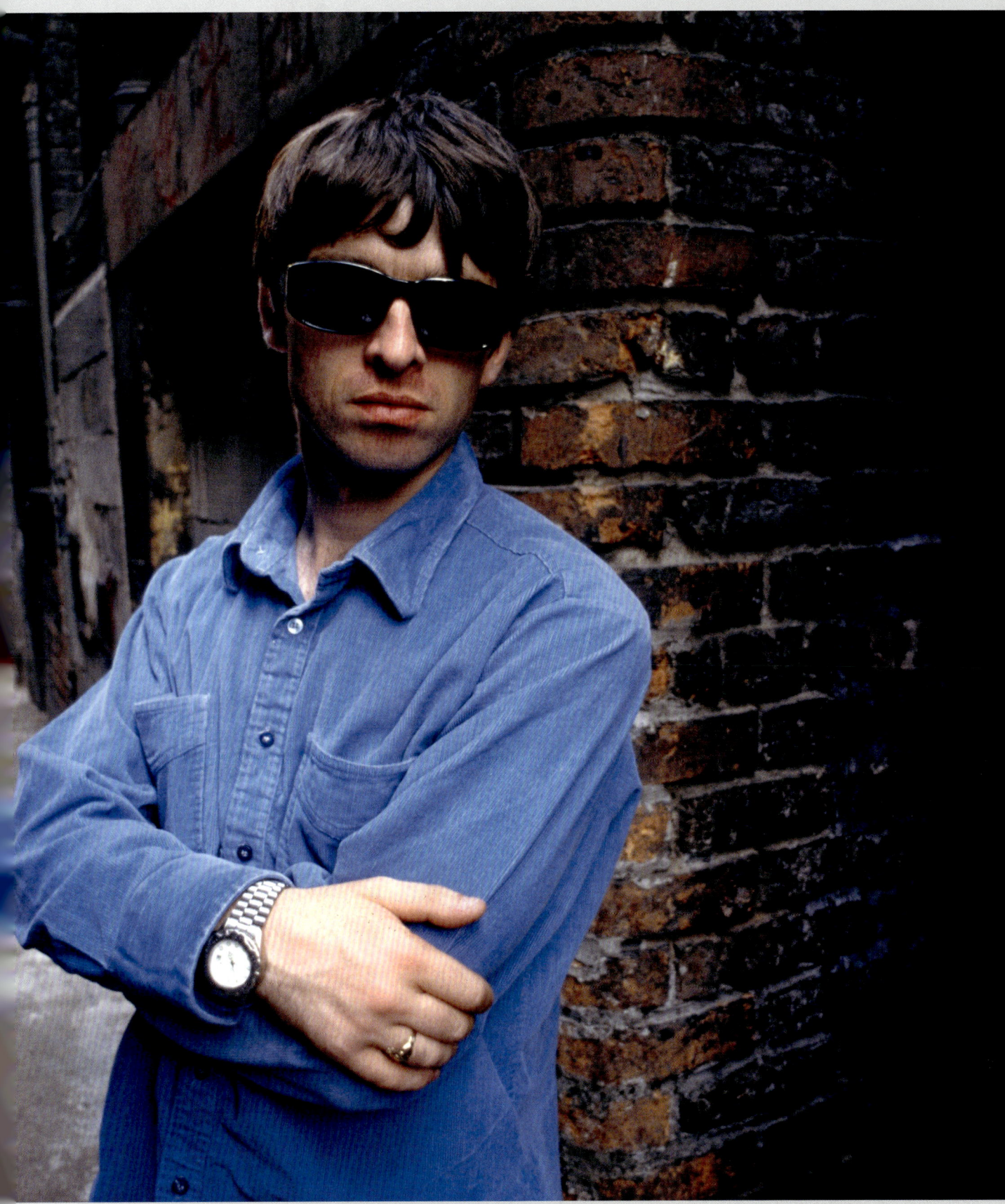

29 JULY

PEVERIL OF THE PEAK, MANCHESTER

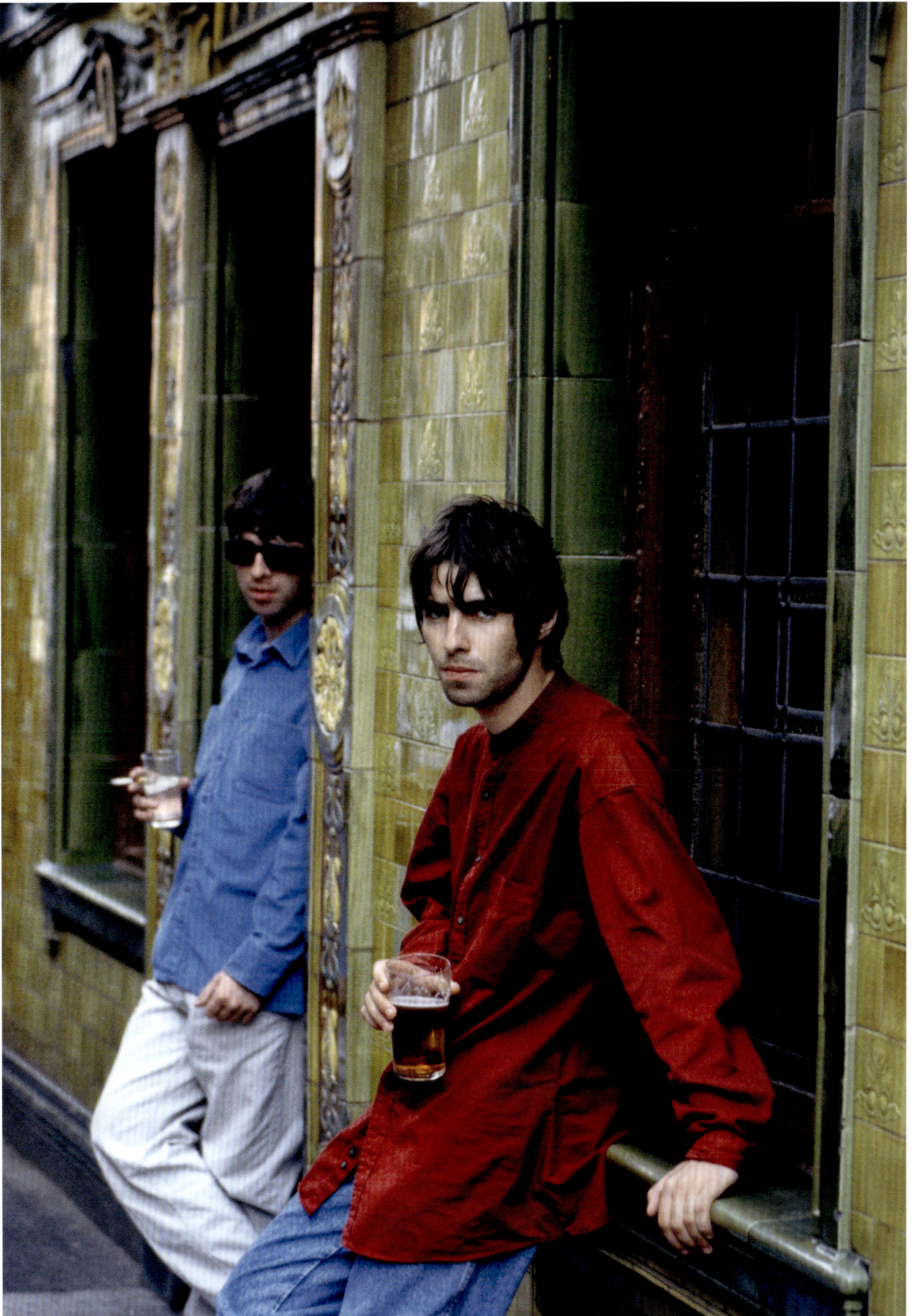

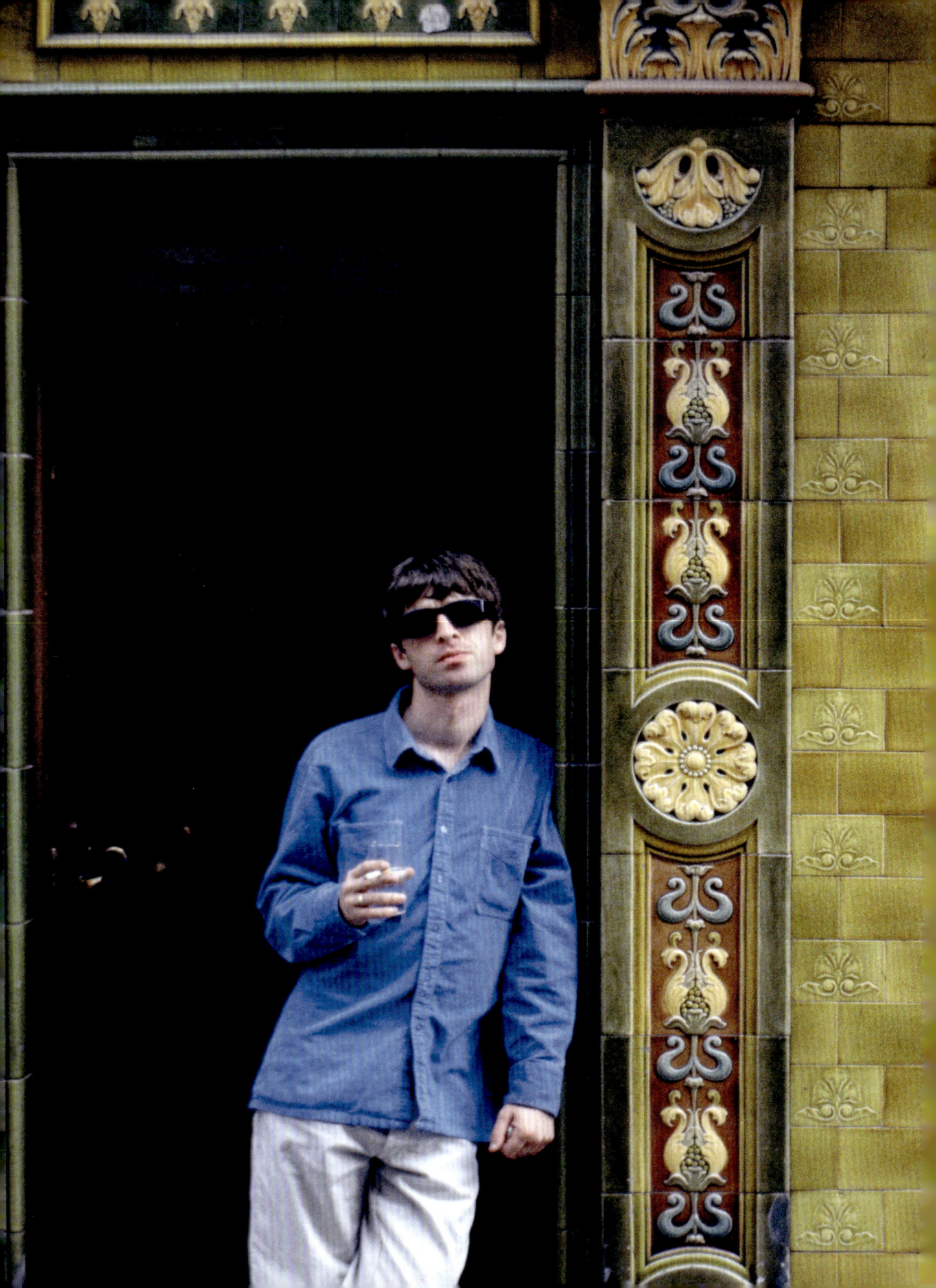

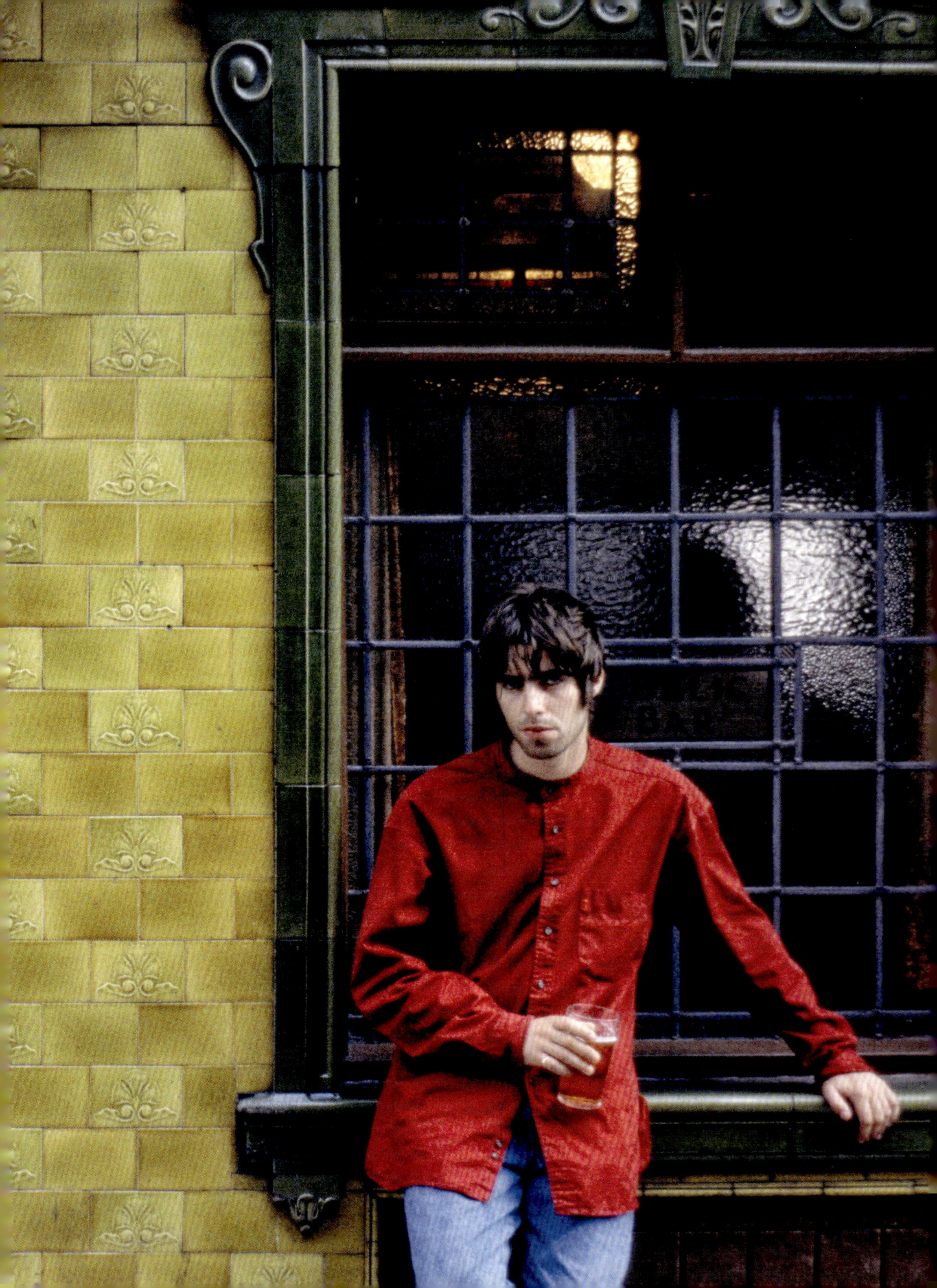

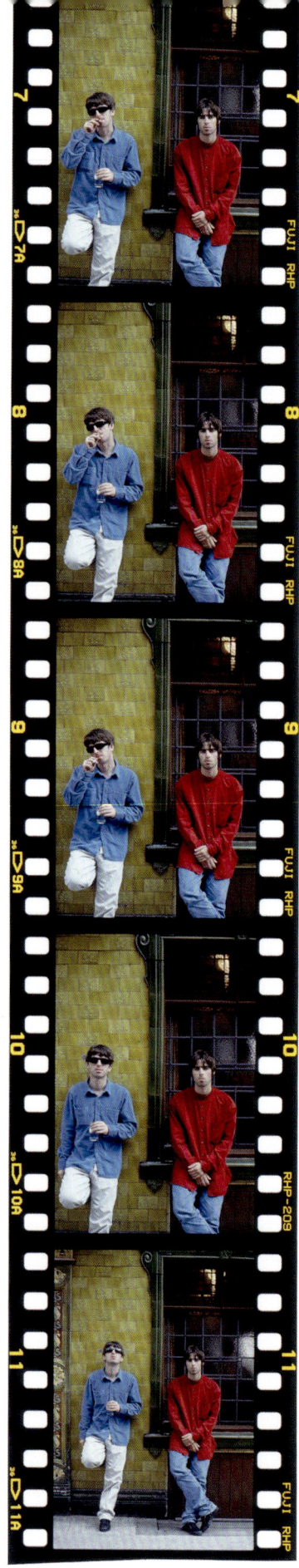

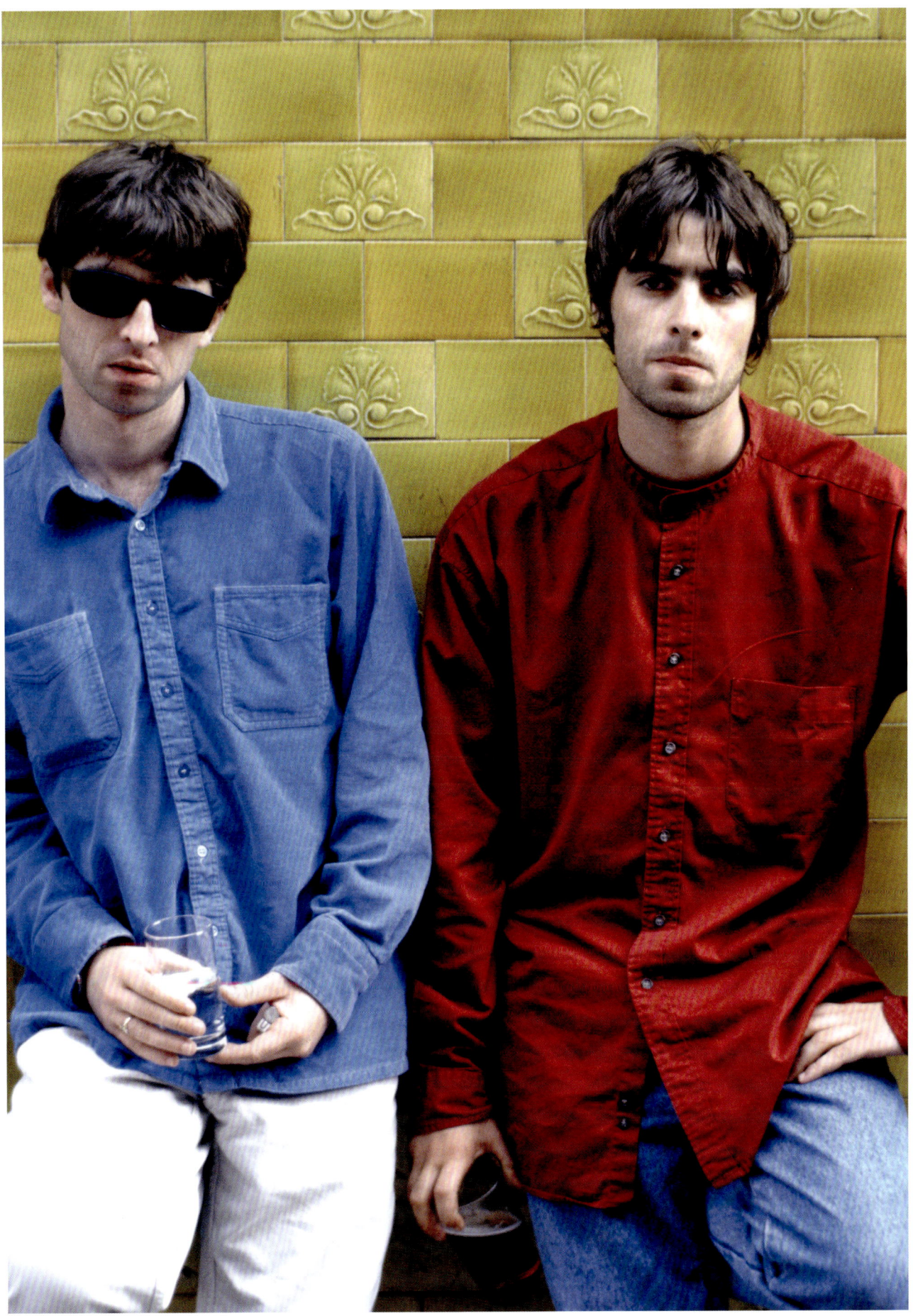

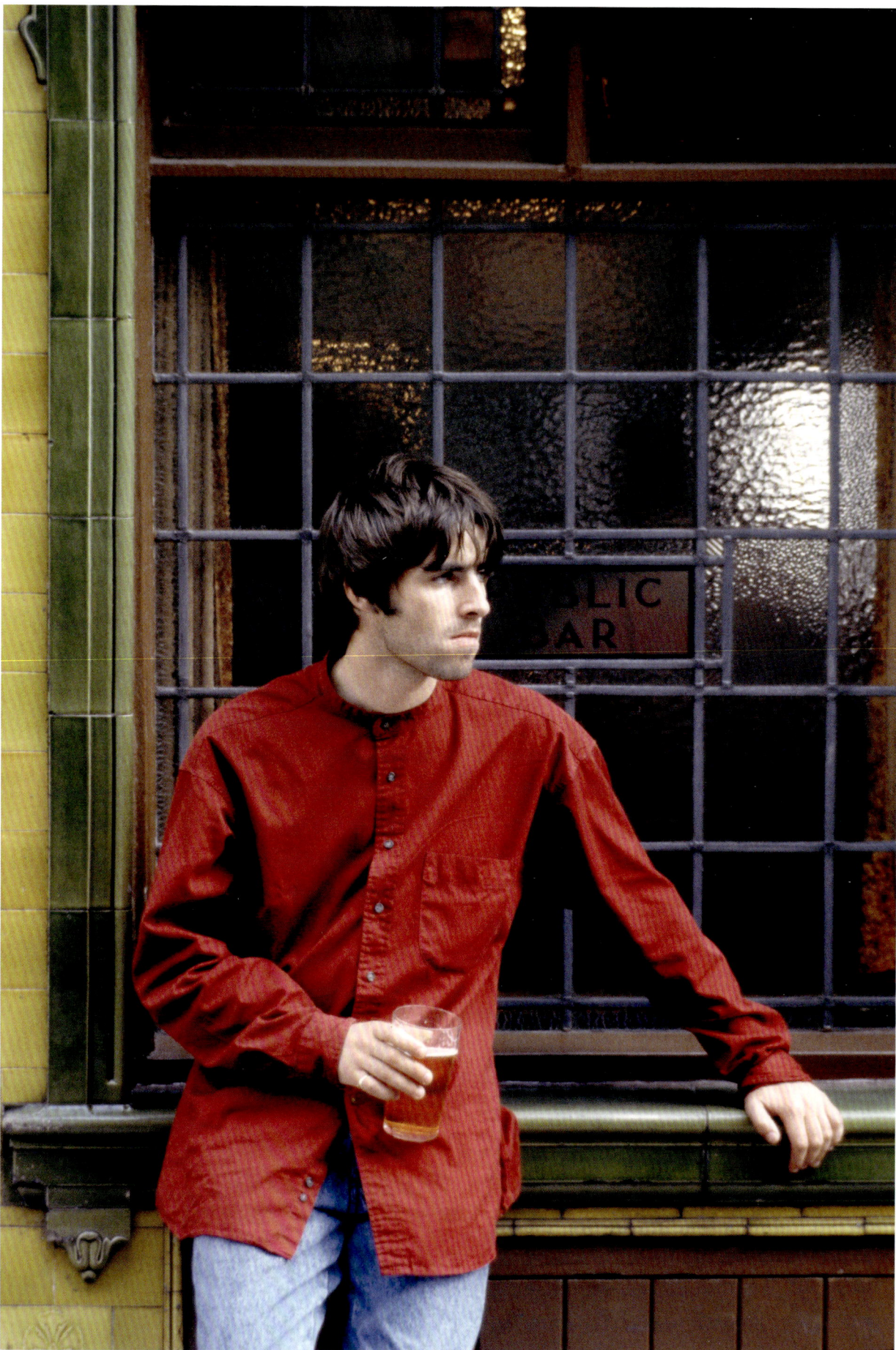

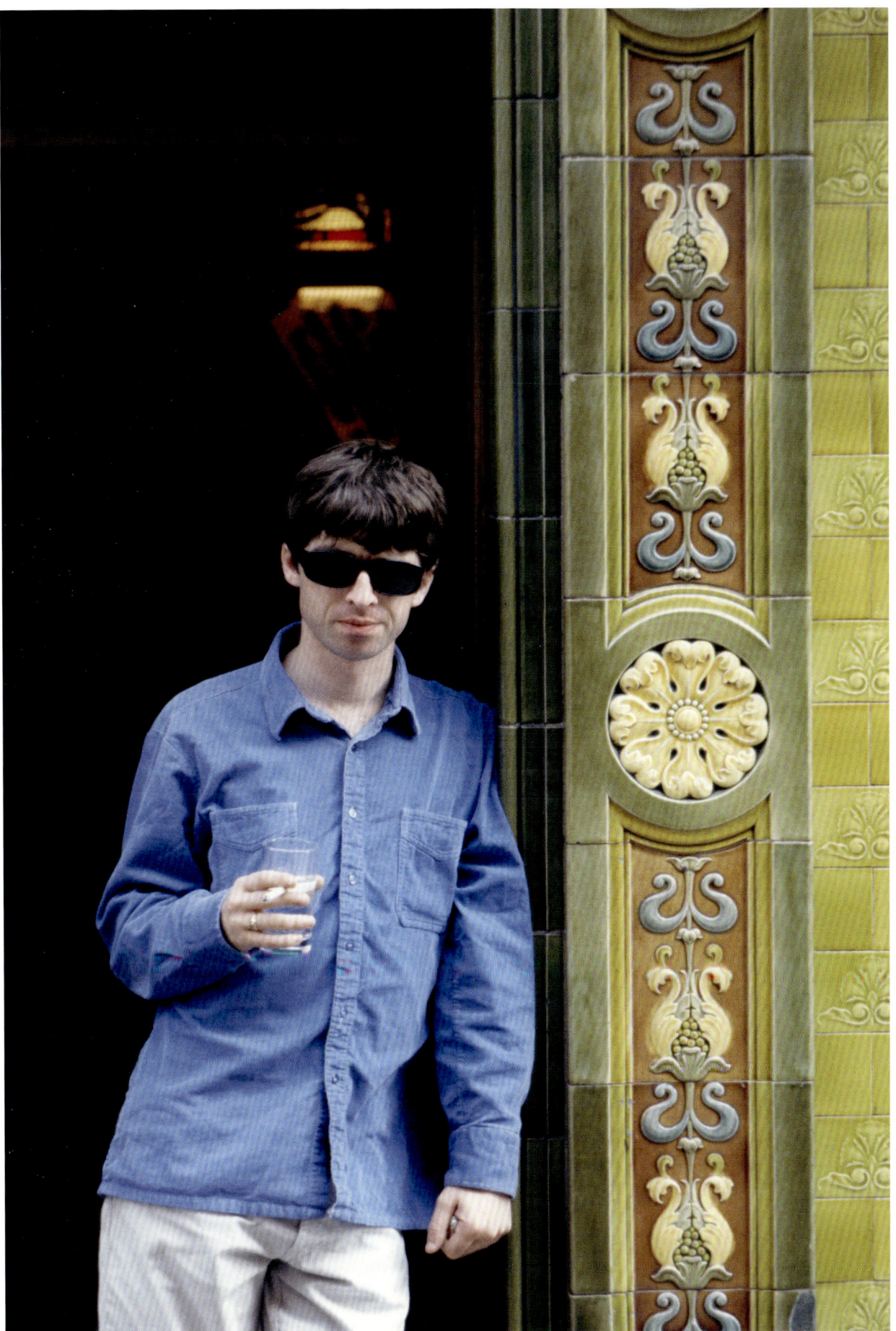

29 JULY

MAINE ROAD, MANCHESTER

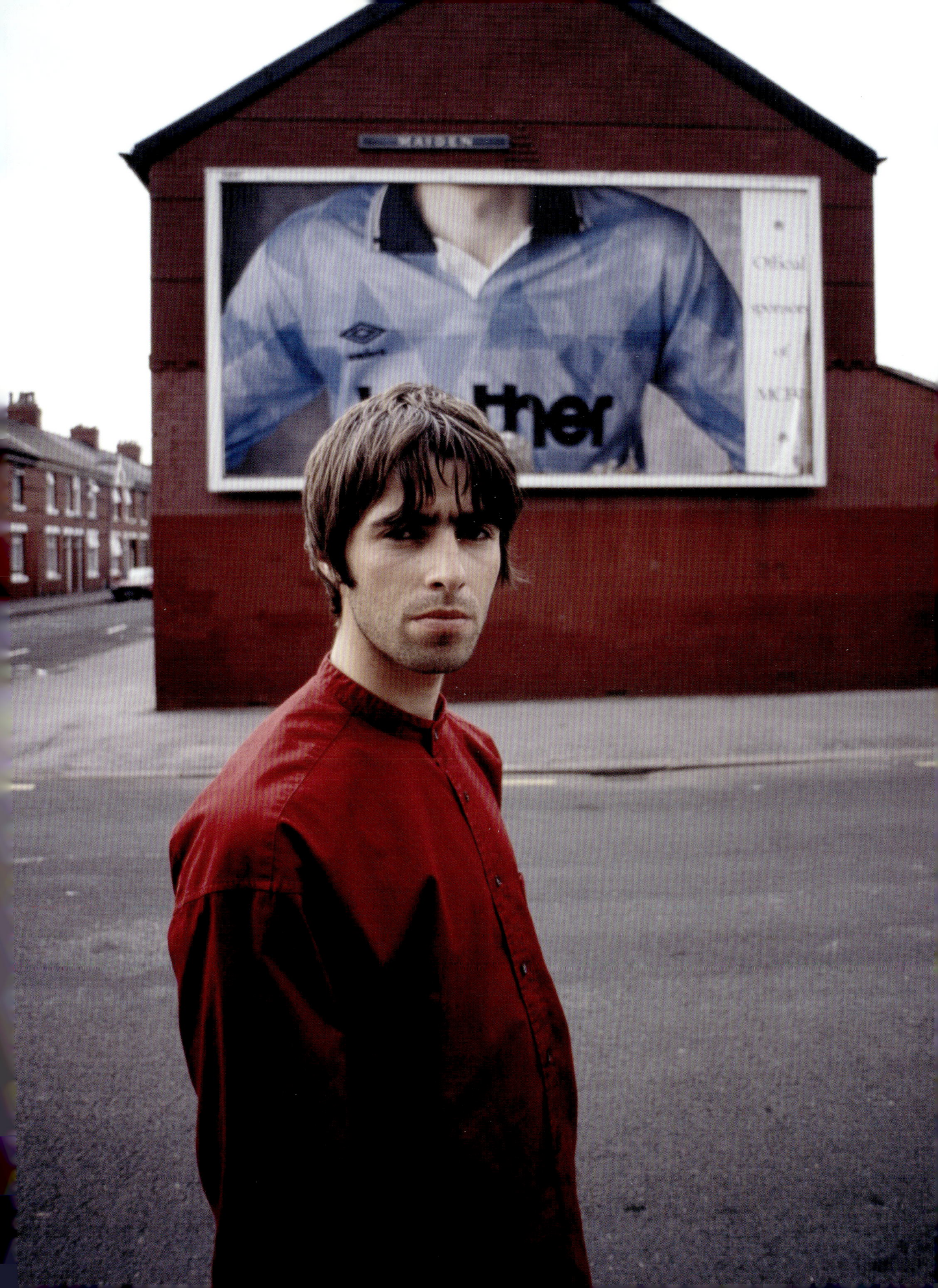

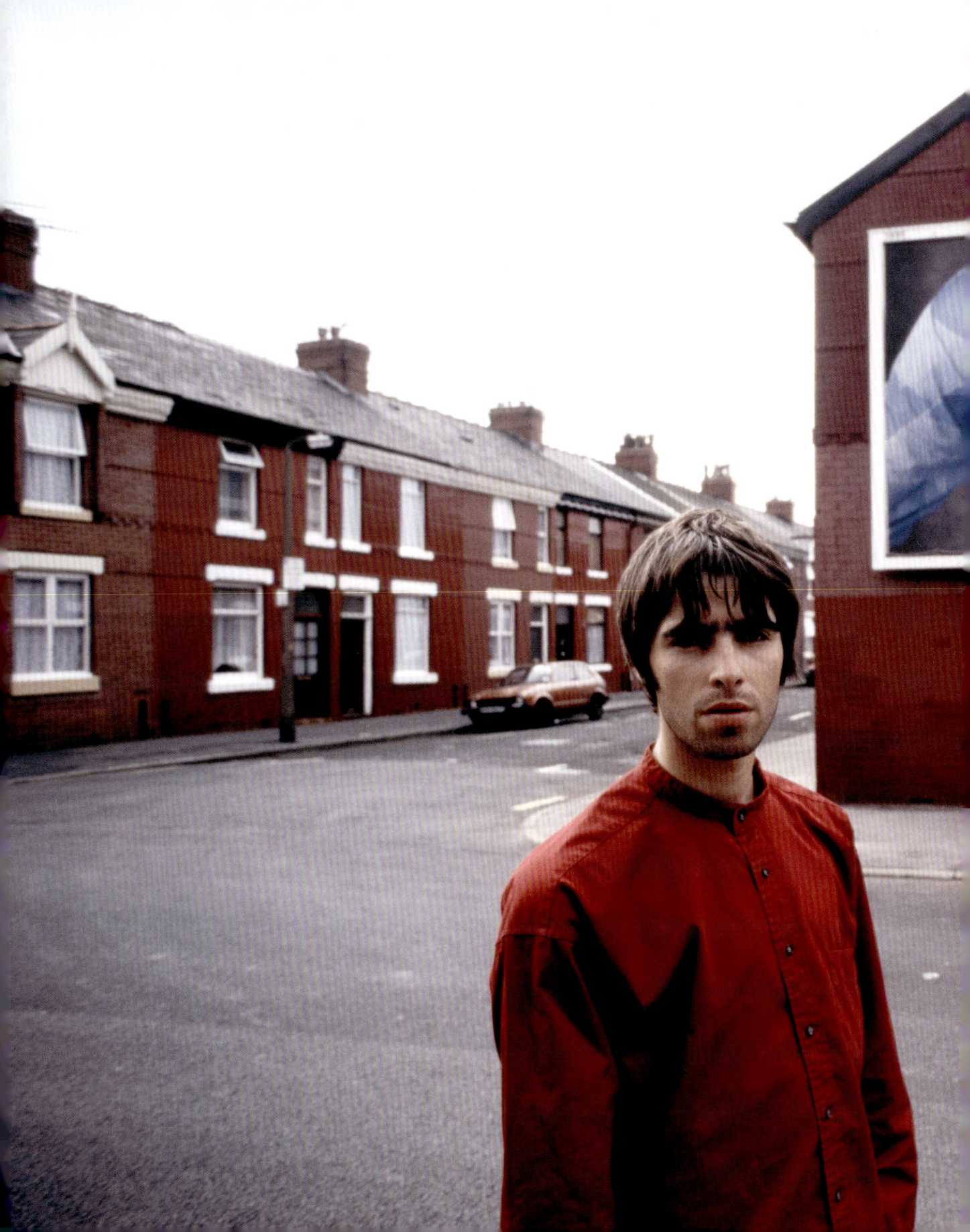

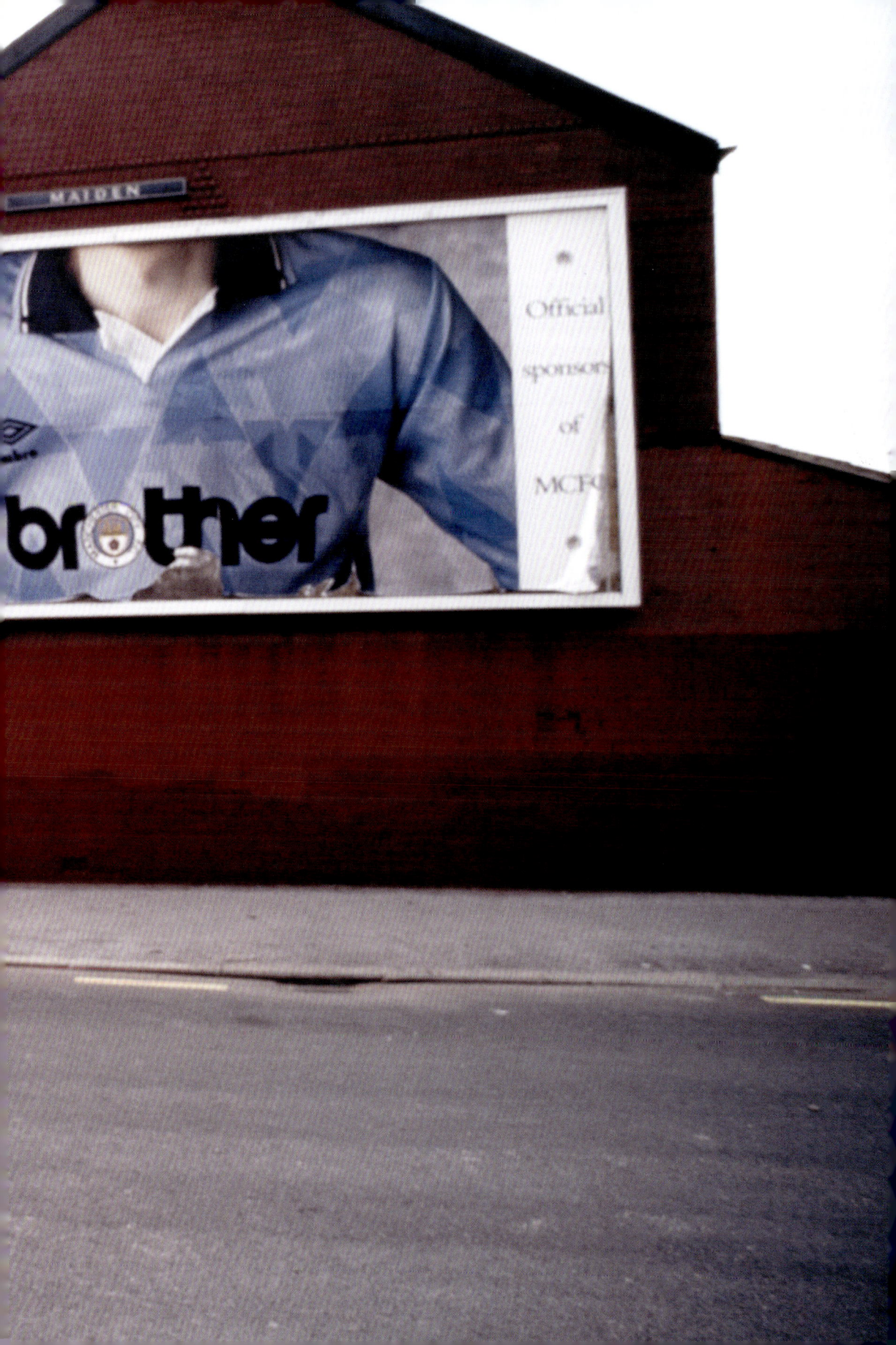

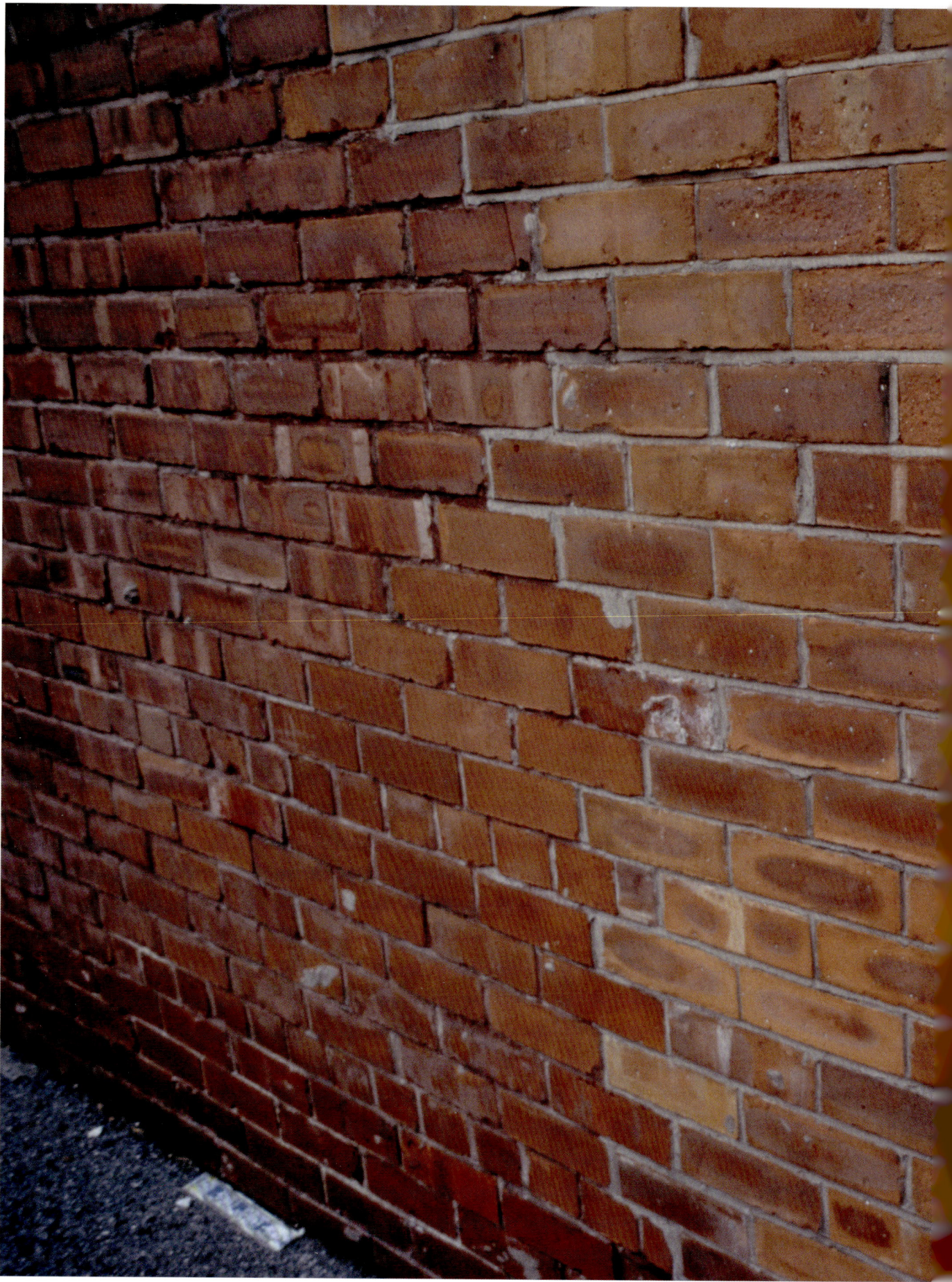

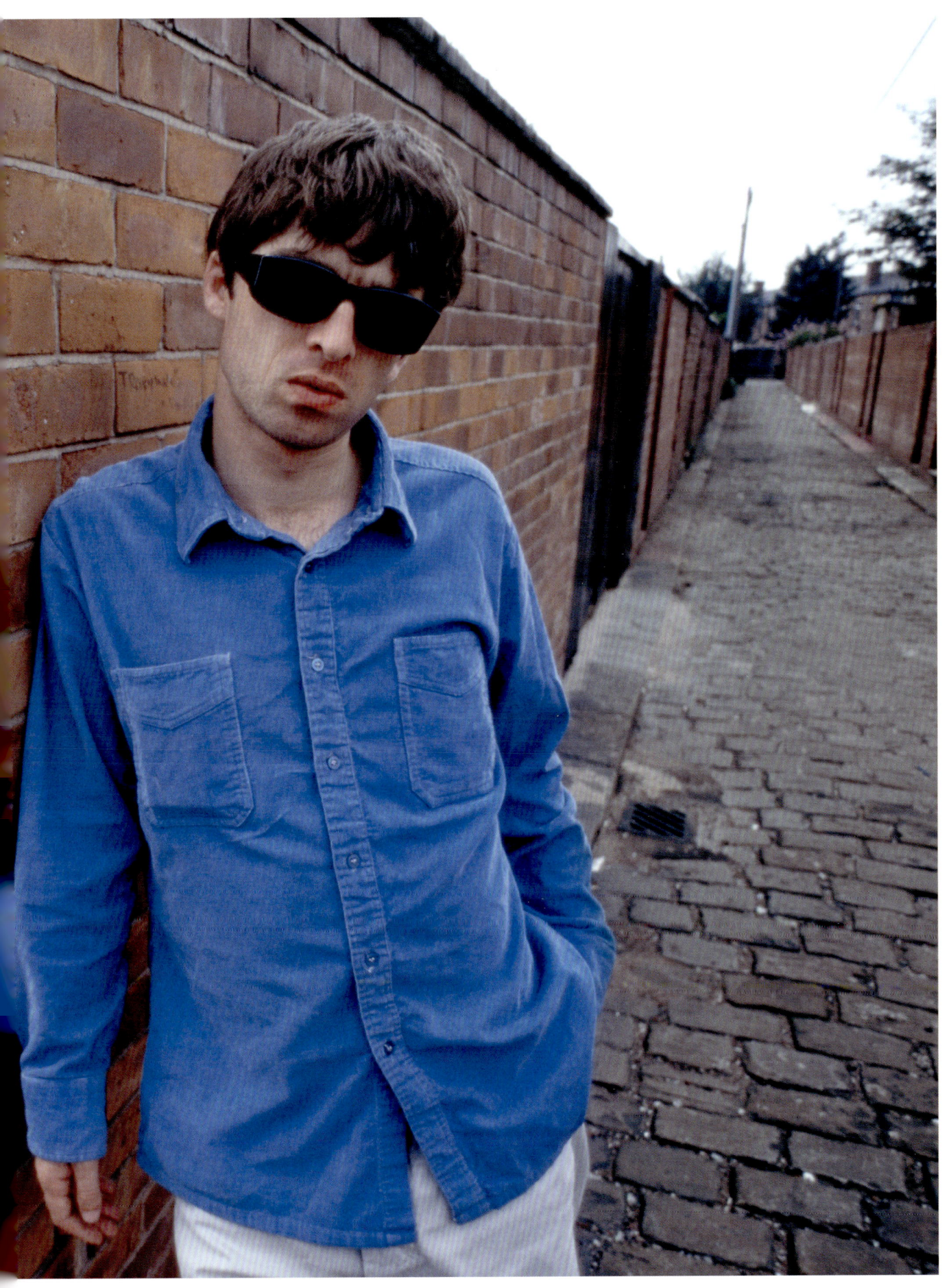

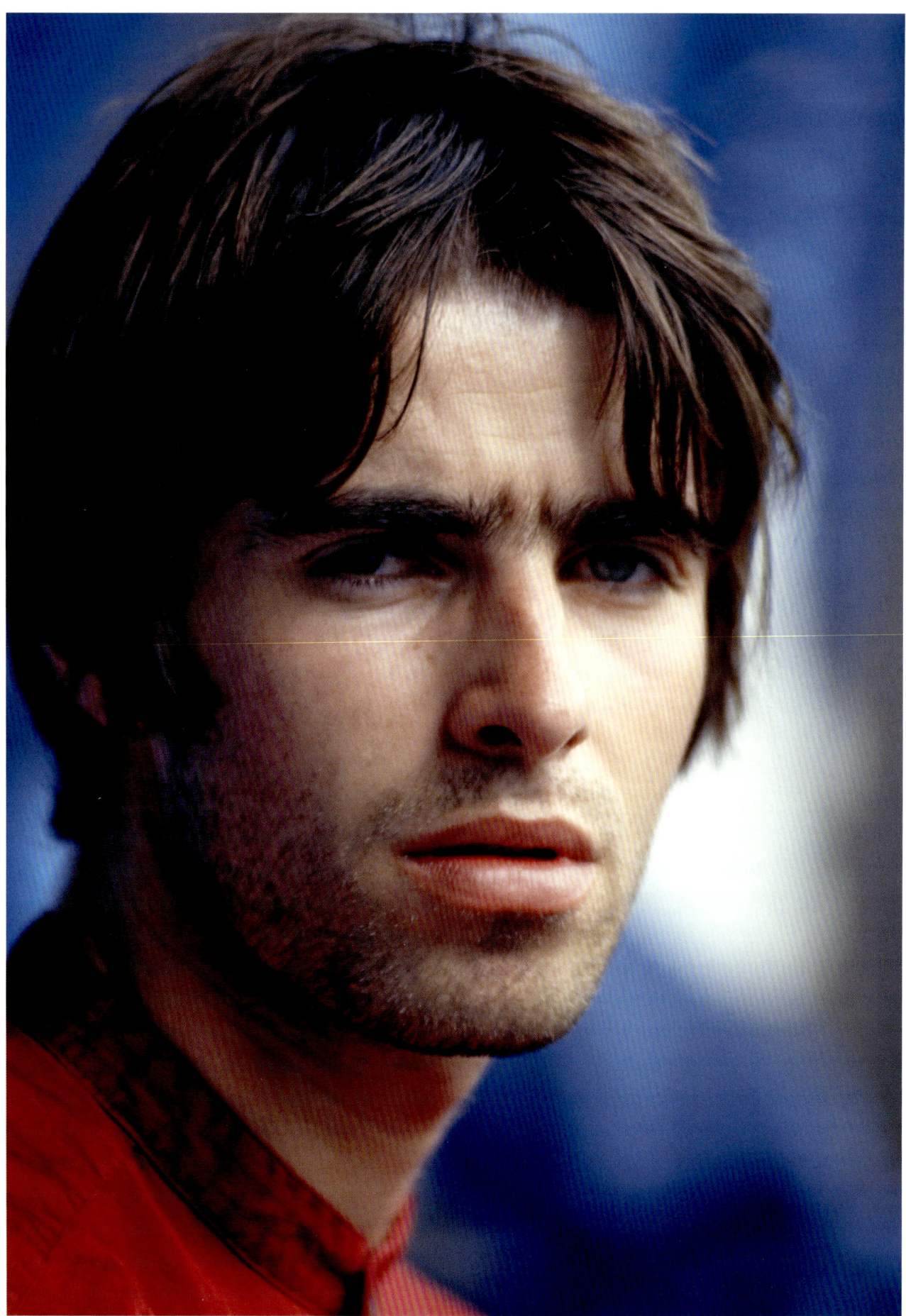

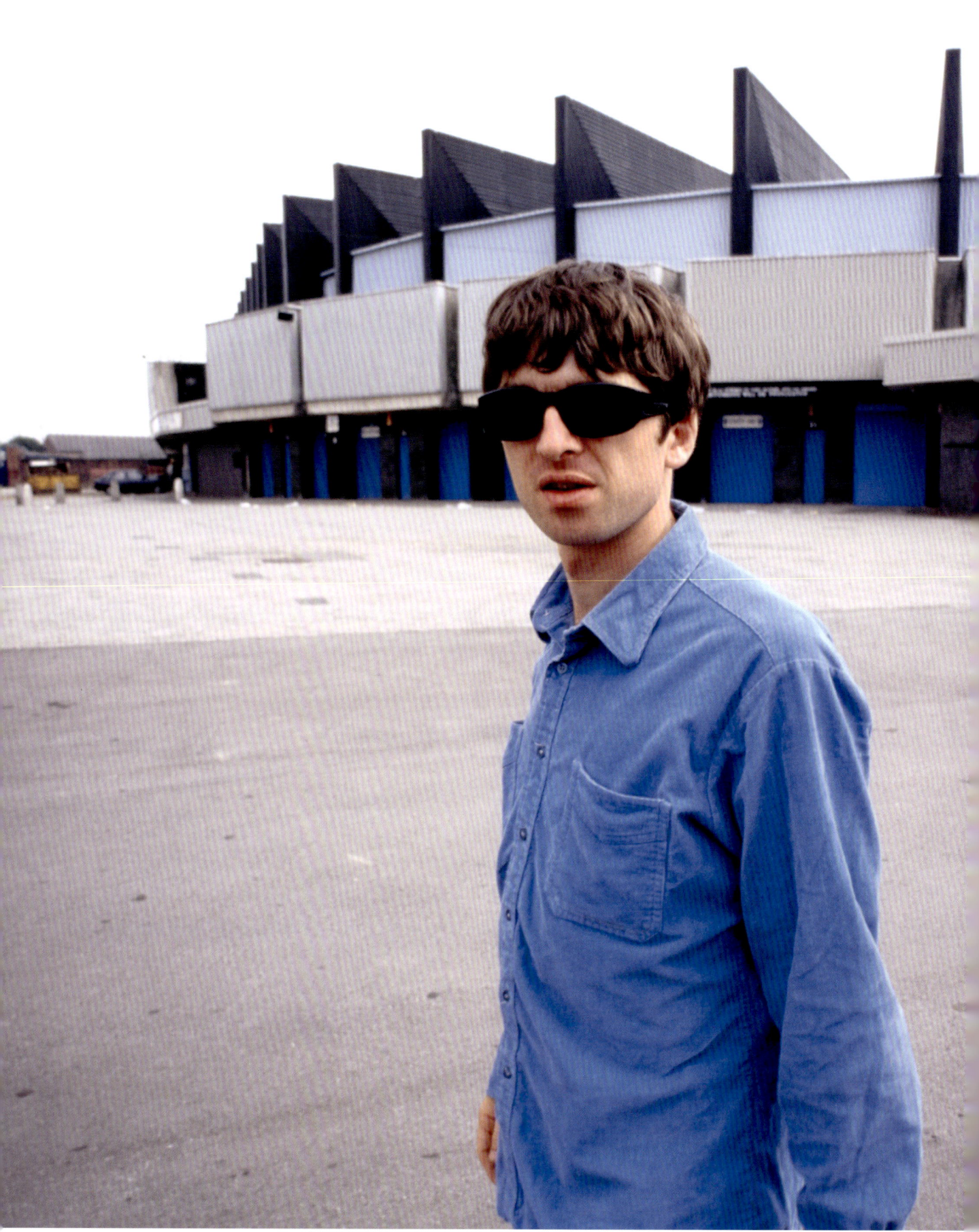

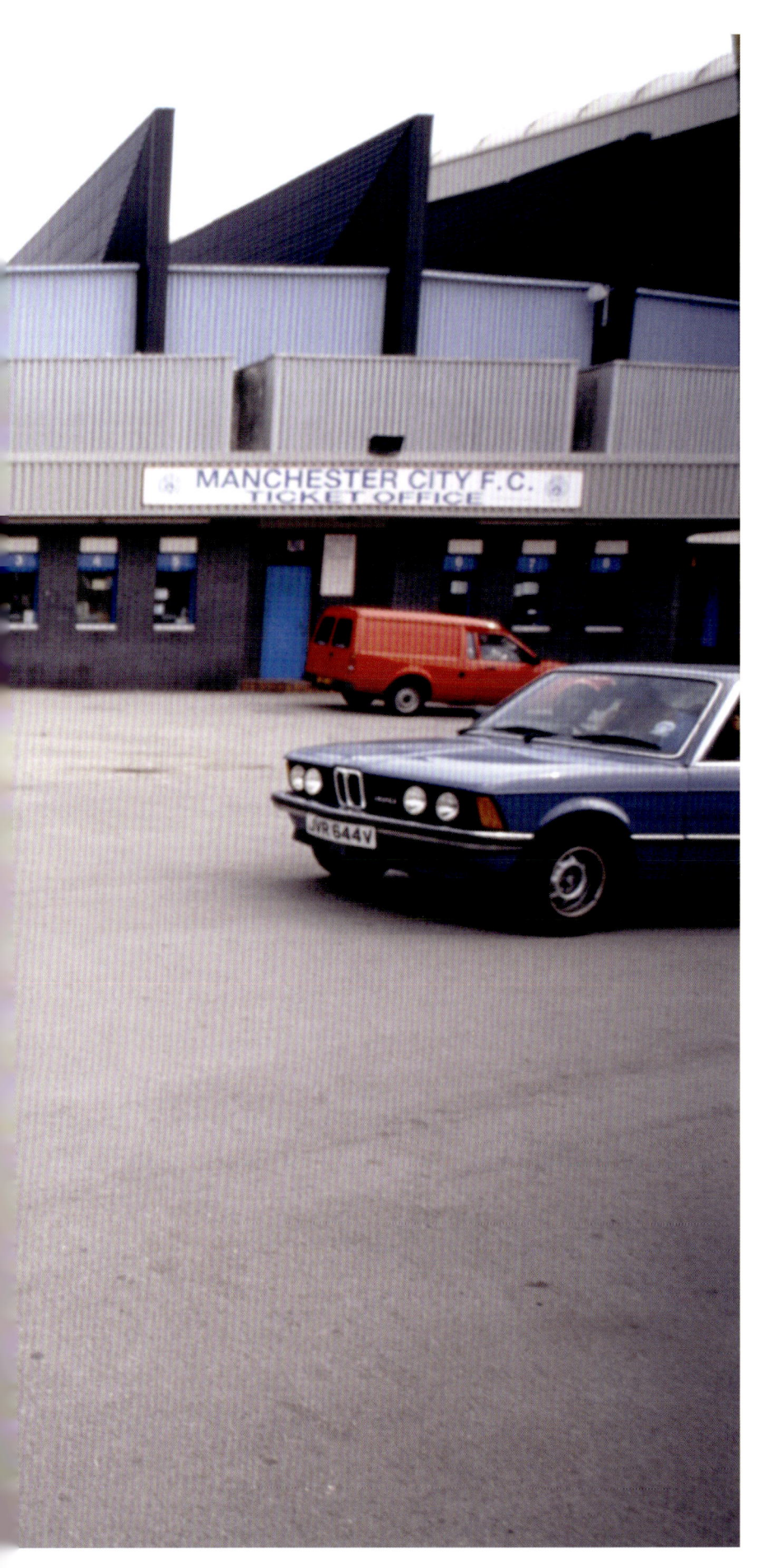

I first got into football like most kids, by playing in the street and at school. Coming from the great North West, football was everything.

My old man watched both City and United – and sometimes (oddly), even Liverpool. He took me to my first game: City v Newcastle at Maine Road in 1974. I don't remember too much about the game, but I do have a clear memory of seeing Bell, Lee and Summerbee play. The stadium seemed enormous to me, and I loved the buzz, the noise and the singing. It was massively overwhelming.

Once you tell everyone at school where you went at the weekend, that's it. You're a Blue for life.

Colin Bell was my absolute hero. He took his place with pride on my bedroom wall among the posters of Franny [Francis Lee], Buzzer [Mike Summerbee], Big Mal [Malcolm Allison] and, erm, The Bay City Rollers – all the greats. I dreamed of being a footballer; what lad didn't?

I played a bit for my school team. Was I any good? Not particularly, no.

But I loved the ritual of going down to Maine Road for a match. Walking from our house, on Stockport Road in Longsight, to the ground, being passed over the turnstiles by a complete stranger, then waiting for my old man to get through. I vividly recall the strong smells of hot dogs and piss. I still associate that pungent cocktail with football, even today.

City fans don't sing many Oasis songs. They've adapted a few, such as "She's Electric" for Éderson: "He's Brazilian, he only cost 30 million…" And I remember a half-arsed "Wonderwall" adaptation back in '95. I never really liked that one really, but it's a real honour when you see the huge banners and flags with some Oasis reference on them. It's the ultimate for me. To have the respect of the lads on the terraces is, well, there's no higher accolade.

I still can't get my head round the fact that so many players are Oasis fans. Sergio Agüero regularly messages me, and I've been with them in the changing room for title celebrations more than once. KdB [Kevin de Bruyne] handing you a beer while singing "Wonderwall" is fucking nuts. Pep [Guardiola] is my mate; actually, for real. I love him so much, it's a fucking joke!

It's a real privilege to be able to wander in to say "Hi" to the lads. It doesn't get any better.

—*Noel Gallagher*

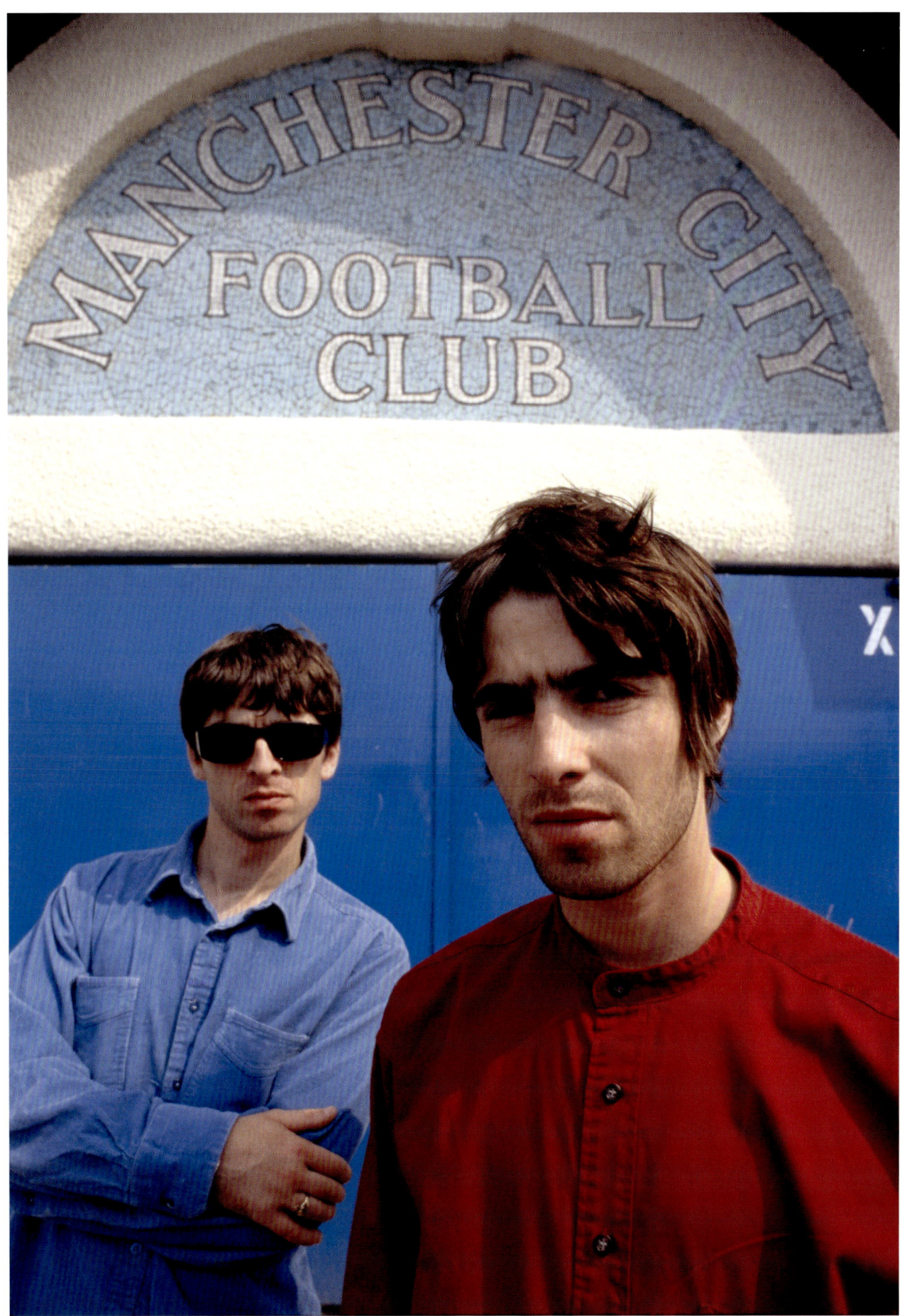

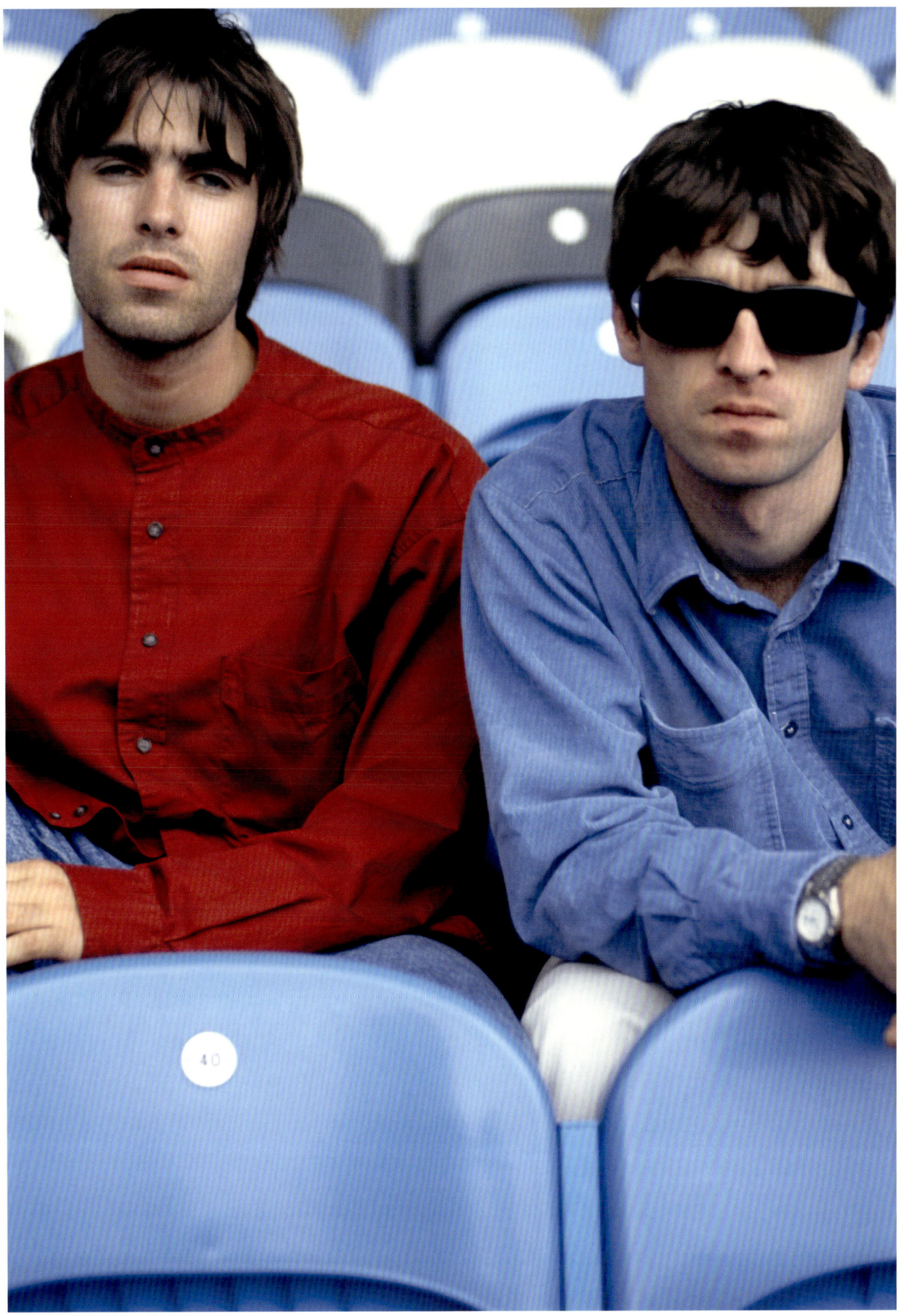

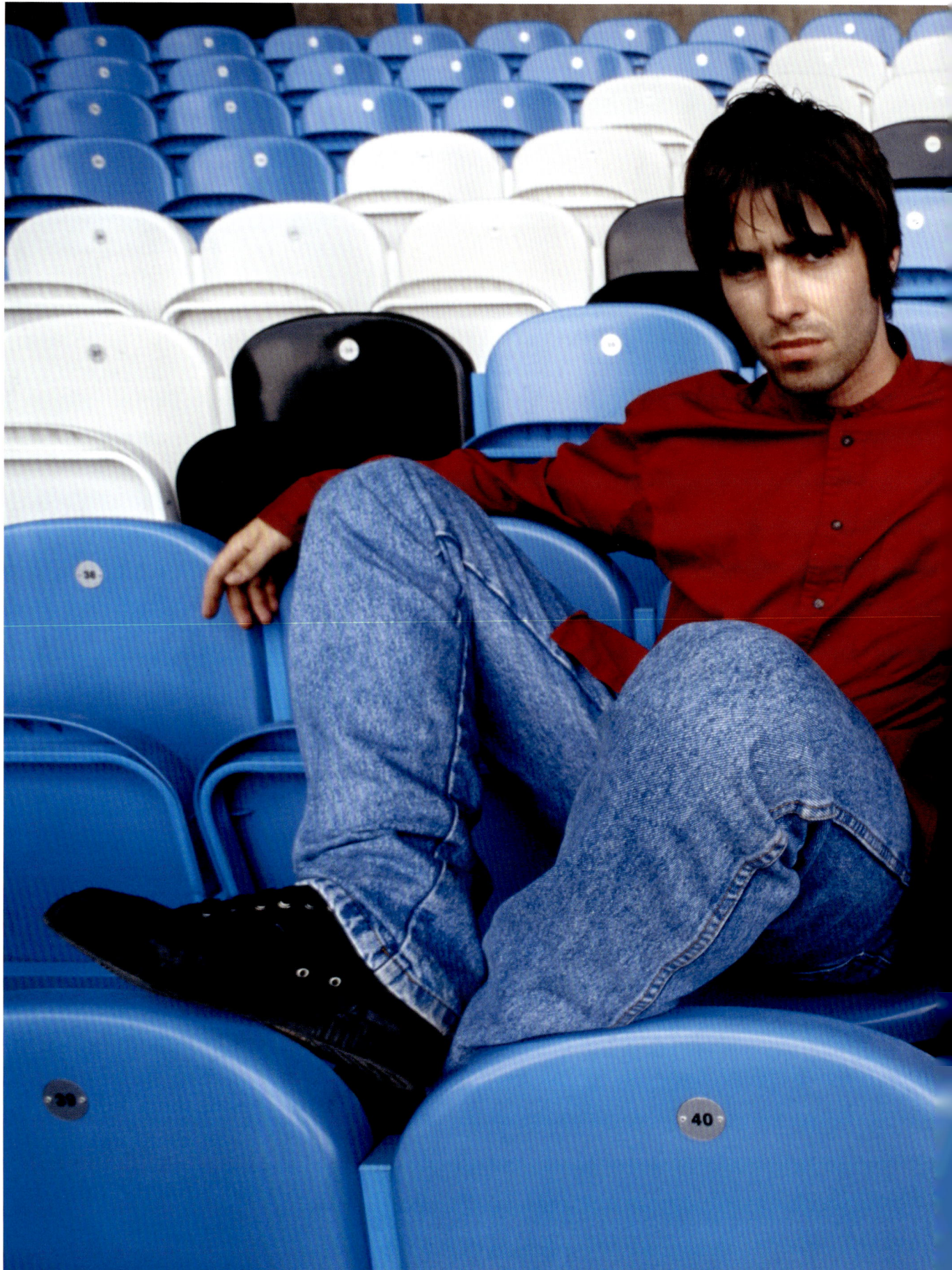

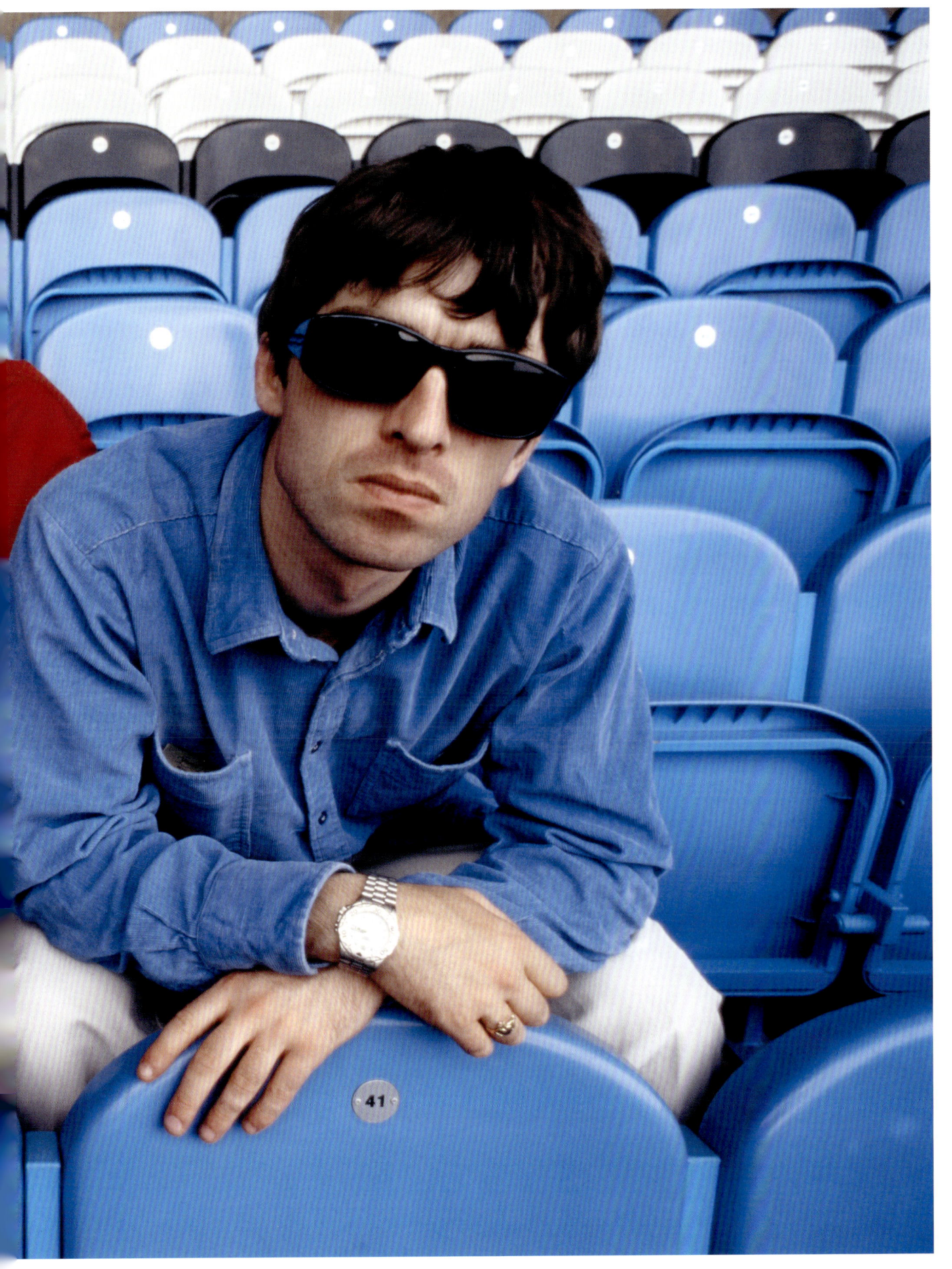

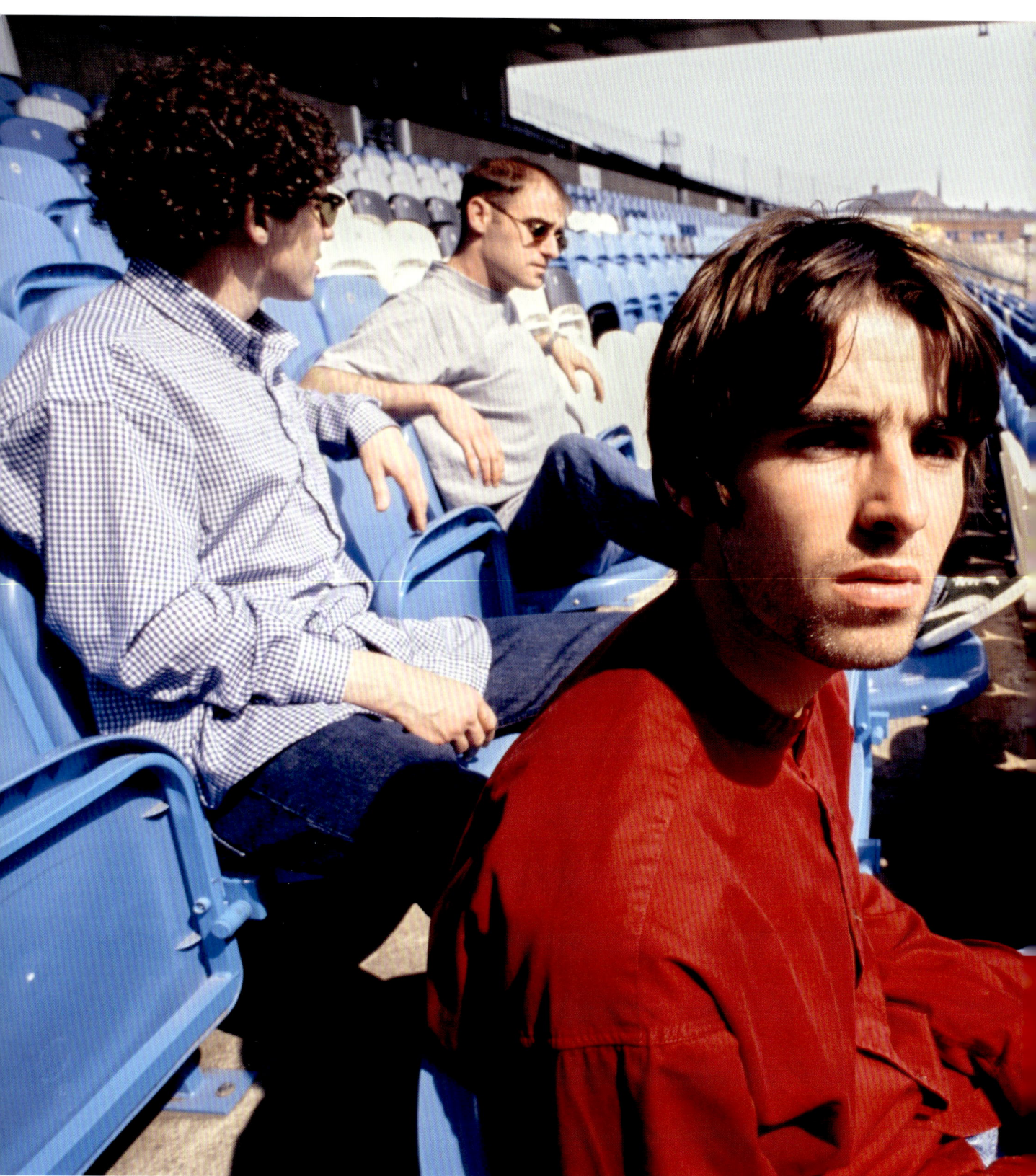

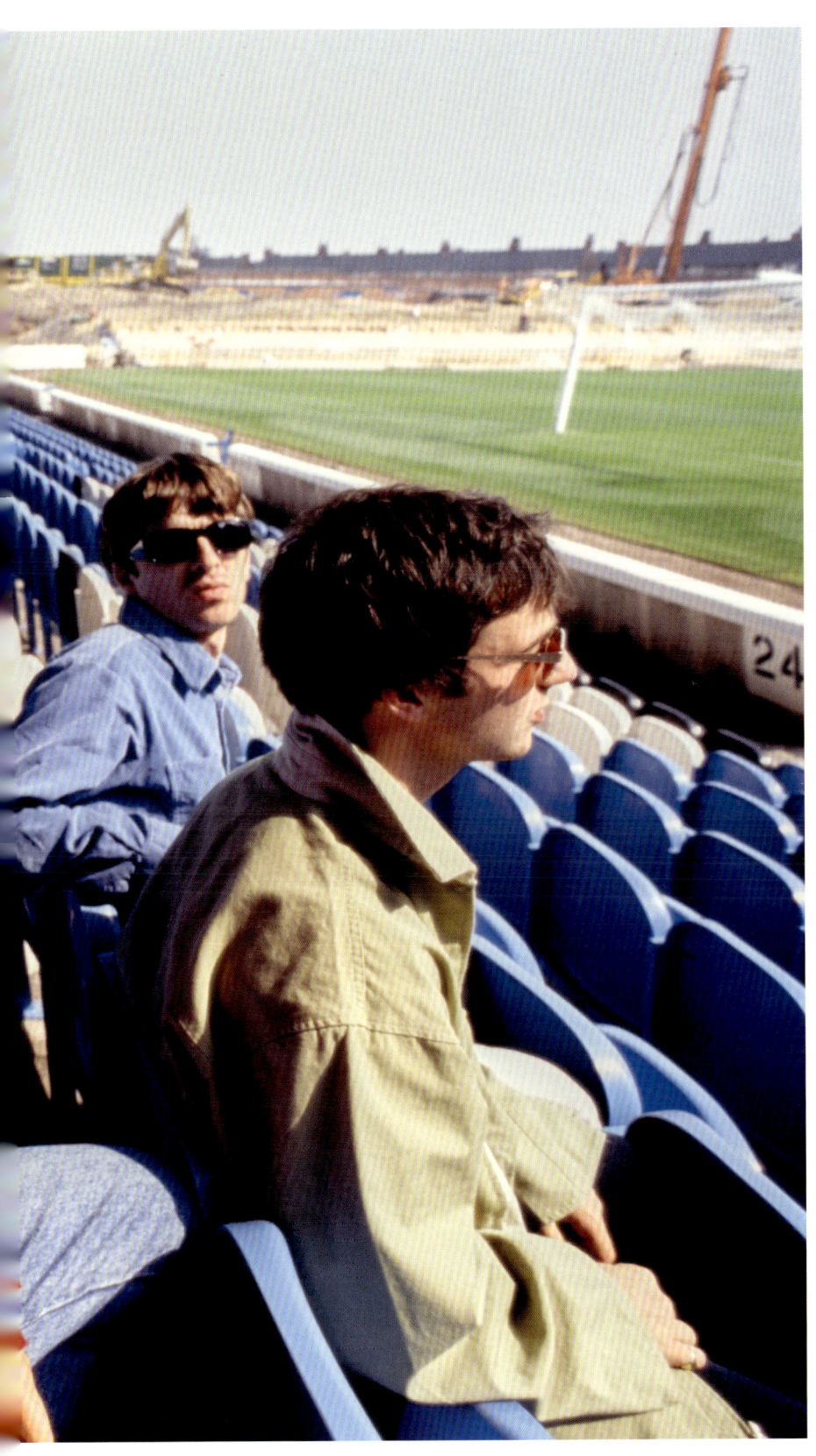

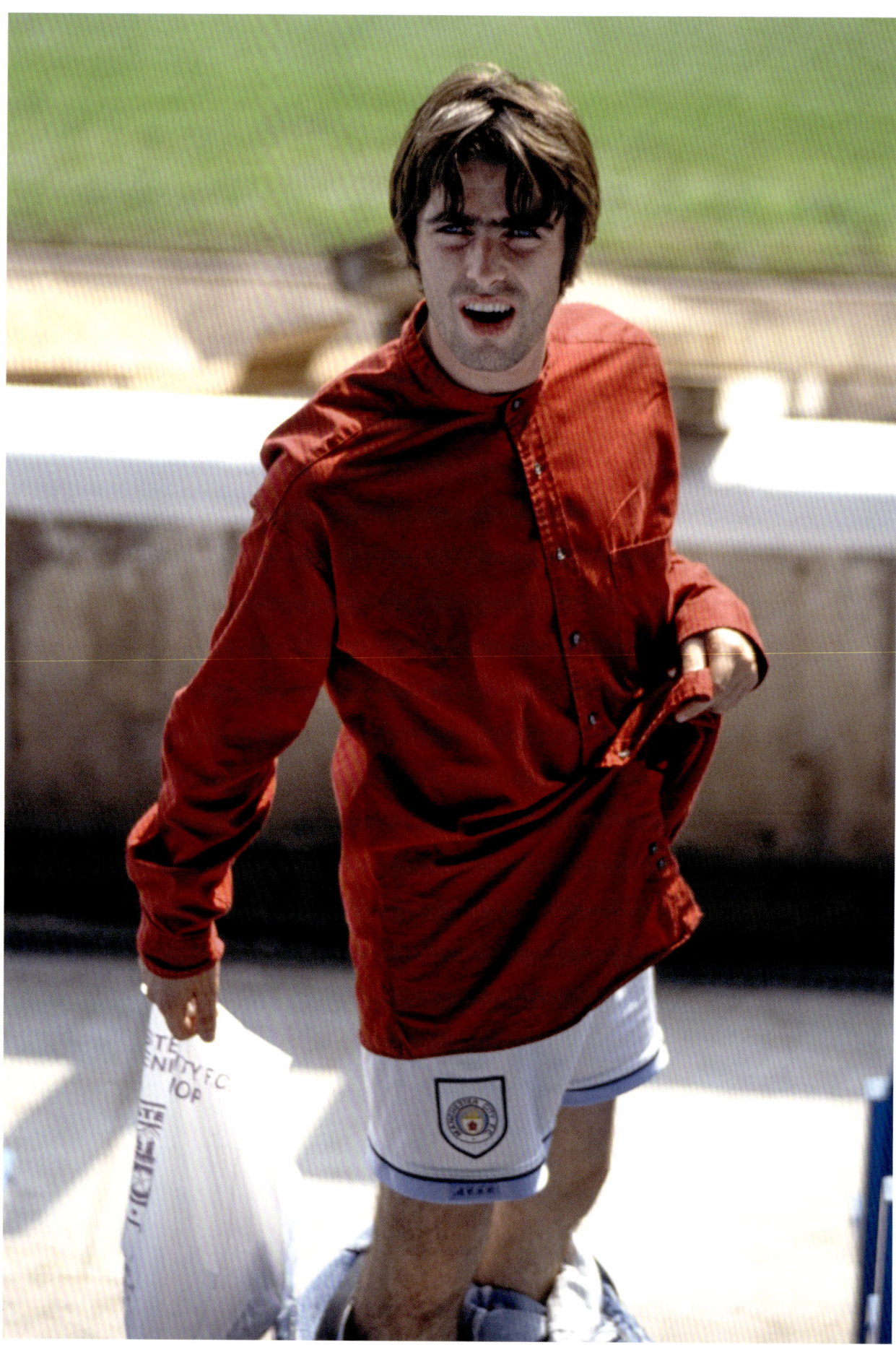

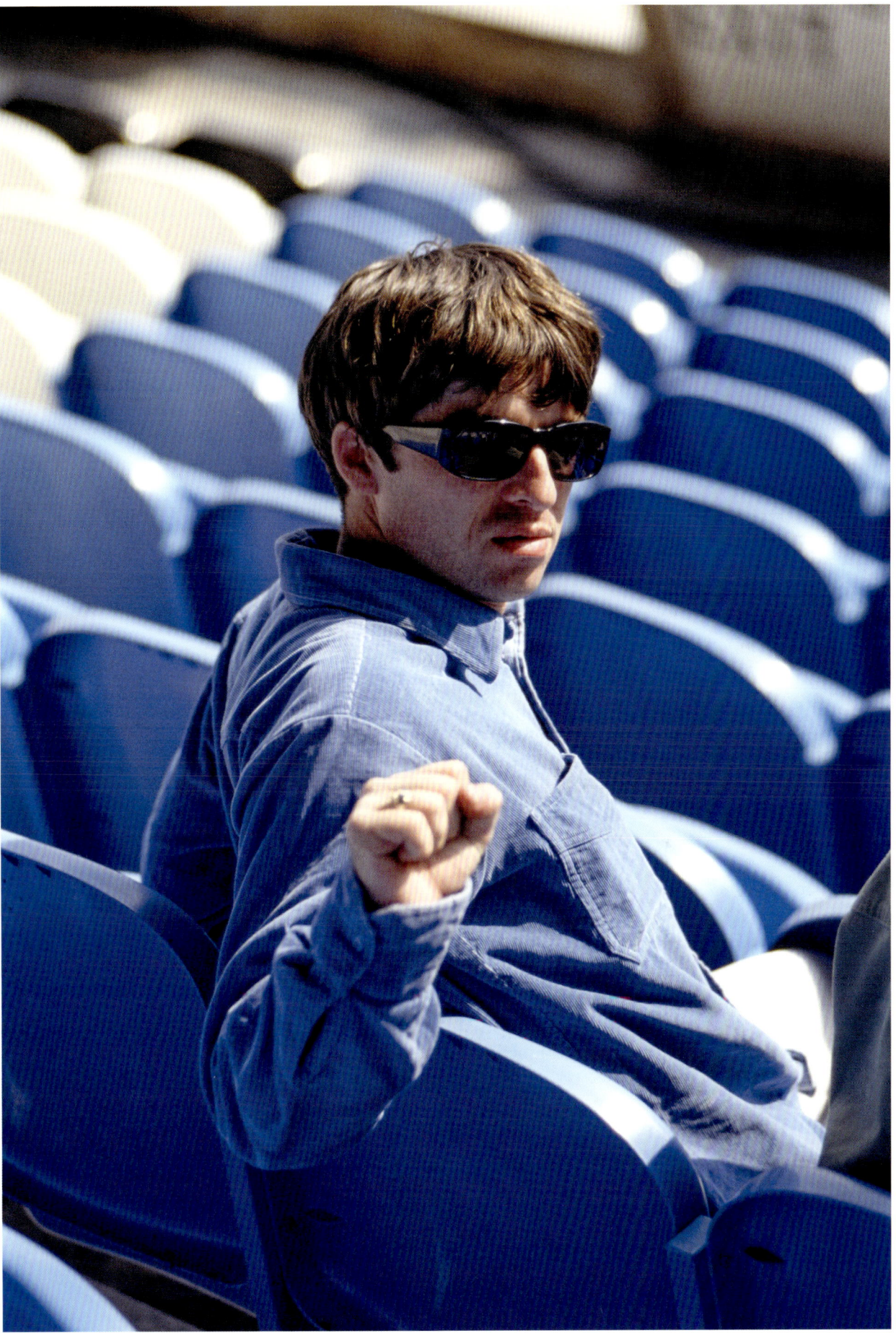

29 JULY
PORTLAND STREET, MANCHESTER

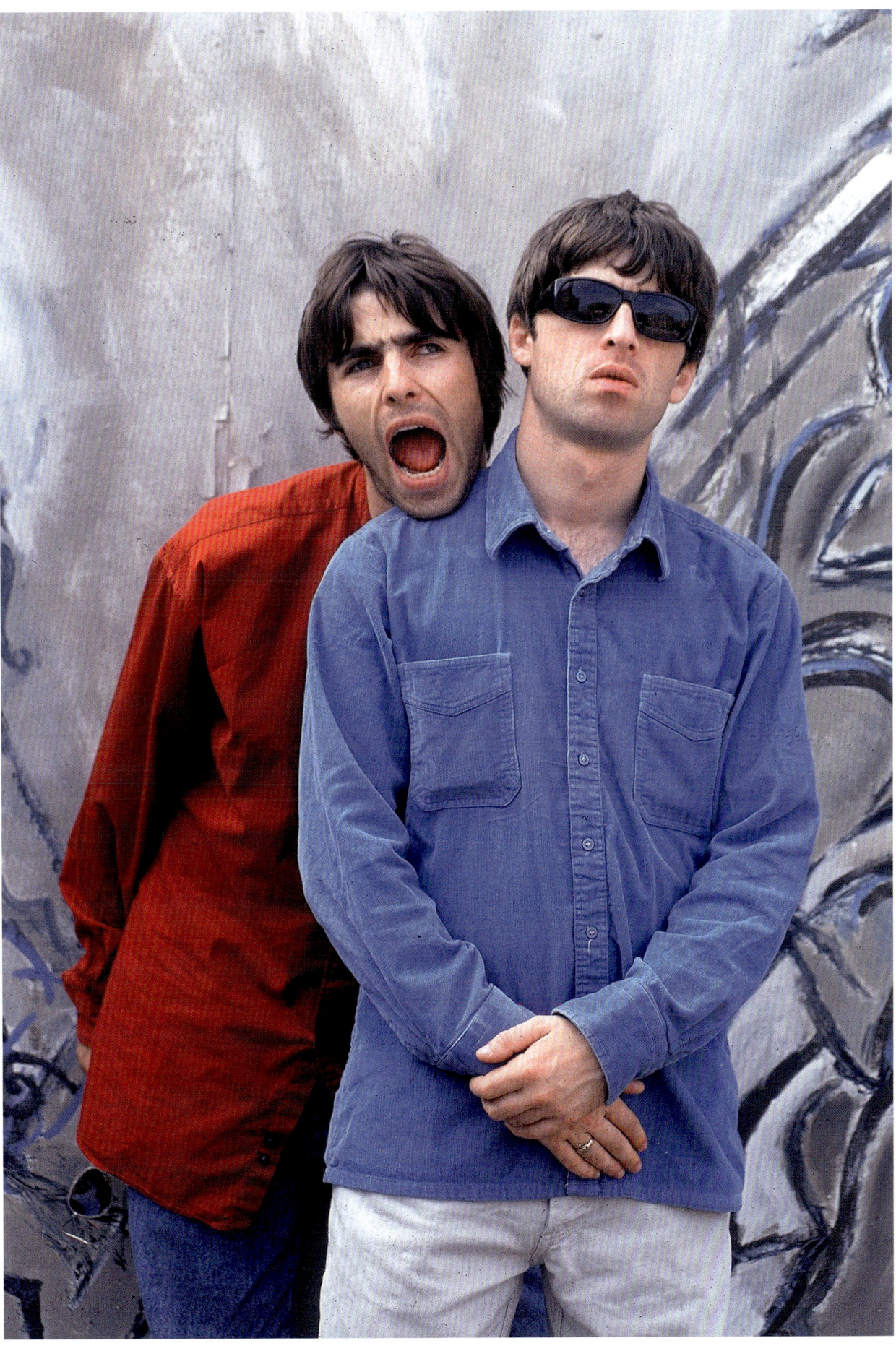

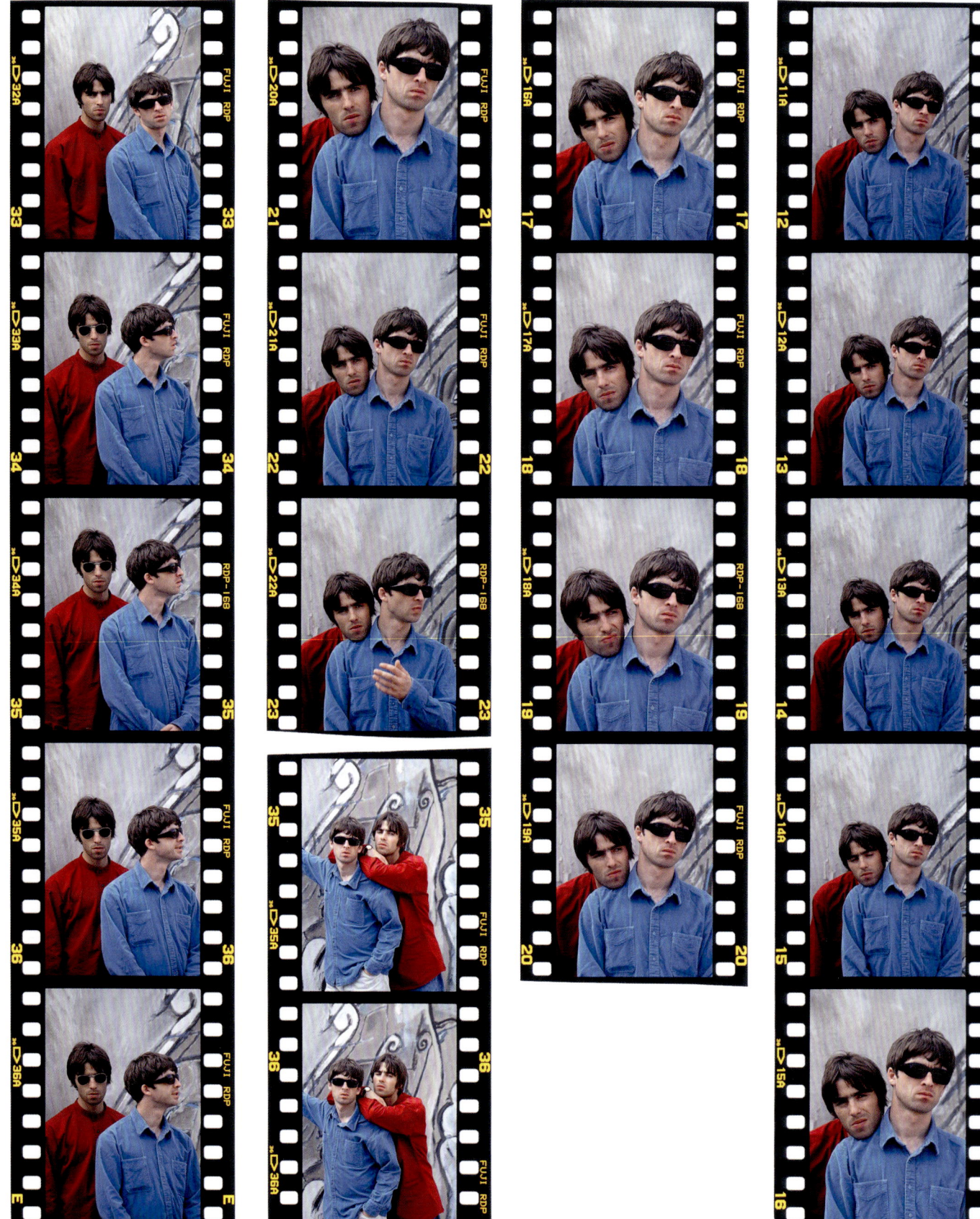

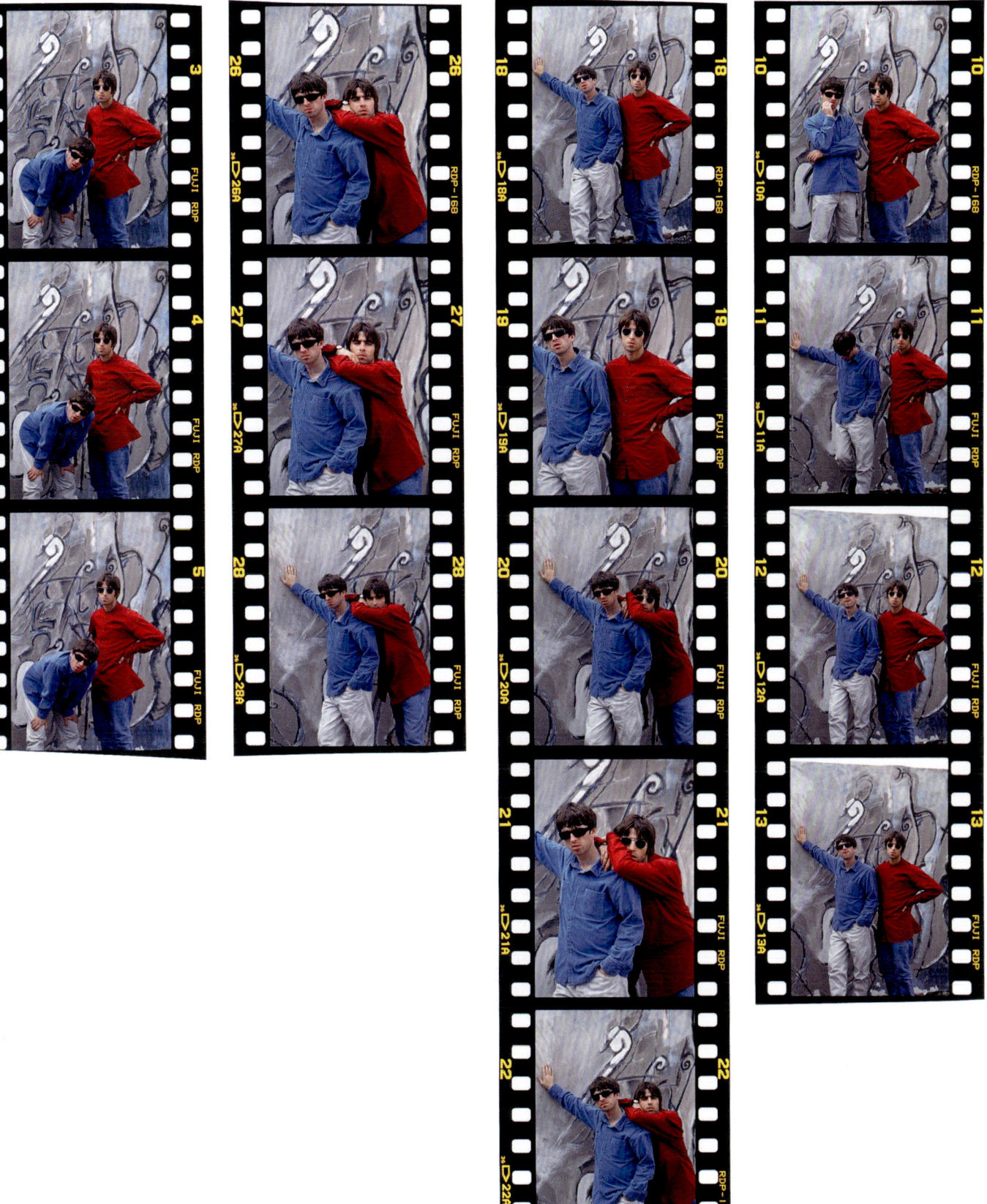

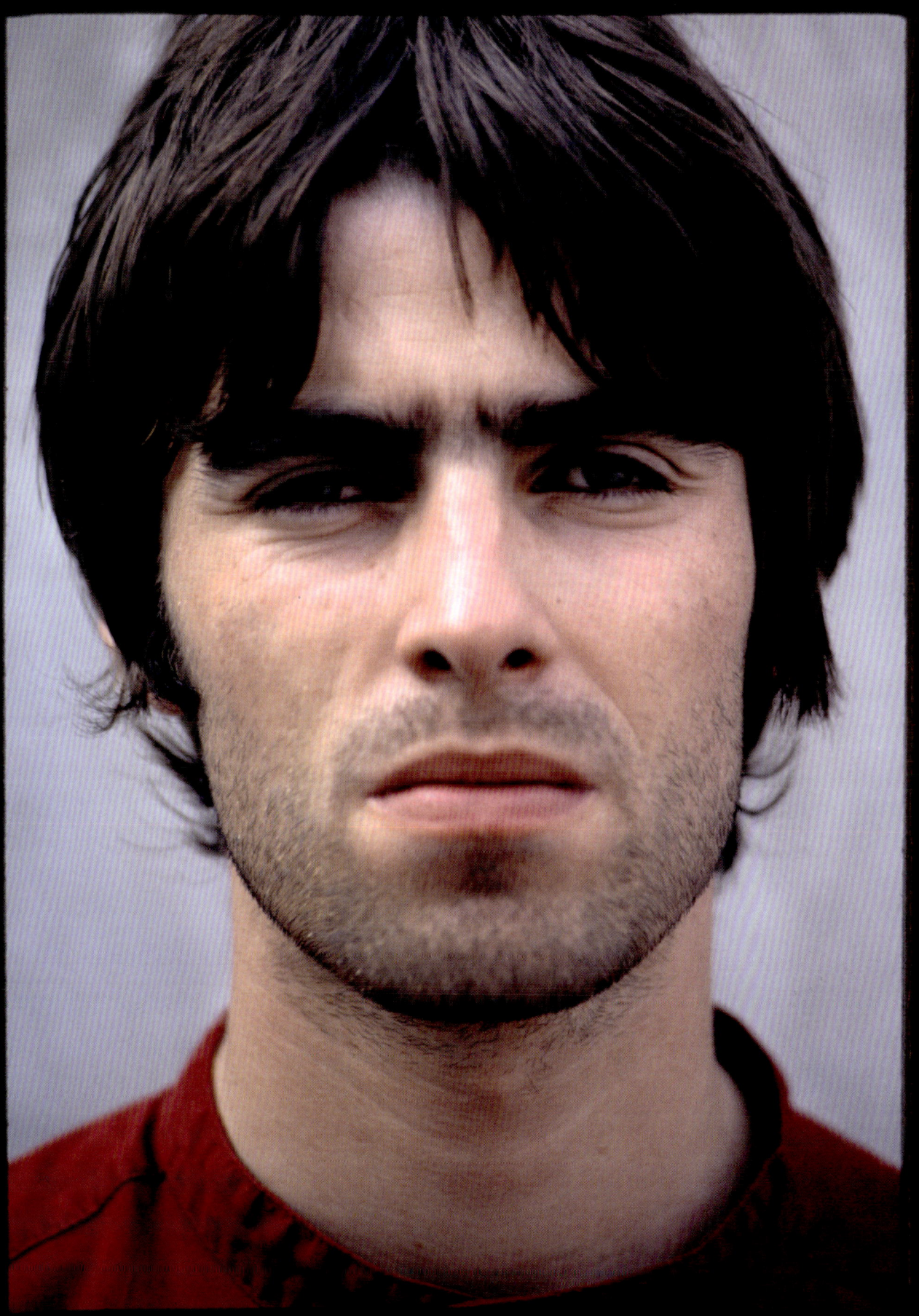

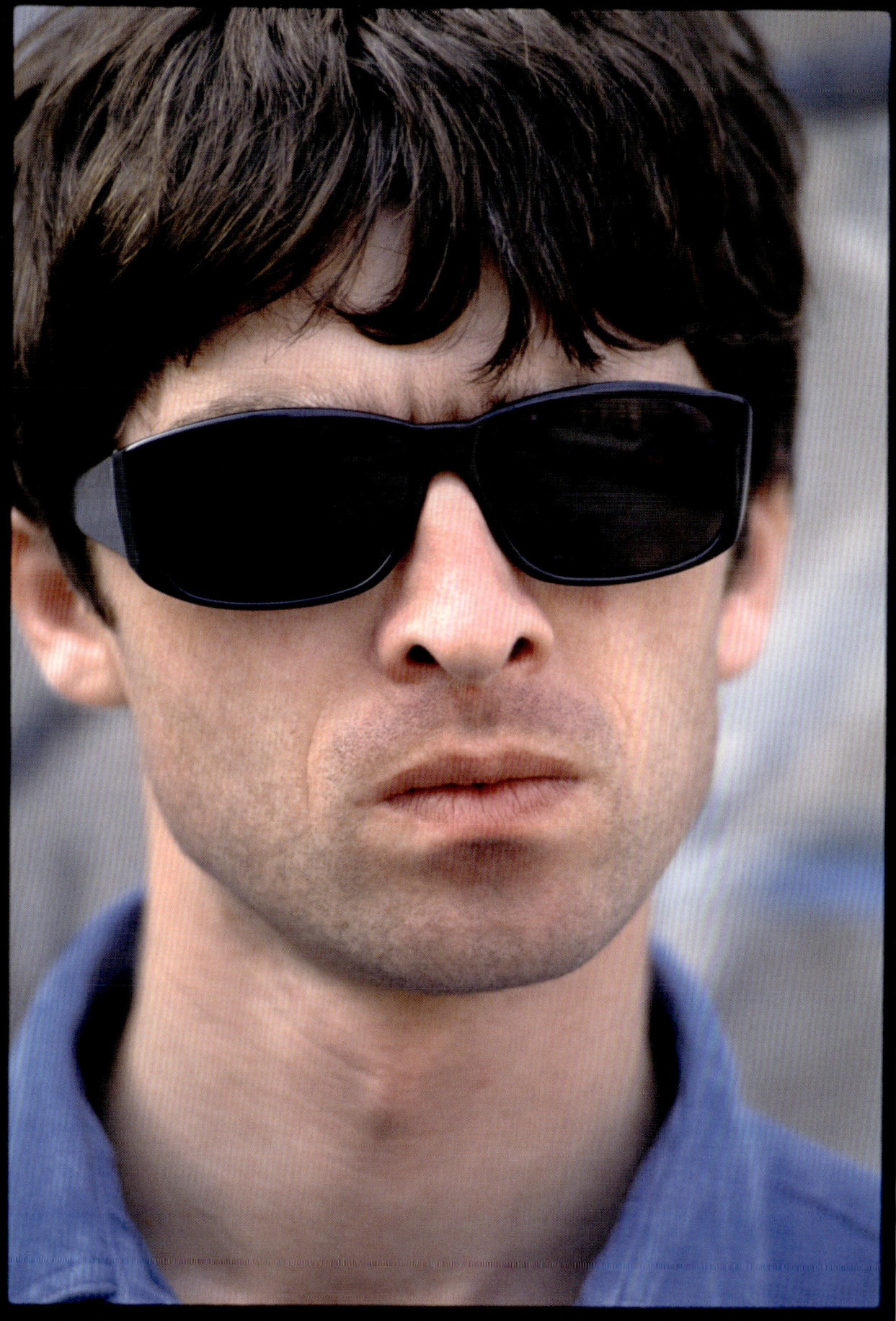

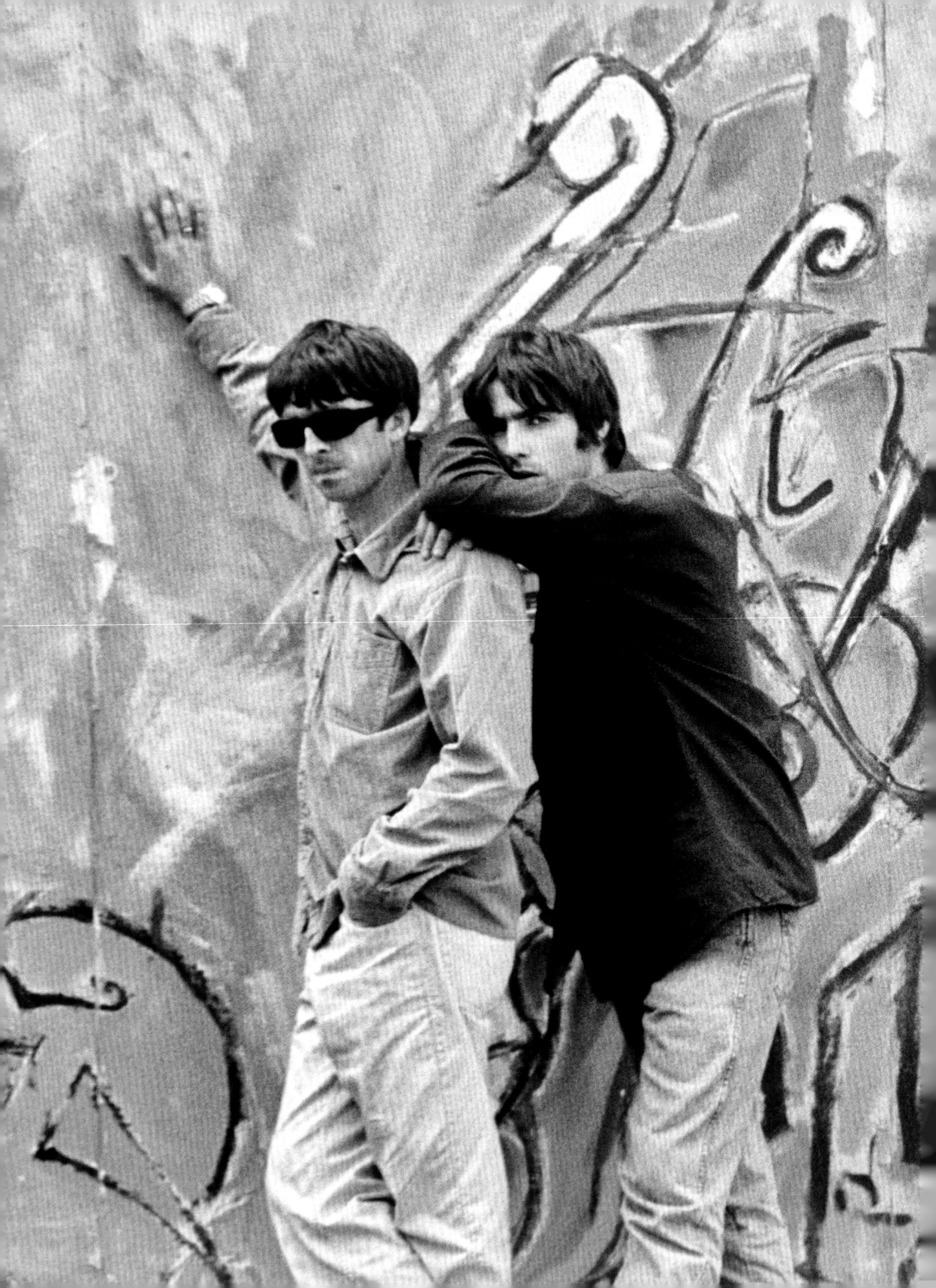

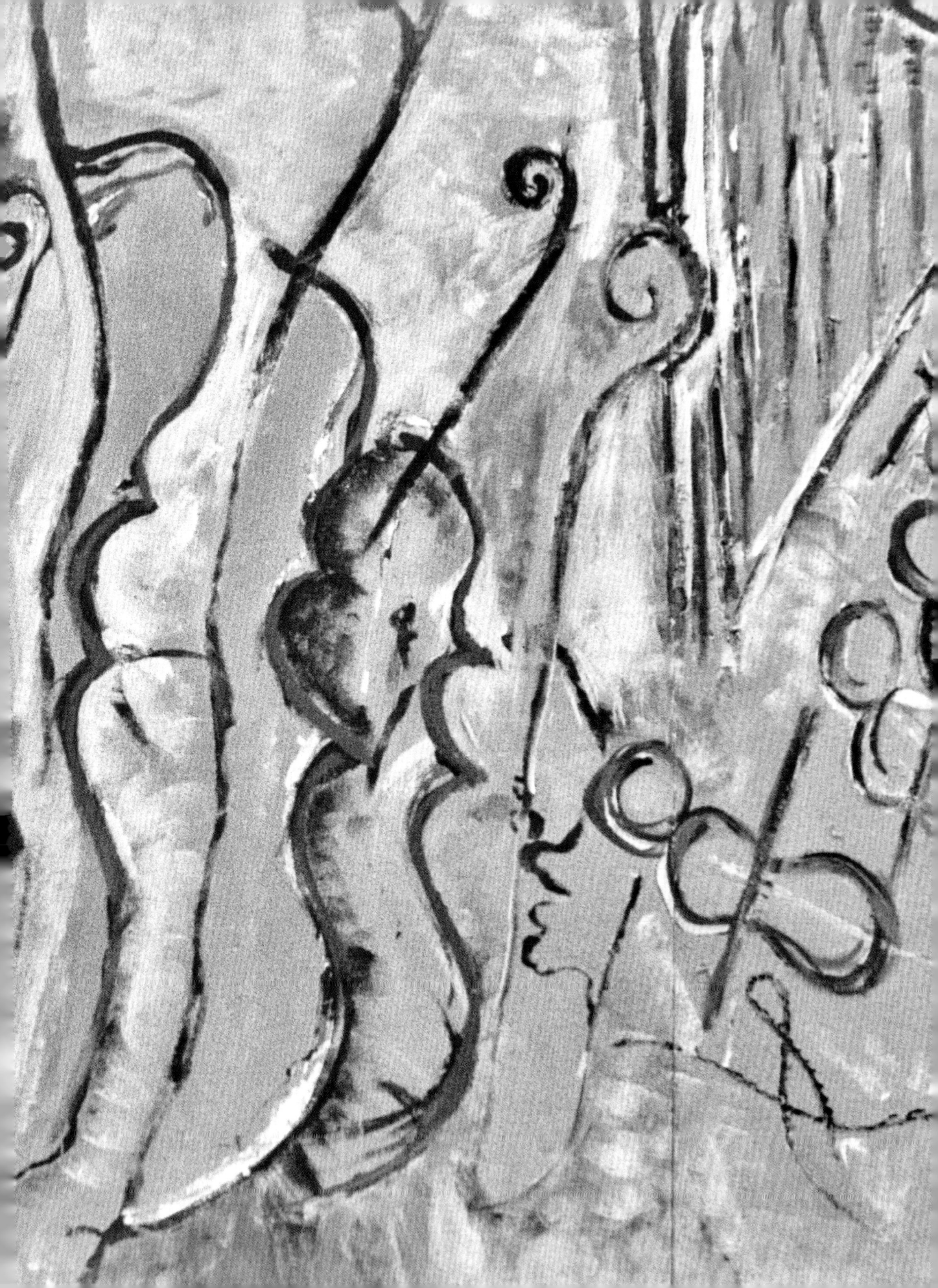

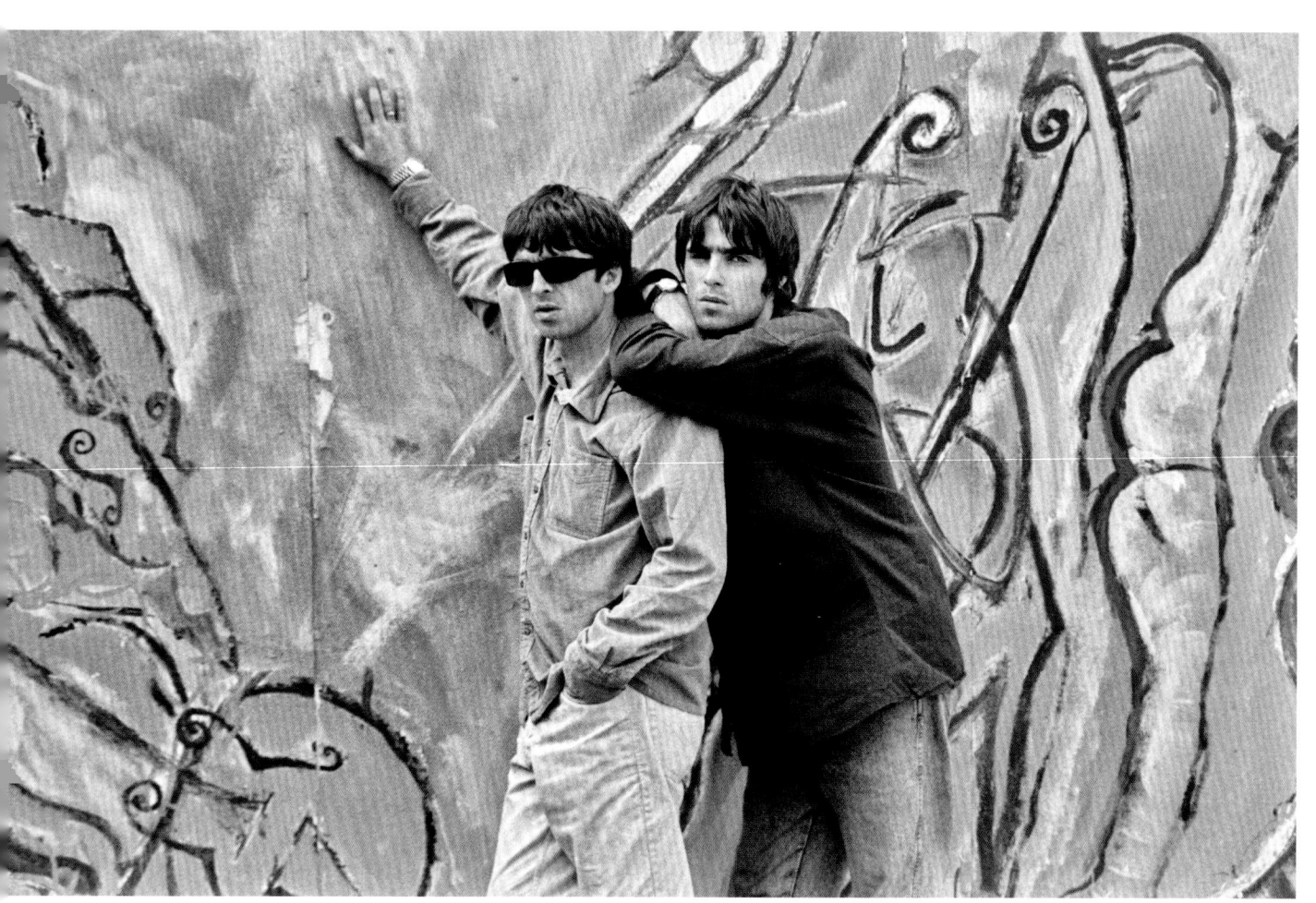

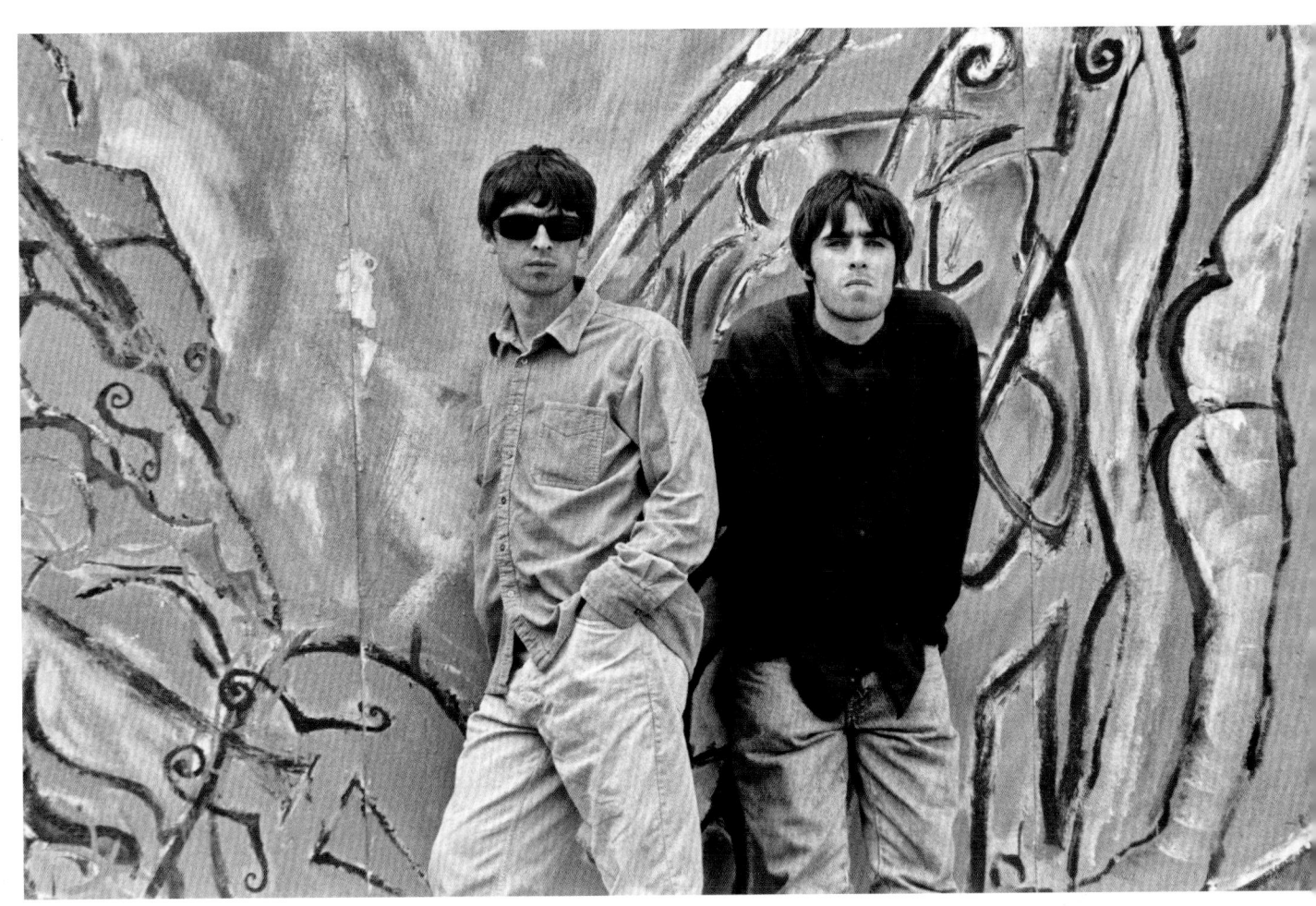

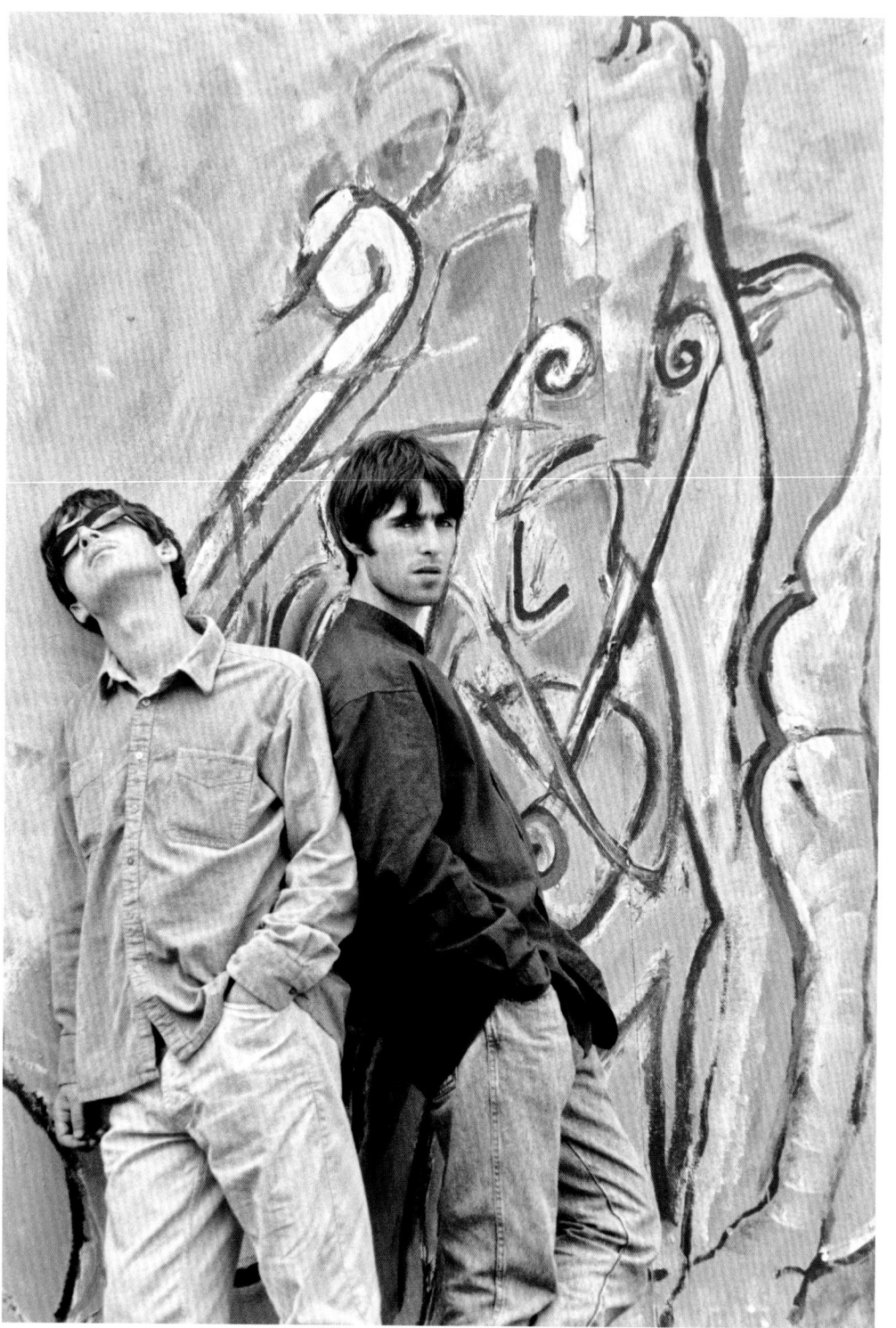

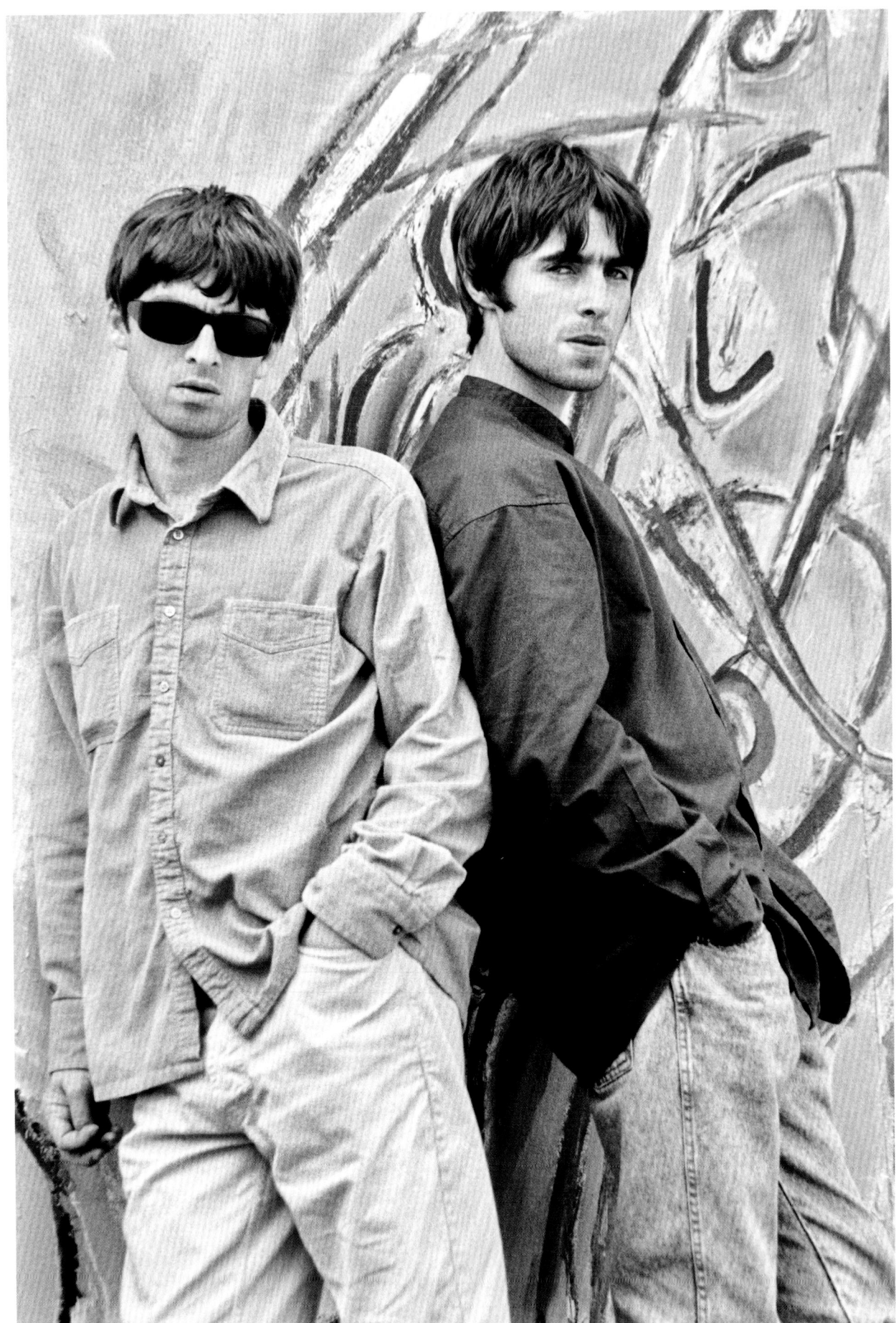

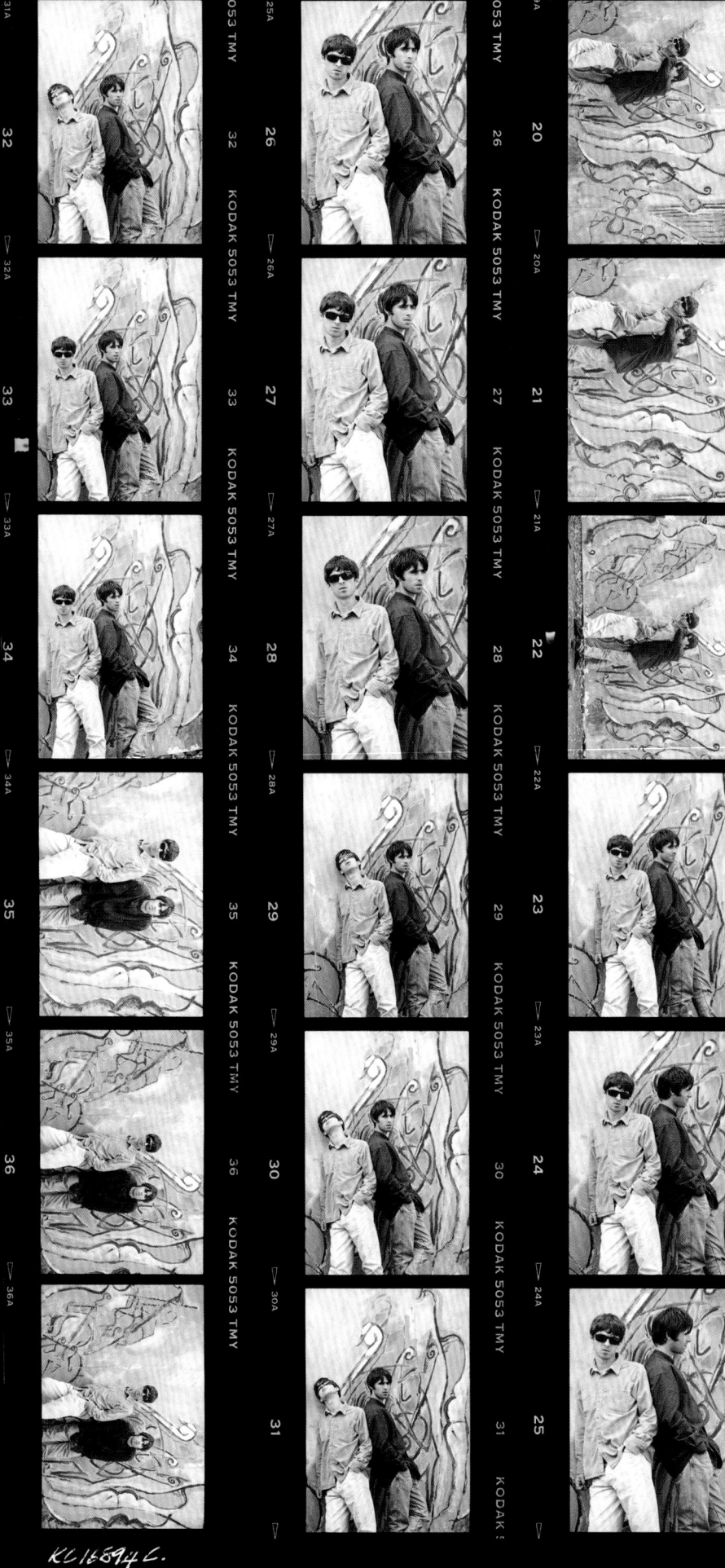

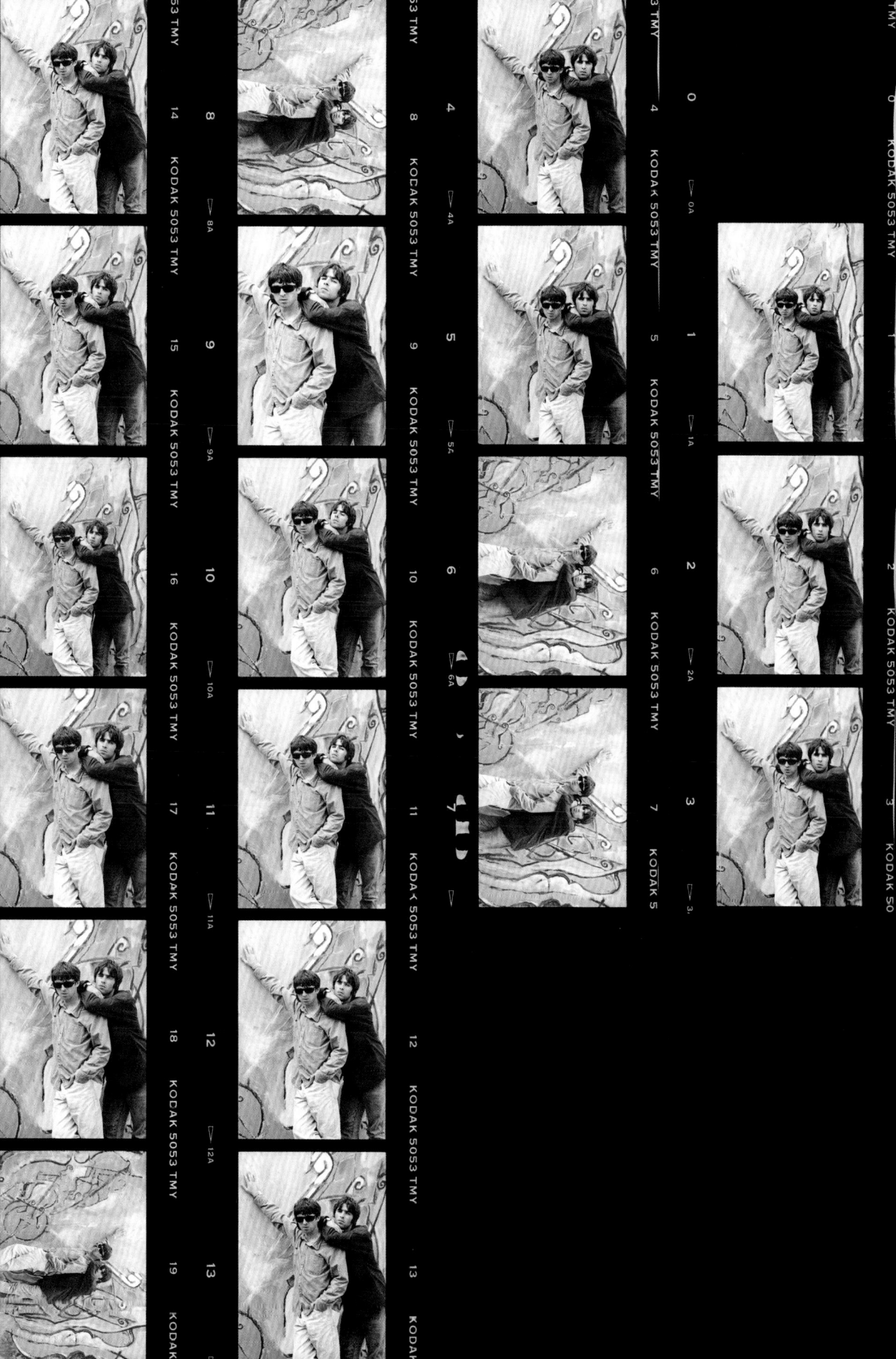

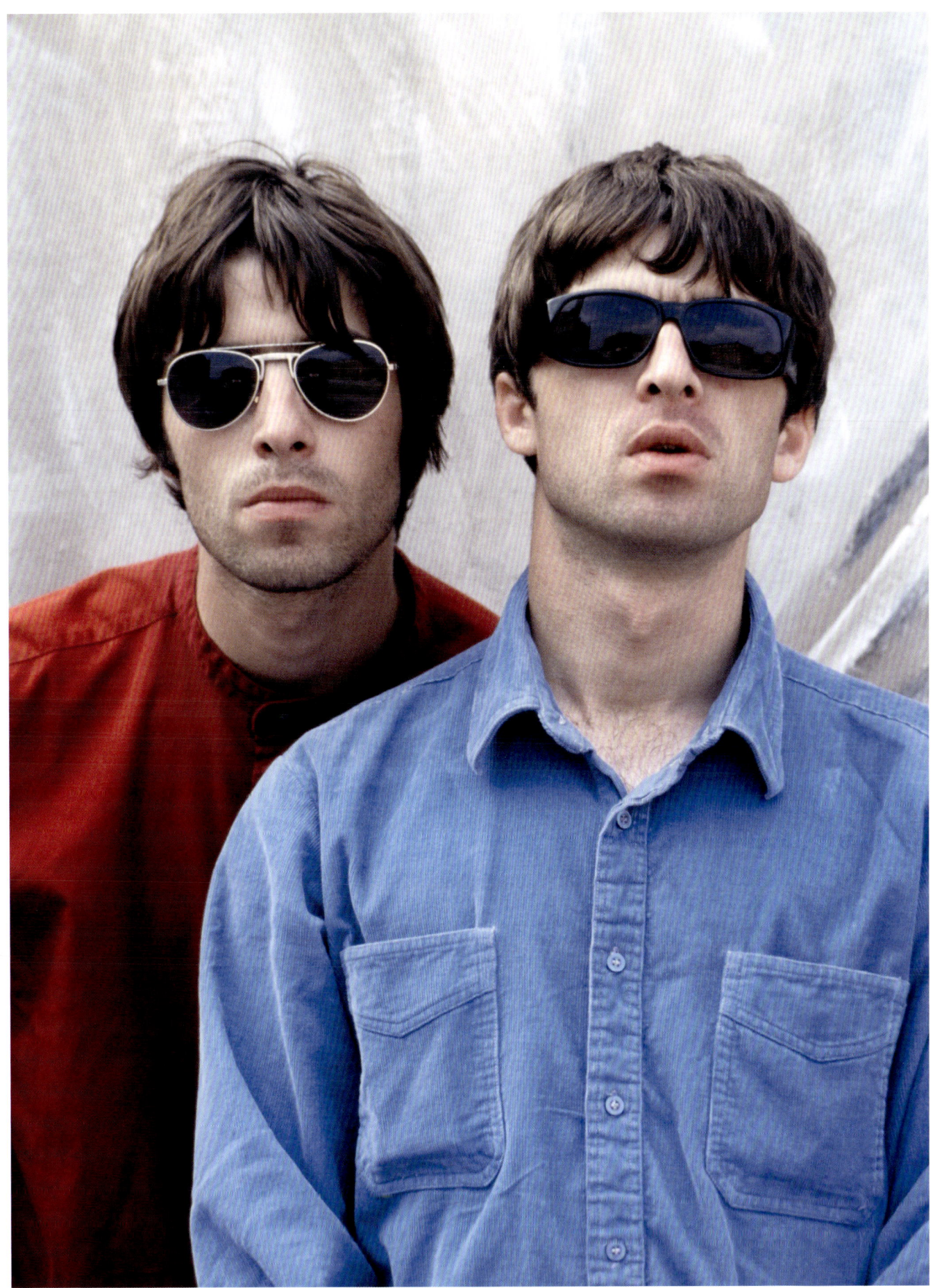

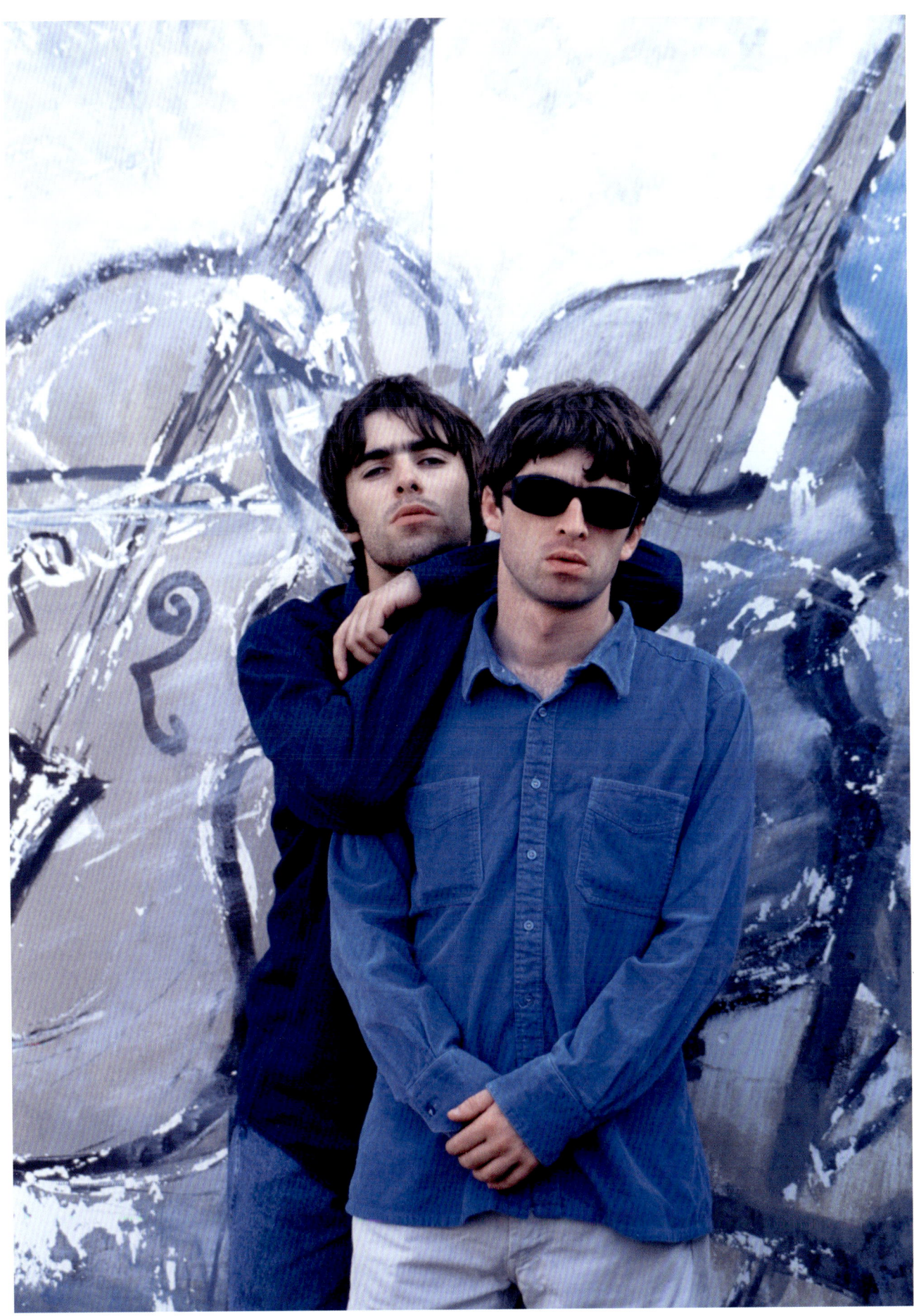

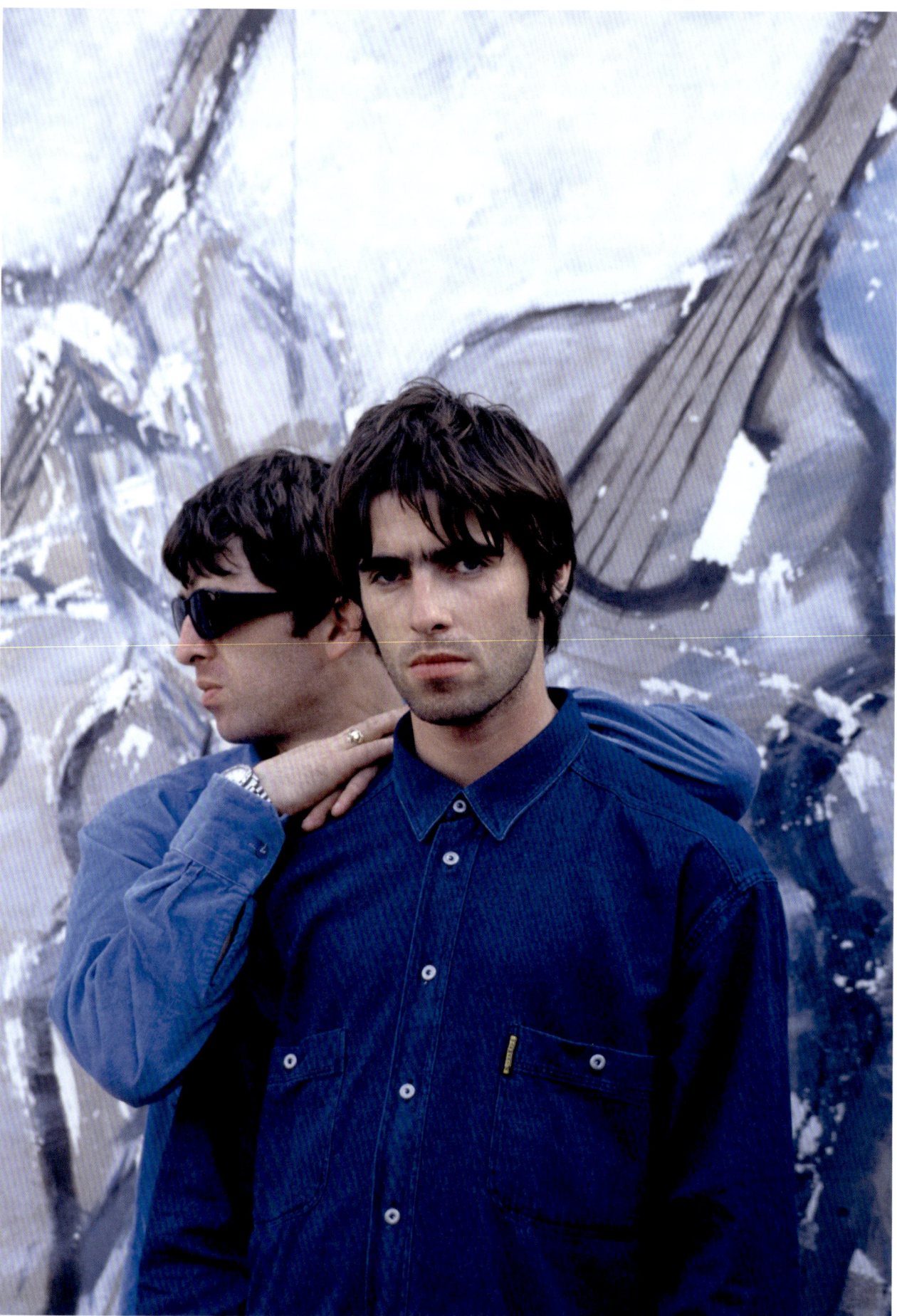

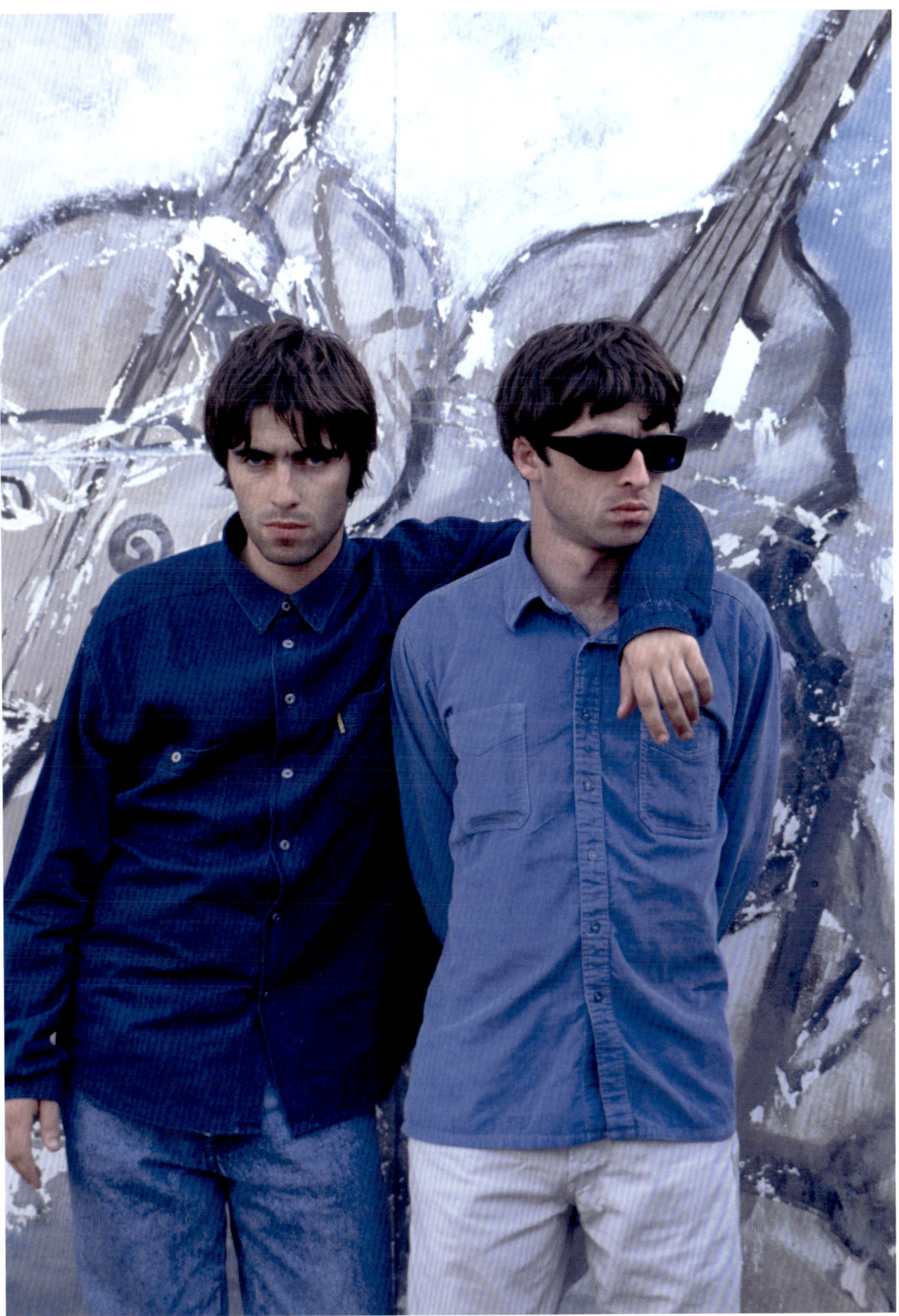

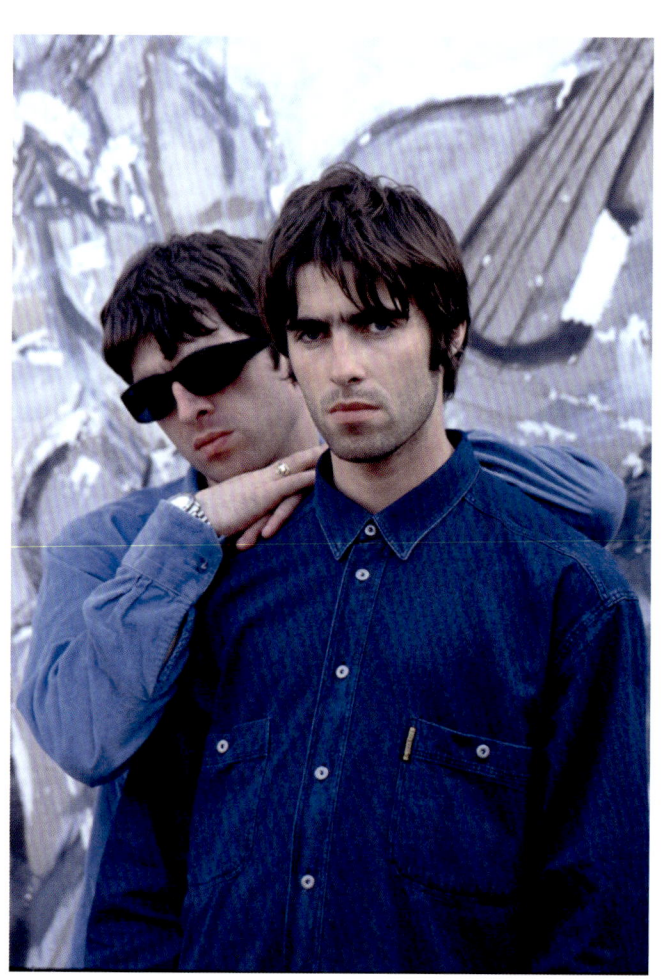
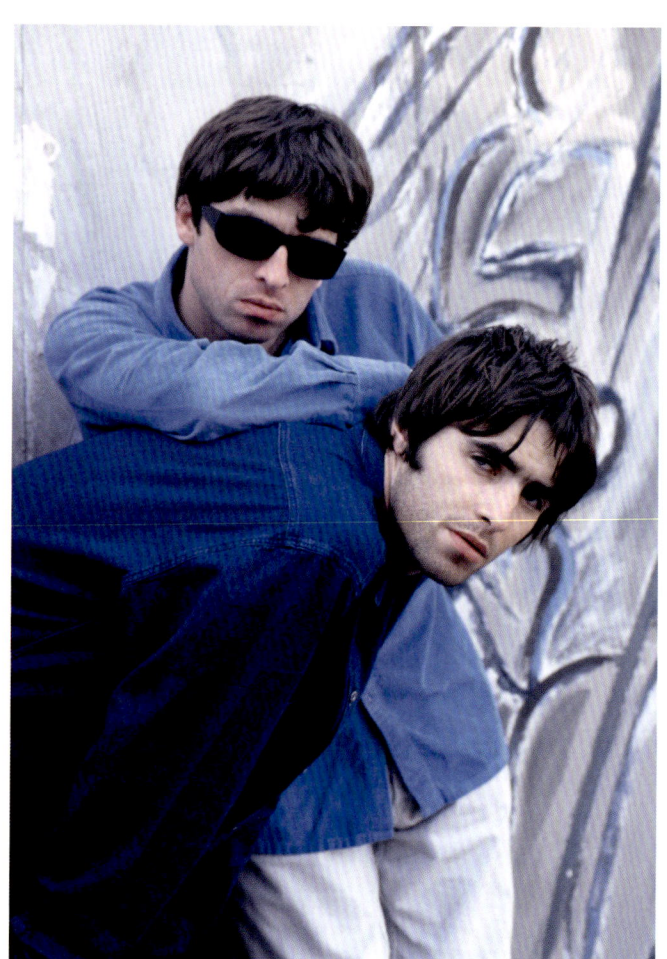

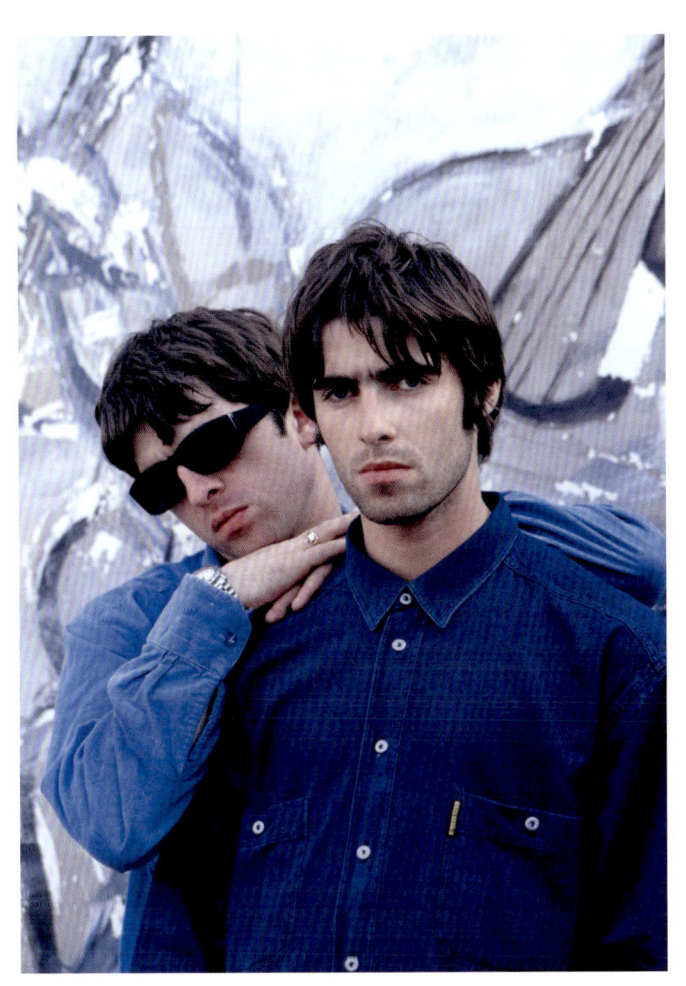
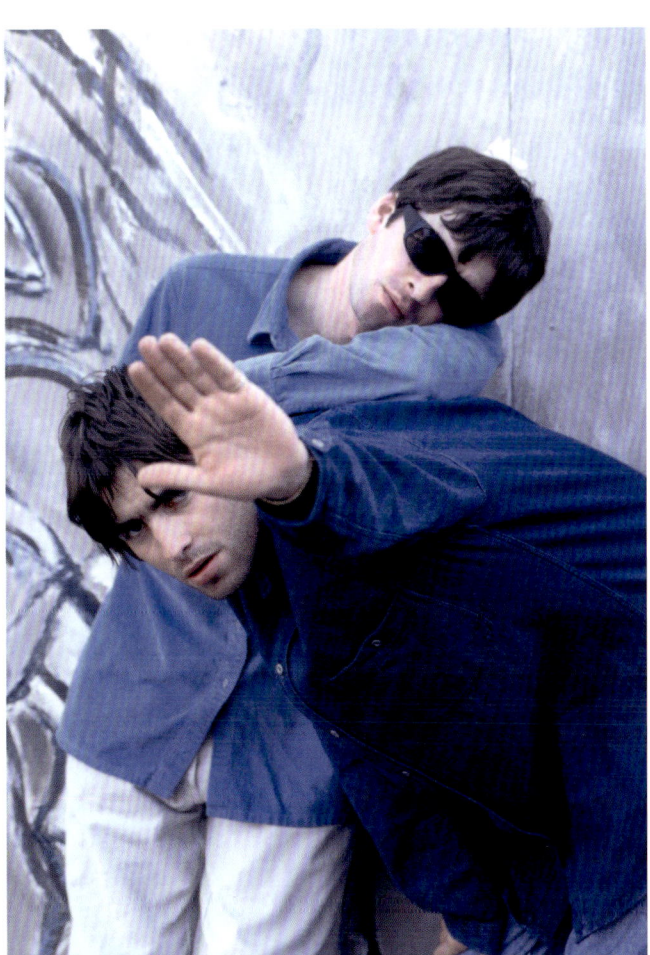

30 AUGUST
VIRGIN MEGASTORE, MARBLE ARCH, LONDON

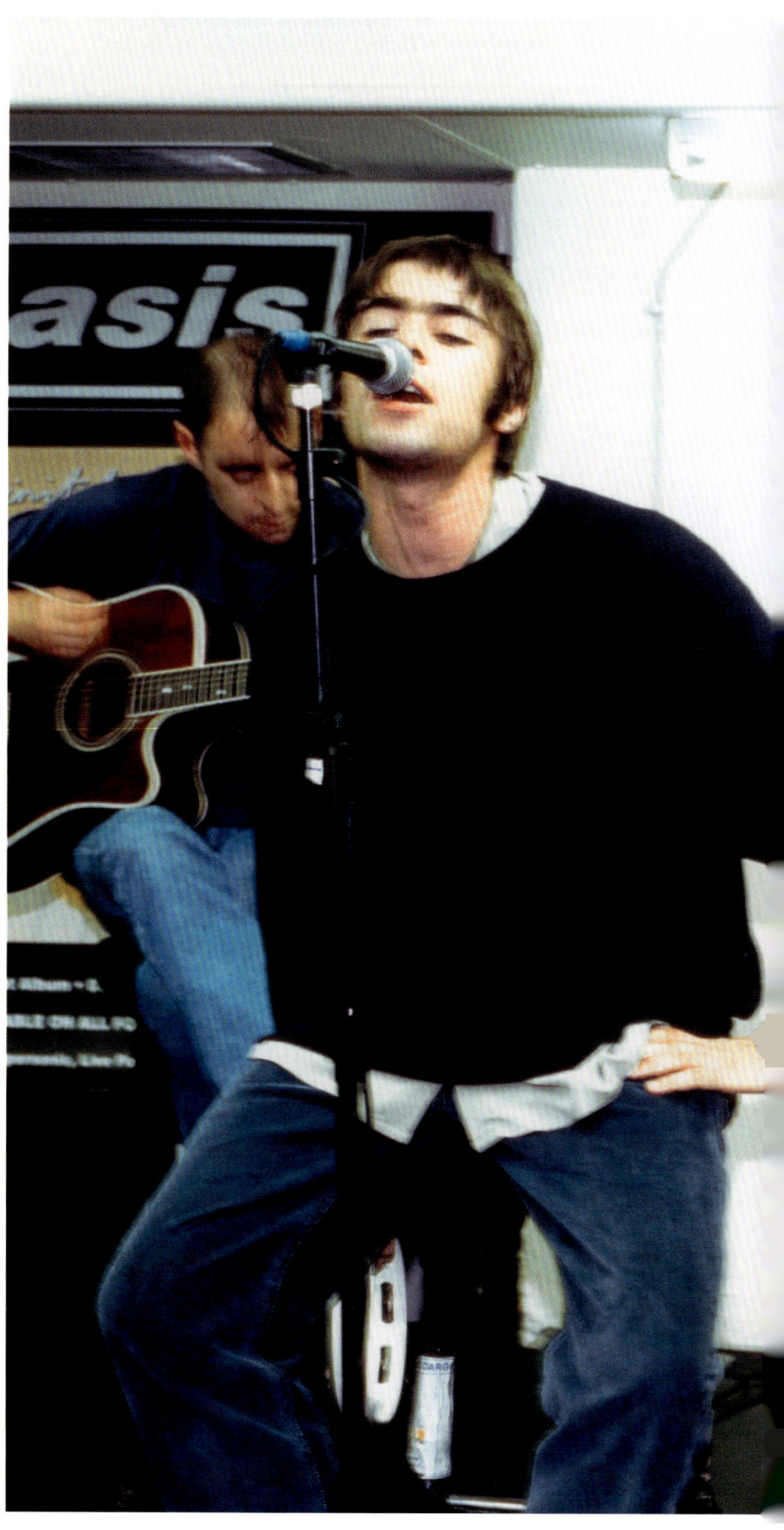

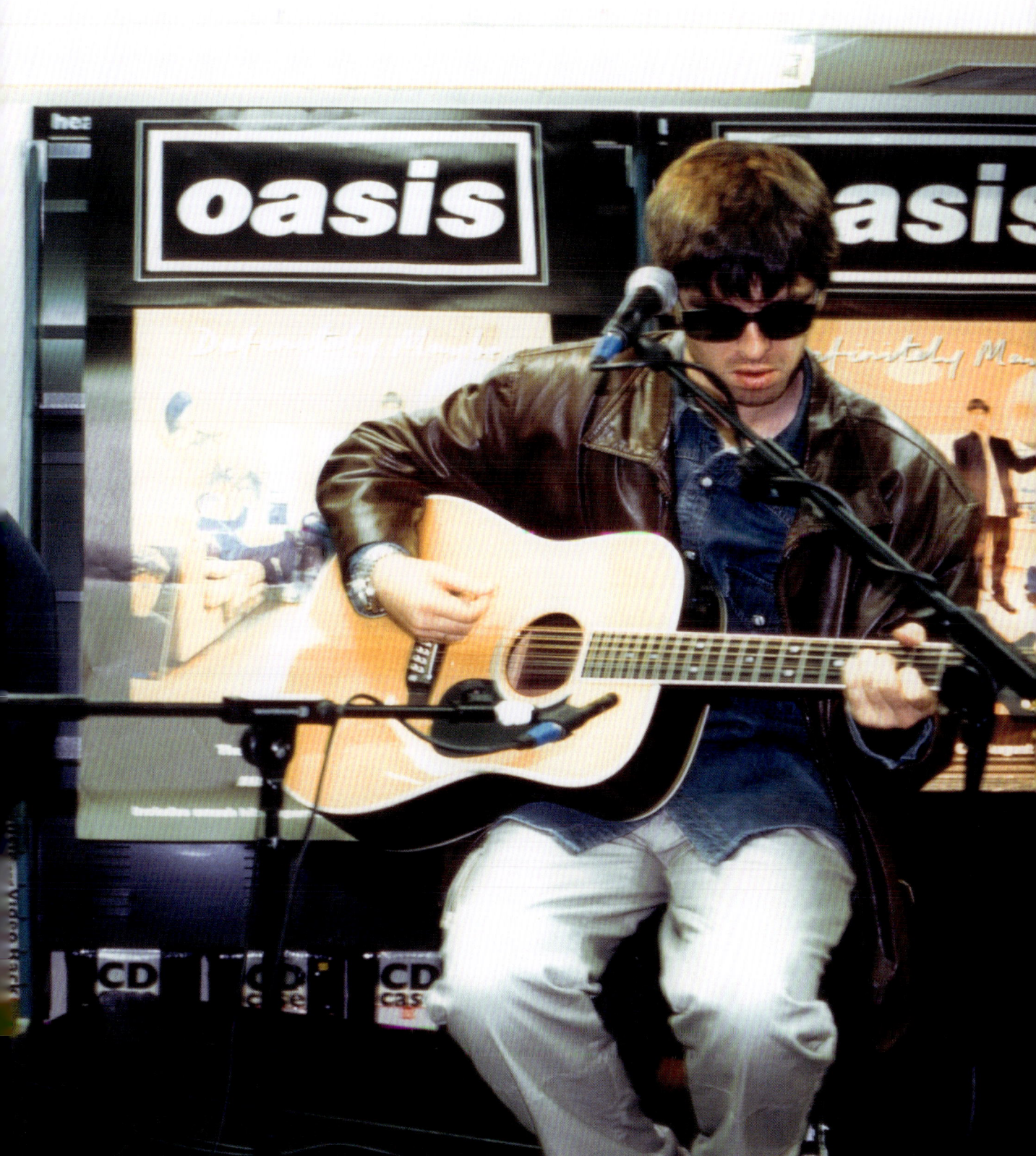

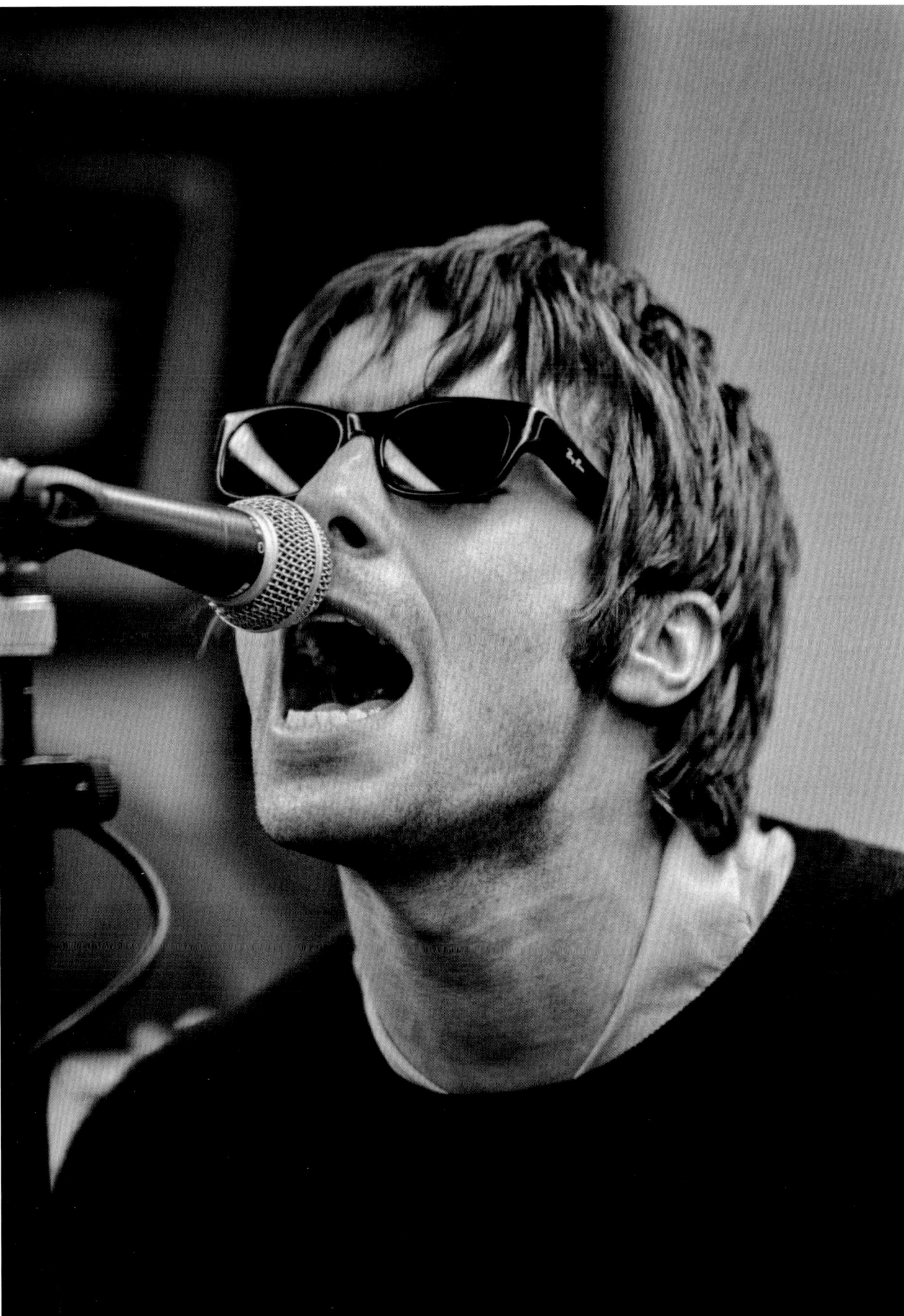

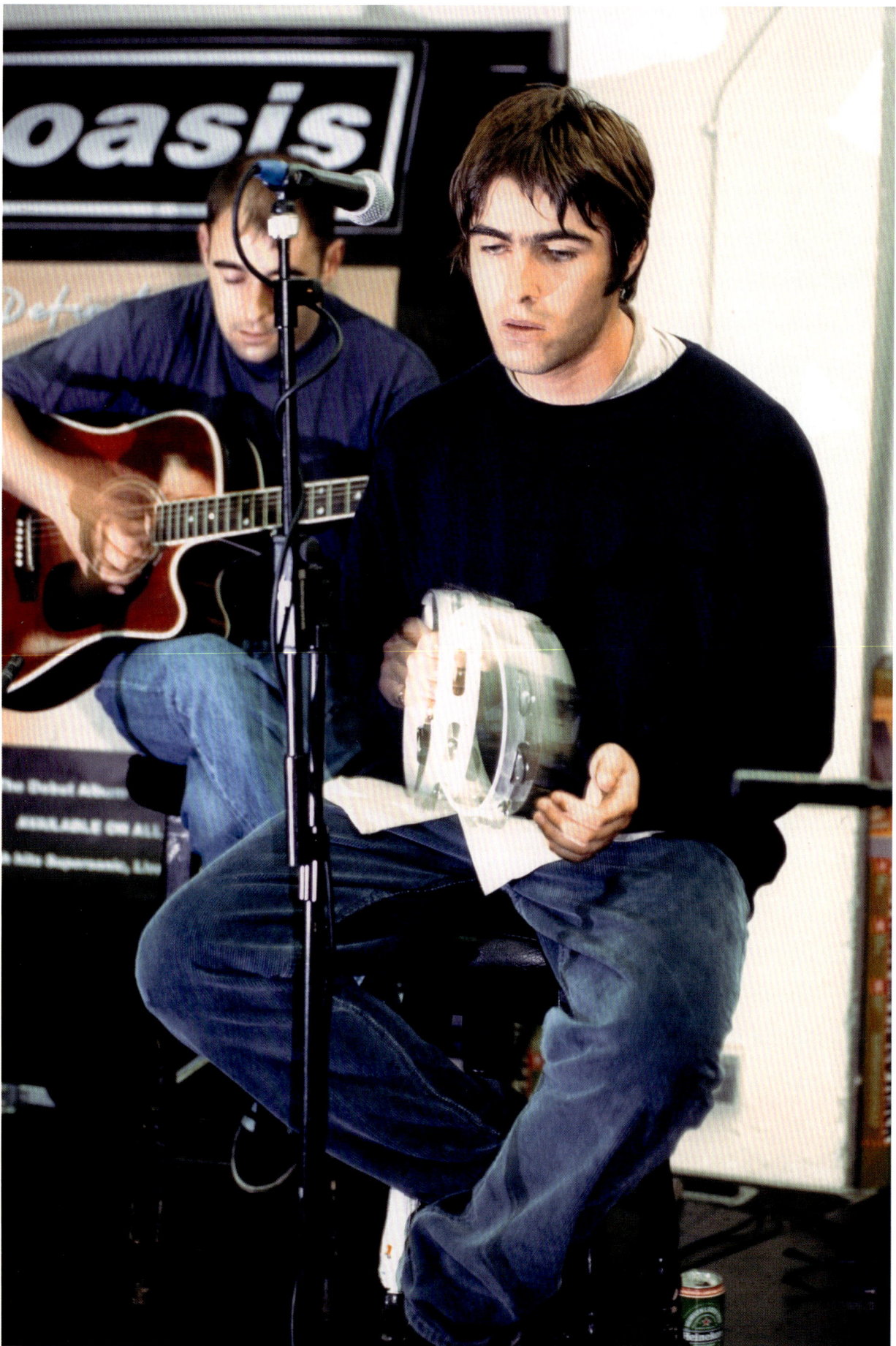

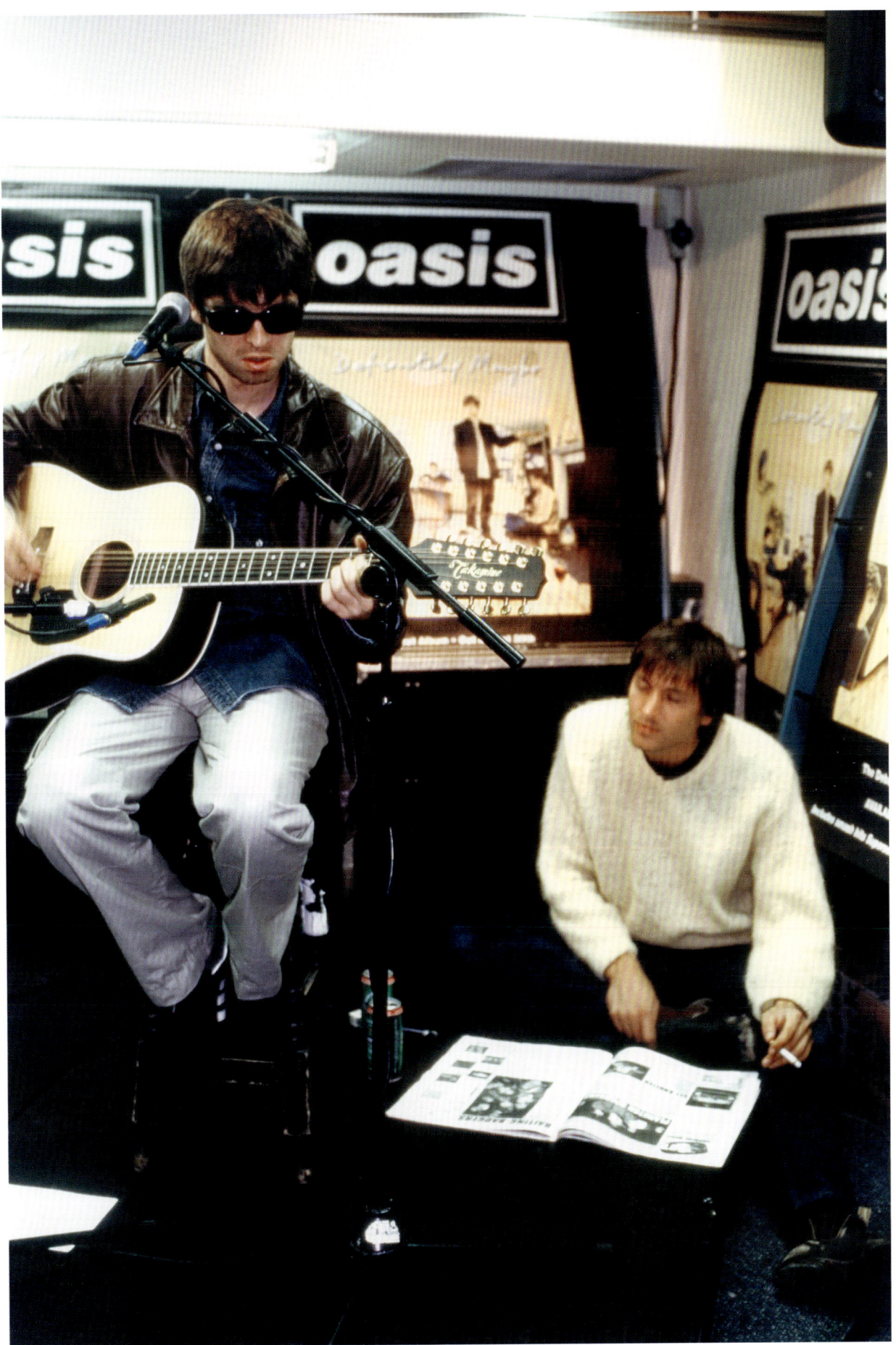

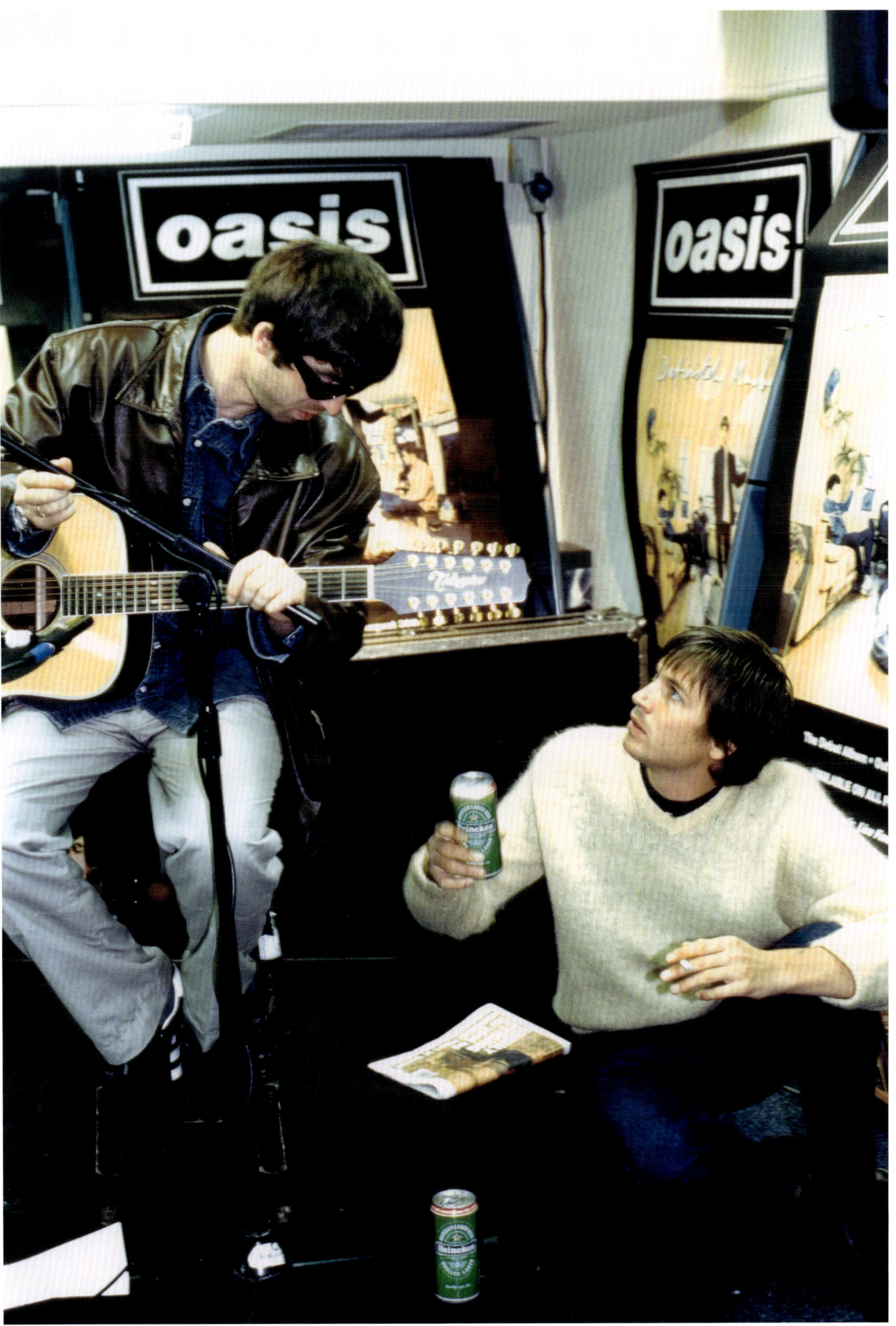

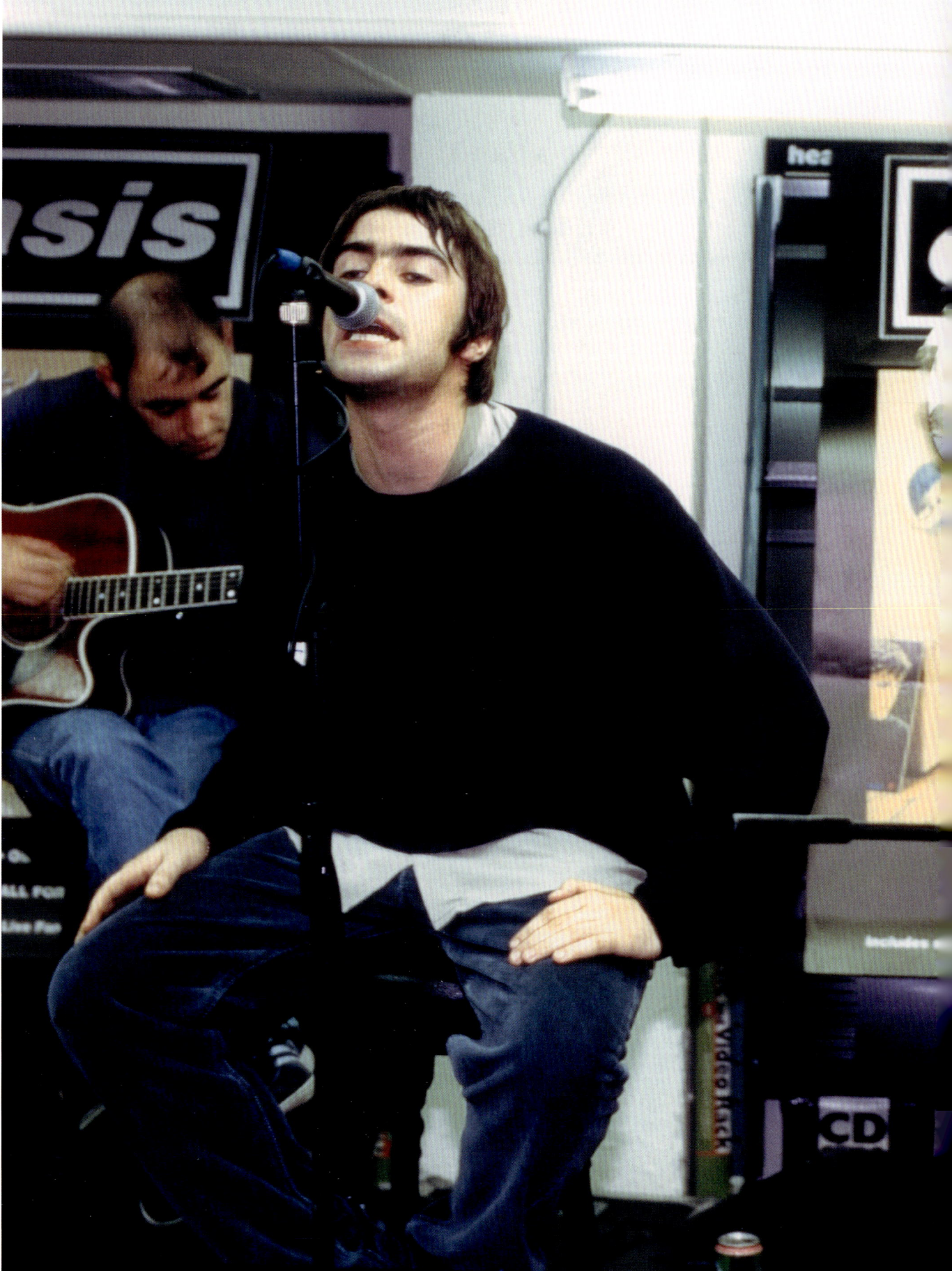

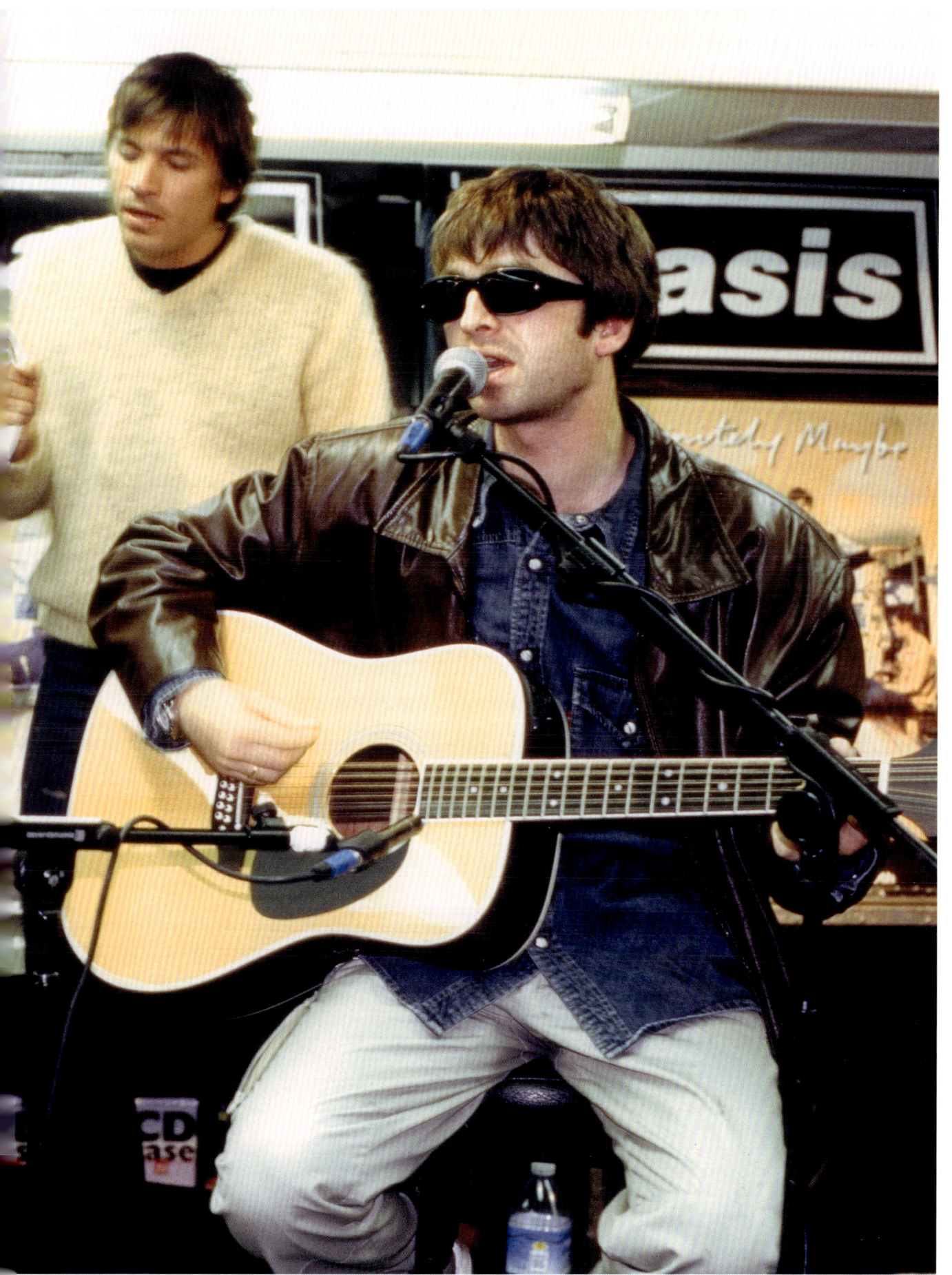

"With the benefit of hindsight, I'd say to the person I was in 1994: Do NOT give these extra tracks away as B-sides and do NOT mix these albums on cocaine. You WILL regret it."

—*Noel Gallagher*

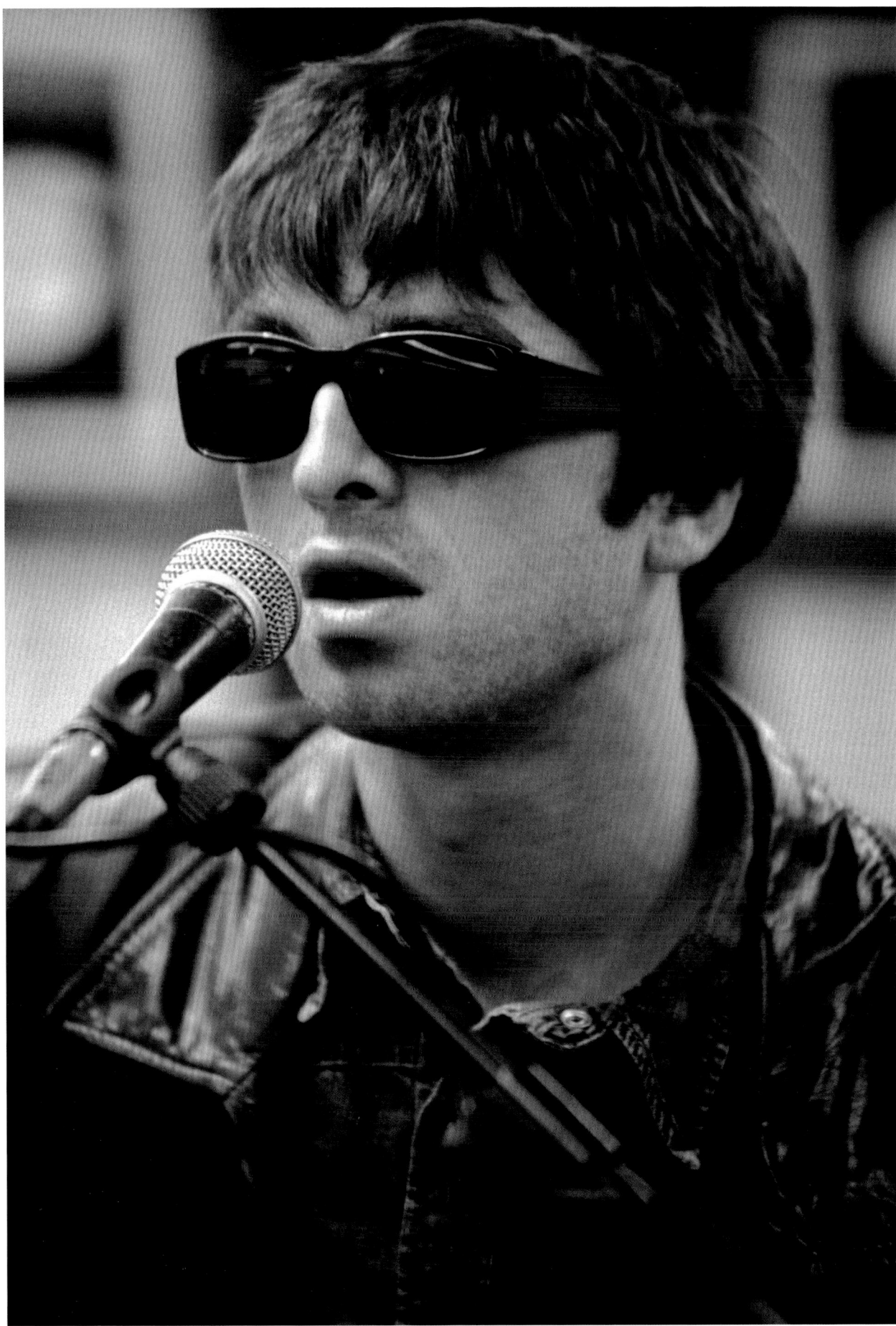

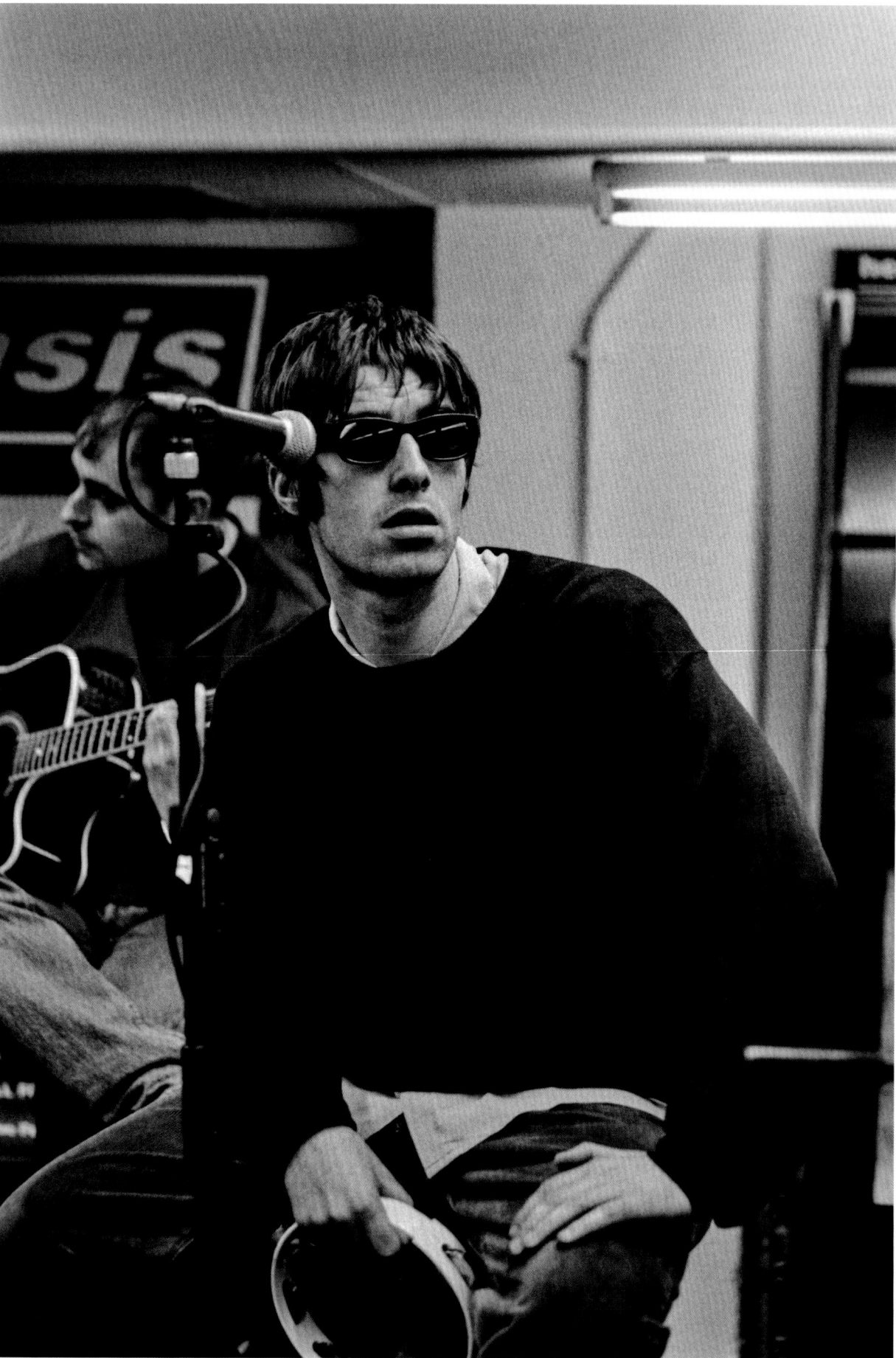

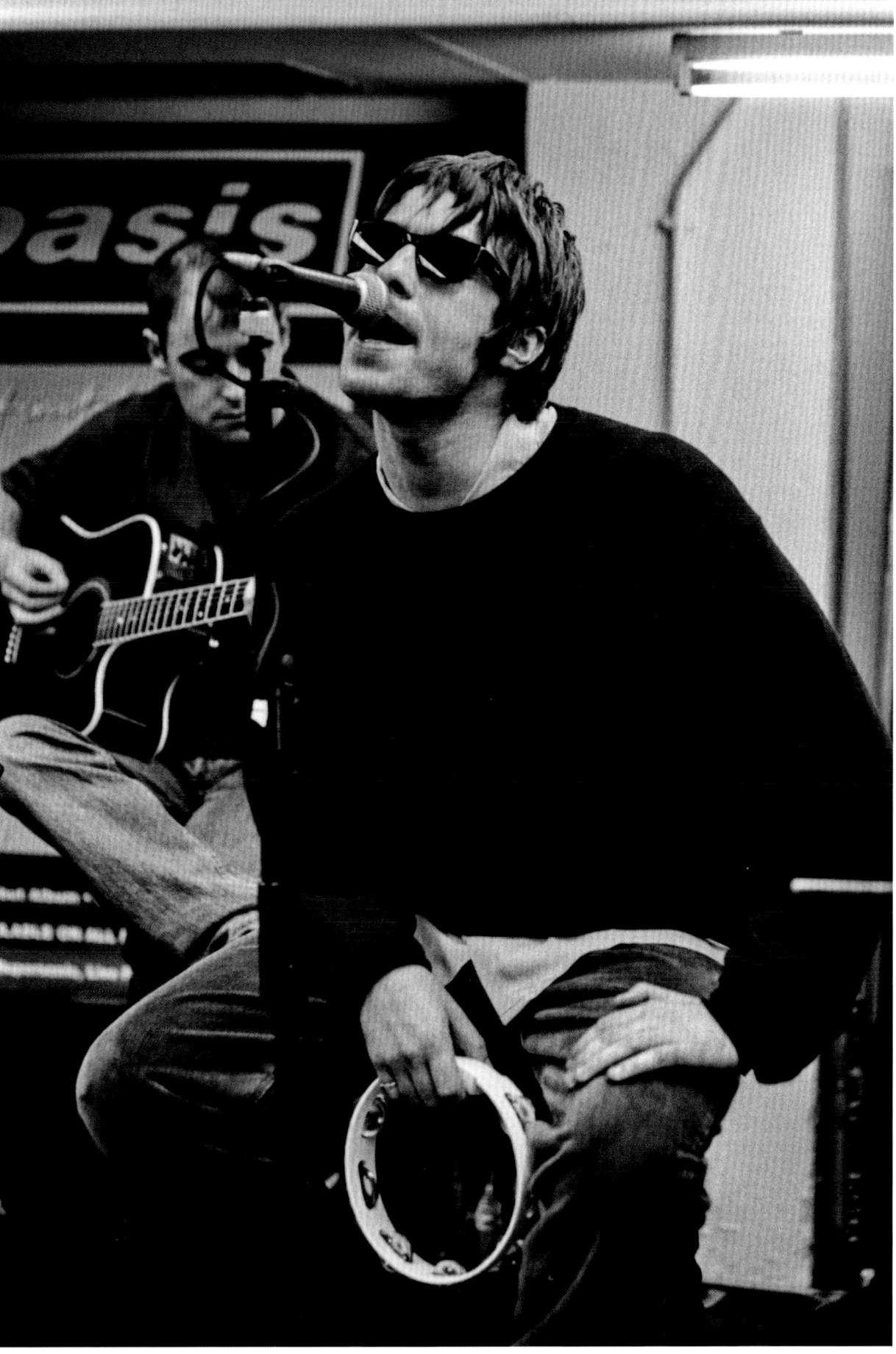

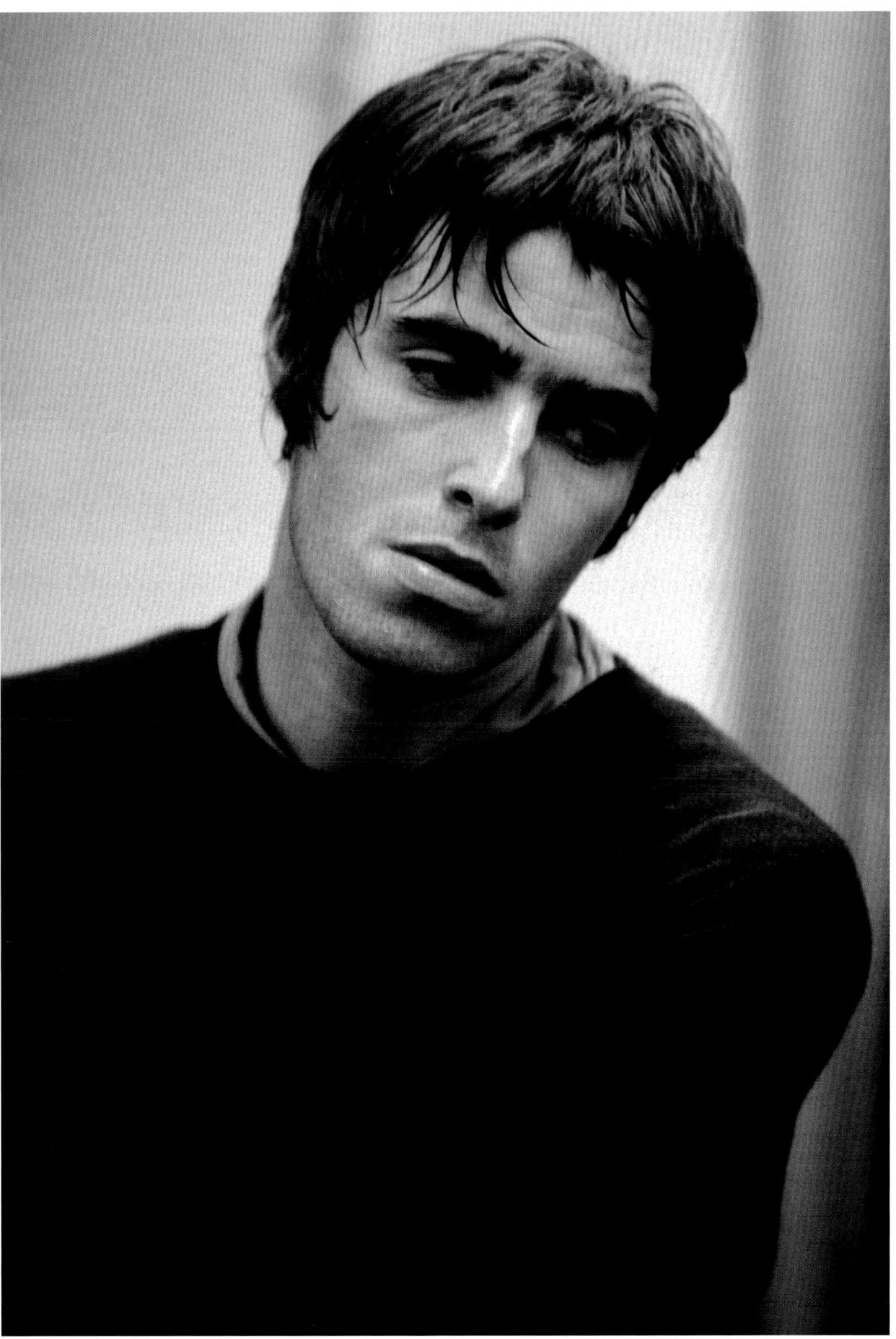

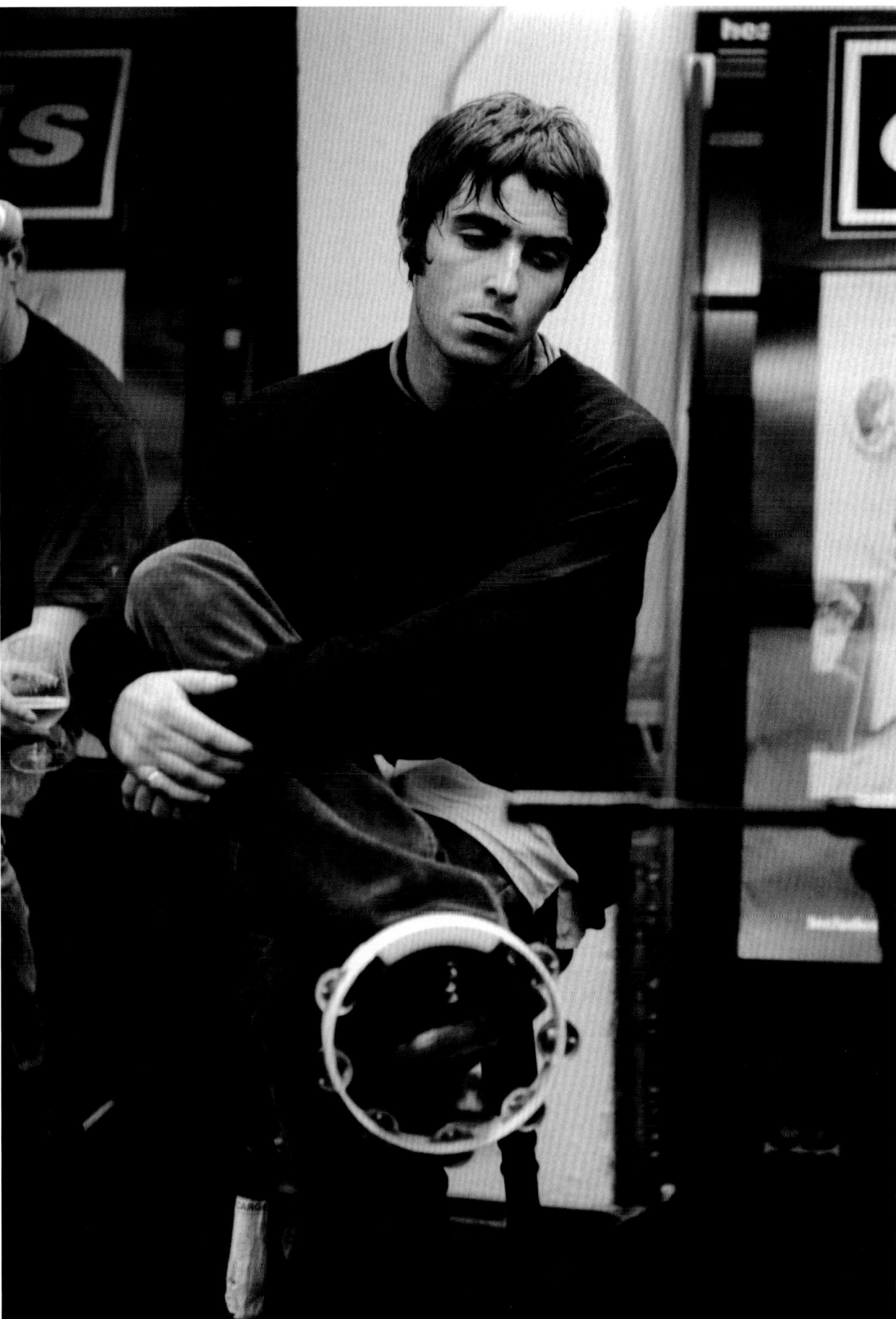

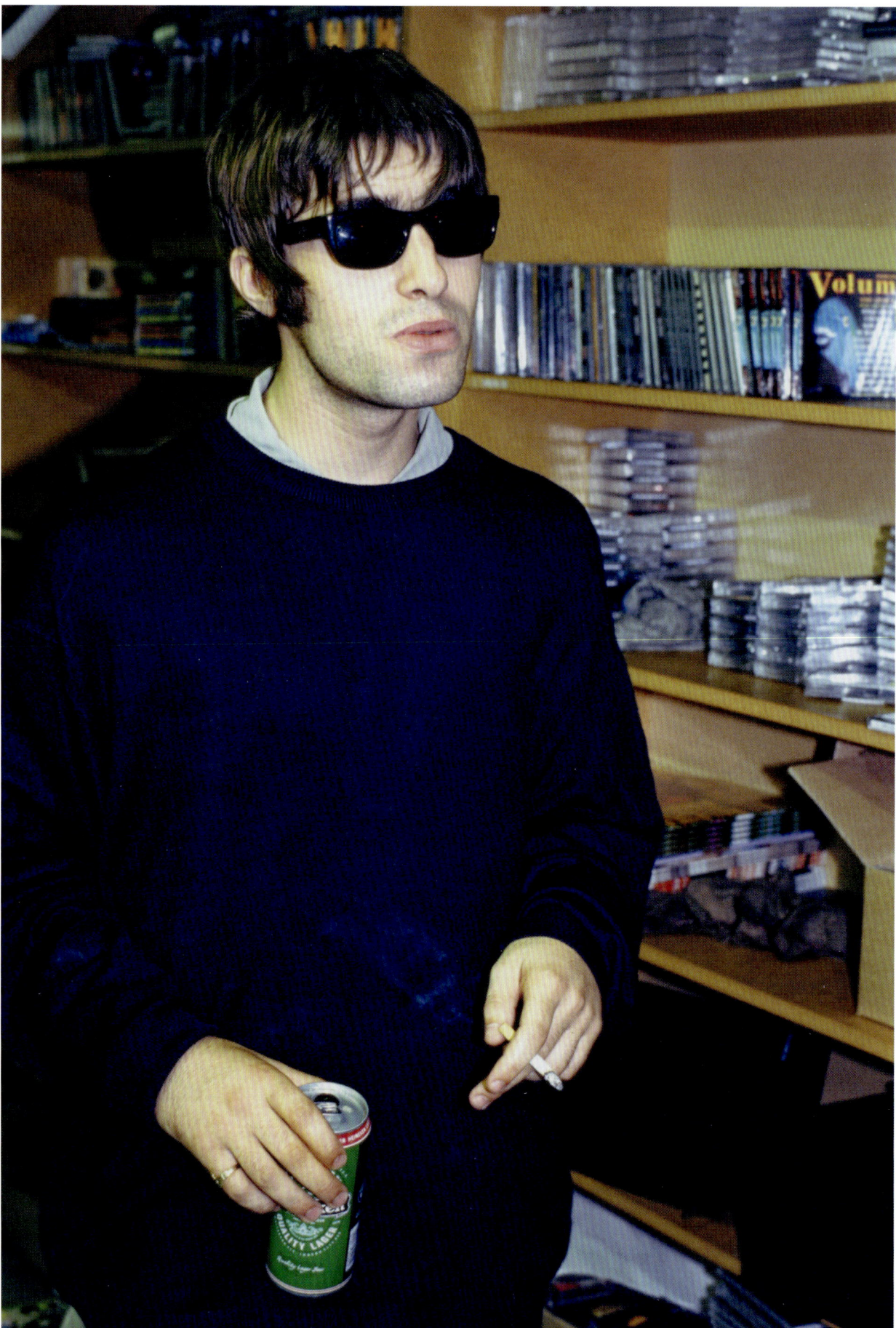

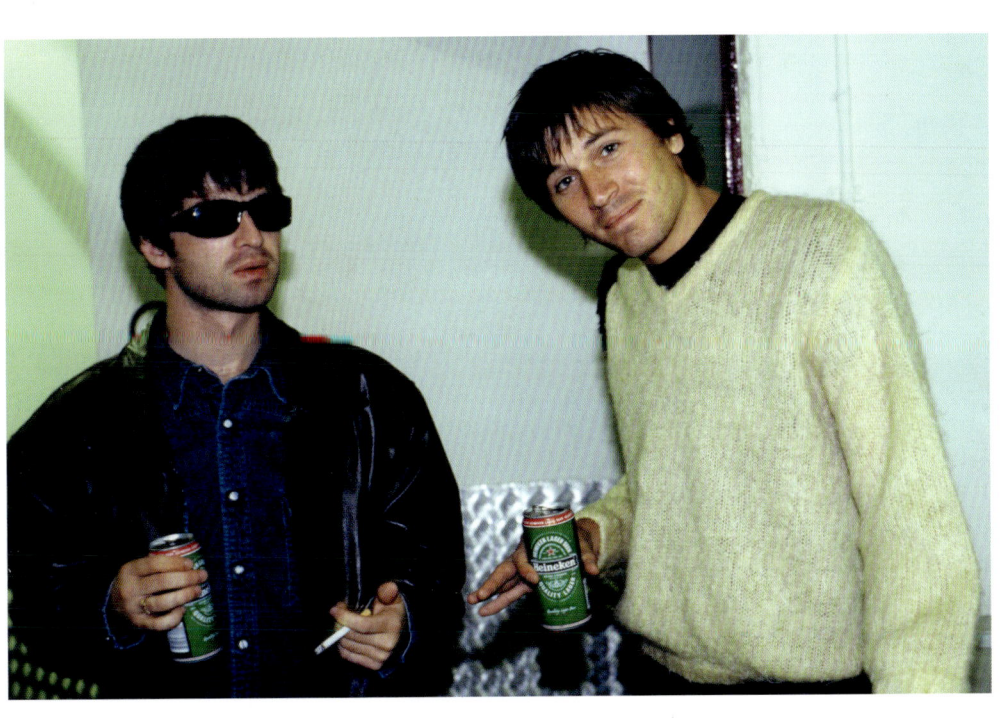

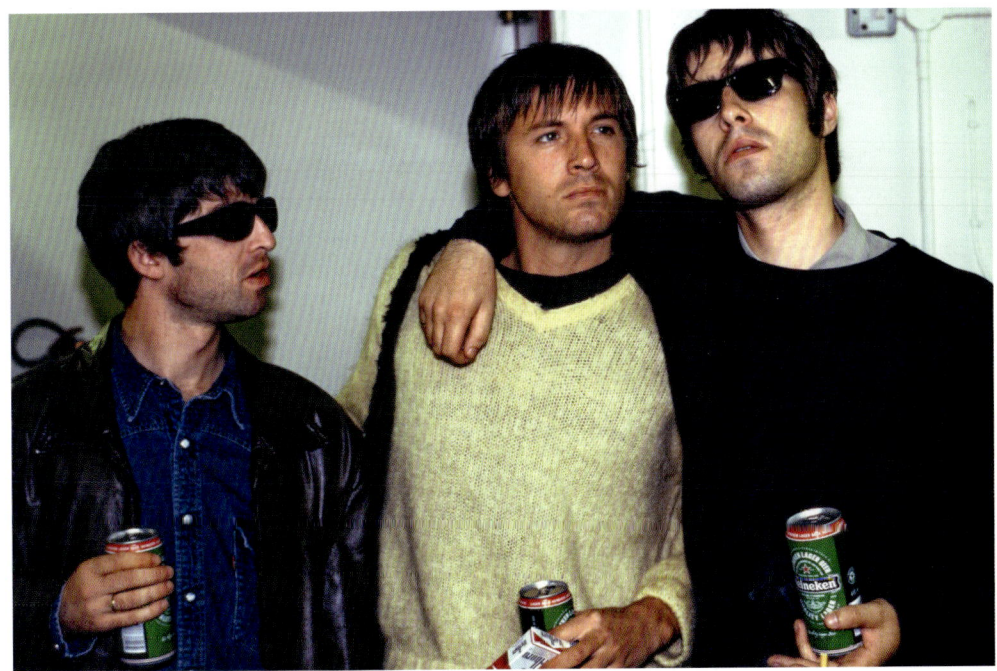

26 DEC
MAINE ROAD, MANCHESTER
CITY V BLACKBURN

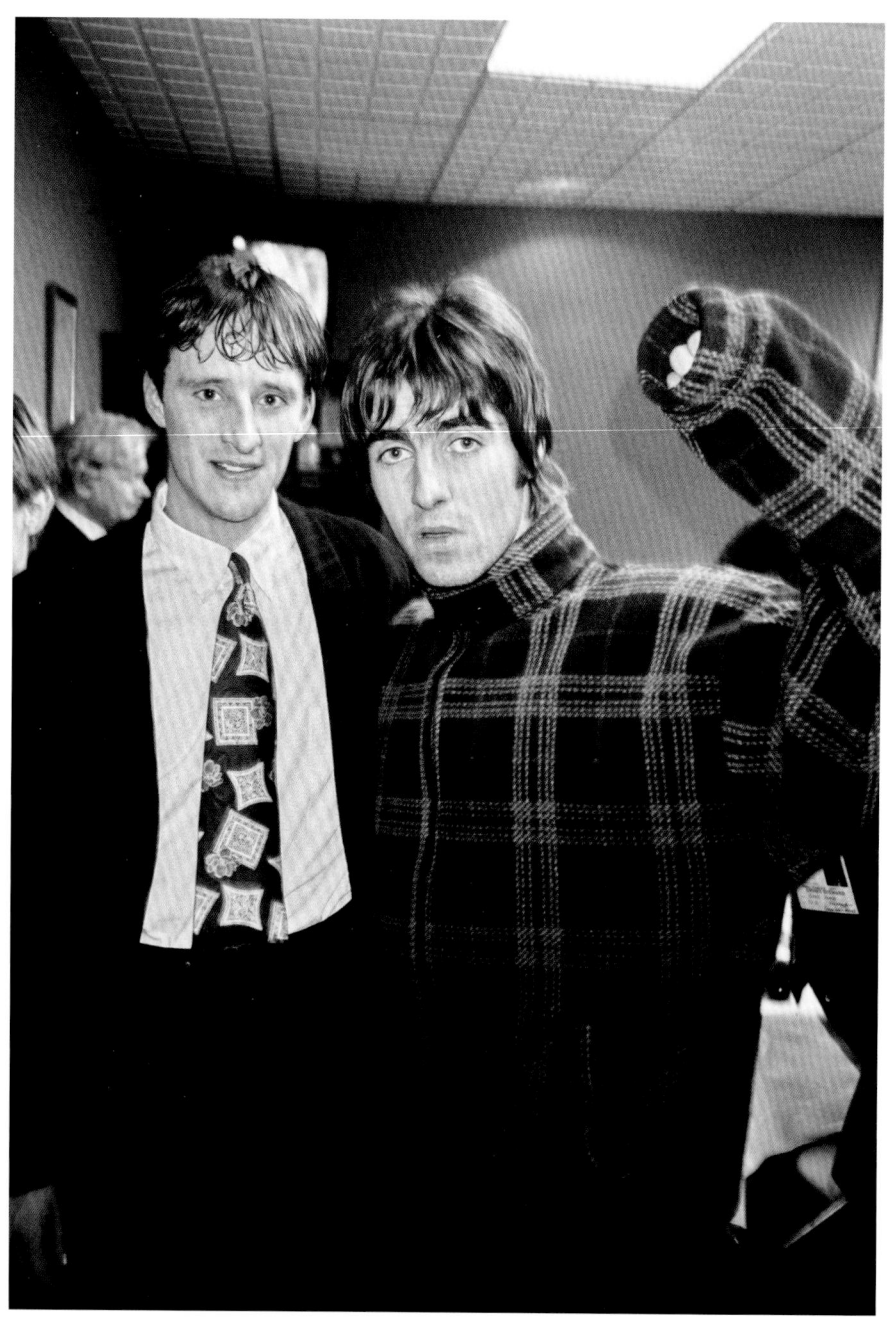

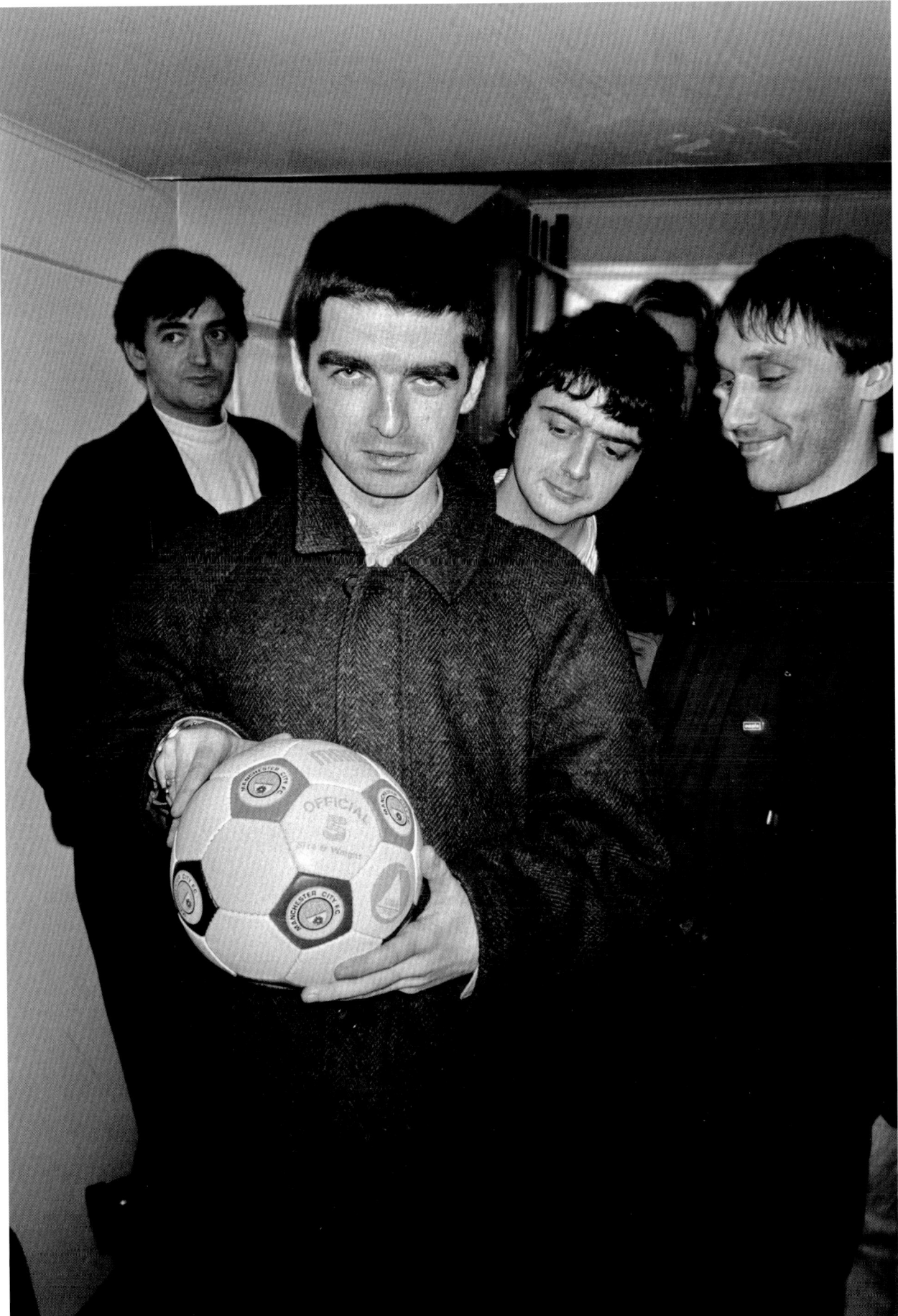

OASIS & MUSIC TODAY
NOEL GALLAGHER
IN CONVERSATION WITH KEVIN CUMMINS

What do you feel music offers people that's unique?
Sadly, in this era, for this generation, virtually nothing. I have teenage kids, and music, for them, wouldn't even be in the top ten things they're interested in.

Who do you listen to for pleasure?
Depends what mood I'm in. I have very eclectic taste, from Buddy Holly to Goldie and almost everything in between. I'm not a fan of metal though, to be honest.

Who is the best live act you've ever seen? When and where?
The best doesn't exist. Live things that I've seen that have stayed with me down the years are: U2, Paul Weller, Neil Young, Goldie, Ennio Morricone, The Strokes, Young Fathers, and countless others too.

Do you prefer vinyl, CD or listening to music digitally?
Not fussed. I'm not really into the science of sound. My phone sounds as good as vinyl to my ears

Do you give your playlists titles?
Absolutely – but I'm not telling you what they are.

Before the ticket sales for the 2025 reunion gigs, did you realize just how popular Oasis are? I mean, I know you know in a way, but the fact that almost half the country tried to buy tickets must be quite startling.
I thought it'd be a big deal, but I was a bit taken aback by just how much of a big deal it was.

Are you still in touch with Evan Dando? Can you remember how he started hanging out with you?
Nah. I did bump into him once, about ten years ago in New York. Oasis and Lemonheads were on the same festival circuit in 1994. We just hit it off.

Years ago, I gave you a 20×16-inch photo of your choice: a photo of OMD's [Orchestral Manoeuvres in The Dark] four-track tape recorder against the Liverpool skyline. What made you choose that?
I just thought it was a great shot. I'm not a huge OMD fan, although I do like them.

Do you ever catch yourself singing one of your own songs when you're driving or doing anything else?
Nope. Actually, when I'm writing, I sometimes go for a walk if I'm stuck and try and work through something in my head.

And finally, what's your favourite Oasis song?
Can I have more than one? Supersonic, Some Might Say, Live Forever and Rock 'n' Roll Star.

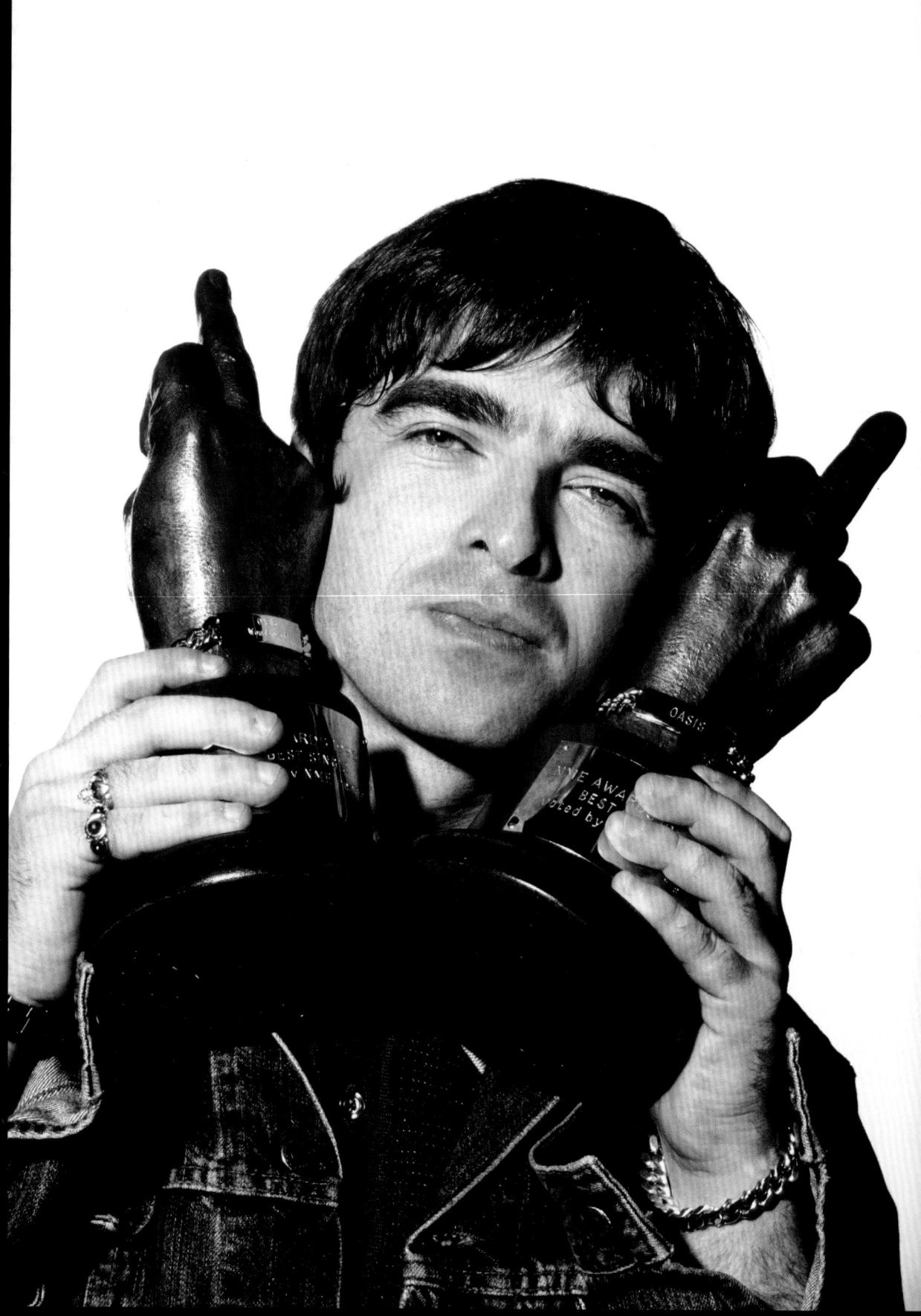

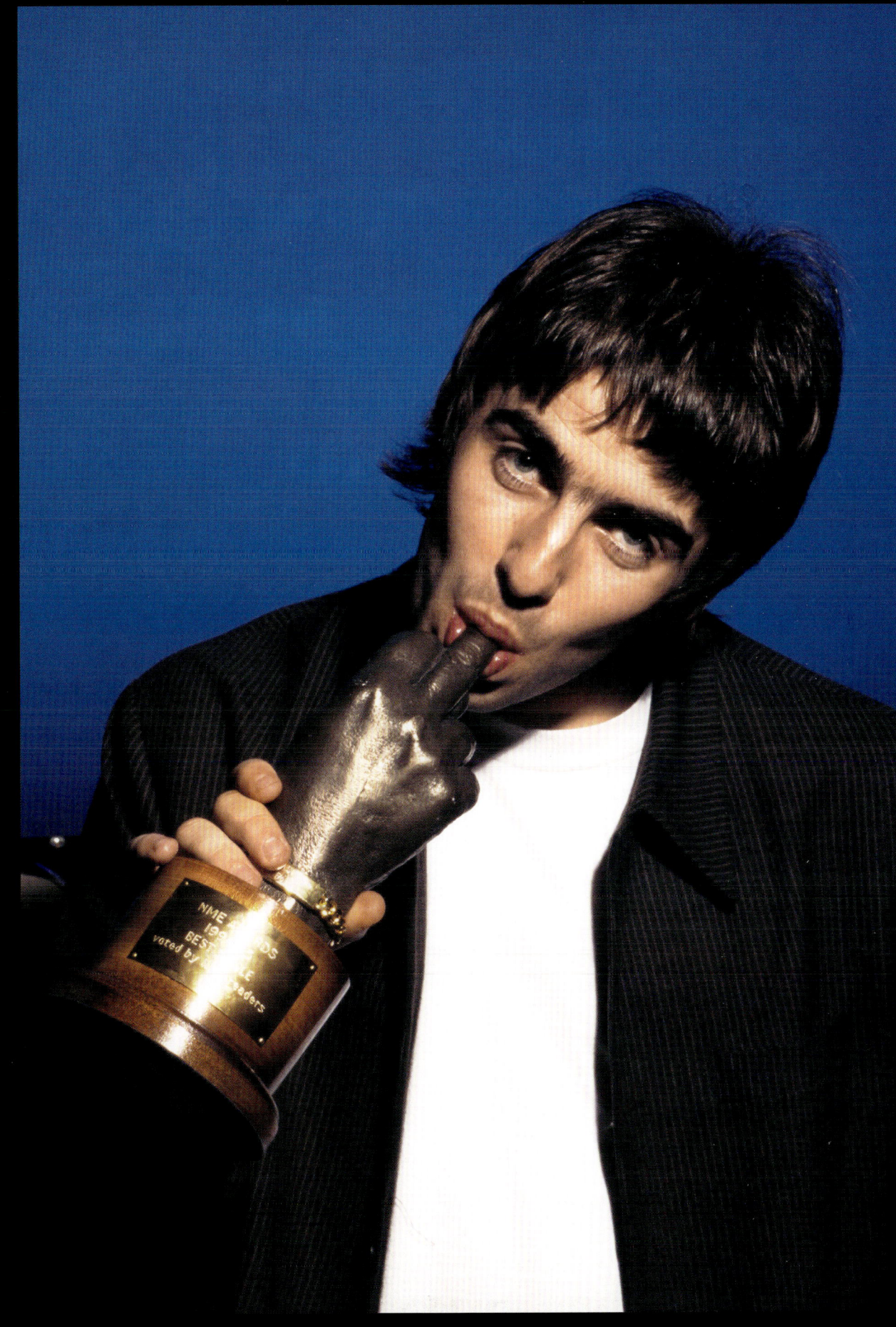

ACKNOWLEDGEMENTS

Putting a book like this together is impossible without a good team around me, and once again I'm lucky to be working with the same core of people at Cassell who I've now worked with for several years.

Thanks to my long-suffering editor, Alison Starling, whose ideas and support proved as invaluable as ever. Her ability to remain relatively calm when deadlines come and go is quite remarkable.

Thanks also to Jonathan and Pauline for helping to make this work, as ever. You're all great to deal with, even if my deadline surfing gives you nightmares. Thanks also to Blake Lewis and Alice Pinson at Iconic for the scanning.

Massive thanks to my agent, Carrie Kania, whose constant support, encouragement and champagne kept me going through the tough winter months. The French House in Soho does a roaring trade every time I'm working on a new book. Although, to be fair, I don't really need an excuse to while away the days there.

I couldn't have produced this book without Gail Crowther. The title was Gail's suggestion, and she is always encouraging me not to settle for the easy options whenever I'm working on a new book. Thanks for all your support with everything, it means the world to me, you know that too.

Thanks to Ella, my daughter, who is a huge Oasis fan. The number of gig tickets she has manged to scrounge off Noel over the years requires a lot of dedication.

Thanks to the Manchester City London Branch Arts Council for good vibes. Thanks to Rob, Geoff, Scully, Mike, Charlie and co for great awaydays in great European cities, and massive thanks to Steve Robinson and Suzanne Heed for making these journeys seamless and fun.

Thanks to Sally, who loves to read everything and suggest fewer commas, before I go to print.

Massive thanks to Noel Gallagher, who always supports my books. His contribution to the text in this one and always offering further support is priceless.

Thanks also to everyone at Ignition, especially Kat, Sarah, Clare and Emily, for always being around to help and offer support too.

Thanks to Gary Aspden and Sam at adidas, and to Shun, Heidi and Nick for all the goodwill.

Thanks to the original band members – Paul Arthurs, Paul McGuigan and Tony McCarroll – your part in this story should never be underestimated.

And thanks to Liam Gallagher too, who, last time I photographed him said, "Bet you're buzzin', photographing me for a change, instead of our kid."

Finally, thanks to all my readers. You're the reason this book exists. I truly hope you all enjoy it – and no, I can't get you tickets for a gig. Sorry, I'd love to, obviously. Maybe next time. Definitely, maybe...

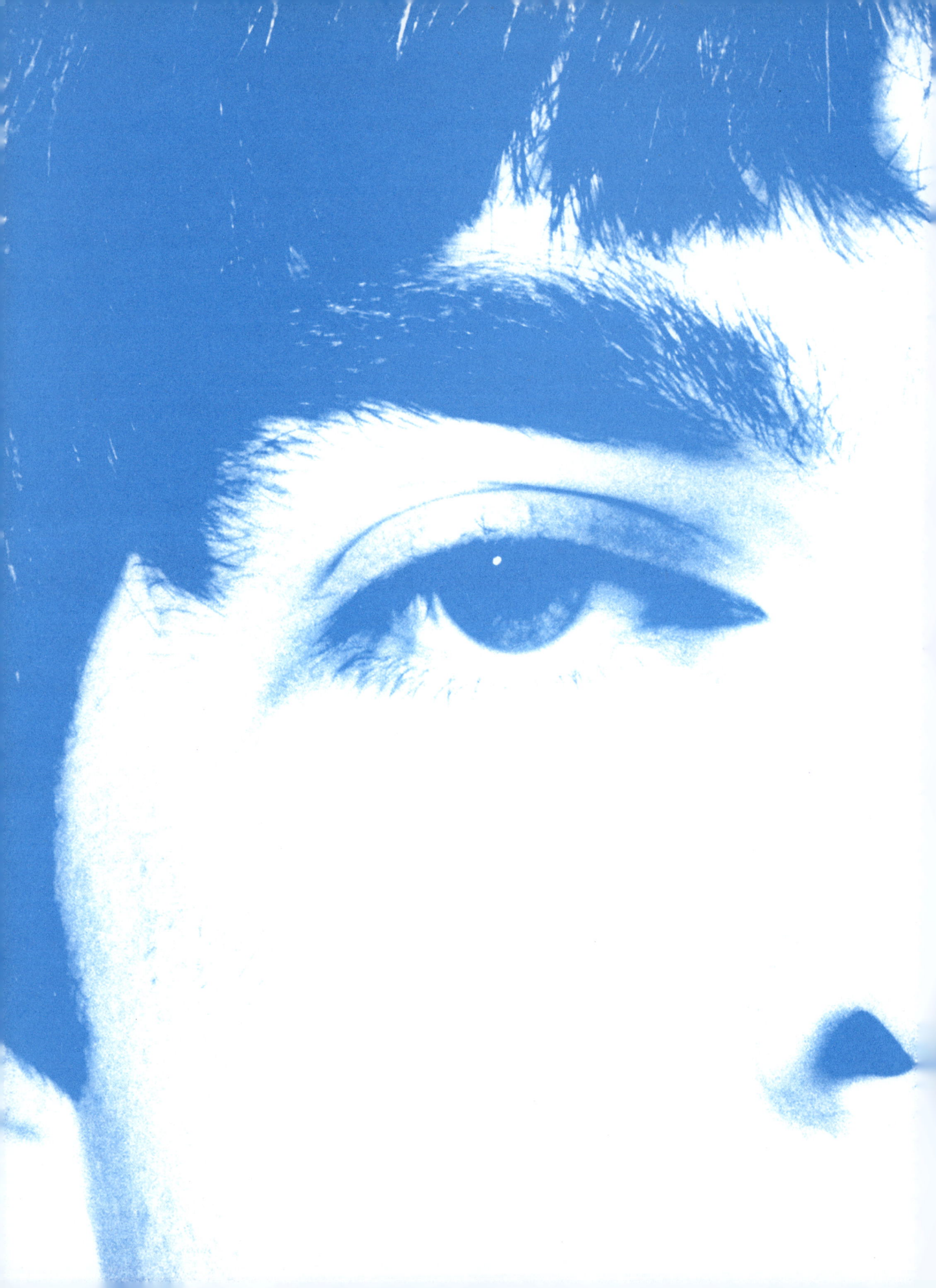